PERSONALITY AND PERSON PERCEPTION ACROSS CULTURES

PERSONALITY AND PERSON PERCEPTION ACROSS CULTURES

Edited by

Yueh-Ting Lee
Westfield State College

Clark R. McCauley
Bryn Mawr College

Juris G. Draguns
The Pennsylvania State University

Psychology Press
Taylor & Francis Group

New York London

First published by Lawrence Erlbaum Associates, Inc., Publishers

Reprinted 2008 by Psychology Press

Psychology Press
Taylor & Francis Group
27 Church Road, Hove, East Sussex BN3 2FA, UK
711 Third Avenue, New York, NY 10017

First issued in paperback 2014

*Psychology Press is an imprint of the Taylor and Francis Group,
an informa business*

Cover design by Kathryn Houghtaling Lacey

Library of Congress Cataloging-in-Publication Data
Personality and person perception across cultures / edited by Yueh-Ting Lee,
    Clark R. McCauley, Juris G. Draguns.
        p. cm.
Includes bibliographical references and indexes.

ISBN 978-0-8058-2813-9 (hbk)
ISBN 978-1-138-01246-2 (pbk)

1. Personality and Culture. 2. Ethnopsychology. I. Lee, Yueh-Ting.
    II. McCauley, Clark, R. III. Draguns, Juris G.
BF698.9.C8P54   1998
155.8—dc21

                                                        98–16383
                                                            CIP

Contents

Preface

Human nature cannot be independent of culture. Neither can human personality. Human beings do share certain social norms or rules within their cultural groups. More than 2000 years ago, Aristotle held that man is by nature a social animal. Similarly, Xun Kuang (298–238 B.C.), a Chinese philosopher, pointed out that humans in social groups cannot function without shared guidance or rules. Therefore, each culture or cultural group establishes its own norms. Constantly, these norms and rules are connected with the behavior and personality of members within a culture and society. *Modal personality*, as often studied by anthropological psychologists and *stereotype accuracy* as studied by sociocultural psychologists, are continuing exploration of the links between personality and culture.

This volume is, among other things, the product of our experiences in dealing with the personalities of contributors who are shaped by their respective cultures. For example, the personalities of our African or Chinese contributors are not identical with those of North American authors. Although their personalities are colored by their respective cultures, this does not imply that there are no individual differences within a culture. Nor does it imply that there are no similarities between Africans, Americans, Canadians, Chinese, Germans, Indians, Mexicans, just to name the nations represented in this project. After all, we are human beings and we live in the global village.

Thus, this volume aims to provide readers with a view of how we are different from, and similar to, each other, both within a culture and across cultures. The research on personality in culture presented here is not only a scientific endeavor but also a practical guide for people preparing to interact with those whose cultural background is different from their own.

ACKNOWLEDGMENTS

We received help and support from the following individuals. Linda Albright (Westfield State College of Massachusetts), Dana Bramel (State University of New York at Stony Brook), David Funder (University of California at Riverside), Ryan Kane and Brian Sicard (Westfield State College of Massachusetts), and Dean Peabody (Swarthmore College) assisted us in reviewing manuscripts and provided us with insightful comments and constructive criticisms. Albert Pepitone (University of Pennsylvania) encouraged us with his scholarship and experience when we started this project. Lawrence Erlbaum, Kathleen Dolan, and Robert Kidd were keenly supportive of this project when we first proposed it to LEA. Kate Graetzer, Linda Eisenberg, and other LEA staff helped us in editing and producing this book. Our secretaries, Lucia Sullivan (Westfield State College of Massachusetts), Ann Ogle (Bryn Mawr College), and Helen Gardner (Pennsylvania State University) were of great assistance at all stages of the work. We are grateful to all of these individuals. However, any remaining faults are our responsibility.

Finally, we are very grateful to our family members, particularly our wives, Fong Wei, Lisa Beck McCauley, and Marie Draguns. Their altruism, encouragement, nurturance, and continuous support have inspired optimism and hope in us beyond what can be put into words.

—YTL
—CRM
—JGD

List of Contributors

Winston Allen, Department of Public Health, Philadelphia.

Richard Brislin, College of Business Administration, University of Hawaii, Honolulu.

Rolando Diaz-Loving, National Autonomous University of Mexico, Mexico City.

Juris G. Draguns, The Pennsylvania State University, University Park, Pennsylvania.

C. Harry Hui, University of Hong Kong, China.

Pittu Laungani, South Bank University, London.

Yueh-Ting Lee, Westfield State College of Massachusetts, Westfield, Massachusetts.

Yanfang Liu, Institute of Psychology, Chinese Academy of Sciences, Beijing, China.

Heiner Maier, Max Planck Institute for Human Development and Education, Berlin, Germany.

Clark R. McCauley, Bryn Mawr College, Bryn Mawr, Pennsylvania.

Laura Miller, Loyola University, Chicago.

Gabriele Oettingen, Max Planck Institute for Human Development and Education, Berlin, Germany.

Barnabas Okeke, Department of Public Health, Philadelphia.

Victor Ottati, Purdue University, West Lafayette, Indiana, and Loyola University, Chicago.

Dean Peabody, Swarthmore College, Swarthmore, Pennsylvania.

Lawrence A. Pervin, Rutgers University, Piscataway, New Jersey.

J. Philippe Rushton, University of Western Ontario, London, Ontario, Canada.

Ben Sheku, Department of Public Health, Philadelphia.

Harry C. Triandis, University of Illinois at Champaign–Urbana.

Kan Zhang, Institute of Psychology, Chinese Academy of Sciences, Beijing, China

I

Introduction

1

Why Study Personality in Culture?

Yueh-Ting Lee
Westfield State College

Clark R. McCauley
Bryn Mawr College

Juris Draguns
Pennsylvania State University

> No man ever looks at the world with pristine eyes. He sees it edited by a definite set of customs and institutions and ways of thinking. Even in his philosophical probings he cannot go behind these stereotypes; his very concepts of the true and the false will still have reference to his particular traditional customs. *—Benedict (1934, p. 2)*

In the late 1960s, Child's (1968) influential chapter in the *Handbook of Personality Theory and Research* raised the study of "personality in culture" to the status of a major field of personality research. Unfortunately, as we believe, the potential of this kind of work has largely slipped from view. The study of personality is flourishing, and cross-cultural research is burgeoning, but research that combines these two interests has been relatively sparse and scattered in recent years. This volume brings together a selection of what is new and interesting in cross-cultural study of personality; our goal is to reestablish the value of examining personality in a cross-cultural context.

We begin with a brief look at the concepts of *personality* and *culture* and the history of interest in their relationship. This interest is currently recovering after a long period of decline, and we point to some recent trends in research that we believe will further encourage the recovery. One weakness of current research on personality and culture is that it is dominated by North American issues and investigators. This volume aims to begin righting the balance, and we conclude our introduction by previewing the chapters contributed by a notably international group of investigators.

BASIC CONCEPTIONS OF PERSONALITY AND CULTURE

Defining personality is like defining human nature. It is both easy and difficult. On the one hand, it is easy because everyone understands what personality means without a definition. On the other hand, definitions are controversial. After reviewing 50 different definitions explicitly and implicitly related to personality, Allport (1937) was offered his own definition: "Personality is the dynamic organization within the individual of those psychophysical systems that determine his unique adjustment to his environment" (p. 48).

Even this definition has not ended the attempts to capture the essence of the concept of personality within one defining statement. For instance, somewhat different from Allport, Funder (1997) defined personality as "an individual's characteristic pattern of thought, emotion, and behavior, together with the psychological mechanisms—hidden or not—behind those patterns" (pp. 1–2). For our purposes, what is noteworthy about both of these definitions is the emphasis on intrapsychic systems or mechanisms that make sense of individual differences in cognition, motivation, and behavior.

In line with this emphasis, Draguns (1975) pinpointed three major topics or concerns of personality research: individuality, consistency, and organization. To elaborate, personality theorists and investigators generally aim to answer the following three questions:

1. What is the nature of individual differences among persons?
2. What are the lines of consistency within a person, or what stimuli and/or situations are similar or equivalent from that person's point of view?
3. How are the various tendencies toward behavior hierarchically organized within a person? What are the priorities among the several potential patterns of behavior within that person? How are conflicts within the person reconciled or resolved?

All this helps to understand what personality is.

The concept of culture is at least as complicated as personality. Kroeber and Kluckhohn (1963) presented 150 definitions of culture in their book, *Culture: A Critical Review of Concepts and Definitions*. Although culture is defined in many different ways in cultural anthropology (e.g., Ember & Ember, 1985; Herskovits, 1948; Rohner, 1984) and in cross-cultural psychology (e.g., Brislin, 1993; Segall, Dasen, Berry, & Poortinga, 1990; Triandis, 1994, 1995), researchers seem to agree that culture is learned and shared by the members of a society. As Triandis (1994) put it, "culture is to society what memory is to individuals" (p. 1).

Perhaps the most concise definition of culture was proposed by Herskovits (1955): "Culture is the man-made part of the environment" (p. 305). This pithy statement encompasses both physical artifacts and mental processes,both machine and language, technology as well as etiquette, and architectural structures as well as psychological constructs. Within cross-cultural psychology, Triandis (1972) introduced the concept of *subjective culture* that specifically referred to the psychological and mental aspects of the human-made environment. Subjective culture has provided the vehicle for the way in which "people categorize experience, their ideas about correct behavior, the way they view other people and groups of people, and the way they value entities in their environment" (Triandis, 1994, p. 87). Subjective culture, in short, is the culture within people's minds, as both a reflection of, and a template for, their social environment.

Cultural anthropologists Ember and Ember (1985) also defined culture as the learned behaviors, beliefs, and attitudes that are characteristic of a particular society or population and as the "shared customs of a society" (p. 166). Similarly, Keesing (1981) discussed culture as "the system of knowledge more or less shared by members of a society" (p. 509). Kottak (1991) stated that culture has the following features: "distinctly human; transmitted through learning; traditions and customs that govern behavior and beliefs" (p. 17). Moreover, according to Borofsky (1994) "definitions of the type Kottak and Keesing present above currently pervade the field" [i.e., anthropology] (p. 3).

Thus, personality and culture are both reducible to patterns of human behavior. Personality refers to an individual's characteristic pattern or enduring tendency of thoughts, feelings, and behavior; culture refers to the characteristic configuration of thoughts, feelings, and behaviors shared by members of a group. The origins of at least some aspects of personality may be seen as biological (Eysenck, 1982, 1990, 1995; Rushton, chap. 3 of this volume; Zuckerman, 1990, 1995), whereas culture is generally seen as entirely learned but based on the biological substrate that makes this learning possible. The study of personality explicitly includes the mechanisms that underlie the patterns of individual differences, whereas the study of culture is more often limited to describing the patterns or dimensions of characteristic behavior within groups.

And yet, human beings can be described as a culture-building species. No humans have ever survived and perpetuated themselves except as members of a social group. As Aristotle (384–322 b.c.) observed, "Man is by nature a social animal." Similarly, Xun Kuang (also known as Hsun Kuang, 298–238 b.c.), an ancient Chinese Confucian and Legalist philosopher, pointed out, "Humans cannot function without social groups which cannot exist without the shared guidance or rules of *li* (i.e., customary rules of living or norms of conduct) or *yi* (i.e., a combination of righteousness, faithfulness, fairness, justice, or morality)." Apparently, the ability to communicate and to transmit the social experience of a group (e.g., social norms and rules, *li* or *yi*) across generations is a biological given of the human condition. Thus, functioning and surviving in a culture are human species characteristics. At the same time, the spectrum of human cultures constitutes a virtually inexhaustible source of human variation in behavior, thought, emotion, and experience.

EARLY INTEREST IN PERSONALITY
AND CULTURE: BROAD AND DEEP

The study of personality in culture has long been of interest to anthropologists and psychologists (Allport, 1937; Benedict, 1934; Ichheiser, 1949, 1970; Kluckhohn & Murray, 1948, 1953, 1965; Mead, 1928/1961, 1946; see Pervin, chap. 2 of this volume). In anthropology, an early classic in this area was Benedict's *Patterns of Culture*, which described both differences between tribal cultures and personality differences within a tribe. Despite Allport's contributions, however, personality and culture did not attract the attention of psychologists until Child (1968), a Yale psychologist, wrote his chapter on personality in culture for the *Handbook of Personality Theory and Research*. This landmark chapter gave brief attention to personality understood as the dynamics of beliefs, motives, and behaviors as an individual functions in daily life. Child then focused more specifically on personality understood as consistent individual differences in behavior. Child argued that the nature and origins of personality differences could be illuminated by cross-cultural study, and he reviewed a wide variety of relevant research to suggest the promise of such study in the future.

Child's chapter drew on decades of work on personality and culture. As McCrae, Costa, and Yik (1996) pointed out, "During the first half of this century, many of the best minds in the social sciences—Sigmund Freud, Bronislaw Malinowski, John Dewey, Erich Fromm, Margaret Mead, and Henry Murray among them—focused on the relations between personality and culture" (p. 189). Classic field work by early anthropologists such as Benedict (1934), Malinowski (1927), Mead (1928/1961, 1935/1950, 1953, 1956), and Sapir (1934) was followed up by later cultural or psychological anthropologists, for example, Honigmann (1954), Hsu (1948, 1954, 1972), Hunt (1967), Kaplan (1961), Kluckhohn (see Kluckhohn & Murray, 1948), LeVine (1973, 1974), Spiro (1951), and Wallace (1968). Hsu (1948), a student of Malinowski, did extensive work on Chinese personality and culture. Particularly noteworthy is Honigmann's (1967) book entitled *Personality in Culture.* In the same way, psychologists such as Allport (1937), Klineberg (1954), Murray (Murray & Kluckhohn, 1965), and Cattell (1949, 1982), and psychoanalysts such as Freud (1950), Jung (1959), Fromm (1941), and Erikson (1959) made important contributions to personality from a cross-cultural perspective. In brief, "personality and culture" was a lively field of research from the turn of the century well into the 1960s.

RECENT INTEREST IN PERSONALITY AND CULTURE: WEAK BUT RECOVERING

Unfortunately, research on personality in culture became marginalized almost to the point of disappearance in psychology in the 1970s and 1980s. The decline of interest in this topic may be attributed primarily to a Zeitgeist of behavioral and cognitive psychology, especially in the United States, which left little room for culture in its emphasis on (a) individuo-centrism or individual-orientedness, (b) experimentalism, and (c) psychological reductionism or psychologism (Bond, 1988; Lee, 1994; Pepitone, 1989; Pervin, 1990).

Conceptual and methodological problems within the culture and personality enterprise also became apparent (also see Ichheiser, 1970; Kenny, 1994). Much of this work has rested on the implicit or explicit assumption that, within a culture, one mode of socialization experience prevailed and that it resulted in a single personality type, modal personality structure, or national character. In retrospect, this assumption appears simplistic. In any case, it proved untenable in the long run. Individual differences were glossed over both in the antecedent conditions of socialization and in the purportedly resulting personality variables. Other possible sources of influence on personally distinctive behavior were overlooked or disregarded. Moreover, Wallace (1970) demonstrated that, even in traditional small-scale tribal groups, personality characteristics were multimodally distributed. This recognition is a fortiori applicable to the populous and complex contemporary nation states from Japan to Argentina, and from Great Britain to Thailand. Thus, the attempt to identify a single pattern of personality characteristics within these cultural entities under the label of national character turned out to be an exercise in futility.

In the 1990s, scholars from many disciplines (e.g., Aguirre & Turner, 1995; C. C. Chen, 1995; Fiske, 1992, 1995; Fiske, Kitayama, Markus, & Nisbett, 1997; Hall & Hall, 1996; Huntington, 1993; Kitayama & Markus, 1994; Lee, Kleinbach, Hu, Peng, & Chen, 1996; Smith & Bond, 1994; Triandis, 1996) have again become interested in the study of culture and cultural differences in groups of many different kinds, including ethnic and national groups. This interest in culture has been extended to institutions such as private corporations and public bureaucracies. In the marketplace of ideas, consumers have become bullish about issues of culture and cultural difference (Lee & Seligman, 1997; Moghaddam, 1998; Rosen, 1991). According to cross-cultural researchers and consultants (e.g., Bond, 1996; Brislin, 1993; Landis & Bhagat, 1996; Lee, 1995; Leung, 1996; Moghaddam, 1987), concerns about intercultural sensitivity and cross-cultural interactions have arisen in two settings. First, these concerns appear in interactions between people from culturally diverse groups within the United States—between African Americans, Asian Americans, Euro-Americans, Hispanic Americans, Native Americans, and other Americans. Second, these concerns are stimulated as modern technology, communication, and transportation bring people together in a global village—people emigrating from one country to another, students seeking educational opportunities in other parts of the world, businesspeople conducting business internationally. All of these intercultural contacts and interactions suggest that human beings share not only an ecological environment and a mutual relationship to the same earth, but increasingly a common social milieu in which groups and individuals with different personalities, characters, attitudes, beliefs, values, communicative styles, behaviors, economic systems, and political systems must live and interact with one another.

Although American psychology—including American mainstream personality and social psychology—has historically neglected the role of culture in its theories and research (see Campbell, 1975; Pepitone, 1994), an increasing number of psychologists have come to realize the influence of culture on social behavior. They have begun to recognize that American psychology needs to be globalized theoretically and practically in order to meet the needs and challenges of a multicultural world (e.g., Bond, 1997; Draguns, 1994, 1996; Fowers & Richardson, 1996; Lee, 1993; Lee & Duenas, 1995; Lee, Jussim & McCauley, 1995; McCauley, Jussim, & Lee, 1995).

Thus far, however, the renewed interest in cross-cultural issues has not brought research on personality and culture into the mainstream of American personality and social psychology of the 1990s. Table 1.1 shows that, since 1990, flagship personality journals in the United States (*Journal of Personality, Journal of Personality and Social Psychology*, and *Personality and Social Psychology Bulletin*) each devoted less than 2.5% of articles to personality in culture. The results in Table 1.1 show that the *Journal of Cross-Cultural Psychology* has published relatively more articles related to personality in culture (about 15%) than the mainstream personality journals. However, Table 1.2 shows some of the limitations of this work.

First, little research has been done in Third World or underdeveloped countries such as in Africa and South Africa and South America. A majority of the studies related to personality in culture have been conducted in Western cultures, and only a few of them investigated Asian cultures. Although China and India have almost 2 billion people (45%

TABLE 1.1
Summary of Recent Research on Personality in Culture (PinC)

Journal	Time Duration (yr. month)	Total No. of Articles Published	Articles Related to PinC	% of Articles Related to PinC
JCCP	1989.6–1995.7	183	28	15.3
JP	1989.6–1995.6	197	3	1.5
JPSP	1989.9–1995.10	1121	27	2.4
PSPB	1989.6–1995.10	482	9	1.9

Note. JCCP = Journal of Cross-Cultural Psychology, JP = Journal of Personality, JPSP = Journal of Personality and Social Psychology, PSPB = Personality and Social Psychology Bulletin. The data related to JP, PSPB, and PSPB were obtained by search for the "CROSS-CULTURAL" term in the PsycLit of the American Psychological Association (APA). The data related to JCCP were obtained by search for the "PERSONALITY" term in the PsycLit of the American Psychological Association (APA).

TABLE 1.2

Personality (P) Research in the *Journal of Cross-Cultural Psychology* (see References)

Author(s)	Date	About What or Content	Area or Geography	No. of Non-U.S. Ss	No. of Ss matched
Ben-Porath et al.	1995	P measures & structure	Israeli	583	1644
G. M. Chen	1995	Self-disclosure	Taiwan	144	200
Roseman et al.	1995	Emotional appraisals & responses	India	306	160
Taylor & Oskay	1995	Identity & self	Turkey	82	101
Tuss, Zimmer & Ho	1995	Attribution & achievement	China Japan	18 44	24 same
Ben-Ari et al.	1994	Attribution style & stereotyping	Israeli	582	a
Hamid	1994	Self-monitor & locus of control	China New Zealand	65 54	0 0
Schaufeli & Janczur	1994	P & burnout	Poland Netherlands	200 183	0 0
Ying & Liese	1994	Adjustment & CPI	Taiwan	172	0
Ellis et al.	1993	Trier P inventory	W. Germany	213	203
Y. Lee & Ottati	1993	Nationality, stereotyping,, & homogeneity	China	182	182
Peng et al.	1993	Traits & impression	Korea	48	32
Gudykunst et al.	1992	Self-monitor & values	b	b	b
V. Lee & Dengerink	1992	Sex, nationality, & locus of control	Sweden	113	142
Tobacyk & Pirttila-Backman	1992	Paranormal belief & P	Finland	117	351
Tobacyk & Tobacyk	1992	Beliefs & P	Poland	149	136
Carden & Feicht	1991	Emotion, homesick, & P	Turkey	69	75
Dake	1991	Risk taking & dispositions	c	c	300
Khan & Alvi	1991	Holland's typology	Pakistan	376	0
Minsel et al.	1991	P & mental health	d	d	d
Osterweil & Nagano	1991	Separateness & independence	Japan Israeli	60 60	0 0
Scott et al.	1991	Children P & family relations	e	e	e
Bontempo et al.	1990	compliance, internal values, & prosocial behavior	Brazil	232	147

10

Dion et al.	1990	P traits & stereotyping			
		physical attractiveness	f	f	f
Stiles et al.	1990	Characteristics & ideal opposite sex person	Mexico	89	99
Wagner et al.	1990	Dominance & dependence	g	g	g
Edelmann et al.	1989	Embarrassment	h	h	h
Lara-Cantu	1989	Masculine–feminine P	Mexico	1301	0

Note.

a. A total of 582 high schoolers were Euro-American descent and African-Asian descent living in Israeli.

b. A total of 850 college students were recruited from Hong Kong, Korea, United States, and Australia.

c. This study only included a U.S. sample but was related to personality and culture.

d. There were 595 students and teachers from France, Germany, Greece, and the United States.

e. A total of 1,686 graders, parents, and teachers were from Hong Kong, Taipei, Osaka, Berlin, Winnipeg, Phoenix, and Canberra).

f. Fifty-three different Chinese students were studying in Canada.

g. A total of 304 Ss were from Austria, India, Turkey, and the United States.

h. There were 700 students from Greece, Italy, Spain, Britain, and West Germany.

to 50% of the world population), there have been few publications related to Chinese or Indian personality in their culture. Second, most of the studies in Table 1.2 involved one culture in comparison with the U.S. culture. Obviously, U.S. culture has been thoroughly studied, whereas other cultures are only occasionally explored for comparison with U.S. culture. Third, almost all studies involved the readily available college students, which strongly points to a sample bias in cross-cultural research on personality. Finally, there is much emphasis on "attribution" (or locus of control, see Table 1.2) and "self" (see Table 1.2 and a special issue by Kashima, 1995), whereas there is relatively little other research on personality in culture. In other words, research on personality in culture has been somewhat narrow in its sampling of both cultures and theoretical issues.

Simply put, psychology, including personality psychology, is an enterprise primarily dominated by Western researchers (especially U.S. scholars) and dealing with Westerners (see Gabrenya & Hwang, 1996; Lee & Ottati, 1993, 1995; Segall et al., 1990). As Triandis (1994) pointed out, psychology is a product of European and North American cultural contexts: "Almost all that we know systematically about social behavior was derived by studying individuals and groups from those regions of the world. However, 70 percent of the earth's population lives outside Europe and North America; in cultures that are quite different from those of the 'West'" (p. xv).

FUTURE INTEREST IN PERSONALITY IN CULTURE:
THE IMPETUS OF THREE RECENT RESEARCH
DIRECTIONS

Despite growing interest in cross-cultural issues, then, the intertwining of culture and personality is not yet a salient topic in the current psychological literature. We believe our topic is likely to become more important in the near future, however, because of interest and excitement associated with three recent developments in interrelated areas of research.

The Nature of the Self

A major focus of interest is the nature and quality of self-experience across cultures. How and where are the boundaries drawn between the self and the external world? How permeable and flexible are they? At the dawn of scientific psychology, James (1891/1952) defined the *self* as the sum of what a person called his or her own. Does the self end at our skin or does it extend into the home, family, community, and beyond? And how articulate and specific are a person's self-descriptions? These are abstract questions, yet they are posed in a highly personal manner, and in a variety of different ways, by persons around the world. Moreover, they are related to actions, preferences, and decisions by specific persons in real-life situations.

The recognition of the importance of the self as a source of cultural variation permeates contemporary clinical psychology and related fields (Chang, 1988; Hsu, 1971, 1983; Kashima, 1995; Kimura, 1995; Landrine, 1992; Markus & Kitayama, 1991; Nathan, 1994; Partridge, 1987; Roland, 1988; Triandis, 1989). Observations on which these formulations are based have variously come from psychotherapeutic practice, social interaction, experimental studies, and multivariate statistical research. All of these diverse perspectives converge toward the recognition of two polarities of self-experience. At one end of the continuum, there is the tightly encapsulated self that sets the individual apart from other people (Chang, 1988). At the other extreme, self-experience is highly permeable, and the boundaries between self and others are not clearly delineated. The self is principally manifested in social interactions, especially with the "significant others" within one's family. The former mode of self-experience is prominent in North America, and in northern and western Europe. The latter mode of self-experience probably prevails in much of the rest of the world, but has been intensively studied in the major Asian cultures of China, Korea, Japan, and India. The implications of these cultural differences in self-experiences are major and far-reaching for the understanding of personality characteristics and personality structure, not just in Euro-American social contexts but around the world. Their exploration is in progress and will probably occupy researchers and theorists of the next decades.

To this end, however, connections have to be specified, and links need to be forged between these empirically based cultural dimensions and a host of personality traits that psychologists in North America and western Europe have been investigating over the last several decades. Moreover, Marin and Triandis (1985) cautioned cross-cultural researchers against being too quick to equate cultural dimensions with personality traits. Take, for example, individualism-collectivism. This construct is applicable on both the cultural-institutional and personal-psychological planes. Its manifestations, however, are subtly, yet detectably different on these two levels, and its respective indicators are expected to yield significant, but imperfect correlations. That is why Marin and Triandis differentiated allocentrism and idiocentrism as personality constructs from the cultural dimensions of collectivism and individualism, respectively.

Dimensions of Variation Across Cultures

Dimensions have been discovered that may constitute the major sources of psychological variation across cultures. The worldwide investigations of work-related attitudes by Hofstede (1980, 1991) have resulted in the identification of four such dimensions: individualism-collectivism, power distance, uncertainty avoidance, and masculinity-femininity. These dimensions have been extended to a variety of other contexts: social interaction (Hofstede, 1991), teacher–pupil relationships (Hofstede, 1986), expression of mental disorder (Draguns, 1990), and experience of psychotherapy (Draguns, 1995). Are they then relevant for the understanding of personality? Individualism-collectivism, in particular, has acquired its own momentum and is being actively investigated as a major variable of social psychology between and within cultures (Triandis, 1996). Do the other three dimensions that Hofstede has introduced have the same potential? Looking toward the future, one may envisage cross-cultural and personality psychology mutually enriching one another. Personality variables, identified within a culture, could be applied in cross-cultural comparisons. Conversely, dimensions derived in multicultural research projects could be investigated for their relevance and usefulness closer to the home base. They could be useful for within-culture investigations of individual differences.

The collectivist versus individualist contrast does not constitute the only source of difference in culturally mediated self-experience. While psychoanalyzing Indian and Japanese clients, Roland (1988) discovered subtle cultural variations in self-concepts. Indian selves were much more open to intrusions by magic, mythology, and intuition; Japanese clients described and expressed their selves in much more concrete and pragmatic terms. A related kind of distinction between pragmatism and idealism was identified by Kumar (1997) in relation to the styles of entrepreneurial activity in India and China. These findings are complemented by a wealth of information on the differences as well as similarities that Cheng (1997) discovered between Chinese, Japanese, and Korean samples, even though all of these three cultures share a strong Confucian influence. And in the West, McClelland, Sturr, Knapp, and Wendt (1958) called attention to the different balances of obligations to self and society in German and U.S. subjects.

Cultural Variations in Conceptions of Individual Differences

Another point of departure for personality-oriented investigations has been to explore intensively the informal, prescientific terms and concepts used in various cultures to describe and explain aspects of personality functioning. Take the concept of *amae*, a common Japanese verb translated "to presume upon other people's benevolence" (Doi, 1973). As described by Doi, amae constitutes an important lifelong psychodynamic in Japan that makes a great variety of actions and experiences meaningful and intelligible. Does it have any explanatory value outside of Japan? Is it a personality dynamic that is waiting to be discovered in North America? Whatever the answer to these questions, the example of amae illustrates the potential value of looking for personality traits and their antecedents, correlates, and consequents, not only in the modern, mostly Western, psychologists' formal theories and systematic data, but in the folk experience of other cultures and our own. Some psychologists in Third World countries, for example, Enriquez (1990) in the Philippines and Yang (1996) in Taiwan, have worked toward the development of indigenous personality theories, to be first tested on their respective home grounds and then explored for their applicability in the rest of the world.

Perhaps the most ambitious undertaking of this kind was initiated by an international team of researchers (Chinese Culture Connection, 1987). These investigators started out with a set of 40 statements explicitly derived from Chinese Confucian values and then applied in many cultures around the world. Independently, Cheng (1990) began with observations of Chinese clients in individual and family therapy. On this basis, he developed an attitude scale based on Confucian maxims and principles, which was then administered to numerous samples of Chinese, other East Asian, Australian, and U.S. samples. The results of these two efforts point to an impressive degree of construct validity for these instruments derived from indigenous Chinese prescriptions of moral conduct, but applicable in many other cultures as well (Cheng, 1997).

Once the aforementioned three trends are absorbed into the mainstream psychology of personality, which at this point remains a lopsidedly North American enterprise, we believe that personality in culture will reemerge and reassert itself as a central, indeed indispensable component of the study of personality. Toward this end, we have sought in this volume to overcome the bias toward North American research by bringing together an international group of psychologists, studying a variety of national groups including China, India, Germany, Africa, and Mexico, in addition to the United States and Canada. In sum, personality in culture is an area of research that has had relatively little attention or review in recent years, and we hope the present volume can help this area participate in the recent resurgence of interest in cross-cultural research.

PREVIEW OF THIS VOLUME

This volume has 14 chapters. The first two chapters deal with the basic issues of personality in culture. Our introductory chapter (chap. 1) examines why we study personality and person perception in culture. Next, Pervin (chap. 2) examines the history of this kind of study in relation to the challenge represented by those who believe that personality does not exist. According to the deconstructionist critique, there is no pattern of behavior nor any internal dynamics of behavior that transcends cultural variation. One does not have to accept this critique in order to profit from the its focus on the difficulty of asking the same question in different cultures.

The next three chapters deal empirically with basic personality difference between social and cultural groups (e.g., nations, ethnicities, or regions). Taking a biological perspective, Rushton (chap. 3) reviews important research on racial differences in temperament. Are Whites somewhere between Africans and Asians in domains as different as sexual behavior, self-esteem, and socialization? Although it is politically controversial, this chapter will catch the attention of many readers. Peabody (chap. 4) offers another controversial hypothesis: that the Big Three personality dimensions are conflated with evaluation and that, purified of evaluation, there are two descriptive dimensions of personality both within and across cultures. McCauley, Ottati, and Lee (chap. 5) examine national differences in economic development from an interdisciplinary perspective. Does culture determine economic development or vice versa? Though controversial among political and sociological scientists, this chapter reviews evidence that cultural values and motivations are substantially related to economic success.

The following six chapters focus on personality differences between two cultures, for a variety of pairs of cultures. Diaz-Loving and Draguns (chap. 6) review research on cultural differences between Mexico and the United States. Broad in its approach, this chapter looks at contrasts in domains of friendship, love, family, marriage, community, economics, and politics. Zhang, Lee, Liu, and McCauley (chap. 7) present results of a recent survey study of how Chinese college students see the differences between Americans and Chinese. For some of the perceived differences, the chapter suggests evidence supporting the validity of the assessed stereotypes. Okeke, Draguns, Ben, and Allen (chap. 8) have tried to transcend the stereotypes of Africans by White Europeans and North Americans. The research, based on information the authors have reviewed, emphasizes the distinctness of African personality characteristics, but calls into question many traditional beliefs, still widespread in the West, about African social and personal traits. Oettingen and Maier (chap. 9) review their program of research on self-efficacy to suggest how one aspect of cultural difference—political ideology—may produce variation in self-perception. Particularly striking are their data showing that Communist regime has in some respects had more impact in East Berlin than in Moscow. In his research on cultural identity and behavior, Laungani (chap. 10) examines cultural differences between India and Britain. This chapter focuses on four dimensions of differences: individualism-communalism, cognitivism-emotionalism, freewill-determinism, and materialism-spiritualism. As a cultural anthropologist, Miller (chap. 11) criticizes common perceptions of the differences between Japanese and Americans. Although acknowledging the existence of a substantial cultural difference between Americans and Japanese, she emphasizes the extent to which these differences depend on contact, context, and social relationship.

The final three chapters deal with practical and academic implications of studying personality and person perception in culture. Ottati, Hui, and Triandis (chap. 12) contrast traits and perception of supervisor–subordinate relations for Hispanic and mainstream (primarily White) recruits in the U.S. Navy. Using Hosfstede's four dimensions (i.e., individualism, power distance, masculinity, and uncertainty avoidance), this chapter provides a powerful example of the extent to which cultural differences can be moderated by selection into a powerful subculture. Brislin (chap. 13) describes the growing popularity of cross-cultural training and a number of the techniques used in this training. He emphasizes the importance of dealing with both intracultural and cross-cultural differences in training, and gives some indication of the extent to which good training depends on the judgment of the trainer to go beyond the limitations of current research. Finally, McCauley, Draguns, and Lee (chap. 14) bring the preceding chapters together in placing research on personality in culture in the more familiar context of theory and research on person perception. We try to suggest some fruitful directions for future research.

CONCLUSION

In brief, we believe that the study of personality and culture is timely and desirable for the following reasons. First, this research is consistent with the academic Zeitgeist and with the growth of cross-cultural contacts both within and between nations. Second, it leads to a theoretically integrated account of person perception that renews and builds on Child's construction of the importance of cross-cultural study of personality. Finally, it can offer practical assistance to the individual who is preparing to visit, study, or work in a different culture. The contributors to this volume join us in the hope that the present volume will make cross-cultural study of personality and person perception a significant and dynamic part of the renaissance of interest in cross-cultural research.

ACKNOWLEDGMENTS

Thanks are extended to David Funder for his helpful comments on the earlier version of this chapter.

REFERENCES

Aguirre, A., & Turner, J. H. (1995). *American ethnicities: The dynamics and consequences of discrimination*. New York: McGraw-Hill.

Allport, G. W. (1937). *Personality: A psychological interpretation*. New York: Holt.

Ben-Ari, R., Schwarzwald, J., & Horiner-Levi, E. (1994). The effects of prevalent social stereotypes on intergroup attribution. *Journal of Cross-Cultural Psychology, 25,* 489–500.

Benedict, R. (1934). *Patterns of culture*. Boston: Houghton Mifflin.

Ben-Porath, Y-S., Almagor, M., Hoffman-Chemi, A., & Tellegen, A. (1995). A cross-cultural study of personality with the Multidimensional Personality Questionnaire. *Journal of Cross-Cultural Psychology, 26,* 360–373.

Bond, M. (1988). *Cross-cultural challenge to social psychology*. Newbury, CA: Sage.

Bond, M. (1996). Chinese values. In M. Bond (Ed.), *The handbook of Chinese psychology* (pp. 208–226). Hong Kong: Oxford University Press.

Bond, M. (1997). *Working at the interface of cultures*. London: Routledge.

Bontempo, R., Lobel, S., & Triandis, H. (1990). Compliance and value internalization in Brazil and the U.S.: Effects of allocentrism and anonymity. *Journal of Cross-Cultural Psychology, 21,* 200–213.

Borofsky, R. (1994). *Assessing cultural anthropology*. New York: McGraw-Hill.

Brislin, R. (1993). *Understanding culture's influence on behavior*. New York: Harcourt Brace.

Campbell, D. T. (1975). On the conflict between biological and social evolution and between psychology and moral tradition. *American Psychologist, 30,* 1103–1126.

Carden, A. I., & Feicht, R. (1991). Homesickness among American and Turkish college students. *Journal of Cross-Cultural Psychology, 22,* 418–428

Cattell, R. B. (1949). The dimensions of cultural patterns by factorization of national characters. *Journal of Abnormal and Social Psychology, 44,* 279–289.

Cattell, R. B. (1982). *Inheritance of personality and ability*. New York: Academic Press.

Chang, S. C. (1988). The nature of self: A transcultural view. Part I: Theoretical aspects. *Transcultural Psychiatric Research Review, 25*(3), 169–224.

Chen, C. C. (1995). New trends in rewards allocation preferences: A Sino-U.S. comparison. *Academy of Management Journal, 38,* 408–428.

Chen, G.-M. (1995). Differences in self-disclosure pattern among Americans versus Chinese: A comparative study. *Journal of Cross-Cultural Psychology, 26,* 84–91.

Cheng, S. K. (1990). Understanding the culture and behavior of East Asians: A Confucian perspective. Australia and New Zealand. *Journal of Psychiatry, 24,* 510–515.

Cheng, S. K. (1997). *The need for approval: A psychological study of the influence of Confucian values on the social behavior of East Asians*. Unpublished doctoral thesis, Murdock University, Australia.

Child, I. (1968). Personality in culture. In E. F. Borgatta & W. W. Lambert (Eds.), *Handbook of personality theory and research* (pp. 82–145). Chicago: Rand McNally.

Chinese Culture Connection. (1987). Chinese values and the search for culture-free dimensions of culture. *Journal of Cross-Cultural Psychology, 18,* 143–164.

Dake, K. (1991). Orienting dispositions in the perception of risk: An analysis of contemporary worldviews and cultural biases. *Journal of Cross-Cultural Psychology, 22,* 61–82.

Dion, K. K., Pak, A. W., & Dion, K. L. (1990). Stereotyping physical attractiveness: A sociocultural perspective. *Journal of Cross-Cultural Psychology, 21,* 158–179.

Doi, L. T. (1973). *The Anatomy of Dependence* (J. Bester, Trans.). Tokyo: Kodansha.

Draguns, J. G. (1975). Assessment of personality. In C. N. Cofer & H. E. Fitzgerald (Eds.), *Psychology: A programmed modular approach* (pp. 517–538). Homewood, IL: Learning Systems Company.

Draguns, J. G. (1990). Culture and psychopathology: Toward specifying the nature of the relationship. In J. Berman (Ed.), *Cross-cultural perspectives: Nebraska Symposium on Motivation 1989* (pp. 235–277). Lincoln: University of Nebraska Press.

Draguns, J. (1994). Pathological and clinical aspects. In L. L. Adler & U. P. Gielen (Eds.), *Cross-cultural topics in psychology* (pp. 165–178). Westport, CT: Praeger.

Draguns, J. G. (1995). Cultural influences upon psychopathology: Clinical and practical implications. *Journal of Social Distress and the Homeless, 4,* 79–103.

Draguns, J. (1996). Abnormal behavior in Chinese societies: Clinical, epidemiological, and comparative studies. In M. Bond (Ed.), *The handbook of Chinese psychology* (pp. 412–428). Hong Kong: Oxford University Press.

Edelmann, R. J., Asendorpf, J., Contarello, A., Zammuner, V; et al. (1989). Self-reported expression of embarrassment in five European cultures. *Journal of Cross-Cultural Psychology, 20,* 357–371.

Ellis, B. B., Becker, P., & Kimmel, H. D. (1993). An item response theory evaluation of an English version of the Trier Personality Inventory (TPI). *Journal of Cross-Cultural Psychology, 24,* 133–148.

Ember, C. R., & Ember, M. (1985). *Cultural anthropology.* Englewood Cliffs, NJ: Prentice-Hall.

Enriquez, V. G. (Ed.). (1990). *Indigenous psychology: A book of readings.* Quezon City, Philippines: Akademya NG Sikolohiyang Pilipino.

Erikson, E. H. (1959). *Identity and life cycle.* New York: International Universities Press.

Eysenck, H. J. (1982). *Personality genetics and behavior.* New York: Praeger.

Eysenck, H. J. (1990). Biological dimensions of personality. In L. A. Pervin (Ed.), *Handbook of personality: Theory and research* (pp. 244–276). New York: Guilford.

Eysenck, H. J. (1995). Creativity as product of intelligence and personality. In D. H. Saklofske & M. Zeidner (Eds.), *International handbook of personality and intelligence* (pp. 231–248). New York: Plenum.

Fiske, A. (1992). The four elementary forms of sociability: Framework for a united theory of social relations. *Psychological Review, 99,* 689–723.

Fiske, A. (1995). The cultural dimensions of psychological research: Method effects imply cultural mediation. In P. Shrout & S. Fiske (Eds.), *Personality research, methods and Theory: Festschrift for Donald Fiske* (pp. 271–294). Hillsdale, NJ: Lawrence Erlbaum Associates.

Fiske, A., Kitayama, S., Markus, Z., & Nisbett, R. (1997). The cultural matrix of social psychology. In D. Gilbert, S. Fiske, & G. Lindzey (Eds.), *Handbook of social psychology* (4th ed; pp. 915–981). New York: McGraw-Hill.

Fowers, B. J., & Richardson, F. C. (1996). Why is multiculturalism good? *American Psychologist, 51,* 609–621.

Freud, S. (1950). *Totem and taboo* (J. Strachey, Trans.). New York: Norton.

Fromm, E. (1941). *Escape from freedom.* New York: Rinehart.

Funder, D. (1997). *The personality puzzle.* New York: Norton.

Gabrenya, W. K., & Hwang, K. K. (1996). Chinese social interaction: Harmony and hierarchy on the good earth. In M. Bond (Ed.), *The handbook of Chinese psychology* (pp. 309–321). Hong Kong: Oxford University Press.

Gudykunst, W. B., Gao, G., Schmidt, K. L., Nishida, T. et al. (1992). The influence of individualism-collectivism, self-monitoring, and predicted-outcome value on communication in ingroup and outgroup relationships. *Journal of Cross-Cultural Psychology, 23,* 196–213.

Hall, E. T., & Hall, E. (1996). How cultures collide. In G. R. Weaver (Ed.), *Culture, communication and conflict* (pp. 5–14). Needham Heights, MA: Simon & Schuster.

Hamid, P. N. (1994). Self-monitoring, locus of control, and social encounter of Chinese and New Zealand students. *Journal of Cross-Cultural Psychology, 25,* 353–368.

Herskovits, M. J. (1948). *Man and his works: The science of cultural anthropology.* New York: Knopf.

Herskovits, M. J. (1955). *Cultural anthropology.* New York: Knopf.

Hofstede, G. (1980). *Culture's consequences: International differences in work related values.* Beverly Hills, CA: Sage.

Hofstede, G. (1986). Cultural differences in teaching and learning. *International Journal of Intercultural Relations, 10,* 301–320.

Hofstede, G. (1991). *Cultures and organizations: Software of the mind.* London: McGraw-Hill.

Honigmann, J. J. (1954). *Personality and culture.* New York: Harper & Row.

Honigmann, J. J. (1967). *Personality in culture.* New York: Harper & Row.

Hsu, F. L. K. (1948). *Under the ancestor's shadow: Chinese culture and personality.* New York: Columbia University Press.

Hsu, F. L. K. (1954). *Aspects of culture and personality.* New York: Abelard-Schuman.

Hsu, F.L.K. (1971). Psychological homeostasis and jen: Conceptual tools for advancing psychological anthropology. *American Anthropologist, 73,* 23–33.

Hsu, F. L. K. (1972). *Psychological anthropology.* Cambridge, MA: Schenkman.

Hsu, F. L. K. (1983). *Rugged individualism reconsidered.* Knoxville: University of Tennessee Press.

Hunt, R. (1967). *Personalities and cultures.* Garden City, NY: The Natural History Press.

Huntington, S. P. (1993). *The clash of civilizations?* (Working Paper Series No. 4). Cambridge, MA: Harvard University, The John M. Olin Institute.

Ichheiser, G. (1949). Sociopsychological and cultural factors in race relations. *American Journal of Sociology, 54,* 395–401.

Ichheiser, G. (1970). *Appearances and realities: Misunderstanding in human relations.* San Francisco: Jossey-Bass.

James, W. (1952). *The principles of psychology.* Chicago: Encyclopaedia Brittanica. (Original work published 1891)

Jung, C. G. (1959). *The basic writing of C. G. Jung* (V. de Laszlo, Ed.). New York: Random House.

Kaplan, B. (1961). *Studying personality cross-culturally.* Evanston, IL: Row, Peterson & Co.

Kashima, Y. (1995). Introduction to the special section on culture and self. *Journal of Cross-Cultural Psychology, 26,* 603–605.

Keesing, R. M. (1981). *Cultural anthropology: A contemporary perspective.* New York: Holt, Rinehart & Winston.

Kenny, D. (1994). *Interpersonal perception: A social relations analysis.* New York: Guilford.

Khan, S. B., & Alvi, S. A. (1991). The structure of Holland's typology: A study in a non-Western culture. *Journal of Cross-Cultural Psychology, 22,* 283–292.

Kimura, B. (1995). *Zwischen Mensch und Mensch* [Between one human being and another]. Darmstadt, Germany: Steinhoff.

Kitayama, S., & Markus, H. (Eds.). (1994). *Emotion and culture: Empirical studies of mutual influence.* Washington, DC: American Psychological Association.

Klineberg, O. (1954). How far can the society and culture of a people be gauged through their personality characteristics? In F. L. K. Hsu (Ed.), *Aspects of culture and personality* (pp. 29–42). New York: Abelard-Schuman.

Kluckhohn, C., & Murray, H. (1948). *Personality in nature, society and culture* (2nd ed.). New York: Knopf.

Kluckhohn, C., & Murray, H. (1965). *Personality in nature, society and culture.* (3rd ed.). New York: Knopf.

Kluckhohn, C., & Murray, H. (1953). *Personality in nature, society, and culture.* New York: Knopf.

Kottak, G. P. (1991). *Anthropology: The exploration of human diversity.* New York: McGraw-Hill.

Kroeber, A. L., & Kluckhohn, C. (1963). *Culture: A critical review of concepts and definitions.* New York: Random House.

Kumar, R. (1997, July). *Confucian pragmatism vs. Brahmanical idealism: Understanding the divergent roots of Indian and Chinese economic performance.* Paper presented at European Organizational Studies Group Symposium, Budapest.

Landis, D., & Bhagat, R. (1996). *Handbook of intercultural training* (2nd ed.). Thousands Oaks, CA: Sage.

Landrine, H. (1992). Clinical implications of cultural differences: The referential versus the indexical self. *Clinical Psychology Review, 12,* 401–415.

Lara-Cantu, M. A. (1989). A sex role inventory with scales for "machismo" and "self-sacrificing woman." *Journal of Cross-Cultural Psychology, 20,* 386–398.

Lee, V. K., & Dengerink, H. A. (1992). Locus of control in relation to sex and nationality: A cross-cultural study. *Journal of Cross-Cultural Psychology, 23,* 488–497.

Lee, Y. T. (1993). Cultural sensitivity and psychological open-mindedness: Understanding ourselves in the global village. *Contemporary Psychology, 38,* 794–795.

Lee, Y. T. (1994). Why does psychology have cultural limitations? *American Psychologist, 49,* 524–525.

Lee, Y. T. (1995). A comparison of politics and personality in China and in the U. S.: Testing a "kernel of truth" hypothesis. *The Journal of Contemporary China, 9,* 56–68.

Lee, Y. T., & Duenas, G. (1995). Stereotype accuracy in multicultural business. In Y. T. Lee, L. Jussim, & C. McCauley (Eds.), *Stereotype accuracy: Toward appreciating group differences* (pp. 157–186). Washington, DC: The American Psychological Association.

Lee, Y. T., Jussim, L., & McCauley, C. (Eds.). (1995). *Stereotype accuracy: Toward appreciating group differences.* Washington, DC: The American Psychological Association.

Lee, Y. T., Kleinbach, R., Hu, P., Peng, Z. Z., & Chen, X. Y. (1996). Cross-cultural research on euthanasia and abortion. *The Journal of Social Issues, 52*(2), 131–148.

Lee, Y. T., & Ottati, V. (1993). Determinants of ingroup and outgroup perception of heterogeneity: An investigation of Chinese-American stereotypes. *Journal of Cross-Cultural Psychology, 24,* 298–318.

Lee, Y. T., & Ottati, V. (1995). Perceived group homogeneity as a function of group membership salience and stereotype threats. *Personality and Social Psychology Bulletin, 21*(6), 612–621.

Lee, Y. T., & Seligman, M. E. P. (1997). Are Americans more optimistic than the Chinese? *Personality and Social Psychology Bulletin, 23*(1), 32–40.

Leung, K. (1996). The role of beliefs in Chinese culture. In M. H. Bond (Ed.), *The handbook of Chinese psychology* (pp. 247–262). Hong Kong: Oxford University Press.

LeVine, R. A. (1973). *Culture, behavior and personality.* Chicago: Aldine.

LeVine, R. A. (1974). *Culture and personality: Contemporary readings.* Chicago: Aldine.

Malinowski, B. (1927). *Sex and repression in savage society.* London: Routledge.

Marin, G., & Triandis, H. (1985). Allocentrism as an important characteristic of the behavior of Latin Americans and Hispanics. In R. Diaz-Guerrero (Ed.), *Cross-cultural and national studies in social psychology* (pp. 85–104). Amsterdam: North Holland.

Markus, H. R., & Kitayama, S. (1991). Culture and the self: Implications for cognition, emotion, and motivation. *Psychological Review, 98*(2), 224–253.

McCauley, C., Jussim, L., & Lee, Y. T. (1995). The time is now: Stereotype accuracy and intergroup relations. In Y. T. Lee, L. Jussim, & C. McCauley (Eds.), *Stereotype accuracy: Toward appreciating group differences* (pp. 293–312). Washington, DC: American Psychological Association.

McClelland, D. C., Sturr, J. F., Knapp, R. H., & Wendt, H. W. (1958). Obligations to self and society in the United States and Germany. *Journal of Abnormal and Social Psychology, 56,* 245–255.

McCrae, R. R., Costa, P. T., & Yik, M. S. (1996). Universal aspects of Chinese personality structure. In M. Bond (Ed.), *The handbook of Chinese psychology* (pp. 189–207). Hong Kong: Oxford University Press.

Mead, M. (1946). Research on primitive children. In L. Carmichael (Ed.), *Manual of child psychology* (pp. 667–706). New York: Wiley.

Mead, M. (1950). *Sex and temperament in three primitive societies.* New York: Mentor. (Original work published 1935).

Mead, M. (1961). *Coming of age in Samoa.* New York: Morrow. (Original work published 1928).

Mead, M. (1953). National character. In A. L. Kroeber (Ed.), *Anthropology today* (pp. 642–667). Chicago: University of Chicago Press.

Mead, M. (1956). The cross-cultural approach to the study of personality. In J. L. McCary (Ed.), *Psychology of personality* (pp. 201–252). New York: Grove Press.

Minsel, B., Becker, P., & Korchin, S. J. (1991). A cross-cultural view of positive mental health: Two orthogonal main factors replicable in four countries. *Journal of Cross-Cultural Psychology, 22,* 157–181.

Moghaddam, F.M. (1987). Psychology in the three worlds: As reflected by the crisis in social psychology and the move toward indigenous third-world psychology. *American Psychologist, 42*(10), 912–920.

Moghaddam, F. M. (1998). *Social psychology: Exploring universals across cultures.* New York: Freeman.

Murray, H. A., & Kluckhohn, C. (1965). Outline of a conception of personality. In C. Kluckhohn & H. Murray (Eds.). *Personality in nature, society and culture* (2nd ed., pp. 3–67). New York: Knopf.

Nathan, T. (1994). *L'influence qui quérit* [The healing influence]. Paris: Odile Jacob.

Osterweil, Z., & Nagano, K. N. (1991). Maternal views on autonomy: Japan and Israel. *Journal of Cross-Cultural Psychology, 22,* 362–375.

Partridge, K. (1987). How to become Japanese: A guide for North Americans. *Kyoto Journal, 29*(3), 12–15.

Peng, Y., Zebrowitz, L. A., & Lee, H.-K. (1993). The impact of cultural background and cross-cultural experience on impressions of American and Korean male speakers. *Journal of Cross-Cultural Psychology, 24,* 203–220.

Pepitone, A. (1989). Toward a cultural social psychology. *Psychology and Developing Societies, 1,* 5–19.

Pepitone, A. (1994). Beliefs and cultural social psychology. In L. L. Adler & U. P. Gielen (Eds.), *Cross-cultural topics in psychology* (pp. 139–152). Westport, CT: Praeger.

Pervin, L. A. (1990). *Handbook of personality: Theory and research.* New York: Guilford.

Rohner, R. (1984). Toward a conception of culture for cross-cultural psychology. *Journal of Cross-Cultural Psychology, 15*, 111–138.

Roland, A. (1988). *In search of self in India and Japan.* Princeton, NJ: Princeton University Press.

Roseman, I. J., Dhawan, N., Rettek, S. I., Naidu, R. K. et al. (1995). Cultural differences and cross-cultural similarities in appraisals and emotional responses. *Journal of Cross-Cultural Psychology, 26*, 23–48.

Rosen, L. (1991). The integrity of cultures. *American Behavioral Scientist, 34*, 594–617.

Sapir, E. (1934). The emergence of the concept of personality in a study of cultures. *Journal of Social Psychology, 5*, 408–415.

Schaufeli, W., & Janczur, B. (1994). Burnout among nurses: A Polish-Dutch comparison. *Journal of Cross-Cultural Psychology, 25*, 95–113.

Scott, W. A., Scott, R., Boehnke, K., Cheng, S. et al. (1991). Children's personality as a function of family relations within and between cultures. *Journal of Cross-Cultural Psychology, 22*, 182–208.

Segall, M. H., Dasen, P. R., Berry, J. W., & Poortinga, Y. H. (1990). *Human behavior in global perspective.* New York: Pergamon.

Smith, P. B., & Bond, M. H. (1994). *Social psychology across cultures.* Boston: Allyn & Bacon.

Spiro, M. E. (1951). Personality and culture: The natural history of a false dichotomy. *Psychiatry, 14*, 19–46.

Stiles, D. A., Gibbons, J. L., & de-la-Garza-Schnellmann, J. (1990). Opposite-sex ideal in the U.S.A. and Mexico as perceived by young adolescents. *Journal of Cross-Cultural Psychology, 21*, 180–199.

Taylor, R. D., & Oskay, G. (1995). Identity formation in Turkish and American adolescents. *Journal of Cross-Cultural Psychology, 26*, 8–22.

Tobacyk, J. J., & Tobacyk, Z. S. (1992). Comparisons of belief-based personality constructs in Polish and American university students: Paranormal beliefs, locus of control, irrational beliefs, and social interests. *Journal of Cross-Cultural Psychology, 23*, 311–325.

Tobacyk, J. J., & Pirttila-Backman, A. M. (1992). Paranormal beliefs and their implications in university students from Finland and the United States. *Journal of Cross-Cultural Psychology, 23*, 59–71.

Triandis, H. C. (1972). *The analysis of subjective culture.* New York: Wiley.

Triandis, H. C. (1989). The self and social behavior in differing cultural contexts. *Psychological Review, 96*, 506–520.

Triandis, H. (1994). *Culture and social behavior.* New York: McGraw-Hill.

Triandis, H. C. (1995). *Individualism and collectivism.* Boulder, CO: Westview Press.

Triandis, H. (1996). The psychological measurement of cultural syndromes. *American Psychologist, 51*, 407–415.

Tuss, P., Zimmer, J., & Ho, H.-Z. (1995). Causal attributions of underachieving fourth grade students in China, Japan, and the United States. *Journal of Cross-Cultural Psychology, 26*, 408–425.

Wagner, W., Kirchler, E., Clack, F., Tekarslan, E. et al. (1990). Male dominance, role segregation, and spouses' interdependence in conflict: A cross-cultural study. *Journal of Cross-Cultural Psychology, 21*, 48–70.

Wallace, A. C. (1968). *Culture and personality.* New York: Random House.

Wallace, A. (1970). *Culture and personality* (2nd ed.). New York: Random House.

Yang, K. S. (1996). Psychological transformation of the Chinese people as a result of societal modernization. In M. Bond (Ed.), *The handbook of Chinese psychology* (pp. 457–478). Hong Kong: Oxford University Press.

Ying, Y.-W., & Liese, L. H. (1994). Initial adjustment of Taiwanese students to the United States: The impact of postarrival variables. *Journal of Cross-Cultural Psychology, 25*, 466–477.

Zuckerman, M. (1990). The psychophysiology of sensation-seeking. *Journal of Personality, 58*, 313–345.

Zuckerman, M. (1995). *Good and bad humors: Biochemical bases of personality and its disorders. Psychological Science, 6*, 325–332.

2

The Cross-Cultural Challenge to Personality

Lawrence A. Pervin
Rutgers University

This chapter considers issues relevant to the cross-cultural challenge to the study of personality. The title, and ensuing discussion, follow from issues raised in Bond's (1988) edited book, *The Cross-Cultural Challenge to Social Psychology*. In this book questions were raised concerning the contribution of cross-cultural research to social psychology. For example, Messick (1988b) argued that cross-cultural replications of social-psychological experiments probably were unwise. Although recognized as potentially useful for evaluating the generality of phenomena and as a theoretical variable, Messick nevertheless concluded that cross-cultural research was an "unadvisable" research strategy to delimit the generality of an empirical relationship. Reasons given for this position included the potential for negative results to have multiple causes (i.e., lack of replication produces an uninterpretable result), the fact that such research is difficult and costly, and that results are open to multiple interpretations (e.g., is it culture? language?). In his response to discussion of the importance of such research by other contributors, Messick (1988a) again questioned whether the payoff was worth the time, money, and effort, further asked what we mean by culture, and called for examination of the processes by which culture influences behavior.

I must say that I was surprised by Messick's challenge to the role of cross-cultural research. First, the beginnings of my training in the field were influenced by a strong cultural emphasis. As a student in Harvard's social relations program, I took course work with anthropologists such as William Caudill, Cora DuBois, Florence Kluckhohn, and Evon Vogt. Thus, for my entire career the importance of cross-cultural research has been unquestioned. Second, through the work of individuals such as Markus and

23

Kitayama (1991; see also Kitayama & Markus, 1994), Shweder (1990; see also Shweder & Sullivan, 1990), and Triandis (1989), it seemed to me that there had been a growing awareness of a cross-cultural challenge to both personality and social psychology. Nevertheless, Messick's own challenge must be taken seriously and it raises a number of issues worthy of consideration: Is there a cross-cultural challenge to personality psychology? If so, what is the nature of the challenge? Given that culture and personality has been a topic of research interest for at least 50 years (Kluckhohn, 1954; Kluckhohn, Murray, & Schneider, 1956; Linton, 1945; Whiting, 1954; Whiting & Child, 1953), why has it taken so long for the relation between personality and culture to be specified?

Before addressing these questions, it may be useful to consider the role of culture in the current major theoretical approaches to personality and to consider some of the evidence for the importance of culture in personality variables.

CULTURE AND PERSONALITY THEORY

Today there are three major approaches to personality theory: psychoanalytic theory, trait theory, and social-cognitive theory (Pervin, 1996; Pervin & John, 1997). Although much of the research in the field is not dictated by hypotheses that follow directly from these theories, they remain the major approaches to broad conceptualizations of personality. Consideration can be given, then, to the role of culture in each conceptualization.

Psychoanalytic Theory

Psychoanalytic theory has a long history of a relationship with cultural anthropology. This is interesting because, despite his interest in cultural differences, Freud's intent was to develop a universal theory of personality based in large part on biological principles (Sulloway, 1979). The relation between psychoanalysis and cultural anthropology is noteworthy in at least three ways. First, a number of analysts attempted to use psychoanalytic insights to interpret cultural phenomena (e.g., Abraham, Devereaux, Kardiner, Roheim). Beyond this, the study of cultures by analysts led to the development of concepts such as *basic personality structure* (Kardiner, 1939, 1945) and *national character* (Gorer, 1950; Inkeles, 1997; Inkeles & Levinson, 1954).

Second, although anthropological studies had little impact on classical psychoanalytic theory, a number of neo-Freudians, such as Fromm (1941, 1944) and Horney (1937), did attempt to revise psychoanalytic theory in the light of a cultural perspective. Note can also be made of the efforts of Erikson (1950) who, although attempting to remain within a traditional analytic framework, emphasized the importance of social and cultural variables.

Third, and perhaps of greatest relevance to the issues under consideration, for a period of three decades or so psychoanalysis had a significant impact upon research in cultural anthropology. For example, Hall and Lindzey (1954) stated that "in relative amount the impact of psychoanalysis upon cultural anthropology has probably been greater than upon any other social science discipline" (p. 170) and Kluckhohn (1954) stated that "psychoanalysis provided anthropology with a general theory of psychological processes that was susceptible of cross-cultural testing by empirical means and with clues that might be investigated as to the psychological causes of cultural phenomena" (p. 964). This is not to say that all such research was conducted along lines sympathetic to psychoanalytic theory. Indeed, as Kluckhohn noted, many cultural anthropologists were positive that the theory was culture-bound to an important degree and set out to demonstrate that this was the case. At the same time, many anthropological researchers were sympathetic to psychoanalysis and psychoanalytic methods of investigation (Tapp, 1981). As an illustration of the former, Whiting and Child (1953) used cross-cultural data to study Freudian hypotheses concerning the relation between child-training practices as antecedent variables and beliefs concerning causes and cures of illnesses as consequent variables. As an illustration of the latter, Hallowell (1945) used the Rorschach with members of different cultures and LeVine (1973), although recognizing the danger of assuming parallel significance of tests in different cultures, suggested that psychoanalysis is a valuable method for studying personality cross-culturally.

As noted, findings from cultural anthropology appeared to have little impact upon classical psychoanalytic theory. And, apparently with time psychoanalysis ceased to have as significant an impact on anthropological investigation as once was the case (Tapp, 1981). This probably was due to many contributing factors, including a more general diminution of interest in psychoanalytic-based research, the cognitive revolution and a turn toward interest in cognitive variables, and a turn toward an emphasis on the meaning of phenomena within specific cultural contexts as opposed to the search for broad universals (Geertz, 1973, 1975). We return to this issue later but it may be worthwhile to note at this point that a similar emphasis on meaning and context was occurring within the field of social psychology (Gergen, 1973).

Trait Theory

The personality field is witnessing a resurgence of interest in traits and many suggest that a consensus is emerging concerning the basic structure of personality in the form of the *Big Five* or the *Five-Factor Model* (FFM) (Digman, 1990; Goldberg, 1993; McCrae & Costa, 1990). Support for this view comes primarily from factor analytic studies of rating and questionnaire data, with some support also coming from studies indicating an important genetic contribution to these traits. Relevant to the model is Goldberg's (1990) *fundamental lexical hypothesis*: "the most important individual differences in human transaction will come to be encoded as single terms in some or all of the world's languages" (p. 1216). In an important review of the cross-cultural generalizability of the FFM, McCrae and Costa (1997) suggested that evidence in support of the universality of the FFM personality structure is strong. As I have noted elsewhere (Pervin, 1994), the issues here are complex and the data open to varying interpretations and conclusions. Thus, for example, Digman concluded that there is something quite fundamental involved in the Big Five and asked: "Is this the way people everywhere construe personality, regardless of language or culture?" (pp. 433–434). John (1990) took a more cautious view and suggested that although the data are impressive, "conclusions about the linguistic, or even cultural universality of the Big Five would be premature" (p. 78).

My own view is that the cross-cultural replicability of factors in ratings and questionnaires is surprising and noteworthy, particularly given the fact that some of the studies involve non–Indo-European languages and a few use adjectives generated by subjects in different cultures as opposed to exclusive reliance upon a standard list of adjectives that are translated into the language of each culture. At the same time, the data are nowhere nearly as conclusive as many trait theorists would suggest. For example, one can ask whether traits are necessarily the units of choice in descriptions of people. In a relevant study, Shweder and Bourne (1984) asked subjects in India and the United States to describe the personality of a close acquaintance. Responses were coded according to whether they referred to an abstract trait, an action, or an evaluative term. They also were coded for whether contextual qualifications were used for the descriptors. The data indicated that Americans are more likely to use trait terms, whereas Indians are more likely to describe people in terms of their actions. In addition, the Indians were much more context dependent in their person descriptions. The suggestion made was that the Indian view of the person is much more embedded in a social matrix, whereas the individualistic American culture treats the person as separate from group contexts and social norms. In addition, the extent of agreement among factors across cultures is open to question (Block, 1995; Pervin, 1994). Although Bond (1994), who has conducted research on the existence of the Big Five in Chinese personality descriptors, is supportive of the fundamental lexical hypothesis, he also stated that indigenous materials need to be "coaxed" into the five-factor solution, that local languages can be "culled" for these terms, and that they are "amenable" to five-factor solutions. Along the same lines, recent research (see Hofstee, Kiers, deRaad, Goldberg, & Ostendorf, 1997) suggests that the Big Five factors are only weakly replicable cross-nationally and that few trait adjectives have the same precise meaning even across closely related languages.

In addition to the question of whether the same factors emerge cross-culturally, A. P. Fiske (1995) asked the following question and provided his own answer: "Do the facets that comprise an American trait like dominance coincide across cultures, and exhibit similar profiles of correlations with other variables? Probably not" (p. 282). In other words, Fiske suggested that the behaviors relating to a personality trait (e.g., dominance) vary cross-culturally and therefore questioned the existence of traits with invariant features across cultures. Because according to Fiske every culture operates in a cultural medium that informs and directs it, one can expect the meanings of traits and their interrelationships to differ cross-culturally. Similarly, Zebrowitz-McArthur (1988) suggested the meaning of behavior and interrelationships among behaviors differs for each cultural group: "In short, the culturally divergent perceptions of people may reflect the education of attention to different realities" (p. 252).

In sum, the issue of cross-cultural generality of the Big Five and the universality of the underlying structure of trait interrelationships, as well as the assumption of traits as basic units of personality description, remain controversial issues at this time.

Social-Cognitive Theory

The main representatives of social-cognitive theory are Bandura (1986) and Mischel (Mischel & Shoda, 1995). For purposes of comparison, however, included within this theory category are cognitive, social-cognitive, and cognitive information-processing approaches to personality. This is because representatives of these approaches share most points of emphasis and often these terms are used interchangeably with one another. One has the sense that social-cognitive theorists are among those personality psychologists most cognizant of and responsive to the importance of cultural differences. Some, such as Mischel, have conducted research in different cultures, and others, such as Markus, have worked closely with cultural anthropologists (e.g., Shweder) and psychologists from non-Western cultures (e.g., Kitayama). In addition, Bandura (1995) has displayed an interest in the relation of social-cognitive variables, particularly self-efficacy, to adaptive functioning in different cultures. At the same time, it is interesting that *culture* is not indexed in Bandura's (1986) major theoretical work or in Mischel's (1993) most recent edition of his personality text. In other words, although the social-cognitive approach displays a sympathy to cultural differences, this does not necessarily translate into direct consideration of culture as an important theoretical variable.

One root of social-cognitive theory is S-R (stimulus-response) learning theory. Along with psychoanalytic theory, S-R learning theory played a role in many early anthropological studies of culture and personality (e.g., Gorer, 1950; Whiting, 1941). In these cases culture was used as a variable in relation to learning theory and learning theory was used to explain cultural differences. In the main, the content of culture was assumed to vary (e.g., specific child-training processes) but the fundamental learning processes were assumed to be universal. Another root of social cognitive theory is Kelly's (1955) personal construct theory. A major contribution of Kelly was his emphasis on the individuality of personal constructs along with the universality of principles of construct system functioning. In other words, although fundamentally different in many ways, both S-R theory and personal construct theory suggest a distinction between content and process, with content assumed to be highly idiosyncratic and process universal. Where concepts such as structure fit in is not clear, in part because a distinction between structure and process is not always made. For example, is a schema a structure or a process? However, it is likely that most social cognitive theorists would leave room for the possibility of universal schema or categories, but it also is likely that they would emphasize that many schema are culturally distinct and that even those that are universal are culturally specific in their salience, contexts, and specific contents (Rhee, Uleman, & H. K. Lee, 1996; Zebrowitz-McArthur, 1988).

More recently, some social-cognitive psychologists appear to take the position that there may not be universal categories or units of personality (e.g., Markus, Kitayama, & Heiman, 1996). Such a position, related to the emphasis on meaning noted earlier, raises fundamental questions concerning the concepts of culture and personality, as well as the potential for a science of personality. Discussion of these issues is once more be reserved for later consideration. At this point, discussion can be summarized by suggesting that social-cognitive theory appears to be the personality theory most open to recognition of the importance of cultural differences. In contrast with psychoanalytic theory, it appears to have had little impact on anthropological research. Rather, it appears to share with some anthropological research a heritage in cognitive psychology (D'Andrade, 1981, 1984). However, also in contrast with psychoanalytic theory, it appears to be significantly influenced by cross-cultural research. This is true both in terms of the content of schema and, in more recent formulations, perhaps in terms of the very formulation of the concept of personality itself.

CULTURE AND BEHAVIOR

In his 1954 review of the literature on culture and behavior, Kluckhohn considered nine areas of research: biological functioning, sexual behavior, motor habits (e.g., gestures), perception (e.g., time), cognition (e.g., categories, language and thought), affect (e.g., expressions of emotions and circumstances of occurrence), fantasy and unconscious processes, abnormal behavior, and values. His conclusion was that "The underlying 'genotype' of all cultures is the same; the 'phenotypic' manifestations vary greatly" (p. 955). I refer to Kluckhohn's review before considering recent research on culture and behavior to once more point out that research in this area has a long history. In this section I highlight four areas of personality functioning that have received considerable attention in the recent literature and that serve as a foundation for consideration of the cross-cultural challenge to personality psychology.

The Concept of the Self

Throughout the history of the field there has been a waxing and waning of interest in the self (Pervin, 1984). Over the past 15 years perhaps no other topic has received as much interest as that of the self. Of central concern in this regard has been cultural differences in the conceptualization of the self (DeVos, Marsella, & Hsu, 1985; Geertz, 1975; Hsu, 1985; Roland, 1988; Shweder & Levine, 1984), with perhaps the greatest influence associated with the articles by Markus and Kitayama (1991) and Triandis (1989). The major contrast drawn by Markus and Kitayama is that between the independent self and the interdependent self. Whereas the Western or Euro-American view emphasizes a bounded, individualized self that transcends situations and contexts, the Asian view of selfhood emphasizes interdependence with others (see Miller, chap. 11 of this volume).

Although the distinction between independent and interdependent self seems useful, the situation in regard to understanding the concept of the self clearly is more complicated. First, it does not appear that individuals have *either* an independent self *or* an interdependent self but may have *both* selves (Singelis, 1994). Similarly, *collectivism* and *individualism* appear to be two dimensions rather than opposite ends of one dimension (Rhee et al., 1996). I am reminded here of discussion of the self in a personality seminar at the University of Hawaii, a wonderful place for studying cultural differences in action. Discussion led to the distinction between a public self and a private self, with some students associating the public self with a phony self. A student who just recently had come from living in Japan was quite perplexed by this. The distinction between a public or outer self and a private or inner self made sense to him but, for him, neither was more real or phony than the other. That is, if I understood what he was saying correctly, to express certain attitudes and behaviors publicly that did not match "inner" attitudes and beliefs was not an indication of "phoniness" but rather an expression of proper social behavior and respect for others. Thus, rather than having one or the other self, members of different cultures may differ in the extent to which their self is independent or interdependent.

Second, the independent-interdependent distinction may not even fit members of other cultures. For example, the Indian sense of self appears to be defined by the coexistence of contradictions and an emphasis on context (Bharati, 1985; Roland, 1988; Sinha & Tripathi, 1994). In other words, the construct independent-interdependent may not apply to the Indian self. Thus, Markus et al. (1996) were led to conclude that "the rapidly expanding volume of studies on culture and self suggest that many current generalizations about the nature and function of self-knowledge will have to be modified. ... Self-knowledge or self-referent thought does not appear to be universally organized by trait attributes and is often situationally variable" (p. 884). Indeed, reading Geertz's (1975) descriptions of concepts of the person in the cultures of Java, Bali, and Morocco makes one wonder about just what kinds of categories are universal and whether any culture's concept of the self can be disentangled from the cultural fabric within which it is embedded.

Cognition

To the extent that one views the self as a schema, we already have been considering cultural differences in cognition. The importance of such differences can be further highlighted by attention to research concerning the *fundamental* attribution error. For many years research on the fundamental attribution error was a major focus of social psychologists. In addition, the fundamental attribution error was used, inappropriately I believe, as an argument against the trait position. That is, it was suggested that trait psychologists take the view of the observer and therefore err in their emphasis on the consistency of behavior across situations. In any case, in what I view as one of the major illustrations of the cost of not testing principles of psychological functioning cross-culturally, it turns out that the fundamental attribution error is not so fundamental. Miller (1984) noted the tendency for Indians to give contextual descriptions of behavior and Morris and Peng (1994) demonstrated that Chinese subjects did not make the fundamental attribution error. In the latter study, although American and Chinese subjects did not differ in their causal explanations for physical events, they did differ in the causal perceptions of social events, with Chinese subjects making more situational attributions and American subjects more dispositional attributions. Interestingly enough, these authors began their article with the following question: "If causal inference is the 'cement of the universe', do cultures construct their models of the universe with different kinds of cement?" (p. 949). Y-T. Lee and Seligman (1997) found differences in explanatory style or causal explanations among mainland Chinese, Chinese-Americans, and White Americans, with mainland Chinese having the most pessimistic explanatory style. White Americans were found to attribute their success to themselves and their failure to others or circumstances to a greater extent than mainland Chinese. Additional evidence of cultural differences in attributions was found by F. Lee, Hallahan, and Herzog (1996) in their analysis of sports articles and editorials in American and Hong Kong newspapers. What remains to be seen is the extent to which cultures differ in their concern with causal explanations and the universality of causal dimensions of explanation.

Before leaving this section it may be worth noting a recent study of cultural differences in the use of rating scales because of its broad research implications. This study of response style differences among high school students from Japan, Taiwan, Canada, and the United States found that American students were more likely to use extreme values on 7-point Likert-type scales whereas the Japanese and Chinese students were more likely to use midpoint values. Canadian students fell between the two groups (C. Chen, S. Lee, & Stevenson, 1995). This study is important because it indicates that members of different cultural groups are responding not only in terms of the content of questionnaires but to the format of responses as well. This is in accord with the point made some time ago by D. W. Fiske (1971) concerning the importance of the meaning of test situations and stimuli for subjects, a point recently extended to the cultural realm by A. P. Fiske (1995).

Motives

One of the most frequently found effects in the personality and social psychological literature is what has been called the self-enhancement bias (e.g., the tendency to attribute success to the self and failure to the situation). A variety of studies now suggest that such an effect does not show up in all cultures (Brockner & Y. Chen, 1996; Heine & Lehman, 1995; Kashima & Triandis, 1986; Kitayama, Markus, Matsumoto, & Norasakkunkit, 1997; Y-T. Lee & Seligman, 1997; Markus et al., 1996). Apparently, the importance of maintaining self-esteem and the ways in which this is done vary considerably cross-culturally, with Asian subjects generally showing less of a self-enhancement bias than American subjects. Similarly, not only may there be cultural differences in the strength of a motive (e.g., need for achievement), but the manifestations of the motive may differ significantly. For example, Doi (1982) suggested that whereas achievement motives are associated with individual attainment and power over others in individualistic cultures, such motives are associated with collective goals and group efforts in collectivist cultures.

Recently, a number of anthropologists have become interested in the question of how we get from culture to motivation, from what the culture values to what members of the culture are motivated to do (D'Andrade, 1992; Strauss, 1992). The search here is not for universal motives but instead for an understanding of the process by which cultural values become internalized into individual goals. This has been an issue of long-standing concern to personality psychologists (Pervin, 1983). In discussing the issue, D'Andrade noted the problems associated with an analysis of motives in a culture: How does one recognize motives? How is context to be considered? How can we be sure that our measures are reliable and valid? Illustrative of the problem he asked: "When a Trobriander spends much time and effort piling up yams in a yam house, how can one tell which drives and goals are really involved?" (p. 27). In a critical comment on this direction for research, Shweder (1992) suggested that it expresses an artificial distinction between culture (content, cognition) and personality (force, affect). Here Shweder touched upon a fundamental issue to be considered, that is, the relation between culture and personality. The question raised is the following: Can culture and personality be considered separate or distinct from one another?

Affect

As noted, Kluckhohn considered the area of affect in his 1954 review of culture and behavior. Not surprisingly, he found considerable evidence of cultural variation in the expression of emotion and circumstances for experiencing emotion. Although dormant for a considerable period of time, the area of affect has been of increased interest for psychologists and anthropologists (Kitayama & Markus, 1994). One can speak of a controversy between those who emphasize the concept of *basic emotions* (Ekman, 1992; Izard, 1994) and those who take a more social constructivist point of view (Markus et al., 1996; White, 1993). In part the controversy involves a definition as to what constitutes affect or emotion. Mesquita and Frijda (1992) suggested a cognitive-process model of emotion with cultural differences playing a greater or lesser difference at various points in the process. Such a model may be helpful, but I suspect that it cannot mask the fact that fundamental differences exist concerning the nature of the phenomena, how they are to be understood, and how they are to be studied. For example, White recognized that there are universal physiological components to emotion, but rejected the view that these are the essential defining aspect of emotional experience. Similarly, although Markus et al. recognized that emotion is grounded in bodily sensations, they suggested that emotional experience is primarily social and cultural. Beyond this, they suggested that the study of universal facial expressions of emotion, as in the research conducted by Ekman and Izard, commits the error of considering the expression of an emotion as located in the bounded person rather than in patterns of social relationships. Perhaps even extending the argument further, White suggested that the very conception of emotion as a subject for strictly psychological research reflects a Western folk psychology that "conceives of persons primarily as autonomous individuals rather than as actors whose subjectivity is continually formed in and through interactions with others" (p. 29). In sum, he argued for a semiotic rather than an objective, individuated conception of emotion.

In considering the area of cross-cultural aspects of emotion, once more we are confronted with an appreciation not only of vast differences in behavior but of fundamental questions concerning how phenomena should be conceptualized and studied. We now return to the issue of the cross-cultural challenge to personality psychology and attempt to address these fundamental questions.

THE CHALLENGE AND THE PROBLEMS

Having considered the role of culture in personality theory and research, we can return to the questions posed at the beginning of this chapter. Given the vast cultural differences that exist in every aspect of personality functioning, and the errors that have been made in assuming universals based on research done within one culture or context, it is clear that cross-cultural research presents both challenges and opportunities for personality theory and research. These challenges and opportunities can be described as follows:

1. Are the observed principles of personality functioning universal?
2. Can cultural variation be used as a variable to test hypotheses?
3. What kind of concept of the person is possible within the context of cross-cultural research? Within such a context, what is the relation between person and culture?

Going back and reading the personality and culture literature, it is clear that these questions have been with us for some time. Recalling Messick's (1988b) view, consider the following question raised by Whiting in 1954: "It might be asked at this point why ethnographic material should be drawn upon to test psychological principles. Why not stick to materials gathered in one's own society, where the language and culture are familiar and where more adequate control of the process of data collection is possible?" (p. 524). Responding to his own question, Whiting suggested that the cross-cultural method had two advantages. First, it ensures that findings were relevant to other cultures. Second, it increases the range of variation of many variables. These sound strikingly like what has been suggested previously. And, Whiting went on to conclude: "In sum, then, the cross-cultural method, although it is still in its infancy, shows promise of being a useful adjunct to other research methods designed for the development of a general science of human behavior " (p. 531).

If we are still considering the same questions, what happened to the promise of the cross-cultural method? Note can be made here of some assumptions and potential problems spelled out by Whiting (1954). For example, he raised the question of sampling problems, particularly in nonhomogeneous societies, and wondered whether customs could be compared from one society to another, suggesting that cross-cultural comparisons required *equivalence in meaning* rather than *formal equivalence.* Consider as well a critique by Lindesmith and Strauss (1950) of the culture and personality literature of the time. These authors suggested that whereas traditional ethnology emphasized specific modes of overt behavior in delineated situations, the culture and personality view emphasized the characterization of societies in psychological terms as functioning wholes or configurations. Thus, the effort to capture the "essence" of culture in psychological terms led to concepts such as *modal personality, basic personality structure,* and *national character.* Critical of these efforts, Lindesmith and Strauss suggested the following:

1. The characterizations of societies and cultures were oversimplified. How could a society be boiled down to one theme or type, as if everyone fit the theme or type?
2. Often there was an inadequate sampling of the population.
3. Personality interpretations were made in terms of psychological processes and states while disregarding behavior as expressive of cultural roles and norms.
4. Observed behaviors were interpreted in biased ways from the standpoint of Western vocabulary and culture.
5. Methods were used (e.g., projective tests) that were of questionable utility.

Thus, it is clear the cross-cultural research and the conclusions to be drawn from it are not simple matters. In doing such research, are we sure that equivalent samples are being drawn? That the test stimuli have the same meaning in the two cultures? In making interpretations, are we sure that we understand the variables of interest within each culture's context and that we are not using biased concepts and categories? In drawing causal connections, can we separate out the specific variable being measured from other variables that may be of greater causal significance (Draguns, 1979, 1995)?

Despite these problems, my own view is that cross-cultural research has value both in the testing of universals and as a variable. Although these problems may be magnified in the study of very different cultures, and where an investigator from one culture studies another culture, one could argue that the same problems arise in research done in any heterogeneous society. In the United States, do those from the North, South, Midwest, and West function the same? Those from urban areas and those from rural areas? Blacks, Hispanics, and Whites? Protestants, Catholics, and Jews? Men and women? College sophomores and everyone else? In other words, any time we think we are establishing a general principle of personality functioning, we have to be aware of possible biases in our sample and different meanings of stimuli and the entire testing situation for different groups of individuals (D. W. Fiske, 1971). I can still recall my experience in 1962 of going from Harvard, where it seemed as if all students were interested in Erikson and felt they were going through an identity crisis, to Princeton, where students hardly seemed to resonate to Erikson at all. And, I can think back to the late 1960s and early 1970s when most of my Rutgers students viewed everything in political terms, in contrast with the present where a political interpretation seems foreign to them. What I am suggesting, then, is that the problems faced in cross-cultural research are serious but that many of them are not fundamentally different from those faced in all personality research. Thus, often I have thought that, before any article is accepted for publication in a personality journal, it should demonstrate replicability across a different population, preferably across different cultures. Where differences emerge, they should be explained in a theoretically meaningful way that forms the basis for further research (e.g., Oettingen, Little, Lindenberger, & Baltes, 1994).

Having maintained support for cross-cultural research in the testing of universals and as a research variable, it is time to come to a more fundamental issue raised by cross-cultural research: What is personality? What is culture? What is the relation between personality and culture? Although hints of such questions appear earlier in the literature, my sense is that more fundamental questions are being raised now concerning the very concept of personality and the kind of science of personality that is possible. Consider, for example, the following passage:

It is the contention of this paper that the concept of personality is an expression of the western ideal of individualism. It does not correspond even to the reality of how the western man lives in western culture, far less any man in any other culture. The stranglehold of the western ideal of individualism on our intellectual deliberations must at least be loosened. Many social scientists of non-western origin, like myself, have in this regard essentially acted like intellectual uncle Toms. I am of the conviction that the time has come for us to replace this concept with something more serviceable and get off the demi-scientific carousel called culture and personality. (Hsu, 1985, p. 25)

Or, consider the following:

It may be that the psychology which European and American investigators, and those trained in these contexts, have jointly elaborated in the past 50 years, is a psychology rooted in one set of largely unexamined ontological assumptions about what it means to be a person, to be a self. ... We can now ask whether the current view of human social behavior is at this point primarily a partial view, limited to the behavior of people within particular sociocultural and historical contexts. (Markus et al., 1996, p. 858)

What some are suggesting is that the individual cannot be separated from the culture, that there is no person without culture, no processing mechanism devoid of meaning (A. P. Fiske, 1995; Markus et al., 1996; Shweder, 1990). Not only does this raise fundamental questions concerning the nature of personality but questions concerning the nature of culture, and the relationship between the two. In other words, what these authors were suggesting is that there is no person without culture, no culture without person, no culture and personality because they are part and parcel of one another.

I can recall the time I read a preprint of Shweder's (1990) presentation of his semiotic point of view and critique of the *central processing mechanism* view of the person. In this article Shweder suggested that general psychology presumes a central processing mechanism that is independent of context and culture. Even if such a mechanism exists, Shweder suggested that the idea of a context-free, meaning-free event is an impossible notion. The article "blew me away" because it challenged many of my basic assumptions and my entire view of a science of personality. I think that this is the current challenge of cross-cultural research to the field of personality. That is, the current challenge is the kind of definition of the person and kind of science of personality that are possible. I must say that, although profoundly challenged by the semiotic point of view, I remain somewhat conventional and conservative in my belief that a bounded view of the person and a science of personality are possible. We must be wiser and more enlightened now of the limits of this view, but I think that it still is possible to talk about universal units and universal processes of personality functioning. I do not think we know what these units and processes are as yet but, for example, I think that the contrast of conflicted as opposed to integrated system functioning is a principle that will be applicable across members of all cultural groups. At the same time, clearly the contents of conflict or integration within the system will vary enormously between individuals, and on a broader scale between members of different cultures.

Perhaps I am back to a distinction between content and process, emphasizing the idiosyncratic aspects of content and the universal aspects of process. Of course, to know the individual one must be aware of content and meaning. However, to know the nature of personality functioning one need not know each and every person. As a practicing clinician, I need to know the content of what is of concern to the person, but as a personality scientist, I am able to attempt to abstract common principles of personality functioning. Whether such principles represent an adequate level of understanding I suspect will be a matter of personal preference and taste. Thus, I remain a believer in a central processing mechanism that always is influenced by culture, just as it always is influenced by context, but can be defined by structural units and system processes that are independent of culture and context. The challenge of cross-cultural research, then, is to define the boundaries of this central processing mechanism that we call personality, including the possibility that the boundaries are so narrow that it is not worth preserving the concept at all.

REFERENCES

Bandura, A. (1986). *Social foundations of thought and action.* Englewood Cliffs, NJ: Prentice-Hall.

Bandura, A. (Ed.). (1995). *Self-efficacy in changing societies.* New York: Cambridge University Press.

Bharati, A. (1985). The self in Hindu thought and action. In A. J. Marsella, G. deVos, & F. L. K. Hsu (Eds.), *Culture and self* (pp. 185–230). New York: Tavistock.

Block, J. (1995). A contrarian view of the five-factor approach to personality description. *Psychological Bulletin, 117,* 187–215.

Bond, M. H. (1988). *The cross-cultural challenge to social psychology.* Newbury Park, CA: Sage.

Bond, M. H. (1994). Trait theory and cross-cultural studies of person perception. *Psychological Inquiry, 5,* 114–117.

Brockner, J., & Chen, Y. (1996). The moderating roles of self-esteem and self-construal in reaction to a threat to the self: Evidence from the People's Republic of China and the United States. *Journal of Personality and Social Psychology, 71,* 603–615.

Chen, C., Lee, S., & Stevenson, H. W. (1995). Response style and cross-cultural comparisons of rating scales among East Asian and North American students. *Psychological Science, 6,* 170–175.

D'Andrade, R. G. (1981). The cultural part of cognition. *Cognitive Science, 5*, 179–195.

D'Andrade, R. G. (1984). Cultural meaning systems. In R. A. Shweder & R. LeVine (Eds.), *Culture theory: Essays on the social origins of mind, self, and emotion* (pp. 88–123). Chicago: University of Chicago Press.

D'Andrade, R. G. (1992). Schemas and motivation. In R. G. D'Andrade & C. Strauss (Eds.), *Human motives and cultural models* (pp. 23–44). Cambridge, England: Cambridge University Press.

DeVos, G., Marsella, A. J., & Hsu, F. L. K. (1985). Introduction: Approaches to culture and self. In A. J. Marsella, G. DeVos, & F. L. K. Hsu (Eds.), *Culture and self* (pp. 2–23). New York: Tavistock.

Digman, J. M. (1990). Personality structure: Emergence of the five-factor model. *Annual Review of Psychology, 41*, 417–440.

Doi, K. (1982). A two dimension theory of achievement motivation: Affiliative and non-affiliative. *Japanese Journal of Psychology, 52*, 344–350.

Draguns, J. G. (1979). Culture and personality. In A. J. Marsella, R. Tharpe, & T. J. Ciborowski (Eds.), *Perspectives on cross-cultural psychology* (pp. 179–207). New York: Academic Press.

Draguns, J. G. (1995). Cultural influences upon psychopathology: Clinical and practical implications. *Journal of Social Distress and the Homeless, 4*, 79–103.

Ekman, P. (1992). An argument for basic emotions. *Cognition and Emotion, 6*, 169–200.

Erikson, E. (1950). *Childhood and society.* New York: Norton.

Fiske, A. P. (1995). The cultural dimensions of psychological research: Method effects imply cultural mediation. In P. E. Shrout & S. T. Fiske (Eds.), *Personality research, methods, and theory* (pp. 271–294). Hillsdale, NJ: Lawrence Erlbaum Associates.

Fiske, D. W. (1971). *Measuring the concepts of personality.* Chicago: Aldine.

Fromm, E. (1941). *Escape from freedom.* New York: Farrar & Rinehart.

Fromm, E. (1944). Individual and social origins of neurosis. *American Sociological Review, 9*, 380–384.

Geertz, C. (1973). *Interpretation of cultures.* New York: Basic Books.

Geertz, C. (1975). "From the native's point of view": On the nature of anthropological understanding. *American Scientist, 63*, 47–53.

Gergen, K. J. (1973). Social psychology as history. *Journal of Personality and Social Psychology, 26*, 309–320.

Goldberg, L. R. (1990). An alternative "description of personality": The big-five factor structure. *Journal of Personality and Social Psychology, 59*, 1216–1229.

Goldberg, L. R. (1993). The structure of phenotypic personality traits. *American Psychologist, 48*, 26–34.

Gorer, G. (1950). The concept of national character. *Science News, 18*, 105–123.

Hall, C. S., & Lindzey, G. (1954). Psychoanalytic theory and its applications in the social sciences. In G. Lindzey (Ed.), *Handbook of social psychology* (pp. 143–180). Cambridge, MA: Addison-Wesley.

Hallowell, A. I. (1945). The Rorschach technique in the study of personality and culture. *American Anthropologist, 47*, 195–210.

Heine, S. J., & Lehman, D. R. (1995). Cultural variation unrealistic optimism: Does the West feel more vulnerable than the East? *Journal of Personality and Social Psychology, 68*, 595–607.

Hofstee, W. K. B., Kiers, H. A., deRaad, B., Goldberg, L. R., & Ostendorf, F. (1997). A comparison of Big-Five structures of personality traits in Dutch. English, and German. *European Journal of Personality, 11*, 15–31.

Horney, K. (1937). *The neurotic personality of our time.* New York: Norton.

Hsu, F. L. K. (1985). The self in cross-cultural perspective. In A. J. Marsella, G. DeVos, & F. L. K. Hsu (Eds.), *Culture and self* (pp. 24–55). New York: Tavistock.

Inkeles, A. (1997). *National character: A psychosocial perspective.* New Brunswick, NJ: Transaction Publishers.

Inkeles, A., & Levinson, D. J. (1954). National character. In G. Lindzey (Ed.), *Handbook of social psychology* (pp. 143–180). Cambridge, MA: Addison-Wesley.

Izard, C. E. (1994). Innate and universal facial expressions: Evidence from developmental and cross-cultural research. *Psychological Bulletin, 115*, 288–299.

John, O. P. (1990). The "Big Five" factor taxonomy: Dimensions of personality in the natural language and in questionnaires. In L. A. Pervin (Ed.), *Handbook of personality: Theory and research* (pp. 66–100). New York: Wiley.

Kardiner, A. (1939). *The individual and his society.* New York: Columbia University Press.

Kardiner, A. (1945). *The psychological frontiers of society.* New York: Columbia University Press.

Kashima, Y., & Triandis, H. C. (1986). The self-serving bias in attribution as a coping strategy: A cross-cultural study. *Journal of Cross-Cultural Psychology, 17,* 83–97.

Kelly, G. A. (1955). *The psychology of personal constructs.* New York: Norton

Kitayama, S., & Markus, H. R. (Eds.). (1994). *Emotion and culture.* Washington, DC: American Psychological Association.

Kitayama, S., Markus, H. R., Matsumoto, H., & Norasakkunkit, V. (1997). Individual and collective processes in the construction of the self: Self-enhancement in the United States and self-criticism in Japan. *Journal of Personality and Social Psychology, 72,* 1245–1267.

Kluckhohn, C. (1954). Culture and behavior. In G. Lindzey (Ed.), *Handbook of social psychology* (pp. 920–976). Cambridge, MA: Addison-Wesley.

Kluckhohn, C., Murray, H., & Schneider, D. (1956). (Eds.). Personality in nature, society, and culture. New York: Knopf.

Lee, F., Hallahan, M., & Herzog, T. (1996). Explaining real-life events: How culture and doman shape attributions. *Personality and Social Psychology Bulletin, 22,* 732–741.

Lee, Y-T., & Seligman, M. E. P. (1997). Are Americans more optimistic than the Chinese? *Personality and Social Psychology Bulletin, 23,* 32–40.

LeVine, R. A. (1973). *Culture, behavior, and personality.* Chicago: Aldine.

Lindesmith, A. R., & Strauss, A. L. (1950). A critique of culture-personality writings. *American Sociological Review, 15,* 587–600.

Linton, R. (1945). *The cultural background of personality.* New York: Appleton–Century.

Markus, H. R., & Kitayama, S. (1991). Culture and the self: Implications for cognition, emotion, and motivation. *Psychological Review, 98,* 224–253.

Markus, H. R., Kitayama, S., & Heiman, R. J. (1996). Culture and "basic" psychological principles. In E. T. Higgins & A. Kruglanski (Eds.), *Social psychology: Handbook of basic principles* (pp. 857–913). New York: Guilford.

McCrae, R. R.. & Costa, P. T., Jr. (1990). *Personality in adulthood.* New York: Guilford.

McCrae, R. R., & Costa, P. T., Jr. (1997). Personality trait structure as a human universal. *American Psychologist, 52,* 509–516.

Mesquita, B., & Frijda, N. H. (1992). Cultural variations in emotions: A review. *Psychological Bulletin, 112,* 179–204.

Messick, D. M. (1988a). Coda. In M. H. Bond (Ed.), *The cross-cultural challenge to social psychology* (pp. 286–289). Newbury Park, CA: Sage.

Messick, D. M. (1988b). On the limitations of cross-cultural research in social psychology. In M. H. Bond (Ed.), *The cross-cultural challenge to social psychology* (pp. 41–47). Newbury Park, CA: Sage.

Miller, J. G. (1984). Culture and the development of everyday social explanation. *Journal of Personality and Social Psychology, 46,* 961–978.

Mischel, W. (1993). *Introduction to personality.* New York: Harcourt Brace.

Mischel, W., & Shoda, Y. (1995). A cognitive-affective system theory of personality: Reconceptualizing the invariances in personality and the role of situations. *Psychological Review, 102,* 246–286.

Morris, M. W., & Peng, K. (1994). Culture and cause: American and Chinese attributions for social and physical events. *Journal of Personality and Social Psychology, 67,* 949–971.

Oettingen, G., Little, T. D., Lindenberger, U., & Baltes, P. B. (1994). Causality, agency and control beliefs in East versus West Berlin children: A natural experiment on the role of context. *Journal of Personality and Social Psychology, 66,* 579–595.

Pervin, L. A. (1983). The stasis and flow of behavior: Toward a theory of goals. In M. M. Page (Ed.), *Personality: Current theory and research* (pp. 1–53). Lincoln: University of Nebraska Press.

Pervin, L. A. (1984). *Current controversies and issues in personality.* New York: Wiley.

Pervin, L. A. (1994). A critical analysis of current trait theory. *Psychological Inquiry, 5,* 103–113.

Pervin, L. A. (1996). *The science of personality.* New York: Wiley.

Pervin, L. A., & John, O. P. (1997). *Personality: Theory and research* (7th ed.). New York: Wiley.

Rhee, E., Uleman, J. S., & Lee, H. K. (1996). Variations in collectivism and individualism by ingroup and culture: Confirmatory factor analyses. *Journal of Personality and Social Psychology, 71,* 1037–1054.

Roland, A. (1988). *In search of self in India and Japan.* Princeton, NJ: Princeton University Press.

Shweder, R. A. (1990). Cultural psychology—What is it? In J. W. Stigler, R. A. Shweder, & G. Herdt (Eds.), *Cultural psychology: Essays on comparative human development* (pp. 1–43). Cambridge, England: Cambridge University Press.

Shweder, R. A. (1992). Ghost busters in anthropology. In C. Strauss & R. G. D'Andrade (Eds.), *Human motives and cultural models* (pp. 45–58). Cambridge, England: Cambridge University Press.

Shweder, R. A., & Bourne, L. (1984). Does the concept of the person vary cross-culturally? In R. A. Shweder & R. A. LeVine (Eds.), *Culture theory: Essays on mind, self, and emotion* (pp. 158–199). New York: Cambridge University Press.

Shweder, R. A., & LeVine, R. A. (Eds.). (1984). *Culture theory: Essays on mind, self, and emotion.* New York: Cambridge University Press.

Shweder, R. A., & Sullivan, M. A. (1990). The semiotic subject of cultural psychology. In L. A. Pervin (Ed.), *Personality: Theory and research* (pp. 399–418). New York: Guilford.

Singelis, T. M. (1994). The measurement of independent and interdependent self-construals. *Personality and Social Psychology Bulletin, 20,* 580–591.

Sinha, D., & Tripathi, R. C. (1994). A case of coexistence of opposites. In U. Kim, H. C. Triandis, C. Kagitcibasi, S-C. Choi, & G. Yoon (Eds.), *Individualism and collectivism* (pp. 123–136). Newbury Park, CA: Sage.

Strauss, C. (1992). Models and motives. In C. Strauss & R. G. D'Andrade (Eds.), *Human motives and cultural models* (pp. 1–20). Cambridge, England: Cambridge University Press.

Sulloway, F. J. (1979). *Freud: Biologist of the mind.* New York: Basic Books.

Tapp, J. L. (1981). Studying personality development. In H. C. Triandis & A. Heron (Eds.), *Handbook of cross-cultural psychology* (pp. 343–423). Boston: Allyn & Bacon.

Triandis, H. C. (1989). The self and social behavior in differing cultural contexts. *Psychological Review, 96,* 506–520.

White, G. M. (1993). Emotions inside out: The anthropology of affect. In M. Lewis & J. Haviland (Eds.), *Handbook of emotions* (pp. 29–39). New York: Guilford.

Whiting, J. W. M. (1941). *Becoming a Kwoma.* New Haven, CT: Yale University Press.

Whiting, J. W. M. (1954). The cross-cultural method. In G. Lindzey (Ed.), *Handbook of social psychology* (pp. 523–531). Cambridge, MA: Addison-Wesley.

Whiting, J. W. M., & Child, I. L. (1953). *Child training and personality.* New Haven, CT: Yale University Press.

Zebrowitz-McArthur, L. (1988). Person perception in cross-cultural perspective. In M. H. Bond (Ed.), *The cross-cultural challenge to social psychology* (pp. 245–265). Newbury Park, CA: Sage.

II

Basic Personality Differences Between Social and Cultural Groups

3

Ethnic Differences in Temperament

J. Philippe Rushton
University of Western Ontario

Over a century ago, Sir Francis Galton began modern questionnaire research into temperament with his study of "Good and Bad Temper in English Families" (Galton, 1865). He was also the first to advocate the study of human twins and of selective breeding studies of animals to disentangle the effects of heredity and environment. And it was Galton who first contrasted the taciturn reserve of American Indians, and the complacency of the Chinese, with the talkative impulsivity of Africans. He further noted that these temperamental differences persisted irrespective of climate (from the frozen north through the equator), and religion, language, or political system (whether self-ruled or governed by the Spanish, Portuguese, English, or French). Anticipating later studies of transracial adoptions, Galton observed that the majority of individuals adhered to racial type even after being raised by White settlers. Modern evidence shows that Galton's views were largely correct.

Temperament refers to an individual's characteristic or habitual modes of behavioral and emotional responding that are present at an early age and often believed to have some basis in biological processes partly determined by heredity. It is typically discernible at birth. That infants differ systematically is shown by research observations starting in the first few days or weeks of life and extending, in some cases, for over a decade. In their book, Temperament and Behavior Disorders in Children, Thomas, Chess, and Birch (1968) were able to classify babies shortly after their birth into three types—"easy children" (adaptable, cheerful, regular in habits), "difficult children" (irritable, crying, withdrawn, irregular in habits), and "slow-to-warm-up children" (inactive, slow to adapt, gentle). About 70% of the difficult babies later developed behavioral problems calling for psychiatric attention; only 18% of the easy ones had such problems (Thomas & Chess, 1984).

GENETICS AND TEMPERAMENT

One of the best known analyses of genetics and temperament was published in 1974 by Daniel G. Freedman. He observed 20 pairs of newborn twins of the same gender, some identical (monozygotic, sharing 100% of their genes), and others fraternal (dizygotic, sharing at least 50% of their genes). Until their observations were complete, the investigators did not know which type of twin they were studying (and neither, at the time, did the parents). The investigators rated the infants for behavioral tendencies such as being responsive to others, displaying fear of a new situation, and having a long attention span. Overwhelmingly, the identical twins were more similar in behavior than the fraternal twins, especially with regard to fearfulness, social awareness, and the tendency to smile and vocalize.

Other twin studies confirm the heritability of temperament. Several investigators have videotaped toddlers to determine how shy they were in dealing with new situations (such as a stranger arriving at the home or a stranger offering toys). A study of activity level in 3- to 12-year-olds counted the number of times children "got up and down" while "watching television" and "during meals." In all these studies, identical twins were found to be much more similar than fraternal twins, with the genetic contribution typically ranging from 27% to 56% (Rowe, 1994).

Several studies have been carried out on temperament traits in adults. In one, my colleagues and I gave questionnaires to 573 pairs of 19- to 60-year-old twins measuring nurturant and aggressive tendencies. The questionnaires included a 20-item altruism scale, a 33-item empathy scale, a 16-item nurturance scale, and many items assessing aggression. As shown in Table 3.1, 50% of the variance on each scale was associated with genetic effects, virtually 0% with the twin's common environment, and the remaining 50% with each twin's specific environment. When the estimates were corrected for unreliability of measurement, the genetic contribution increased to 60% (Rushton, Fulker, Neale, Nias, & Eysenck, 1986).

High heritabilities were also found in an examination of violent reactions such as the destruction of property, fighting, carrying and using a weapon, and struggling with a police officer (Rushton, 1996). At least the heritabilities were high for men. In this study, however, environmental factors were predominant for women. More generally, women averaged a significantly gentler temperament than men; they were typically more empathetic, less prone to anger, less prone to aggression, and less prone to acts of violence. Women also had a smaller variance of scores on measures of violence.

TABLE 3.1

Genetic and Environmental Contributions to Altruism and Aggression Questionnaires
in 573 Adult Twin Pairs

Trait	Additive Genetive Variance		Common Environmental Variance		Specific Environmental Variance	
Altruism	51%	(60%)	2%	(2%)	47%	(38%)
Empathy	51%	(65%)	0%	(0%)	49%	(35%)
Nurturance	43%	(60%)	1%	(1%)	56%	(39%)
Aggressiveness	39%	(54%)	0%	(0%)	61%	(46%)
Assertiveness	53%	(69%)	0%	(0%)	47%	(31%)

Note. From Rushton, Fulker, Neale, Nias, & Eysenck (1986). Altruism and aggression: The heritability of individual differences. *Journal of Personality and Social Psychology, 50,* 1194. Copyright © 1986 by the American Psychological Association. Adapted by permission. Estimates in parentheses are corrected for measurement unreliability.

Corroborating the twin work on antisocial behavior are several American, Danish, and Swedish adoption studies. Children who were adopted in infancy were at greater risk for criminal convictions if their biological parents had been convicted of a crime than if their adoptive parents had been. For example, in a Danish study of some 14,000 adoptees, if boys had neither adoptive parents nor biological parents who were criminals, their rate of criminal conviction was 14%. If the adoptive, but not the biological parents were criminals, boys still had a conviction rate of only 15%. But if the biological, but not the adoptive parents were criminal, the rate increased to 20%. And, if both biological and adoptive parents were criminals, the rate increased to 25%. Moreover, whereas siblings raised apart showed 20% concordance for criminality, half-siblings showed only 13% concordance, and pairs of unrelated children reared together only 9% concordance (Mednick, Gabrielli, & Hutchings, 1984).

ETHNIC DIFFERENCES IN TEMPERAMENT

I cannot emphasize enough that the profiles I am about to describe reflect *average* differences. Not all Africans or East Asians (and their descendants) are the same as each other and different from Europeans (and their descendants). There is much overlap and the full range of temperament and behavior is found in every ethnic group. Moreover, I obviously engage in much oversimplification by dividing all the world's people into just three categories: East Asian, European, and African (although I do provide a wide sampling from the home continents as well as the United States). Also, although the data suggest that genetic factors contribute to differences between human groups, it is clear that environmental factors do so too (Rushton, 1995).

Temperamental differences are not randomly distributed in the population. Again Daniel Freedman (1974, 1979) was one of the first to provide evidence in support of Galton's insights. Freedman examined 24 newborn Chinese-American babies and 24 newborn White babies who were similar in weight, physical vitality, mother's age, length of labor, and use of drugs during labor. Though there was a substantial overlap between the two groups: The Chinese-American babies, within (on the average) 33 hours of being born, were less perturbable, more placid, and more easily consoled than the White babies. The Euro-American infants had a greater tendency to be changeable, move back and forth between states of contentment and upset, and reach the peak of excitement sooner, whereas the Chinese-American infants were calmer and more consolable when upset.

Similar findings have been reported by Jerome Kagan and his coworkers (Kagan, Arcus, Snidman, Feng, Hendler, & Greene, 1994) at Harvard University. In a comparison of 106 Irish 4-month-olds born in Dublin and 80 Chinese infants who were born in Beijing, Kagan et al. recorded motor activity, vocalization, fretting, crying, and smiling. A total motor score was calculated based on the frequency of movements of both arms, both legs, bursts of movement of either arms or legs, or arches of the back. Vocalization, smiling, and fretting were coded in terms of the seconds the child cried. Analysis of the videotapes of the infants' behavior revealed a dramatic difference between the White and the Chinese infants. The Chinese infants were significantly lower in motor activity, irritability, and vocalization compared with either the Irish infants or the White American infants.

Interestingly, Amerindian infants tend to be temperamentally and motorically similar to Chinese babies. In a study of Amerindian infants, Brazelton, Robey and Collier (1969) reported that Amerindian neonates exhibited almost none of the normally occurring spasmodic movements common in White newborns, and maintained smoother gross motor movements throughout the first year. DNA analysis suggests that Amerindians and Chinese are two branches of the Mongoloid race, thought to have become differentiated from Whites about 41,000 years ago and from each other about 30,000 years ago (Stringer & Andrews, 1988; see more later). The common Mongoloid-Caucasoid split from African Negroids is believed to have occurred about 110,000 years ago.

By 2 years of age, Caucasoid children show greater behavioral inhibition than do Mongoloid children. One cross-cultural laboratory study comparing 118 Chinese toddlers from the People's Republic of China with 82 White Canadian children, found the Chinese children spent more time in physical contact with their mothers during free play and had a longer latency to approaching a stranger or an exciting toy than did the White children (Chen et al., in press). By 3 and 4 years of age, White children readily engage in approach and interaction behavior whereas East Asian children spend more time on individual projects and generally demonstrate low noise levels, quiet serenity, and few aggressive or disruptive behaviors (Freedman, 1974, 1979). African-descended (or Negroid) children are even more uninhibited than Whites.

A study carried out in Quebec, Canada, with preschoolers, showed how generalizable the racial pattern in temperament is. A sample of 825 4- to 6-year-old children from 66 different countries speaking 30 different languages were assessed by 50 teachers. All the children were in preschool French language immersion classes for immigrant children in Montreal used to facilitate integration into the school system. Only 20% of the children were born in Canada, with the Black children typically coming from French-language countries like Haiti, the White children from Spanish-speaking countries like Chile, and the Oriental children from what was once French Indo-China (now Vietnam and Kampuchea). Teachers reported better social adjustment and less hostility-aggression from Mongoloid children than from Caucasoid children, who in turn were better adjusted and less hostile than Negroid children (Tremblay & Baillargeon, 1984).

Comparing three groups of Chinese 5-year-olds in Beijing with three groups of White Canadians in Ottawa, using continuous observation on four separate occasions, Orlick, Zhou, and Partington (1990) also found significant differences in prosocial and antisocial behavior. Whereas 85% of peer interactions documented in China were cooperative in nature, 78% of those in Canada involved conflict. Similar results emerged from a study of 10-year-olds in the People's Republic of China compared with children from Sweden on the Olweus' Aggression Inventory. Ekblad and Olweus (1986) found that the Chinese were less aggressive and higher in prosocial behavior than were the Swedes.

These results do not vary, regardless of the age of the subjects, the trait studied, or the method of measurement. Typically, studies of infants and young children use observer ratings, whereas studies of adults use paper-and-pencil tests. Researchers have investigated the personality of the Chinese and Japanese, both in their homelands and in North America, giving university students standardized tests such as Cattell's Sixteen Personality Factor Questionnaire, the Eysenck Personality Questionnaire, the Edwards Personal Preference Schedule, and the Minnesota Multiphasic Personality Inventory (Vernon, 1982). The evidence showed that, on average, East Asians were more introverted and more anxious, though less dominant and less aggressive than White Americans. Studies carried out on Africans and Black Americans show greater aggressiveness, dominance, impulsivity, and displays of masculinity compared to Whites (Wilson & Herrnstein, 1985).

In one study, I indexed behavioral restraint by low Extraversion (sociability) and high Neuroticism (anxiety) scores from the Eysenck Personality Questionnaire for a worldwide database of thousands of subjects from 25 different countries (Rushton, 1985). Asian samples averaged less extraversion and more anxiety than did the European samples, who averaged less extraversion and more anxiety than did the African samples. Of course studies of subjects who are not neonates, even studies of children as young as 6 months of age, may be assessing heredity–environment interaction rather than only inherited differences in temperament. But when studies of neonates and older subjects converge on the same pattern of results—Europeans consistently between Africans and East Asians—we are entitled to suggest that heredity makes some contribution to this pattern.

Self-Esteem.   Self-esteem may be one aspect of temperament. Surprisingly, African-American youth have higher general self-esteem than Whites or Asians (Levin, 1997). In one of the larger studies, 11- to 16-year-olds were examined in two small southern towns (Tashakkori, 1993). Respondents read along on each question while the teacher read it aloud. Items measuring self-esteem were from the Rosenberg Self-Esteem Scale and included "I take a positive attitude toward myself," "I feel I am a person of worth, on an equal basis with others," "At times I think I am no good at all," "On the whole, I am satisfied with myself," and "I am able to do things as well as most people." Assessments were also made concerning beliefs about general competence with items such as "I am intelligent" and "I can learn almost anything if I set my mind on it," as well as more specific beliefs about attractive appearance, physical ability, and academic self-perceptions like reading and mathematics and personal control over events.

Tashakkori (1993) found the general self-esteem scores on the Rosenberg Scale as well as other indices of self-attitudes showed African Americans scored from one half to two thirds of a standard deviation higher than White

Americans. This finding is confirmed by a study of older adolescents in national studies (see Tashakkori, 1993). African-American groups consistently showed more positive scores on the majority of specific self-belief indices, particularly regarding appearance and attractiveness, but also regarding competence in reading, science, and social studies (but not mathematics), despite their lower self-reported (and actual) academic achievement. The only beliefs in which the African Americans scored lower than the Whites were those that reflected self-efficacy and control of events that happened to self.

Crime. Crime is partly based on temperament. In *Crime and Human Nature*, Wilson and Herrnstein (1985) noted that the East Asian underrepresentation in U.S. crime statistics posed a theoretical problem. The solution proposed by criminologists as early as the 1920s was that the Asian "ghetto" protected members from the disruptive tendencies of the outside society. For African Americans, however, the ghetto is said to foster crime. Even though they make up less than one eighth of the population, African Americans account for half of all arrests for assault and murder and two thirds of all arrests for robbery in the United States. Because about the same proportion of African-American and White crime victims report that their assailant was African American (Levin, 1997), the arrest statistics cannot be attributed only to racist police.

Female-perpetrated homicides tell a similar story. In one study (Mann, 1996), 75% of arrests were of African-American women, 13% were White women, whereas no Asian women at all were arrested. Contrary to some popular sociocultural explanations, African Americans also make up a disproportionate share of those arrested for white-collar offenses. For example, about one third of those arrested for fraud, forgery, counterfeiting, and receiving stolen property, and about one fourth of those arrested for embezzlement are African American. African Americans are underrepresented only for crime in the executive suites—those white-collar offenses (tax fraud, securities violations) that by definition are restricted to individuals in high-status occupations.

A similar racial pattern is found in other industrialized Western countries. In London, England, for example, African-descended people make up 13% of the population, but account for 50% of the crime. A government commission in Canada reported that Blacks were 5 times more likely to be in jail than were Whites, and 10 times more likely than Asians (Ministry of the Solicitor-General and Correctional Services, 1996).

I have carried out several analyses of INTERPOL Yearbooks including for the years 1983–1984, 1985–1986, and 1989–1990. The results are consistent. The rate of violent crime (murder, rape, and serious assault) was three times lower in Asian or Pacific Rim countries than in African or Caribbean countries, with European countries intermediate. Aggregating the data for Asian, European, and African countries from the 1990 INTER-POL Yearbook yielded the following crime rates per 100,000 population: Asian = 32, European = 75, and African = 240. Of course, these data, by themselves, do not (and cannot) address the issue of whether the behaviors are genetic or cultural in origin.

STEREOTYPES OR ACCURATE PERCEPTIONS?

Daniel Freedman (1979), Ottati and Lee (1995), and Lee, Jussim, and McCauley (1995), among others, have examined the question of whether so-called "stereotypes" may sometimes be accurate perceptions of real group differences. For example, Eskimos, Amerindians, and Asians alike (all of whom are of Mongoloid origin) are perceived by Europeans as placid and behaviorally restrained whereas Eskimos and Asians sometimes characterize Whites as "emotionally volatile" (LeVine, 1975).

In my book, *Race, Evolution, and Behavior* (Rushton, 1995), I described three distinct racial profiles that apply to over 60 anatomical and social variables, including temperament and personality, in which East Asians are at one end of the continuum, Africans are at the other, and Europeans regularly fall between the two. These results show that Galton's original assessments of race differences extend beyond temperament (Table 3.2). Temperament is best seen as one element in a suite of behaviors that make up what is known in evolutionary biology as a "life-history."

While conducting my research on mean race differences on the various traits listed in Table 3.2, I carried out a survey (Rushton, 1992) of the opinions of 73 Asian and 211 non-Asian (mainly White) students at the University of Western Ontario concerning the ranking of the races on that list of traits. There was substantial agreement of the rankings by the Asian and non-Asian students. Asians (and Whites) viewed Asians as having more intelligence, industry, anxiety, and rule-following behavior than either Whites or Blacks, while being significantly lower in activity level, sociability, aggressiveness, strength of the sex drive, and genital size. Whites were ranked intermediate to Asians and Blacks. This gradient parallels that

TABLE 3.2

Relative Ranking on Diverse Variables

Variable	Asians	Whites	Blacks
Temperament			
Activity	Lower	Intermediate	Higher
Aggressiveness	Lower	Intermediate	Higher
Cautiousness	Higher	Intermediate	Lower
Dominance	Lower	Intermediate	Higher
Impulsivity	Lower	Intermediate	Higher
Self-concept	Lower	Intermediate	Higher
Sociability	Lower	Intermediate	Higher
Maturation rate			
Gestation time	Later	Later	Earlier
Skeletal development	Later	Intermediate	Earlier
Motor development	Later	Intermediate	Earlier
Dental development	Later	Intermediate	Earlier
Age of first intercourse	Later	Intermediate	Earlier
Age of first pregnancy	Later	Intermediate	Earlier
Life-span	Longer	Intermediate	Shorter
Social organization			
Marital stability	Higher	Intermediate	Lower
Law abidingness	Higher	Intermediate	Lower
Mental health	Higher	Intermediate	Lower
Administrative capacity	Higher	Higher	Lower
Reproductive effort			
Two-egg twinning (per 1000 births)	4	8	16
Hormone levels	Lower	Intermediate	Higher
Secondary sex characteristics	Smaller	Intermediate	Larger
Intercourse frequencies	Lower	Intermediate	Higher
Permissive attitudes	Lower	Intermediate	Higher
Sexually transmitted diseases	Lower	Intermediate	Higher
Intelligence			
IQ test scores	106	100	85
Decision times	Faster	Intermediate	Slower
Brain size			
Autopsy data (cm^3 equivalents)	1,351	1,356	1,223
Endocranial volume (cm^3)	1,415	1,362	1,268
External head measures (cm^3)	1,356	1,329	1,294
Cortical neurons (billions)	13.767	13.665	13.185

Note. Adapted from J. P. Rushton (1995). *Race, evolution, and behavior* (p. 5), New Brunswick, NJ: Transaction Publishers. Copyright © 1995 by Transaction Publishers, All rights reserved. Reprinted by permission.

found for the objective measures. (The only exception to the general tendency is that Asians, but not Whites, viewed Whites as more aggressive than Blacks.)

RELATED RACIAL TRAITS

It is important to examine at least briefly some of the other differences listed in Table 3.2. The relationship between these differences and the levels of various hormones (especially testosterone) may help to order the biological basis of behavior. If temperament differences are rooted in the genes, they must also be mediated by neurophysiological mechanisms. Even more, they must be rooted in evolutionary processes where, of course, genes originate.

Physical Maturation.   In the United States, Asian and White babies have a longer gestation period than African-American babies. By week 39, 51% of African-American children have been born, but only 33% of Asian or White babies. Similar differences are found in Europe where women of European ancestry have been compared with women of (often middle-class) African ancestry (Papiernik, Cohen, Richard, de Oca, & Feingold, 1986). Although Black babies are born earlier than White babies, they are physiologically more mature at birth (as measured by pulmonary function and amniotic fluid).

The relative Asian delay in physical maturation continues through life. Asian children typically do not walk until 13 months, compared with 12 months for White children, and 11 months for Black children (Freedman, 1974, 1979). Well-standardized tests such as Bayley's Scales of Mental and Motor Development and the Cambridge Neonatal Scales show that Black babies from Africa, the Caribbean, and the United States mature faster on measures taken from birth to 12 months (coordination and head lifting, muscular strength and turning over, and locomotion) and 15 to 20 months (putting on clothing).

Asian children begin the first phase of permanent tooth eruption at 6.1 years and finish at 7.8 years; Europeans begin at 6.1 years and finish at 7.7 years; and Africans begin at 5.8 years and finish at 7.6 years (Eveleth & Tanner, 1990; Tompkins, 1996). East Asians also reach sexual maturity (measured by age at first menstruation, first sexual experience, and first pregnancy) later than do Europeans, who in turn sexually mature slower than do Africans. One large U.S. survey showed that by age 12, 19% of African-American girls had reached the highest stages of breast and pubic hair development, compared to 5% of White girls (Herman-Giddens, Slora, Wasserman, Bourdony, Bhapkar, Koch, & Hasemeier, 1997). By age 11, 2% of African-American boys had experienced coitus, figures not reached by White boys for another 1.5 years. Asians, in turn, lag 1 to 2 years behind their (White) American counterparts in sexual development and onset of sexual interest.

Sexuality. World Health Organization as well as national surveys show that Asians are sexually less active and precocious than Europeans, who are sexually less active and precocious than Africans (Centers for Disease Control and Prevention, 1992). One typical U.S. study carried out in Los Angeles found the average age at first intercourse was 16.4 years for East Asians and 14.4 years for African Americans, with Whites intermediate (Moore & Erickson, 1985). The percentage of students who were sexually active was 32% for East Asians and 81% for African Americans, with Whites again intermediate. A self-report study recently carried out in Canada, found that Asians were significantly more sexually "restrained," even on items measuring fantasy and masturbation that do not require the presence of a sexual partner (Meston, Trapnell, & Gorzalka, 1996). Further, Asian students born in Canada were as restrained as those who had only recently immigrated.

Sexual activity after marriage reveals a similar pattern. A meta-analysis of a number of surveys showed that for married couples in their 20s, the average frequency of intercourse per week is 2.5 for the Japanese and Chinese in Asia; 4 for American Whites, and 5 for African Americans (Rushton, 1995). Similar differences are found on measures of sexual permissiveness, amount of thinking about sex, and sex guilt. One study observed that each of three generations of Japanese Americans, as well as Japanese students in Japan, reported less interest in sex than did European samples. In studies carried out in Britain and Japan, using a sex-fantasy questionnaire, British men reported twice as many such fantasies as Japanese men. British women admitted to four times as much sex fantasy as did Japanese women (Iwawaki & Wilson, 1983). Asians were the most likely to believe sex has a weakening effect. By contrast, Blacks reported not only having had intercourse with more casual partners but also fewer second thoughts than did Whites.

The hypothesis that the racial differences in sexual behavior go deeper than culture is supported by their linkage to reproductive physiology.

Whereas the average woman produces one egg every 28 days, in the middle of the menstrual cycle, some women have shorter cycles than others, and some produce two eggs in a cycle. Either behavior produces greater opportunities for conception and therefore can lead to greater population growth. Occasionally, each egg in a double ovulation is fertilized by a separate sperm, producing dizygotic (two-egg) twins. The races differ in their rates of double ovulation. The frequency of dizygotic twins is less than 4 per 1,000 births for Mongoloids, 8 for Caucasoids, and 16 or greater for Negroids (Bulmer, 1970). Studies of Mongoloid-Caucasoid crosses in Hawaii and Caucasoid-Negroid crosses in Brazil have established that the rate of multiple birthing is determined by the race of the mother, not the father.

Family Functioning.   Marital stability can be measured by rates of divorce, out-of-wedlock birthing, child abuse, and delinquency. On each of these measures, Asians are more stable than Whites or Blacks. The 2 million East Asians in the United States are rarely perceived as a "social problem." They have significantly fewer divorces, out-of-wedlock births, or incidences of child abuse than do Whites. Perhaps this is why they are very seldom studied. African-American family structure, on the other hand, has been studied intensively. About 75% of births to African-American teenagers are out of wedlock compared with 25% of births to White teenagers. Overall, over 50% of new mothers are teenagers (Jaynes & Williams, 1989).

However, the female-headed family structure is not unique to the United States, the legacy of slavery, or the result of inner-city decay. It is also found in many areas of Black Africa (Draper, 1989). The female-headed family is part of an overall life-history pattern that consists of: (a) early onset of sexual activity, (b) loose emotional ties between spouses, (c) expectation of sexual union with many partners, and children by them, (d) lowered maternal nurturing with long-term "fostering" of children, sometimes for several years, with the stated reason sometimes being to remain sexually attractive, (e) greater competition by males for females, (f) less paternal involvement in child rearing, and (g) higher fertility, despite education and urbanization (which in other regions and among other groups produce a decline in fertility).

Even when compared to others in the developing world, African women stop caring intensively for their children relatively early in the child's life (Draper, 1989). Once breast feeding is stopped, ovulation resumes and the mother can conceive again. This allows a relatively high number of births per woman at relatively short birth intervals. Once a child is a year or so old, other children and grandparents do much of the caretaking. Children learn to look to older children for basic needs during the day. Groups of preteens and teenagers are left relatively free of adult supervision.

Intelligence Test Scores. Although this chapter is concerned with temperament, intelligence is certainly an important facet of character. As Galton recognized early on, intelligence interacts with differences in temperament to produce socially desirable outcomes such as educational achievement and the avoidance of crime. East Asian populations both in the United States and in Pacific Rim countries average IQs in the range of 101 to 111; White populations in the United States, Europe, and India average from 85 to 117, with an overall mean of 100; and African populations in the United States, Britain, the Caribbean, and sub-Saharan Africa average from 70 to 90 (Herrnstein & Murray, 1994; Jensen, 1998; Levin, 1997).

Voice Dominance. Asians have lighter voices than do Whites and Whites lighter than do Blacks. In one study, Hudson and Holbrook (1982) gave a reading task to 100 Black men and 100 Black women volunteers ranging in age from 18 to 29 years. The fundamental vocal frequencies were measured and compared to White norms. The frequency for Black men was 110 Hz, lower than the 117 Hz for White men; the frequency for Black women was 193 Hz, lower than the frequency of 217 Hz for White women.

HOW ARE THE TEMPERAMENT DIFFERENCES MEDIATED?

Testosterone. Is there then some neurohormonal "master switch" that sets each person's and the racial average position on the overall suite of characters? One possible trigger is testosterone level. Testosterone level correlates with temperament, self-concept, aggression, altruism, crime, and sexuality, in women as well as in men (Harris, Rushton, Hampson, & Jackson, 1996). Testosterone is also involved in secondary sexual characteristics such as muscularity and deepening of the voice, and even the organization and structure of the brain.

Race differences in testosterone (male hormone) level may explain other behavior differences. The testosterone rate was found to be 19% higher in a sample of Black U.S. college students than in their White counterparts. In an older group of U.S. military veterans, Blacks had a testosterone level

3% higher than Whites (Ellis & Nyborg, 1992). A study of testosterone metabolites showed a 10% to 15% higher incidence in African Americans than in White Americans and a still lower incidence among the Japanese (in Japan).

Hormones and other biological factors may influence sexual behavior more among Blacks than they do among Whites or Asians. For example, there is a greater frequency of intercourse at mid-cycle (the time most likely to result in pregnancy) among Black women than among White women. When East Asian and White students at a Canadian university were compared, the Asian women reported less periodicity of sexual response than did White women (Rushton, 1992). Biological factors similarly predict the onset of sexual interest, dating, first intercourse, and first pregnancy better for Blacks than they do for Whites or for Asians. Conversely, social factors such as religious beliefs and gender-role attitudes predict the sexual behavior of White women better than they do for Black women.

Neurobehavioral Activation and Inhibition Systems.   For several decades British psychologist Jeffrey Gray (1987) has been investigating the areas of the brain responsible for the control of emotional behavior. These include a behavioral inhibition system (BIS) and a behavioral activation system (BAS). In Gray's theory antisocial behavior is especially linked to underactivation of the BIS and the failure to learn a conscience or the conditioned emotional response of anxiety to antisocial thoughts. Behavioral inhibition is especially linked to the prefrontal cortex, and damage here often results in antisocial responding.

The racial gradient in decreasing mean brain size, going from East Asians to Europeans to Africans, has been independently established using three different procedures: wet brain weight at autopsy, volume of empty skulls using filler, and volume estimated from external head sizes. Recently, more sophisticated techniques including magnetic resonance imaging (MRI) have confirmed the findings by in vivo three-dimensional images of the brain. The results from all these studies converge on the conclusion that the brains of East Asians and their descendants average about 17 cm3 (1 in3) larger than those of Europeans and their descendants whose brains average about 80 cm3 (5 in3) larger than those of Africans and their descendants (Rushton & Ankney, 1996).

Kagan et al. (1993) suggested that the differences in motor activity and crying between the two groups lie in the excitability of the amygdala and its circuits to the corpus striatum, cingulate, central gray, and hypothalamus. The differences in ease of motor activity and crying suggest a muting or modulation of these circuits in the Chinese infants. It is relevant that Asian-American patients with symptoms of anxiety require lower concentrations of psychotropic medication than do White American adults with the same symptoms (Levy, 1993).

TRANSRACIAL ADOPTIONS

In the early part of this chapter behavior genetic evidence was presented showing substantial heritability for temperament traits. The question arises as to whether findings based on studies carried out within populations (mostly White, but also including Asian and African American; Lynn & Hattori, 1990; Osborne, 1980), generalize to differences between populations. One crucial type of evidence are multiracial adoption studies. Most of these have assessed IQ, but some have examined temperament.

Studies of Korean and Vietnamese children adopted into White American and White Belgian homes have been conducted (e.g., Clark & Hanisee, 1982). As babies, many adoptees had been hospitalized for malnutrition. Nonetheless they went on to develop IQs 10 or more points higher than their adoptive national norms. By contrast, Black and mixed-race (Black–White) children adopted into White middle-class families typically perform at a lower level than similarly adopted White children. For example, in the well-known Minnesota Transracial Adoption Study, by age 17, adopted children with two White biological parents had an average IQ of 106, adopted children with one White and one Black biological parent had an average IQ of 99, and adopted children with two Black biological parents had an average IQ of 89 (Weinberg, Scarr, & Waldman, 1992). These results, showing that Black and Asian babies register neither gains (for Blacks) nor losses (for Asians) in IQ by being adopted by Whites, provide direct evidence for a genetic basis for the ethnic differences.

Less well known (and much less established) are the transracial adoption results on temperament. Two unpublished doctoral theses have been carried out. Under the direction of Dan Freedman at the University of Chicago, Brooks (1989) assessed activity level and temperament in Korean children raised by White American families. She found that the adopted children scored partway between the other two groups. In collaboration with Sandra Scarr at the University of Virginia, DeBerry (1991) analyzed the Minnesota Transracial Adoption Study. She found that fully two thirds of the interracial

(Black and mixed-race) adoptees, who took the Minnesota Multiphasic Personality Inventory, had higher than average scores, thereby indicating impulsivity, outgoingness, aggressiveness, rebelliousness, and hedonism. Individuals with this profile typically report difficulty in marital or family relationships and have trouble with the law or authority in general.

EVOLUTIONARY SELECTION

In 1758, Caroleus Linneus classified four subspecies of *Homo sapiens*: American Indians, Asians, Europeans, and Africans. Most subsequent classifications recognize at least the three major subdivisions considered in this chapter: Mongoloid, Caucasoid, and Negroid. This classification does not rule out making finer distinctions within these major races. I have provided an evolutionary hypothesis that explains why so many variables correlate so consistently and why East Asians average the most quiescent temperament, Africans average the least quiescent, and Europeans average intermediately (Rushton, 1995).

The currently most accepted view of human origins posits a beginning in Africa some 200,000 years ago, an African/non-African split about 100,000 years ago, and a Caucasian/East Asian split about 40,000 years ago (Cavalli-Sforza, Menozzi, & Piazza, 1993; Stringer & McKie, 1996). Evolutionary selection pressures were different in the hot savanna where Africans evolved than in the cold Arctic where East Asians evolved. I hypothesize that the farther north the populations migrated, out of Africa, the more they encountered the cognitively demanding problems of gathering and storing food, gaining shelter, making clothes, and raising children successfully during prolonged winters. Similarly, the winters were socially demanding, putting a premium on cooperation and impulse control. As the original African populations evolved into present-day Europeans and East Asians, they did so in the direction of larger brains, slower rates of maturation, and lower levels of sex hormone with concomitant reductions in sexual potency and aggression and increases in family stability and longevity.

CONCLUSION

The scientific study of ethnic differences in temperament began with Galton's contrast between the Chinese, the Amerindians, and the Africans. Since then, most of the research has been carried in Europe or the United

States, where various groups have been viewed through a Eurocentric lens. Increasingly, however, scientists of non-European ancestry have been adding to our store of knowledge and thereby broadening our perspective. By doing so, research on ethnic differences in temperament and behavior may help to promote mutual understanding and cooperation.

REFERENCES

Brazleton, T. B., Robey, J. S., & Collier, G. A. (1969). Infant development in the Zincanteco Indians of southern Mexico. *Paediatrics, 44,* 274–290.

Brooks, L. (1989). *Adopted Korean children compared with Korean and Caucasian non-adopted children.* Unpublished doctoral dissertation, University of Chicago, Chicago.

Bulmer, M. G. (1970). *The biology of twinning in man.* Oxford, England: Clarendon.

Cavalli-Sforza, L. L., Menozzi, P., & Piazza, A. (1993). Demic expansions and human evolution. *Science, 259,* 639–646.

Centers for Disease Control and Prevention. (1992). Selected behaviors that increase risk for HIV infection among high school students—United States, 1990. *Morbidity and Mortality Weekly Report* (No. 14), pp. 231–240.

Chen, X., Hastings, P. D., Rubin, K. H., Chen, H., Cen., G., & Stewart, S. L. (in press). Child-rearing attitudes and behavioral inhibition in Chinese and Canadian toddlers: A cross-cultural study. *Developmental Psychology.*

Clark, E. A., & Hanisee, J. (1982). Intellectual and adaptive performance of Asian children in adoptive American settings. *Developmental Psychology, 18,* 594–599.

DeBerry, K. M. (1991). *Modeling ecological competence in African American transracial adoptees.* Unpublished doctoral dissertation, University of Virginia, Charlottesville.

Draper, P. (1989). African marriage systems: Perspectives from evolutionary ecology. *Ethology and Sociobiology, 10,* 145–169.

Ekblad, S, & Olweus, D. (1986). Applicability of Olweus' Aggression Inventory in a sample of Chinese primary school children. *Aggressive Behavior, 12,* 315–325.

Ellis, L., & Nyborg, H. (1992). Racial/ethnic variations in male testosterone levels: A probable contributor to group differences in health. *Steroids, 57,* 72–75.

Eveleth, P. B., & Tanner, J. M. (1990). *Worldwide variation in human growth* (2nd ed.). London: Cambridge University Press.

Freedman, D. G. (1974). *Human infancy: An evolutionary perspective.* New York: Wiley/Halstead.

Freedman, D. G. (1979). *Human sociobiology.* New York: The Free Press.

Galton, F. (1865). Hereditary talents and character. *Macmillan's Magazine, 12,* 157–166, 318–327.

Galton, F. (1883). *Inquiries into human faculty and its development.* London: Macmillan.

Gray, J. A. (1987). *The psychology of fear and stress.* Cambridge, England: Cambridge University Press.

Harris, J. A., Rushton, J. P., Hampson, E., & Jackson, D. N. (1996). Salivary testosterone and self-report aggressive and pro-social personality characteristics in men and women. *Aggressive Behavior, 22,* 321–331.

Herman-Giddens, M. E., Slora, E. J., Wasserman, R. C., Bourdony, C. J., Bhapkar, M. V., Koch, G. G., & Hasemeier, C. M. (1997). Secondary sexual characteristics and menses in young girls seen in office practice: A study from the Pediatric Research in Office Settings Network. *Pediatrics, 99,* 505–512.

Herrnstein, R. J., & Murray, C. (1994). *The bell curve.* New York: The Free Press.

Hudson, A. I., & Holbrook, A. (1982). Fundamental frequency characteristics of young Black adults: Spontaneous speaking and oral reading. *Journal of Speech and Hearing Research, 25,* 25–28.

Iwawaki, S., & Wilson, G. D. (1983). Sex fantasies in Japan. *Personality and Individual Differences, 4,* 543–545.

Jaynes, G. D., & Williams, R. M., Jr. (Eds.). (1989). *A common destiny: Blacks and American society.* Washington, DC: National Academy Press.

Jensen, A. R. (1998). *The g factor.* Westport, CT: Praeger.

Kagan, J., Arcus, D., Snidman, N., Feng, W. Y., Hendler, J., & Greene, S. (1994). Reactivity in infants: A cross-national comparison. *Developmental Psychology, 30,* 342–345.

Lee, Y-T., Jussim, L. J., & McCauley, C. R. (Eds.). (1995). *Stereotype accuracy: Toward appreciating group differences.* Washington, DC: American Psychological Association.

Levin, M. (1997). *Why race matters.* Westport, CT: Praeger.

LeVine, R. A. (1975). *Culture, behavior, and personality.* Chicago: Aldine.

Levy, R. A. (1993). Ethnic and racial differences in response to medication: Preserving individualized therapy in managed pharmaceutical programmes. *Pharmaceutical Medicine, 7,* 139–165.

Linnaeus, C. (1956). *Systema Naturae.* 10th ed. London, England: Royal Society of London. (Original work published 1758).

Lynn, R., & Hattori, K. (1990). The heritability of intelligence in Japan. *Behavior Genetics, 20,* 545–546.

Mann, C. R. (1996). *When women kill.* Albany: State University of New York Press.

Mednick, S. A., Gabrielli, W. F., & Hutchings, B. (1984). Genetic influences in criminal convictions: Evidence from an adoption cohort. *Science, 224,* 891–894.

Meston, C. M., Trapnell, P. D., & Gorzalka, B. B. (1996). Ethnic and gender differences in sexuality: Variations in sexual behavior between Asian and non-Asian university students. *Archives of Sexual Behavior, 25,* 33–72.

Ministry of the Solicitor-General and Correctional Services. (1996). *Report of the commission on systemic racism in the Ontario criminal justice system.* Toronto: Queen's Printer for Ontario.

Moore, D. S., & Erickson, P. I. (1985). Age, gender, and ethnic differences in sexual and contraceptive knowledge, attitudes, and behaviors. *Family and Community Health, 8,* 38–51.

Orlick, T., Zhou, Q. Y., & Partington, J. (1990). Co-operation and conflict within Chinese and Canadian kindergarten settings. *Canadian Journal of Behavioral Science, 22,* 20–25.

Osborne, R. T. (1980). *Twins: Black and White.* Athens, GA: Foundation for Human Understanding.

Ottati, V., & Lee, Y-T. (1995). Accuracy: A neglected component of stereotype research. In Y-T. Lee, L. J. Jussim, & C. R. McCauley (Eds.), *Stereotype accuracy: Toward appreciating group differences* (pp. 29–59). Washington, DC: American Psychological Association.

Papiernik, E., Cohen, H., Richard, A., de Oca, M. M., & Feingold, J. (1986). Ethnic differences in duration of pregnancy. *Annals of Human Biology, 13,* 259–265.

Rowe, D. (1994). *The limits of family influence.* New York: Guilford.

Rushton, J. P. (1985). Differential K theory and race differences in E and N. *Personality and Individual Differences, 6,* 769–770.

Rushton, J. P. (1992). Life history comparisons between Orientals and Whites at a Canadian university. *Personality and Individual Differences, 13,* 439–442.

Rushton, J. P. (1995). *Race, evolution, and behavior.* New Brunswick, NJ: Transaction.

Rushton, J. P. (1996). Self-report delinquency and violence in adult twins. *Psychiatric Genetics, 6,* 87–89.

Rushton, J. P., & Ankney, C. D. (1996). Brain size and cognitive ability: Correlations with age, sex, social class and race. *Psychonomic Bulletin and Review, 3,* 21–36.

Rushton, J. P., Fulker, D. W., Neale, M.C., Nias, D. K. B., & Eysenck, H. J. (1986). Altruism and aggression: The heritability of individual differences. *Journal of Personality and Social Psychology, 50,* 1192–1198.

Stringer, C. B., & Andrews, P. (1988). Genetic and fossil evidence for the origin of modern humans. *Science, 239,* 1263–1268.

Stringer, C. B., & McKie, R. (1996). *African exodus.* London: Random House.

Tashakkori, A. (1993). Race, gender and pre-adolescent self-structure: A test of construct-specificity hypothesis. *Personality and Individual Differences, 14,* 591–598.

Thomas, A., & Chess, S. (1984). Genesis and evolution of behavioral disorders: From infancy to early adult life. *American Journal of Psychiatry, 141,* 1–9.

Thomas, A., Chess, S., & Birch, H. G. (1968). *Temperament and behavior disorders in children.* New York: New York University Press.

Tompkins, R. L. (1996). Human population variability in relative dental development. *American Journal of Physical Anthropology, 99,* 79–102.

Tremblay, R. E., & Baillargeon, L. (1984). Les difficultés de comportement d'enfants immigrants dans les classes d'accueil, au préscolaire. [Behavioral difficulties of immigrant children in preschool classrooms]. *Canadian Journal of Education, 9,* 154–170.

Vernon, P. E. (1982). *The abilities and achievements of Orientals in North America*. New York: Academic Press.

Weinberg, R. A., Scarr, S., & Waldman, I. D. (1992). The Minnesota Transracial Adoption Study: A follow-up of IQ test performance at adolescence. *Intelligence, 16*, 117–135.

Wilson, J. Q., & Herrnstein, R. J. (1985). *Crime and human nature*. New York: Simon & Schuster.

4

Nationality Characteristics: Dimensions for Comparison

Dean Peabody
Swarthmore College

Why does British television devote considerable amounts of time to the weather, when British weather itself is relatively predictable (cloudy)? "We're obsessed by the weather because it's a wonderful opening gambit for a shy race," said Bill Giles, the BBC's senior broadcaster.

"It's the only way we'd talk to anyone without being introduced," he said. "With Americans, you can know their life history within 10 minutes of meeting them, but here we can sit in a train compartment for five hours and just say, 'It's a fine day, isn't it?' " (from *The New York Times,* September 15, 1996, Section 4, p.2).

This example is not dramatic, but it serves to illustrate the possibility of comparisons using national characteristics. This chapter considers such characteristics, and the "dimensions" along which such comparisons may be made.

The two most important questions concern the selection of nationalities, and the selection of characteristics (variables). Among the variables, the first problem is to avoid confusing possible characteristics of individuals with those of the society or culture itself. The recent collection of the writings of Inkeles (1997) reiterates this point, which he had stated already in 1954.

Among the possible characteristics are (a) personality characteristics or "traits" (Peabody, 1985), (b) "values" (Schwartz, 1994; Schwartz & Bilsky, 1987), (c) types of "social relations" (Fiske, 1992, 1993), (d) "dimensions of cultures" (Hofstede, 1980, 1991). This chapter considers primarily a comparison between the dimensions derived from personality traits, and those of Hofstede. (Smith & Bond, 1993, considered all of the aforementioned.)

PERSONALITY TRAITS

Selection of Variables

The research on personality traits made use of the "lexical hypothesis." This is an assumption that the important personality traits have become encoded in language as single terms. Thus, one can list something over 4,000 terms for stable personality characteristics in English; perhaps 400–600 would be familiar to college students (Peabody, 1987). One then needs only to select variables to represent these. Judgments using such terms can be summarized in five large factors (the "Big Five"):

- Factor I. "Surgency"—for example, *self-confident* (vs. *unassured*).
- Factor II. "Agreeableness"—for example, *warm* (vs. *cold*).
- Factor III. "Conscientiousness"—for example, *thorough* (vs. *careless*).
- Factor IV. "Emotional Stability"—for example, *relaxed* (vs. *tense*).
- Factor V. "Intellect"—for example, *intelligent* (vs. *unintelligent*).

The Big Five comes close to the traditional objective of a classification system, that the categories should be mutually exclusive and collectively exhaustive. The factor analytic method can ensure that the factors are statistically independent, although a given trait variable may be related to more than one factor. The lexical hypothesis supports a claim that the Big Five are a comprehensive representation of personality characteristics.This provides in principle a solution for the difficult problem of the selection of variables, which is usually somewhat arbitrary. It could be applied independently for different languages. In addition, trait adjectives permit a relatively direct interpretation: Trait adjectives are interpreted according to their "obvious" meanings.

In the previous examples, the trait adjectives that are given before the parentheses are all evaluatively favorable, whereas the contrasting terms inside the parentheses are evaluatively unfavorable. Indeed, any measure using trait adjectives tends to combine (or "confound") an evaluative component (abbreviated "+" vs. "–") with some other ("descriptive") component, but does not tell the importance of either.

The judgment "X is thrifty (+) versus extravagant (–)," can be both evaluative—"X is good versus bad"—and descriptive—"X is unready versus ready to spend." Separating these components would permit a clearer analyis. (E.g., social psychological theories emphasize the evaluative component, but the evidence suggests that the descriptive components are of greater importance—Peabody, 1967, 1990.) In an effort to get around this problem, Peabody (1967) selected *pairs* of trait measures so as to separate the evaluative and descriptive components. Thus, a scale of *thrifty* (+) versus *extravagant* (–) can be paired with another scale of *stingy* (–) versus *generous* (+). To subtract the two scales would tend to cancel the evaluative components, and leave the descriptive component—for example, *thrifty* (+) and *stingy* (–) versus *extravagant* (–) and *generous* (+).The research considered here is based on such pairs of scales.

As just shown, it is possible to counterbalance the evaluative components between two such scales, and to analyze the descriptive components. Such analyses tend to show two large descriptive dimensions, labeled Tight–Loose and Assertive–Unassertive. These two descriptive dimensions plus one of general evaluation correspond to a transformation (rotation) of the first three of the Big Five factors (Peabody & Goldberg, 1989). The Tight–Loose dimension corresponds largely to a contrast between Factor III (Conscientiousness)—for example, thrifty versus extravagant—and Factor II ("Agreeableness")—for example, generous versus stingy. The Assertive–Unassertive dimension corresponds largely to Factor I ("Surgency"), which is itself relatively unrelated to evaluation. For the other two factors, it is not easy to find comparable nonevaluative dimensions—which would require favorable forms of neuroticism ("Emotional Instability"), and unfavorable forms of intelligence ("Intellect"). Moreover, there is evidence that the first three factors are the more important (and so are sometimes called the "Big Three"). They correspond to other three-part distinctions—for example, that of McClelland (1961) into motives for Power (resembling Factor I), Affiliation (Factor II), and Achievement (Factor III).

Figure 4.1 shows some of the relationships. The relevant traits form a circular arrangement, which can be summarized into six groups of traits. Factor I from the Big Five involves favorable traits of Assertiveness (vs. unfavorable traits of Unassertiveness)—for example, *self-confident* (+) versus *unassured* (–); *forceful* (+) versus *passive* (–). For the descriptive dimension of Assertive–Unassertive, these scales would be paired with others representing unfavorable Assertiveness versus favorable Unassertiveness—for example, *conceited* (–) versus *modest* (+); *aggressive* (–) versus *peaceful* (+). The descriptive Assertive–Unassertive dimension would combine the two scales—for example, *self-confident* (+) and *conceited* (–) versus *unassured* (–) and *modest* (+).

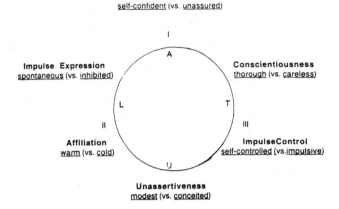

FIG. 4.1 Some relations between trait adjectives. The circular representation emphasizes the evaluatively favorable traits. Each of six groups of traits is capitalized, and one example is given for each group. Big Five factors: I, II, III. Descriptive dimensions: T, L: Tight versus Loose; A, U: Assertive versus Unassertive. Adapted from Peabody (1989). Reprinted with permission of American Psychological Association.

Factor III from the Big Five involves favorable traits for Impulse Control and Conscientiousness. Factor II involves favorable traits for Affiliation, extending to those for Impulse Expression and Unassertiveness. The descriptive dimension of Tight–Loose involves counterbalancing these—for example, *self-controlled* (+) versus *impulsive* (–) with *inhibited* (–) versus *spontaneous* (+); *thrifty* (+) versus *extravagant* (–) with *stingy* (–) versus *generous* (+).

Altogether 14 pairs of such scales were used, and so 28 scales. Each involved a seven-step response scale on which a subject judge could indicate the likelihood that a nationality target would have one or the other of the traits defining the scale.

Selection of Nationalities

The subject judges were groups of students (generally 40–50), mostly from western Europe. Each group judged 8–10 nationalities as target objects. Altogether there were 76 such "cases" (of a group of nationality judges rating a target nationality). A convenient summary of the results came from an analysis of the correlations of these 76 cases across the 28 scales. These results showed two large factors that could be clearly interpreted as reflecting the descriptive dimensions of Tight–Loose and Assertive–Unassertive.

TABLE 4.1

Results on Two Descriptive Dimensions

Target	Judges	Tight–Loose	Assertive–Unassertive
ITALIANS	Self (5 Outgroups)	-79 (-65)	04 (49)
SPANISH	French	-52	52
AMERICANS	5 Outgroups	-49	64
GREEKS	Self	-39	65
IRISH	English	-35	72
FRENCH	Self (5 Outgroups)	-23 (-62)	77 (47)
FILIPINOS	Self	-19	-16
AUSTRIANS	Self	-12	-37
SWEDES	Finns	-12	75
DUTCH	3 Outgroups	26	-14
ENGLISH	Self (5 Outgroups)	37 (76)	16 (18)
JAPANESE	2 Outgroups	43	66
CHINESE[a]	Self	66	00
GERMANS	Self (4 Outgroups)	79 (52)	10 (69)
SWISS	4 Outgroups	80	02
FINNS	Self	80	13

Note. From Peabody (1985). Table 18.1. Results are factor loadings on the analysis of 76 cases across 28 scales. Decimal points omitted.

[a]Chinese living in the Phillipines.

Table 4.1 gives a partial excerpt of the results of this analysis. For purposes of comparison, Table 4.1 includes only nationalities also included by Hofstede. In Table 4.1 each particular nationality target is listed only once (although some were judged by as many as seven groups of judges). Where possible preference is given to the ingroup self-judgments; these seemed to be somewhat more valid than the outgroup ones. (Sometimes, this difference is much more dramatic—cf. Peabody & Shmelyov, 1996.)

Exceptions are for four of the nationality targets—Italians, French, English, Germans—which were judged by a "standard" set of groups of judges. In these cases, Table 4.1 gives results for both the ingroup and—in parentheses—the outgroups. Note that in each of these cases the outgroup results imply a stronger relationship with one of the two dimensions—for example, the FRENCH are only slightly Loose (–.23) in self-judgments, but strongly so (–.62) in outgroup judgments.

In the absence of ingroup judgments, results were averaged, generally for as many outgroups as possible. (E.g., the Swiss were judged by German, French, Italian, and Austrian judges.) Perhaps most debatable are the three cases where a nationality is judged by a single outgroup, and where the outgroup might have a peculiar viewpoint. A plausible example is the judgment of the Swedes as slightly "Loose" by students from an up-country Finnish university.

In Table 4.1, the order of the targets follows the scores on the Tight–Loose dimension. Thus, the targets judged most Loose were the ITALIANS, SPANISH, AMERICANS, GREEKS, IRISH, and FRENCH. This summary index reflects results on the 28 separate scales, where the ITALIANS were judged *generous* and *extravagant*; *spontaneous* and *impulsive*. The targets judged most Tight are the FINNS, SWISS, GERMANS, CHINESE, JAPANESE, and ENGLISH. Thus, in their ingroup self-judgments, the FINNS are *thrifty* and *stingy*; *self-controlled* and *inhibited.* On the Assertive–Unassertive dimension, no nationalities are judged strongly Unassertive. Some are judged Assertive, others as not so Assertive. The former tend to be judged *self-confident* and *conceited*; *forceful* and *aggressive.*

Peabody (1985) compared these results with more traditional reports by experts about "national character." This comparison was made especially for six target nationalities: the English, Germans, French, Italians, Americans, and Russians. The comparison generally showed agreement between the two kinds of evidence. A theory that proved useful was that of Max Weber about the "Protestant ethic." This held that the origin of modern capitalism involved certain Calvinist characteristics of systematic economic activity and impulse control. (In terms of Fig. 4.1, this implies both parts of Factor III: "Conscientiousness" in systematic work, and Impulse Control.) Some nationalities may still have the legacy of a Calvinist/Puritan tradition—for example, the Americans, British, Swiss, Dutch. More often, one could use Weber's rubrics indirectly, by asking about contrasting alternatives. Thus, the Russians and Italians resemble opposites of the Protestant ethic.

How could one summarize this research as regards the selection of characteristics or variables and of nationalities? Regarding the selection of variables, this research is relatively strong: Evidence using the lexical hypothesis enables one to argue that the factors approach being mutually exclusive and collectively exhaustive. Moreover, the use of trait adjectives supports an obvious direct interpretation in terms of their content. The selection of nationalities, although extensive, is less strong. This results especially from the emphasis on European nationalities.

DIMENSIONS OF CULTURE

The opposite is true of the work of Hofstede (1980, 1991). Here, the selection of nationalities is very strong, whereas the selection of variables has limitations.

Selection of Nationalities

Hofstede studied some 88,000 employees of IBM in over 50 countries. One could argue for a more representative selection within each nationality. But one can also argue in favor of having specified and comparable selections. Hofstede's nationalities include representation from east Asia and Latin America. It even includes some from Africa, and is notably lacking only for former Communist countries.

Selection of Variables

The IBM questionnaire was not originally designed for cultural comparisons, but for organizational development. Employees gave self-report responses to about 160 items. Hofstede (1983) analyzed the data with ingenuity. He compared scores not for individuals but between countries, which he called "ecological analysis." He reported four "dimensions of culture."

1. Power distance: "the extent to which the members of a society accept that power in institutions and organizations is distributed unequally"
2. Individualism versus Collectivism: "*Individualism* ... a preference for a loosely knit social framework in society in which individuals are supposed to take care of themselves and their immediate families only; as opposed to *Collectivism* ... a preference for a tightly knit social framework ..."
3. Masculinity versus feminity: "*Masculinity* ... a preference for achievement, heroism, assertiveness, and material success; as opposed to *Femininity* ... a preference for relationships, modesty, caring for the weak, and the quality of life"
4. Uncertainty Avoidance: "the degree to which members of society feel uncomfortable with uncertainty and ambiguity" (Hofstede, 1983, pp. 336–337).

There is no reason to consider that these dimensions approach being mutually exclusive and collectively exhaustive. Hofstede's (1980) careful analysis showed that the same factor combines low Power Distance and Individualism versus high Power Distance and Collectivism. However, Hofstede preferred to keep two separate dimensions, in part because there is a class of exceptions that combine large Power Distance and high Individualism (Latin European countries, in particular France and Belgium).

The items are heterogenous in content; some items concern "values" but others do not. The items do not lend themselves to a direct interpretation, where the content of the items would directly refer to the nature of the dimension. In general, the items do not directly state the preferences for certain types of society as given in the definitions. Thus, two of the dimensions are based on a factor analysis of the relative importance of 14 "work goals." One factor included choosing personal time, freedom of approach, and challenge versus training opportunities, physical conditions, and use of one's skills. The interpretation of this factor as Individualism versus Collectivism does not follow in any direct way from these items. However, Hofstede was subtle and sophisticated in assembling evidence supporting the "construct validity" of his interpretations. It therefore becomes plausible that the proposed construct relates in a *general way* to the index that is scored. However, some nationalities' scores might also result from other reasons, so it would not be justified to treat all scores on an index as due to the proposed interpretation.

Table 4.2 gives results on these dimensions for 50 countries and three regions. The grouping of countries is adapted from Hofstede (1980, 1983). Hofstede noted that within such groups, the nationalities tend to have similar scores.

Hofstede has made unusual efforts to elaborate the conceptual nature of his dimensions. Such extensions have also been made by others (e.g., Draguns, 1996). There is already considerable research concerning these dimensions, mostly regarding individualism-collectivism. The present chapter does not attempt to review this research.

CHINESE VALUES

Nationalities can be different. That is the point of interest here, and is not itself an issue. However, there is an issue regarding the characteristics used in making comparisons. If one says that the English tend to be impulse controlled and the Italians impulse expressive, the issue concerns the basis

TABLE 4.2

Scores on Four Hofstede Dimensions for 50 countries and Three regions

Country or Region	Scores			
	PD	IDV	MAS	UA
Less Developed Latin				
Guatemala	95	6	37	101
Panama	95	11	44	86
Ecuador	78	8	63	67
Venezuela	81	12	73	76
Colombia	67	13	64	80
Mexico	81	30	69	82
Peru	64	16	42	87
Salvador	66	19	40	94
Chile	63	23	28	86
Portugal	63	27	31	104
Asian				
Malaysia	104	26	50	36
Indonesia	78	14	46	48
Philippines	94	32	64	44
Thailand	64	20	34	64
Singapore	74	20	48	8
Hong Kong	68	25	57	29
South Korea	60	18	39	85
Taiwan	58	17	45	69
Pakistan	55	14	50	70
India	77	48	56	40
Africa				
West Africa	77	20	46	54
East Africa	64	27	41	52
Near Eastern				
Arab countries	80	38	53	68
Iran	58	41	43	59
Turkey	66	37	45	85
Greece	60	35	57	112
(Yugoslavia)	76	27	21	88
Japan	54	46	95	92
Jamaica	45	39	68	13
More Developed Latin				
France	68	71	43	86
Belgium	65	75	54	94
Brazil	69	38	49	76
Uruguay	61	36	38	100

continued

Argentina	49	46	56	86
Spain	57	51	42	86
(Italy)	50	76	70	75
Costa Rica	35	15	21	86
Anglo				
USA	40	91	62	46
Great Britain	35	89	66	35
Australia	36	90	61	51
New Zealand	22	79	58	49
Canada	39	80	52	48
Ireland	28	70	68	35
(South Africa—Whites)	49	65	63	49
Germanic				
Germany FR	35	67	66	65
Switzerland	34	68	70	58
Austria	11	55	79	70
Israel	13	54	47	81
Nordic				
Finland	33	63	26	59
Norway	31	69	8	50
Netherlands	38	80	14	53
Sweden	31	71	5	29
Denmark	18	74	16	23

Note. Results from Hofstede (1991). Copyright © 1991 by Geert Hofstede. Reproduced by permission. Scores had been transformed to resemble a 100-point scale. The classification of countries is adapted from Hofstede (1980). The dimensions are abbreviated as follows: PD: Power Distance; IDV: Individualism versus Collectivism; MAS: Masculinity versus Femininity; UA: Uncertainty Avoidance.

for considering the impulse-control versus impulse-expression contrast. In this case, the contrast began with an analysis using trait adjectives in English. But in principle such a contrast might not be relevant for a different culture.

This issue is often discussed under a distinction labeled *etic* versus *emic*. This distinction is borrowed from linguistics. Each language uses distinctive "phonemic" categories of sounds. But these categories are thought to be related to a universal "phonetic" system. It could be a mistake to impose emic distinctions from one culture on another.

It is attractive to adopt this more relativistic position, and oppose comparisons as a kind of intellectual "imperialism." Indeed, one should agree that in principle the analysis of a culture could be imposed from outside in a way that is inappropriate.

However, one needs to pay attention as to how big a problem this is in practice. Thus, the Big Five factors were originally derived from trait adjectives in English. But similar factors have since been found in many languages. Some of these studies initially used translations of the English variables, but others began with those in the other language. (Admittedly, most of the studies so far have used European languages.) Michael Bond (e.g., Bond & Forgas, 1984), working within a Chinese culture, accepted that the Big Three personality dimensions are universal. But, in general, when comparisons between cultures are attempted, "the Furies are released" (Bond, 1988, p. 1009).

Bond himself organized a study of Chinese values to explore the afore-mentioned issue. In an effort to find out whether Chinese cultural values were neglected in existing measures, Bond organized a group that he called the Chinese Culture Connection (1987). Forty Chinese values were gener-ated and responded to by subjects from 22 countries (less than half were East Asian). A factor analysis yielded four factors. These factors were compared with the four dimensions of Hofstede across 20 nations shared by both investigations. Three of the Chinese factors had substantial corre-lations with those of Hofstede. The fourth was called "Confucian dyna-mism" or, later, "long-term" versus "short-term orientation." This factor involved a contrast between high scores for values of (a) persistence (perseverance), (b) ordering relationships by status and observing this order, (c) thrift, (d) having a sense of shame, versus low scores for (e) personal steadiness and stability, (f) protecting your "face," (g) respect for tradition, and (h) reciprocation of greetings, favors, and gifts. This factor showed a strong correlation with economic growth data for the period 1965–1987. There were high scores for all of the economic "Five Dragons" from East Asia—Japan, Taiwan, South Korea, Hong Kong, and Singapore.

It seems unfortunate that the variables included only Chinese values and no contrasting items. The scores could reflect primarily the overall accep-tance of Chinese values. On the other hand, if the scores are standardized so as to have the same overall mean, then the East Asian countries *cannot* generally get higher scores. The secondary *relative* distinctions *among* the Chinese values may be difficult to understand. The evidence supports this interpretation. An initial analysis yielded a very large single factor. The means for the 40 items were then standardized for each nationality sepa-rately before proceeding. Hence, countries with Chinese culture (most obviously, Taiwan, Hong Kong, Singapore) cannot *generally* score high. They do so only on the second factor of "Confucian dynamism." But they score *low* on the first factor called "Integration." This low score indicates a relative emphasis on filial piety, and chastity in women (as opposed to tolerance and harmony with others), and is positively related to Hofstede factors for collectivism and high power distance. Among the other three factors for Chinese values it is only "Confucian dynamism" that reflects a consistent relative choice for Chinese cultures. Scores for 23 countries on this factor are shown in Table 4.3.

Hofstede's (1991) summary is as follows:

Three dimensions dealing with basic human relations seem to be so universal that they show up in whatever multicountry value study we do. These are the equivalents of the power distance, individualism-collectivism, and masculinity-femininity dimensions in the IBM study. A fourth dimension can be found, but its nature depends on the culture of the designers of the questionnaire.

TABLE 4.3
Index Values for 23 Countries on Long-term Orientation (Confucian Dynamism)

Country or Region	Score
China	118
Hong Kong	96
Taiwan	87
Japan	80
South Korea	75
Brazil	65
India	61
Thailand	56
Singapore	48
Netherlands	44
Bangladesh	40
Sweden	33
Poland	32
Germany FR	31
Australia	31
New Zealand	30
USA	29
Great Britain	25
Zimbabwe	25
Canada	23
Philippines	19
Nigeria	16
Pakistan	00

Note. From Hofstede (1991). Copyright 1991 by Geert Hofstede. Reproduced by permission.

With the Western-made questionnaires ... a dimension "uncertainty avoidance" was found; with the CVS another dimension "Confucian dynamism." (pp. 170–171).

RELATIONS BETWEEN THE APPROACHES

What kind of relations might one propose between the approaches considered previously? The simplest answer would be to accept all the proposed dimensions. For personality characteristics, there are three (to five) factors and the corresponding two descriptive dimensions. For the variables of Hofstede and Bond, there are five dimensions altogether. Before reverting to such a "default" option, however, it is worth looking for possible relations.

The comparisons here emphasize the *conceptual* relations between the two sets of dimensions. Hofstede himself also made use of rank-order correlations across the nationalities that are common to the dimensions being compared. Between the personality trait dimensions and the Hofstede–Bond dimensions, I have not found the fairly substantial correlations that Hofstede reported in his analyses. This is at least partly due to the samples of nations involved (e.g., the trait dimensions are mostly for west European nationalities).

Tight–Loose and Uncertainty Avoidance.   One may begin with the descriptive dimension of Tight versus Loose, which is largely a contrast between Big Five Factor III (Conscientiousness in work and Impulse Control) and Factor II (Affiliation and Impulse Expression). Hofstede (1991) made the somewhat paradoxical proposal that *high* Uncertainty Avoidance is related to impulse expression. He first related Uncertainty Avoidance to a factor that Lynn (1971) called "anxiety" or "neuroticism." He continued:

The more anxious cultures tend to be the more expressive cultures. They are the places where it is socially acceptable ... to show one's emotions ... In weak uncertainty avoidance countries anxiety levels are relatively low. ... Aggression and emotions are not supposed to be shown ....

In countries with strong uncertainty avoidance people come across as busy, fidgety, emotional, aggressive, active. In countries with weak uncertainty avoidance people give the impression of being quiet, easy-going, indolent, controlled, lazy. (pp. 114–115)

The first thing to note is that this interpretation seems to be generally consistent with the evidence. Nationalities that score Loose on the Tight–Loose dimension tend to be high on Uncertainty Avoidance. In particular this applies to southern European nationalities such as the French, Italians, Spanish, and Greeks.

What is paradoxical is that it might seem natural to expect cultures where it is more acceptable to express emotions to be *less* avoidant. Such paradoxes are of special interest; if they can be resolved, this can lead to a more profound understanding. A very relevant example: Peabody (1985) found that French (and Italian) cultures put unusual emphasis on impulse control, although these nationalities appear to be relatively impulse expressive. The resolution proposed was that precisely because impulse control was relatively less "internalized," there was more deliberate emphasis on impulse control. In contrast, northern European nationalities would have more internalization of impulse control, and need less explicit emphasis. A similar resolution seems to fit Hofstede's interpretation. Hofstede's account suggests that nationalities with weak uncertainty avoidance have more of something like internalization. This could leave them less anxious about lack of control.

This interpretation (of a possible relation of Uncertainty Avoidance to Loose impulse expression) suggests implications for the Tight–Loose dimension, even for nationalities (such as Latin American and East Asian ones) for which this has not yet been studied directly: Loose Impulse Expression for southern European and Latin American nationalities; Tight Impulse Control for northern European and most east Asian ones.

Tight–Loose and Confucian Dynamism. As shown in Fig. 4.1, Tight involves a combination of Impulse Control and "Conscientiousness" with regard to task performance. There is another dimension that is plausibly related to this: the Chinese dimension called "Confucian dynamism" or "Long-term orientation." This dimension included "thrift" and "persistence (perseverance)." These terms would be classified with the trait groups just mentioned. Mentioned earlier was the proposal of Max Weber that the Protestant ethic led to the origin of modern capitalism. (This may be extended—for example, by McClelland (1961)—to apply to economic growth generally.) The ethic involved systematic economic activity and impulse control—Tight characteristics. If one looked for similar characteristics for the East Asian dragons, one finds them in Confucian dynamism. One can see that persistence and thrift exactly correspond to Weber's formulation. Further, the lack of respect for tradition is consistent with Weber. This is a striking confirmation of a theory developed in a quite different context.

Assertive–Unassertive and Masculinity–Femininity. One may now turn to the descriptive dimension of Assertive–Unassertive, which is closely related to the Big Five Factor I. According to Hofstede's own statements, these should be related to his dimension of Masculinity versus Femininity, which he also labeled "Assertiveness versus modesty" (Hofstede, 1991, pp. 79–80). As seen in Fig. 4.1, Assertive is a label for one end of the Assertive–Unassertive dimension, and modest is an example for the other end.

Among those working with trait adjectives, it is generally agreed that masculinity and femininity relate to Big Five Factors I and II, respectively. A Masculinity–Femininity dimension would therefore be close to the Assertive–Unassertive one.

This is an appropriate place to reexamine Hofstede's method of interpretation. Masculinity–Femininity is actually measured by choices among work goals that do not refer directly to masculinity versus femininity. The score on this dimension involved a choice of earnings, recognition, advancement, and challenge versus relations with one's superior, cooperation, living area, and employment security. There are gender differences on these items. It follows that the scores relate in a general way to gender. However, nations' scores could also derive from some other bases. Hence, one should not necessarily interpret the scores for all nationalities as due to masculinity versus femininity. But such interpretations seem to be made. Thus, it is implied (Hofstede, 1991, pp. 104–105) that the well-known Hispanic hypermasculinity called machismo does not really apply to Spain itself, nor to a majority of Hispanic-American cultures—all of which score in the lower half of the masculinity index. It seems more plausible that these Hispanic nations may respond to the items for some reason other than femininity. (This reason might be economic uncertainty—the Latin countries are all high on Uncertainty Avoidance.) Hofstede's relationships between items and interpretation are actually the probabilistic ones possible in social science; but they are being treated like the more certain ones traditionally looked for in natural science. (Cf. Hofstede, 1991, pp. 133–134.)

One hesitates to make a comparable close examination of the analysis of Chinese values, as this is much more questionable. Masculinity is correlated with a Chinese value factor called "Human heartedness" including *kindness (forgiveness, compassion), patience, courtesy.* One must agree with the comments that it is "perhaps surprising" that the content suggests "feminine" valuing rather than "masculine" (The Chinese Cultural Connection, 1987, p. 152), and that "patience and kindness we would rather expect at the feminine pole" (Hofstede, 1991, pp. 163–164). For human heartedness the factor scores reported are 1.42 for Japan, then for 20 countries positive scores ranging from 1.10 to .27, but finally, a single negative score of −1.09 for the Netherlands. Such a distribution is strange.

The Other Dimensions.   What dimensions remain? Among the Big Five, there are Factor IV (Emotional Stability) and Factor V (Intellect). These factors tend not to provide clear descriptive dimensions independent of evaluation. For similar reasons, they are unlikely to provide interesting national differences. The first three Big Five factors have been considered here indirectly through the descriptive dimensions of Tight versus Loose and Assertive versus Unassertive. In any case, it would be helpful to have additional data for all of the Big Five factors and a wider range of nationalities.

Among Hofstede's dimensions, we have not yet considered relations for the two related ones of Individualism versus Collectivism and low versus high Power Distance. One could find some evidence for these as another counterpart of the Assertive versus unassertive dimension. Trait adjectives such as *individualistic* and *independent* would be classified under Assertiveness. Moreover, the Power Distance acceptance by subordinates of lesser power suggests unassertiveness.

Another possible dimension from the trait research may be still more promising as a counterpart. It was mentioned earlier that, in addition to results on the trait-adjective scales, Peabody (1985) examined other reports about national character. A major dimension from this latter examination was not expressed on the trait-adjective scales. This dimension involved a traditional sociological contrast between Gesellschaft ("society") and Gemeinschaft ("community")—Peabody (1985). This contrast could be expressed using several related variables—for example, *universalism* versus *particularism* (people are treated similarly or differently) and *specificity* versus *diffuseness* (the scope of the relationship is limited or broad). Hofstede (1991) related Individualism versus Collectivism to the first of these. (Smith, Dugan, & Trompenaars, 1996, reported related data.)

One would expect individualist societies to be *universalistic* and *specific*, but collectivist societies to be *particularistic* and *diffuse*. In individualist societies one should treat everybody alike (and the relationship tends to be limited in scope). In collectivist societies one treats relatives and friends preferentially (and the relationship tends to be more broad). Among the six nationalities examined most intensively in Peabody (1985), it seemed that the French and the Germans tended to be universalistic in a public sphere and particularistic in a private sphere. For the Americans and the English, universalism tended to invade the private sphere. In contrast, particularism tended to extend into the public sphere for the Italians and the Russians—and, one would guess, for many collectivist cultures in the non-European rest of the world. Altogether, this dimension seems important, and to show a promising fit with the Hofstede ones.

Conclusion. Pending further evidence, the comparisons considered between the trait dimensions and the Hofstede–Bond ones are only suggestive and based mainly on conceptual similarities. One cannot conclusively consolidate the two sets of dimensions and must therefore provisionally retain them all. At any rate, one can argue that the Hofstede–Bond dimensions are not sufficient, and can be usefully supplemented with those from the trait analyses. Consider differences between the British and the Americans. On the five Hofstede–Bond dimensions these differences are very small. In four cases they range from 2 to 5 points on a scale of about 100, and reach a peak of only 11 points for Uncertainty Avoidance.

In contrast, notable British-American differences were illustrated by the example at the beginning about the weather and readiness to initiate conversation. This example can be explained by the very large differences on the two trait dimensions, where the Americans are Loose and very Assertive (psychologists often call one or both of these "extraverted"); in contrast, the English are Tight and not Assertive. These English-American differences on the trait dimensions are among the largest to be found. This confirms that some such dimensions are needed for cross-cultural comparison.

Implications. What are the implications of the present approach for the general issues of this book? The present approach seems well adapted for dealing with these issues. The trait dimensions are very general, and so applicable to any nationalities. Moreover, the distinction between evaluative and descriptive aspects suggests that different nationalities may agree about the descriptive components of judgment but disagree about the evaluative components (Peabody, 1985). These latter differences could lead to cross-cultural misunderstanding.

The first two issues concern modal characteristics of different nationalities. Consider the evaluative aspects. In some simple cases, the differences would *only* be evaluative—for example, *We* are self-confident, *you* are conceited, and so forth. More common would be cases where descriptive differences are agreed on. Thus, as regards the Tight–Loose dimension, a Loose group could judge "We are *spontaneous* (+), you are *inhibited* (–)," whereas for a Tight group "You are *impulsive* (–), we are *self-controlled* (+)." The initial example about the weather could be an illustration. Americans would consider the English as aloof because of their disinterest in biographical revelations (and boring because of their preoccupation with the weather.) The English would consider the Americans as brash and imperceptive because of their failure to respect the English reserve and privacy.

As regards the Assertive–Unassertive dimension, Hofstede (1991) gave a relevant example from his own biography. American job interviewers expect applicants to oversell themselves, and so interpret the modesty of a Dutch applicant as lack of assurance. In contrast, a Dutch interviewer could interpret an American applicant as a braggart.

The previous examples concern the issues involving the "modal" characteristics of different nationalities. The remaining issues are treated here as regards the covariation *between* characteristics (as they occur in "lay theories of personality"). The principle of "descriptive consistency" proposed that outgroup judgments might exaggerate the descriptive consistency between characteristics (Peabody, 1985). (Linville, Fischer, & Yoon, 1996, gave similar results for age categories.) Examples could come from the four cases in Table 4.1, where both ingroup and outgroup results are presented. As noted earlier, the ingroup self-judgments in each case show a weaker relationship to one of the two descriptive dimensions. For example, for the French the relationship to Loose impulse expression is weak in their ingroup judgments, much stronger in outgroup judgments. Looking at the detailed results from the 28 scales, one finds that the self-judgments recognize some classical examples of French impulse *control*, such as skepticism and thrift. The outgroup judges show less recognition of such exceptions.

Thus, all the issues illustrate the misunderstandings that could arise between different nationalities, and so what one would need to know to try to avoid them. The analysis made here into evaluation and the two descriptive dimensions makes it easier to pinpoint this danger, as well as to provide conceptual clarification in general.

To summarize some advantages of the present approach:

1. The lexical hypothesis provides in principle a solution for the selection of variables, and *could* help deal with the (emic/etic) problem of cross-cultural generality.
2. The separation into evaluative and descriptive components allows for a clearer analysis. For example, theories often emphasize evaluation, but evidence suggests that the descriptive components are generally more important.
3. As has just been shown, a similar point applies to the possibility of cross-cultural misunderstandings. These may involve descriptive agreement but evaluative disagreement.
4. The two descriptive dimensions of Tight–Loose and Assertive–Unassertive contribute to a useful framework for examining national characteristics.

REFERENCES

Bond, M. H. (1988). Finding universal dimensions of individual variation in multicultural studies of values: The Rokeach and Chinese Value Surveys. *Journal of Personality and Social Psychology, 55,* 1009–1015.

Bond, M. H. , & Forgas, J. P. (1984). Linking person perception to behavior intention across cultures. *Journal of Cross-Cultural Psychology, 15,* 337–352.

Chinese Culture Connection. (1987). Chinese values and the search for culture- free dimensions of culture. *Journal of Cross-Cultural Psychology, 18,* 143–164.

Draguns, J. G. (1996). Toward a more sensitive and realistic assessment in multi-cultural settings. In R. T. Carter (Ed.), *What is multiculturalism? 1995 Columbia University Teachers College Cross-Cultural Roundtable Proceedings* (pp. 23–29). New York: Columbia University Teachers College Press.

Fiske, A. P. (1992).The four elementary forms of sociality: Framework for a unified theory of social relations. *Psychological Review, 99,* 689–723.

Fiske, A. P. (1993). *Structures of social life: The four elementary forms of human relations.* New York: The Free Press.

Hofstede, G. (1980). *Culture's consequences: International differences in work-related values.* Beverly Hills, CA: Sage.

Hofstede, G. (1983). Dimensions of national cultures in fifty countries and three regions. In J. B. Deregowski, S. Dziurawiec, & R. C. Annis (Eds.), *Expiscations in cross-cultural psychology* (pp. 335–355). Lisse, Netherlands: Swets and Zeitlinger.

Hofstede, G. (1991). *Cultures and organizations: Software of the mind.* London: McGraw-Hill.

Inkeles, A. (1997). *National character: A psycho-social perspective.* New Brunswick, NJ: Transaction.

Linville, P. W., Fischer, G. W., & Yoon, C. (1996). Perceived covariation among features of ingroup and outgroup members: The outgroup covariation effect. *Journal of Personality and Social Psychology, 70,* 421–436.

Lynn, R. (1971). *Personality and national character.* Oxford, England: Pergamon.

McClelland, D. C. (1961). *The achieving society.* Princeton, NJ: Van Nostrand.

Peabody, D. (1967). Trait inferences: Evaluative and descriptive aspects. *Journal of Personality and Social Psychology Monographs, 7* (Whole No. 644).

Peabody, D. (1985). *National characteristics.* New York: Cambridge University Press.

Peabody, D. (1987). Selecting representative trait adjectives. *Journal of Personality and Social Psychology, 52,* 59–71.

Peabody, D. (1990). The role of evaluation in impressions of persons. In I. Rock (Ed.), *The legacy of Solomon Asch: Essays in cognition and social psychology* (pp. 57–75). Hillsdale, NJ: Lawrence Erlbaum Associates.

Peabody, D., & Goldberg, L. R. (1989). Some determinants of factor structures from personality-trait descriptors. *Journal of Personality and Social Psychology, 57,* 552–557.

Peabody, D., & Shmelyov, A. G. (1996). Psychological characteristics of Russians. *European Journal of Social Psychology, 26,* 507–512.

Schwartz, S. S. (1994). Beyond individualism/collectivism: New cultural dimensions of values. In U. Kim et al. (Eds.), *Individualism and collectivism* (pp. 185–219). Thousand Oaks, CA: Sage.

Schwartz, S. S., & Bilsky, W. (1987). Toward a universal structure of human values. *Journal of Personality and Social Psychology, 53,* 550–562.

Smith, P. B., & Bond, M. H. (1993). *Social psychology across cultures: Analysis and perspectives.* London: Allyn & Bacon.

Smith, P. B., Dugan, S., & Trompenaars, F. (1996). National cultures and the values of organizational employees: A dimensional analysis across 43 nations. *Journal of Cross-cultural Psychology, 27,* 231–264.

5

National Differences in Economic Growth: The Role of Personality and Culture

Clark McCauley
Bryn Mawr College

Victor Ottati
Purdue University

Yueh-Ting Lee
Westfield State College

Political scientists and even a few economists have rediscovered culture. This lost continent was a surprising landfall for investigators seeking explanations of economic growth, in particular explanations for national differences in economic growth since World War II. The differences have been large: From 1960 to 1989, for instance, average yearly growth in real per capita gross domestic product (GDP) ranged from 6.6% for South Korea to .75% for Nigeria (Granato, Inglehart, & Leblang, 1996a). During this period U.S. growth averaged 2.1% per year, a mediocre performance in relation to 5% to 7% growth rates for the "Five Dragons"—Japan, South Korea, Taiwan, Singapore, and Hong Kong (Granato, Inglehart, & Leblang, 1996a; Hofstede & Bond, 1988).

National differences in economic growth are not well predicted by the usual econometric models, which point to factors such as level of development (growth more difficult in a more developed economy, as assesed by per capita GDP), education (growth greater with higher percentage of children in primary school), and investment (growth greater with higher percentage of GDP in domestic investment). For economists, these are the usual suspects when trying to account for economic growth, but the rise of the Five Dragons remains surprising even after these factors have been examined. Hofstede and Bond (1988) noted that an economic forecast in *The American Economic Review* in 1966 greatly overestimated growth in India and Sri Lanka, greatly underestimated growth in Taiwan and South Korea, and ignored Singapore and Hong Kong as economically insignificant.

Thus scholars have been driven to explore more broadly for the predictors of economic growth, and they have landed on cultural differences. This chapter offers a brief review of the results and controversies in research aiming to link national differences in culture with national differences in economic growth. The cultural differences that are the focus of this research include differences in achievement motivation, interpersonal trust, and other social values; these aspects of culture may be of particular interest to anyone who must cross cultural boundaries for economic purposes.

THE RELATION OF CULTURE AND ECONOMICS: WEBER AND MCCLELLAND

Recent studies of culture and economic development all hark back to Weber's *The Protestant Ethic and the Spirit of Capitalism* (1904/1930). Weber noticed that modern industrial development had proceeded faster in Northern Europe, especially in Calvinist nations like England and the Netherlands, than in Catholic France, Italy, and Spain. He argued that the Reformation had led to different values in the Protestant nations, in particular to encouraging hard work and thrift and a concern for worldly success. The Protestant doctrine of predestination might seem to discourage individual efforts, but, according to Weber, Calvinist interpretation of the doctrine had paradoxically encouraged individual achievement. Although the individual could do nothing to merit salvation, worldly success was the sign of divine favor for those predestined to heaven. Thus, compared with Catholics, Protestants worked harder, consumed less, invested more, and were more eager for worldly success. The result was higher economic growth for Protestant nations (see Peabody, 1985, for a more sophisticated explication of Weber's views on this issue).

Weber's thesis linking values with economics was taken up by McClelland (1961), who developed a measure of achievement motivation from content analysis of stories told by individuals in reaction to ambiguous pictures (McClelland, Atkinson, Clark, & Lowell, 1953). The measure proved to be unreliable at the level of the individual (retest correlations about .25), but McClelland was able to use the same kind of content analysis to assess achievement motivation in stories from children's readers. For each of 22 nations, achievement motivation was scored from 21 readers in use in the 1920s and from 21 readers in use in the 1950s. Thus aggregated, the national achievement motivation scores had adequate reliability (split half correlation based on 11 readers vs. 10 readers was .67 for the 1920s readers and .59 for the 1950s readers).

It was McClelland's ambitious idea to test Weber's thesis by relating national level of achievement motivation to economic growth. Using kilowatt hours per capita as a measure of national economic performance, McClelland used 1925 economic level to predict 1950 economic level in a regression model. Then he defined economic achievement in terms of deviation from the regression predictions, such that greater-than-predicted economic level in 1950 received a positive deviation score and less-than-predicted achievement received a negative deviation score. Finally, he correlated 1920s and 1950s achievement motivation with economic over- and underachieving. The result was consistent with Weber's thesis: The 1920s scores correlated .53 with economic over- and underachieving between 1925 and 1950. Of course 1950s schoolchildren would not be expected to have yet had any impact on national economic performance, and, consistent with this expectation, the 1950s achievement motivation scores correlated .03 with economic achievement between 1925 and 1950.

McClelland's research is even today a model of how to test the link between national character or modal personality and economic performance. It is a model that has recently been rediscovered by political economists, and we describe some of this work in the next section. Before moving on, however, it is worth noting that McClelland's work has been extended to predicting a more recent period of economic growth.

Jackman and Miller (1996b) used GDP per capita in 1960 and in 1989 as the measure of national economic development, and were able to get economic data for 19 of the nations for which McClelland had assessed 1950s achievement motivation. Thus Jackman and Miller were able to test the prediction value of 1950s achievement motivation for over- and underachievement in terms of economic growth between 1960 and 1989. Using a more complex regression model than McClelland (1961), Jackman and Miller used not only 1960 economic level but percentage of children in school in 1960 and domestic investment as a percentage of GDP between 1960 and 1989 to predict 1989 economic level. With these three predictors in the regression model, 1950s achievement motivation did not add anything to the prediction of 1989 economic level for these 19 nations; indeed the zero-order correlation between 1950 achievment motivation and economic growth 1960–1989 was –.16.

Thus, although national achievement motivation in 1925 predicted national economic growth between 1925 and 1950, achievement motivation in 1950 did not predict economic growth between 1960 and 1989. This inconsistency in results will not be understood or resolved without additional research, but should at least alert us to the possibility that the cultural traits contributing to economic growth may differ in different periods of history.

CULTURE AND ECONOMICS IN ITALY:
PUTNAM'S DATA

In the 1970s, Italy inaugurated 20 elected regional governments that took over from the national government in Rome a wide range of responsibilities including public health and safety. The borders of these regions were approximately the borders of regions recognized as distinct political and cultural entities since the Middle Ages: Lombardy, Tuscany, Emilia-Romagna, Calabria, and so forth. Since the unification of Italy in 1870, these regions had been governed from Rome by a centralized state; 100 years after unification these regions received comparable constitutions and local responsibilities. Each region also received financial support from Rome, with the poorer regions receiving a little more per capita than the richer regions; by the 1990s, the regional governments were disposing of almost a tenth of Italy's GDP. Putnam (1993) seized the opportunity of this quasi-experiment in institutional formation to track the success of the new regional governments, and to relate differences in government success to differences in civic culture measured in the early 1900s.

Although Putnam (1993) focused on measuring and predicting the political success of regional governments—their responsiveness, their innovations, their support for business, agriculture, health, and housing—he did not neglect the economic success of these regions. In general, the northern regions of Italy are more economically advanced than the southern regions. Putnam showed that the percentage in agriculture is relatively low in the northern regions and relatively high in the southern regions; conversely the percentage in industry is relatively high in the northern regions and relatively low in the southern regions. To understand these regional differences, Putnam went back to the autocratic governance of the Normans who

conquered southern Italy in the Middle Ages, as opposed to the cooperative and more democratic governance of emerging city states in the
northern regions.

More specifically and empirically, Putnam showed that a measure of the
strength of civic traditions in the early 1900s is a better predictor (beta =
$-.73$, $p < .01$) of 1977 percentage working in agriculture than is 1901
percentage working in agriculture (beta = .26, ns). Similarly, strength of
civic traditions in the early 1900s is a better predictor (beta = .82, $p < .01$)
of 1997 percentage working in industry than is 1901 percentage working in
industry (beta = .01, ns). Finally, strength of civic traditions in the early
1900s is a better predictor (beta = $-.75$, $p < .01$) of infant mortality rate
1977–1984 than is 1901–1910 infant mortality (beta = .19, ns). The adjusted
R-squared for these three regressions ($n = 20$ for each regression) are .69,
.63, and .56.

The power of civic traditions circa 1900 as a predictor of economic
development 70 years later is striking, and suggests that Putnam's measure
of civic traditions is worth serious attention. This measure is an aggregation
of five indicators drawn from data of 1860 to 1920: strength of mass parties,
incidence of cooperatives, membership in mutual aid societies, electoral
turnout, and the longevity of local associations. Putnam understood this
measure as an index of civic involvement or social capital: the extent to
which citizens act on mutual obligation, trust, and expectation that the
public domain is a means to individual welfare. The southern regions are
low on this kind of social capital. Edward Banfield (1958) earlier had
described the southern perspective as amoral familism in which the norm
is to "maximize the material, short-term advantage of the nuclear family;
assume that all others will do likewise" (p. 85).

Civic traditions warrant recognition as a measure of culture at least to
the extent that they are quite stable over time. Putnam (1993) derived a
similar measure of civic involvement for 1970, a measure that puts together
regional data on preference voting, referendum turnout, newspaper readership, and the frequency of sports and cultural associations. Across the
20 regions, 1900s civic involvement and 1970s civic involvement are
correlated .93.

Putnam (1993) then used his measure of 1970 civic involvement to
predict economic growth between 1970 and 1989. His measure of economic
success is regional product per capita (RGP) in 1970 and 1989. In a
regression model including both 1970 RGP and 1970 civic involvement as
predictors of 1987 RGP, Putnam showed that both predictors are significant

(beta = .64 for 1970 RGP, beta = .35 for 1970 civic involvement; adjusted R-squared = .92).

Note that cultural differences in civic traditions are differences in relationships rather than differences in personality. Whereas McClelland linked national differences in achievement motivation with differences in economic development, Putnam linked a social psychological variable—civic involvement—with economic development. There is evidence, however, that social psychological variables and personality traits may be linked.

Peabody (1985) obtained trait ratings of target nations by raters from the same and other nations, using a technique of balanced trait pairs (e.g., thrifty-extravagant, stingy-generous) that permits unconfounding evaluation and description. He applied the same techniques to comparing northern versus southern Italians, as seen by both northern and southern Italian raters. Results showed that northerners and southerners were agreed that northerners are higher on impulse control (thrifty, self-controlled, serious, skeptical, persistent). Northerners and southerners also agreed that northerners are more assertive (forceful, self-confident, independent). The content of these north–south differences within Italy are remarkably similar to Weber's description of north–south differences across European nations: Northern Italians have more of the traits that Weber associated with the Protestant ethic.

Thus the personality traits of northern and southern Italians differ in ways that parallel the differences in civic culture that Putnam (1993) focused on. Differences in personality traits and differences in civic relationships are both aspects of cultural difference, and both may be important in understanding variations in economic development. Recent research linking culture with economic growth has further examined individual motives and values by turning to survey results.

CULTURE AND ECONOMICS: INTERNATIONAL SURVEYS OF CORPORATE EMPLOYEES AND STUDENTS

In the 1970s, IBM developed a data bank of employee surveys: over 100,000 questionnaires in 20 languages from 72 nations, obtained between 1967 and 1973. Hofstede (1980) seized the opportunity to analyze 32 items that he thought would tap cultural differences in relation to work. These items had to do with preferences about job characteristics, work goals, management style, competition, and other work-related issues. Hofstede's analyses concentrated on 50 nations and three multinational regions (East Africa, West Africa, and Arab-speaking nations) with sufficent data for comparative purposes. The result was four dimensions of cultural difference: power distance (acceptance of status inequality), individualism-collectivism (individual vs. group definitions of identity and success), uncertainty avoidance (by following rules), and masculinity-femininity (tough vs. tender minded).

Although Hofstede preferred to distinguish them for conceptual reasons, factor analysis results indicated that power distance and individualism-collectivism were strongly related (see Peabody, chap. 4 of this volume). Indeed, we calculate a correlation of +.68 between scores on power distance and collectivism for the 53 nations and regions in Exhibit 2 of Hofstede and Bond (1988). Nations high on acceptance of inequality tend also to be high on collectivism; these nations may be thought of as relatively traditional in social relations, with an emphasis on what Fiske (1992) has referred to as communal-sharing and authority-ranking models of relationships. Hofstede (Hofstede & Bond, 1988) found that nations high on individualism, in particular, tended to be have higher GDP per capital, but his analyses of changes over time indicated that it is wealth that leads to individualism rather than individualism leading to wealth. Hofstede suggested that prosperity makes it possible for people to behave more selfishly.

Another approach to assessing cultural differences by surveys was undertaken by Bond and the Chinese Culture Connection (CCC, 1987), who developed a survey to assess particularly Chinese values and obtained samples of university students from 22 nations. Factor analysis suggested three dimensions identifiable (factors correlating at least .60) with Hofstede's three dimensions, including the correlation between the power distance and individualism-collectivism dimensions. These results offered strong cross-cultural validation of the three dimensions.

A fourth dimension emerged from the CCC results that had no counterpart in Hofstede's results, a dimension that he called "Confucian dynamism." Nations high on this dimension give more importance to persistance, thrift, observing status differences, and having a sense of shame, and give less importance to personal steadiness, protecting face, respect for tradition, and reciprocation of favors. The new dimension was interesting because it was correlated with recent variations in economic growth; in particular the Asian Dragons (South Korea, Japan, Taiwan, Singapore, and Hong Kong) were notably high on Confucian dynamism.

For the 10 nations having the required data (Brazil, Canada, Germany, Great Britain, India, Japan, South Korea, Netherlands, Sweden, United States), we calculate a correlation of +.72 between Confucian dynamism scores (Hosftede & Bond, 1988) and economic growth 1960–1989 (Granato, Inglehart, & Leblang, 1996a).

Hofstede and Bond (1988) interpreted Confucian dynamism in terms of what helps and hurts economic activity, that is, modern flexibility in business versus traditional resistance to innovation. There is some post hoc quality to this interpretation, which certainly did not originate in any theoretical prescription. Although persistance and thrift are familiar candidates for supporting economic activity, it is not clear why observing status differences should help or why reciprocation of favors should harm economic activity. Still, the survey research by Hofstede and Bond has initiated a promising avenue of inquiry into the link between culture and economics.

Other researchers (e.g., Schwartz, 1994; Smith, Dugan, & Trompenaars, 1996) have performed similar cross-national surveys. For example, Smith et al. surveyed over 8,800 organization managers and employees from 43 countries (including eastern European nations unrepresented in previous surveys) and found dimensions of national differences that could be related to Hofstede's individualism-collectivism and power distance and to CCC's Confucian dynamism work. On the basis of their findings, Smith et al. suggested that Hofstede's individualism-collectivism and power distance dimensions may be better understood or defined as "representing varying orientations toward continuity of group membership (loyal involvement/utilitarian involvement) and varying orientations toward the obligations of social relationship (conservatism/egalitarian commitment)" (pp. 231). However interpreted, the two dimensions are not clearly related to economic growth: The two-dimensional plot of nations shows China closest to Bulgaria and Russia, whereas the other "Dragons" (Hong Kong, Singapore, Korea, Japan) are closest to Burkina Faso and the United Arab Emirates.

CULTURE AND ECONOMICS:
THE WORLD VALUES SURVEY

Economic data for various nations are not always reliable or comparable, but the economic data are rock solid by comparison with the measurement of culture. McClelland argued that cultural values must be represented in the stories of children's readers, or these stories would not appeal to the teachers, parents, and students who must agree to buy these readers. This was a plausible assumption that led to interesting results, but a more direct measure of national cultural values would come from surveying a representative sample of a nation's adult population. One need not believe that survey data are the gold standard for assessing cultural values; it may be precisely the deepest and least examined cultural values that are least accessible to survey respondents. Nevertheless, survey data on cultural values of different nations offer an interesting approach to exploring the linkage between values and economics.

The World Values Survey includes a common core of questions administered to a representative sample of respondents, in their native language, in many different nations. Granato et al. (1996a) used results of the 1990 World Values Survey to predict economic growth from 1960 to 1989 for 25 nations. Their measure of economic level in 1960 and in 1989 was real per capita GDP. Their measure of cultural values was a four-item Achievement Motivation Index derived from the following question: "Here is a list of qualities which children can be encouraged to learn at home. Which, if any, do you consider to be especially important?" The list included "Thrift," "Determination," "Obedience," and "Religious Faith," and Granato et al. constructed their Achievement Motivation Index as the sum of the percentages of a national sample saying that Thift and Determination are important, *minus* the sum of the percentages saying that Obedience and Religious Faith are important. Thus the index takes a positive value to the extent that a nation sees Thrift and Determination more important than Obedience and Religious Faith, and takes a negative value to the extent that a nation sees Obedience and Religious Faith as more important than Thrift and Determination.

The correlation between the Achievement Index and mean rate of per capita economic growth was a striking +.66; the nations with values favoring achievement over traditional values showed stronger economic growth. Granato et al. (1996a) went on to test the power of the Achievement Index in a multiple regression model that included the economists' usual suspects: initial economic level (per capita GDP in 1960), percentage of school-age children in primary and secondary education in 1960, and investment (average 1960–1989 of real domestic investment as percentage of real GDP). Taken together, the economic predictors accounted for 55% of the variance in 1989 economic level; with Achievement Motivation added to the regression, 70% of the variance was accounted for. The results suggest that both economic factors and cultural factors are important for economic growth, and that the two kinds of predictors make substantially independent contributions.

Before moving on to consider the implications of these results, it is necessary to consider several criticisms of Granato et al. (1966a) advanced by Jackman and Miller (1996a,1996b).

First and perhaps most telling is that Jackman and Miller (1996b) made salient what Granato et al. (1996a) had buried in an Appendix: that the World Value Survey data came from 1990, although the data were used to "predict" economic growth from 1960 to 1989. Although Granato et al. were not explicit on this point, it appears that they had to use the 1990 World Value Survey because Surveys from previous years did not include the desired questions or did not include enough nations. It might be argued that change in national values proceeds slowly, so slowly that little is lost by using 1990 data in the absence of similar data from 1970. This argument could be strengthened by showing that the results of the crucial questions, or of similar questions, did not change much over time for those nations where the questions had been asked in World Value Surveys earlier than 1990. Unfortunately, Granato et al. did not offer any data to support the stability of Survey results.

Thus Jackman and Miller (1996b) were able to argue that economic growth is, to an unknown degree, the cause rather than the effect of cultural values. Indeed, they were able to show that economic growth 1960–1989, together with percentage of children in secondary education in 1960, are strong predictors (R-squared = .69) of the Achievement Index from 1990.

In addition, Jackman and Miller (1996b) showed, as described previously, that McClelland's 1950 measure of achievement motivation from children's readers does not predict economic growth from 1960 to 1989.

Finally, Jackman and Miller (1996a) wondered about how the 4 items were selected for the index from the list of 11 qualities that children might be encouraged to learn at home. The list offered to World Survey respondents included "Hard Work" and "Independence," and it is not clear why these were not included in the Achievement Index constructed by Granato et al. (1996a).

What can be said about the results offered by Granato et al. (1996b), after taking account of the criticisms raised by Jackman and Miller (1996b)? We believe that there is still some considerable surprise value in the power of the relation between national values and national growth, even if the relationship is postdiction rather than prediction. Suppose that you had the opportunity to write 11 new questions for the next World Values Survey, knowing that you could use the best 4 to try to predict economic growth from 1960 to 1996. How much would you wager that you could do as well as the Achievement Index put together by Granato et al.?

On the other hand, there may be better measures of educational inputs than those used by Granato et al. The percentage of school-age children in primary or secondary education is all too literally an input measure; one might suppose that achievement level of children in primary or secondary education might better assess educational input to economic progress. The IEA Third International Mathematics and Science Study (TIMSS, 1994–1995) provides mean eighth-grade mathematics achievement scores for 17 of the 25 nations studied by Granato et al. These scores correlate .69 with mean rate of per capita economic growth 1960–1989 (vs. .55 correlation of growth with the Achievement Motivation Index of Granato et al. for these 17 nations; both correlations our calculations). For these 17 nations, regression showed the usual suspects (see earlier discussion) accounted for 61% of the variance in 1989 economic level; adding Achievement Motivation to the model raised variance accounted for to 68%; adding eighth-grade mathematics scores raised variance accounted for to 84% (our calculations). It may be that educational achievement (rather than educational exposure) is a more important form of social capital than achievement motivation.

Other kinds of results also suggest that the importance of achievement motivation for national growth remains somewhat uncertain. It is not clear why McClelland's 1950 achievement motivation scores did not predict growth from the period 1960–1989, not clear why teaching children the value of hard work and independence doesn't even postdict growth, and not clear how much national values may be the effect rather than the cause of economic growth.

ARE "DIMENSIONS" OF CULTURAL COMPARISON ILLUSORY?

Whereas Jackman and Miller (1996a) criticized a particular measure of cultural traits, some students of culture criticize the whole enterprise of cross-cultural trait measures. From this perspective, cross-cultural comparison is a false and groundless enterprise because it involves "comparing incomparables" (Goldschmidt, 1996, p. 8). That is, cultures cannot be compared along a common trait dimension because there are no common value dimensions. For example, power distance may be a relevant and salient dimension that underlies human behavior in Nation A, but irrelevant in Nation B. Individuals in Nation B are neither "high" nor "low" on power distance; rather, they simply do not think or act in terms of this dimension and respond on the basis of alternative concerns that are more salient within their culture. This kind of failure to establish "dimensional relevance" or commonality must undermine confidence in cross-cultural comparison.

A second problem associated with cross-cultural comparisons of traits involves the potential failure to establish "scale value equivalence." Some researchers argue that, even when a common trait dimension characterizes human behavior in two distinct cultures, it is impossible to establish a common metric of measurement that enables one to compare the magnitude of this trait in these two cultures. This problem can arise when the scale value associated with a given behavior differs across cultures. For example, the behavior "place your arm around another person's shoulder" might reflect a greater magnitude of intimacy among American men than among Italian men. If Italian men enact this behavior more frequently than American men, it is difficult to know whether this reflects (a) greater intimacy among Italian men than American men, or alternatively, (b) equal intimacy among these two groups—but with differing degrees of intimacy implied by the same behavior. In addition, when comparing trait magnitudes across cultures, one must consider the possibility that cultural differences reflect only differences in response style, social desirability, extreme checking style, or sensitivity to demand characteristics (Berry, 1980). In one study, H. C. Triandis and L. M. Triandis (1962) reported that cultural differences in a number of attitude and personality variables disappeared when acquiescence was statistically controlled.

Given these concerns, one must be cautious when assessing the relation between national character and national economic performance. Yet, several considerations argue against the extreme claim that values cannot be compared across nations (and therefore cannot be associated with national economic performance). First, a variety of empirical tests can be performed to ascertain whether "dimensional identity" does indeed exist across cultures (Hofstede & Bond, 1988; Schwartz & Bilsky, 1990; Peabody, chap. 4 of this volume). For example, one might factor analyze a battery of items purported to measure two trait dimensions; if different cultures yield a similar two-factor solution, dimensional identity is implicated (Irvine & Carroll, 1980). When dimensional identity is empirically established, it may also be possible to guard against violations of scale-value equivalence. For example, one might estimate a national character score for each nation that is adjusted for international differences in response style, acquiescence, social desirability, and so on (Hofstede, 1980; Peabody, 1985; H. C. Triandis & L. M. Triandis, 1962).

Perhaps most important, absence of dimensional identity and scale-value equivalence can only diminish the reliability and validity of measures of national character, which can only diminish the empirical relation observed between national character and national economic performance. Thus, measurement problems suggest that, if anything, current estimates of the relation between national character and national economic performance are likely to be overly conservative.

CONCLUSION

McClelland's early successes in linking national character to national economic growth attracted relatively little attention in the 1970s, but Hofstede and Bond rediscovered this linkage in the 1980s using multinational surveys of ad hoc samples of employees and students. More recently, Inglehart and his colleagues raised the methodological stakes by using multinational polling data as a means of getting at national values related to growth, and found a notable resonance with McClelland's results in the relation between economic growth and values of thrift and determination. Putnam's innovation was to use historical records as indicators of the public involvment and interpersonal trust that may be as important for economic growth as the economic and educational factors favored by econometric models.

In addition to methodological development, these results offer some substantive hints for future research. Putnam's Italian results, in particular, are clear and striking: Civic traditions assessed from turn-of-the-century records are strongly associated with regional economic level assessed in 1977. Civic traditions assessed in 1970 are less strongly but significantly associated with regional economic level in 1987. We have emphasized that Putnam assessed civic traditions in terms of political involvement and participation in self-help associations and cooperatives—that is, Putnam understood social capital in terms more related to social psychology than to personality or individual psychology. Of course, personality differences and social relationship differences are likely to occur together: Peabody's (1985) trait-rating results show that northern and southern Italians are agreed in seeing northerners with more impulse control and more assertiveness than southerners. Nevertheless, we think that Putnam's focus on social relations is potentially very important.

Consider the results of the two-dimensional array of nations that emerged from factor analysis of 1990 polling data by Smith et al. (1996). Ex-Communist nations (Yugoslavia, China, Bulgaria, Russia, Rumania, Hungary, Poland, and Czechoslovakia) appeared together in this array, separated from other nations in a quadrant defined by utilitarian (rather than loyal) relation to work and by ascribed (vs. achieved) status and particularist (vs. universalist) morality. It is difficult to believe that these nations have historically been similar in national character, but less difficult to believe that their 1990 values in regard to social relations have been affected similarly by their experience of a Communist system that emphasized the individual's relation to the state at the expense of relations among family and coworkers. From this point of view, the weak economic growth of these nations (China's current rapid growth only beginning after Deng Xiao-Ping took power after the death of Mao Tze-Tung in 1979) has less to do with similarities of modal personality and more to do with their similarity of social relations—that is, the Communist depression of the kind of social capital Putnam focused on.

Similarly, the economic success of overseas Chinese was notable during a period (1949–1979) in which growth of mainland China was weak (Borthwick, 1992; "The Overseas Chinese," 1992; Redding, 1990; Wang, 1992). For instance, in the mid-1980s Chinese were 4% of the population of Indonesia but owned 75% of assets and controlled 17 of the 25 biggest business groups or corporations ("The Overseas Chinese," 1992). Overseas Chinese in Thailand accounted for less than 10% of its population but owned about 90% of commercial and manufacturing assets and half the bank capital. Chinese in the Philippines accounted for about 60% of the sales of the 67 biggest commercial outfits ("The Overseas Chinese," 1992). It seems likely that culture had something important to do with the success of overseas Chinese, but why did the same culture produce no economic success on the mainland? Again the differences in economic success seem more naturally attributed to differences in social relations and organizations than to differences in modal personality.

In short, it seems to us that Putnam may be correct in emphasizing the importance of social capital understood in terms of relationships. Civic traditions of relationship and trust, private organizations and institutions—these are the channels through which cultural differences in value or modal personalty must flow. In order for individual values to affect economic activity, these values must be expressed in relationships with others. Thus it may be that social psychology is a better predictor or economic activity than personality psychology because the social psychology of relationships is more proximal in the chain of determinants of economic activity. This perspective suggests research aimed at learning more about national differences in social relations and social institutions, perhaps using Fiske's (1992) four models of relationships—communal sharing, authority ranking, equality matching, and market pricing.

Finally, we acknowledge that the research we have discussed is more a signboard to the future than a collection of established facts. Research has begun to uncover the cultural differences that are expressed in a nation's economic life and in national differences in economic success, but the pattern of results across various measures of culture is not yet clear. For the individual preparing to live or work across national boundaries, the strongest implication of this work may be a greater sensitivity to the traits, the values, and the social relationships of economic actors. We have suggested that social relationships and structures may be more important than individual values and traits, and that educational achievement may be a more important form of social capital than educational exposure, but these suggestions will remain only speculation without additional research.

REFERENCES

Banfield, E. C. (1958). *The moral basis of a backward society*. Glencoe, IL: The Free Press.

Berry, J. W. (1980). Introduction to methodology. In H. C. Triandis & J. W. Berry (Eds.), *Handbook of cross-cultural psychology: Methodology* (Vol. 2, pp. 1–28). Boston: Allyn & Bacon.

Borthwick, M. (1992). *Pacific century*. Boulder, CO: Westview.

Chinese Culture Connection. (1987). Chinese values and the search for culture-free dimensions of culture. *Journal of Cross-Cultural Psychology, 18*, 143–164.

Fiske, A. (1992). The four elementary forms of sociability: A framework for a united theory of social relations. *Psychological Review, 99*, 689–723.

Goldschmidt, W. (1996). *Comparative functionalism*. Berkeley: University of California Press.

Granato, J., Inglehart, R., & Leblang, D. (1996b). Cultural values, stable democracy, and economic development: A reply. *American Journal of Political Science, 40*, 680–696.

Granato, J., Inglehart, R., & Leblang, D. (1996a). The effect of cultural values on economic development: Theory, hypotheses, and some empirical tests. *American Journal of Political Science, 40*, 607–631.

Hofstede, G. (1980). *Culture's consequences: International differences in work-related values*. Beverly Hills, CA: Sage.

Hofstede, G., & Bond, M. (1988). The Confucius connection: From cultural roots to economic growth. *Organizational dynamics, 4*(16), 4–21.

Irvine, S. H., & Carroll, W. K. (1980). Testing and assessment across cultures: Issues in methodology and theory. In H. C. Triandis & J. W. Berry (Eds.), *Handbook of cross-cultural psychology: Methodology* (Vol. 2, pp. 181–244). Boston: Allyn & Bacon.

Jackman, R. W., & Miller, R. A. (1996b). The poverty of political culture. *American Journal of Political Science, 40*, 697–716.

Jackman, R. W., & Miller, R. A. (1996a). A renaissance of political culture? *American Journal of Political Science, 40*, 632–659.

McClelland, D. C. (1961). *The achieving society*. Princeton, NJ: Van Nostrand.

McClelland, D. C., Atkinson, J. W., Clark, R. A., & Lowell, E. L. (1953). *The achievement motive*. New York: Appleton–Century.

The overseas Chinese: A driving force. (1992, June 18). *The Economist*, pp. 21–24.

Peabody, D. (1985). *National characteristics*. London: Cambridge University Press.

Putnam, R. D. (1993). *Making democracy work: Civic traditions in modern Italy*. Princeton, NJ: Princeton University Press.

Redding, S. G. (1990). *The spirit of Chinese capitalism*. New York: Walter de Gruyter.

Schwartz, S. H. (1994). Cultural dimensions of values: Toward an understanding of national differences. In U. Kim, H. Triandis, C. Kagitcibasi, S. C. Choi, & G. Yoon (Eds.), *Individualism and collectivism: Theory methods and applications* (pp. 85–119). Thousands Oaks, CA: Sage.

Schwartz, S., & Bilsky, W. (1990). Toward a theory of the universal content and structure of values: Extensions and cross-cultural replications. *Journal of Personality and Social Psychology, 58*, 878–891.

Smith, P. B., Dugan, S., & Trompenaars, F. (1996). National culture and the values of organizational employees. *Journal of Cross-cultural Psychology, 27*, 231–264.

Third International Mathematics and Science Study (TIMSS). (1994–1995). [On-line]. Available: http://wwwcsteep.bc.edu/TIMSS1/HiLightB.html

Triandis, H. C., & Triandis, L. M. (1962). A cross-cultural study of social distance. *Psychological Monographs, 76, 21*, (Whole no. 540).

Wang, G. W. (1992). *China and Chinese overseas*. Singapore: Times Academic Press.

Weber, M. (1930). *The Protestant ethic and the spirit of capitalism*. (T. Parsons, Trans.). New York: Scribner. (Original work published 1904).

III

Personality Across Cultures

6

Culture, Meaning, and Personality in Mexico and in the United States

Rolando Diaz-Loving
National Autonomous University of Mexico

Juris G. Draguns
The Pennsylvania State University

CULTURE IN HUMAN INTERACTION

As Aronson (1995) has pointed out, human beings possess a unique ability to construct, communicate, and change culture. This capacity is perhaps the characteristic of human evolution. Culture, "that complex whole which includes knowledge, belief, art, law, morals, custom, and any other capabilities and habits acquired by humans as a member of society" (Tylor, 1877), plays a predominant role in shaping the human way of life, by ensuring the transmission and communication of thoughts, words, concepts, and feelings. Experiencing, construing, and communicating "reality" thus constitute the building blocks of personal belief and social interaction. Culture then provides the conceptual framework for explaining how groups of individuals arrive at socially shaped yet personally distinctive sets of values, attributes, attitudes, and patterns of social behavior.

Human evolution has produced an interplay of similarities and difference that are traceable to ecological niche, cultural heritage, and personal experience, all of which jointly produce social behavior. In this process, the human-made part of the environment sets the norms, traditions, and expectancies for perceiving, interpreting, and enacting social responses (Herskovits, 1955) that are transmitted to the individual through patterns of socialization, enculturation, and acculturation (Berry, Poortinga, Segall, & Dasen, 1992). This process occurs in constant interaction between the individual's biopsychic needs (Diaz-Guerrero, 1994) and the group's environment (Triandis, 1994). Its objective is to enable people to perceive and construe themselves (and thereby establish their self-concept and identities), and to make sense of the behavior of other human beings (through the formation of stereotypes and prototypes).

Human interaction requires encoding, interpreting, storing, and retrieving verbal, physical, and contextual stimuli. The resulting information in turn is utilized in order to guide and channel sociocultural norms of a specific group. The complexity of this process requires a person to sift heuristically through mountains of information. By means of generalization, integration, discrimination, deletion, accommodation, assimilation, and completion strategies, human beings succeed in navigating through a sea of stimuli, creating expectancies, beliefs, norms, roles, status, traits, values, and attitudes pertaining to their own selves and other persons. As a result of this progression our subjective world acquires both stability and predictablity.

At the dawn of scientific psychology Ezequiel A. Chavez (1901) boldly asserted that not paying attention to culture can only produce a distorted and misleading understanding of human conduct:

> The most relevant human endeavor is lodged in the study of ethnic character. Disregarding this cardinal observation has induced some persons to fall victim to the absurdity of attempting to directly transplant educational, law enforcement or governmental institutions from one culture to another, without even reflecting on the possible incompatibility of intellect, affect and will of the peoples whom they want to improve by offering them a beautiful although impractical reality. It is not enough for laws to pass the test of reason in the abstract, but rather it is indispensable that they concretely adapt to the special conditions of the people for whom they were enacted. Ideas and programs, to some, seem very noble. However, the sad reality is so often experienced in countries of Latin extraction, where marvelous plans are designed on paper, harmonious constitutions are promulgated, yet like Plato's dreams they crash against the harshness of practice and reality. (p. 84)[1].

We must also caution that culture does not necessarily correspond to nationality (Matsumoto, 1994). Being from Mexico does not mean that the

---

[1]Translated from Spanish by the author.

person will behave in a manner that corresponds to an average Mexican's actions and reactions. There are many regional and other group differences that should be considered. Analyzing stereotypes and prototypes must always include consideration of such variability. Discussions of "national cultures" ignore the diversity within people and their respective cultures that may be encompassed within a nation state (see Smith & Bond, 1994).

Once these precautions have been heeded, continued improvement of the ever-growing interaction between the citizens of Mexico and of the United States is crucially dependent on specification and knowledge of the norms that regulate their respective behavior, as well as the concepts and constructs that color their respective subjective worlds, the personal selves that define their attributes, and the prototypes and stereotypes constructed for the explanation of the characteristics of outgroups. Social psychological research on the construction of knowledge and social influence (e.g., Bem, 1970; Bruner, 1990; Hovland, Janis, & Kelly, 1953) indicates that the characteristics of interpersonal relationships are based on knowledge about ourselves and others. The coping strategies for such interactions are then selected on the basis of social construction. Constructive interactions require knowledge of individual and cultural similarities and differences in stereotypes, prototypes, perception, cognitive structures, behavioral patterns, attitudes, and beliefs. To provide a more solid foundation for such interaction, the following sections address Mexican and North American values, the sociocultural premises of the Mexican culture, the subjective world of Mexican and North Americans, and the Mexican self-concept.

MEXICAN AND U.S. VALUES

The definition of culture implies a shared set of values. Hofstede's (1980) cross-cultural work on values in the working environment contributes valuable insight, into both Mexican and U.S. cultures. In research with over 50 countries, Hofstede identified four factorial dimensions, which he labeled respectively: (a) individualism-collectivism, pertaining to the extent to which one's identity is defined by personal choices and achievements or by the character of the collective group, (b) power distance, dealing with the amount of deference and respect accorded to persons in socially superior positions by those of subordinate or lower social status, (c) uncertainty avoidance, referring to the need in a culture for formal rules and structure, and (d) masculinity-femininity, indicative of the relative cultural emphasis given to goals related to productivity or those referring to interpersonal harmony. Based on the factor scores from Hofstede's analysis, it is possible to classify the 50 countries on each of the four dimensions. The scores for Mexico and the United States are given in Table 6.1.

It is clear that Mexico is a country where gender (high masculinity) and social hierarchies (high power distance) are central to interpersonal relationships. The sociocultural premises that ascribe attributions for behavior are moderately high (moderate uncertainty avoidance) and there is a marked tendency to consider the group over individuals (high collectivism). In sharp contrast, in the United States the individual constitutes the center piece of society (high individualism). Given that "all men (relatively high masculinity) are created equal" there is emphasis on individual human rights (low power distance) and few rules are designed for curbing "free spirits" (low uncertainty avoidance).

MEXICAN HISTORIC SOCIOCULTURAL PREMISES

The culture in which individuals grow and develop provides the foundation for the delineation of the norms and rules of acceptable and desirable social behavior and interaction (uncertainty avoidance). Interpersonal behavior is directed and determined, in part, by the extent to which each subject addresses, believes, and internalizes cultural dictates. Given the importance of rules in the Mexican culture, Diaz-Guerrero (1986) extracted the Mexican historic sociocultural premises from sayings, proverbs, and other forms of popular communication. Content analysis of these premises shows the central position that the family occupies within the culture. Two basic principles emerge that capture the essence of Mexican family life: power and supremacy of the father and love and absolute and necessary sacrifice by the mother. In questionnaires constructed around these two cardinal premises, over 80% of large samples of the Mexican population register their approval of these assertions. Moreover, they indicate that these statements constitute the guiding principles of their lives. Interestingly, self-de-

TABLE 6.1
Ranks for Mexico and the United States on Hofstede's Dimensions

	Power Distance	Uncertainty Avoidance	Individualism-Collectivism	Masculinity-Femininity
Mexico	6	18	32	6
United States	38	43	1	15

nial holds true for both men and women who believe that it is important to satisfy the needs of others over self. Thus, self-modification or autoplasticity (Marin & Triandis, 1984; Vexliard, 1968) constitutes the preferred mode of coping of Mexican respondents (Avendano Sandoval & Diaz-Guerrero, 1990). Factor analysis of the responses to these statements has yielded a central traditionalism factor of affiliative obedience versus active self-affirmation ("children should always obey their parents," "when parents are strict children grow up correctly," "everyone should love their mother and respect their father"). According to this factor, children should never disobey parents and they must show respect in exchange for security and love. As would be expected from the family premises, Mexican society is built on a strict hierarchical structure based on "respect" toward others who are higher in the social hierarchy, especially parents and elder relatives (Diaz-Guerrero & Peck, 1963). Status, moreover, is determined by ascription, that is, that which the person is, rather than achievement, that is, the person's cumulative accomplishments. A gender dimension complements the traditionalism factor (machismo vs. virginity-abnegation), stating that "fathers should always be the heads of the home" and that "women should remain virgins until marriage." The importance of the family status quo and the cultural rigidity in relation to the roles played by men and women in the family is operationalized by such statements as: "Most girls would prefer to be like their mothers"; "women should always be protected"; "married women should be faithful to the relationship"; "a young woman should not be out alone at night"; and "when parents are strict, children grow up correctly."

The factors that form the sociocultural premises of the Mexican family depict the rules and norms that specify the ingroup relationships and the expectancies and stereotypes formed by people outside the group. Two lines of research help in understanding the impact and form in which sociocultural premises are transmitted and the manner in which they produce socialization practices that ensure the development of certain personality traits in Mexico. Andrade Palos (1996) reported that Mexican children and adolescents perceive their father as someone who is loving and hardworking, is an authority figure, provides for the family, scolds the children if necessary, demands respect, and gives permission; whereas the mother is described as tender, loving, helpful, protective, and responsible, who scolds children when necessary and is understanding and good; that is to say, she combines all the characteristics needed to induce affiliative obedience in their children. A more direct measure of the type of socialization practice and the impact on personality was presented by Andrade Palos (1987). In this study, the perceptions or parental socialization style by elementary school students was obtained and then regressions were established toward personality characteristics. Andrade Palos found that children who say that their mothers are more punitive and less affectionate and accepting (characteristics of the typically bad Mexican mother) develop fatalistic personality traits, whereas mothers and fathers who are affectionate, accepting, and achievement oriented have children who develop both a more instrumental and a more expressive internal locus of control. Other findings include the interaction of the father and mother and the gender of the child in the development of certain traits. It is noteworthy that in all cases there is emphasis on family, respect, affect, and punishment, which corresponds both to the traditional Mexican sociocultural premises and to the characteristics that describe the prototype of the Mexican self-concept, presented in the future sections of this chapter.

A more basic sociocultural premise was envisaged by Diaz-Guerrero (1967a, 1967b, 1982) in order to capture the contrast between the typical Mexican and Anglo-American learned responses to stress. As Diaz-Guerrero put it, Mexicans want to avoid stress whereas North Americans seek to confront it. In actuality, these broad and only partially verbalized attitudes compel Mexicans to endure stress passively, in line with the culturally inculcated virtues of obedience, patience, and self-abnegation. In the United States, on the other hand, values inculcated in the course of socialization impel the individual toward constant activity. On the basis of observations from a variety of sources, Diaz-Guerrero described the active and passive syndromes of responding to stress, each with their distinctive set of both assets and liabilities from the adaptive point of view. He explicitly emphasized that neither of these two contrasting sociocultural premises was intrinsically superior or inferior; both come with a mixed bag of advantages and disadvantages. The study of children in Mexico City and Austin, Texas, provided the opportunity for a large-scale systematic comparison of these two distinct orientations (Holtzman, Diaz-Guerrero, & Schwartz, 1975). The results of this investigation confirmed that "Americans tend to be more active than Mexicans in their style of coping with life's problems and challenges" (Holtzman et al., 1975, p. 339). By way of related and complementary findings, it was also established that Americans tended toward a more complex and differentiated cognitive style and that Mexicans displayed a more fatalistic and pessimistic outlook. Glimmers of the active–passive dimension are detectable in some aspects of the recent Mexico versus United States psycholinguistic comparison (Diaz-Guerrero & Szalay, 1993), although these findings were overshadowed by differences in individualistic versus sociocentric orientation. In the factor analysis of self-related attitudes, LaRosa and Diaz-Loving (1991) were able to identify one pole of the passivity–activity factor. In this study, a peaceful, serene, calm, and tranquil mode of responding to stress was indeed positively valued. Its negative opposite was marked by largely aimless agitation, low frustration tolerance, and disruptive, disagreeable, and aggressive interaction with other persons. That is very different from the Anglo-American notion of an active, resourceful, energetic, and effective person who embodies and exemplifies the active orientation to stress. Either the active sociocultural premise is distorted in the Mexican view or the dimension discovered in LaRosa and Diaz-Loving's factor analysis is distinctly different from the active–passive dimension as theoretically formulated. It should, however, be remembered that Diaz-Guerrero (1967a, 1967b) construed activity-passivity as an underlying dimension that possibly might not be amenable to detection by means of measures primarily designed to tap surface traits. At this point, the passive versus active dichotomy of sociocultural premises remains a promising and fascinating topic of investigation that may eventually prove to be the bedrock of the Anglo-American versus Mexican cultural contrast.

Effective multicultural relationships may be promoted by considering the findings reviewed to this point. Mexicans would do well to know the rules that govern their behavior and the cultural relativity of these social regulations. North Americans should be conscious of the differing premises permeating the cultures around the world and the core that they provide for the construction of reality for the people who uphold them. Specifically, they should be aware of the sociocultural premises that prevail in neighboring Mexico. Concurrently, we should caution that group premises and stereotypes are indicators of central tendencies in particular groups and that individual differences and variability within the groups are to be expected. Thus, not all humans live by their prescribed sociocultural premises. As stated elsewhere (Draguns, 1979):

The cultural design for their perpetuation is implicitly rational, yet it is rarely, if ever, fully realized. The cultural message is subject to distortion both at the source and at the point of its reception. Different people encode and articulate the cultural message in a distinct manner; it is then decoded and interpreted in a variety of ways. For better or worse, the result of socialization is always discrepant from that which was intended. Therein lie the seeds of cultural change, of innovation, of rebelliousness and alienation, but also of the great variety of personalities that exist within the same culture. (p. 319)[2]

Young rebels in the United States call for peace and love in a society that stresses power and competition, whereas Mexican adolescents call for liberty and equality in a culture built on interdependence and respect. A "proper" stereotype would depend on the extent to which individuals follow their sociocultural norms in a strict fashion. For example, Diaz-Guerrero (1994) presented data that show a negative correlation between adherence to sociocultural premises and years of schooling. Laborers and peasants cling to traditional sociocultural premises, whereas the more highly educated Mexicans value individualism, production, and competition and thereby identify less with traditional Mexican beliefs. However, it should be kept in mind that the norms embodied in the historic sociocultural premises represent a major source of the general Mexican self-prototype and self-stereotype. As such they continue to exercise a substantial influence upon the percepts, constructs, and precepts that guide day-to-day Mexican behavior. It is now time to turn to the more subjective aspects of the Mexican experience of the self in the world.

THE SUBJECTIVE WORLD OF MEXICANS AND NORTH AMERICANS

Diaz-Guerrero and Szalay (1993) have addressed the differences and similarities in the construction of the subjective worlds of Mexican and North American by means of a series of free associations. Several hundred Mexican and North American participants contributed their subjective constructions of a series of concepts, which we examine in this section.

Family, Self, and Friendship. As expected on the basis of the findings presented earlier, Mexican subjects emphasize affiliative interdependent relationships between parents and children, with special attention to the parents' responsibility for providing a "proper" upbringing and socialization for children. They stress intimate relationships and place a higher value on love, respect, and obedience. The value of familism has even been suggested to be one of the most culture specific characteristics among all Hispanics, with strong attachment links of loyalty, reciprocity, and solidar-

---

[2]Translated from Spanish by author.

ity to families, in both their nuclear and extended forms (Triandis, Marin, Betancourt, Lisansky, & Chang, 1982). In contrast, North Americans prize the father–mother or husband–wife relationships as the core of family experience. They place emphasis upon individual rules, and on the attainment of subjective psychological states such as happiness and diversion. Although love is also important for the North American family, it is comparatively less prominent than in Mexico. There is little evidence in Diaz-Guerrero and Szalay's data of how it can be used as an instrument of influence.

The images and social construction of the Mexican self exhibit a collective identity that is dependent on strict social rules. Demands for reciprocity, mutual help, understanding, cohesion and group, family and community unity are the centerpiece and the most important component of an individual. On the other hand, North Americans see themselves as independent and secure individuals. The self is construed by positive social qualities directed by personal interests and guided toward individualism, competition, and self-actualization (Diaz-Guerrero & Szalay, 1993).

The differential construction of self and the family in the two cultures has created different coping styles. In Mexico, a basic purpose of relationships is to make others happy, especially within the family. As a result, the characteristic coping style is geared toward self-modification, and is directed to adapting to the needs and values of others. For North Americans the tradition and norms call for an individualistic style that imposes the self's interests, needs, and lifestyle onto others (Diaz-Loving & Andrade Palos, 1984).

As expected, interaction styles brewed in the family environment spill over into the realms of friends and acquaintances. In Mexico, friends and friendships are reciprocally bound by tight and strong affiliative ties, laden with a host of long-lasting implications. In fact, the family is a central reference point for friendship. A good friend becomes part of the family, someone to help and assist in all areas of life. Friendship has a profound and selective significance; it implies harmony, trust, commitment, and strong long-lasting obligations to a few select individuals. In the United States friendship has a more limited impact. Basically, these relationships are focused on having fun, and in many occasions, on sexual relations. Friendships tend to be shorter and less intimate, built on convenience or the whims of situational determinants such as physical proximity and geographical mobility. They provide a transitory situational tie, to be engaged with almost anybody without any specific social obligations that might interfere with the free action and choice of the individual (Diaz-Guerrero & Szalay, 1993). Remarkably, this finding is anticipated by the observation that Kurt Lewin (1936) contributed after his arrival in the United States from Germany. He too noted that friendships in North America were situation-bound, informal, and entailed few commitments or obligations nor were they expected to last for a long period or even for lifetime. By contrast, in more tradition-based cultures—presumably including Mexico—friendship is marked by rituals, entailing far-reaching mutual obligations, and it is expected to be lifelong, unless terminated unilaterally or bilaterally, usually on the basis of nonfulfillment of obligations. As in other collectivist and traditional societies (Hui, 1990), Mexicans see others as permanent "objects" in their lives, with stringent and lasting loyalty to extended family and friends.

Love and Marriage

In Mexico, perhaps more than elsewhere, the belief prevails that love and marriage go together. Their conjunction includes affect, sentiments, comprehension, and attachment toward someone whose intrinsic qualities, behaviors, social roles, and status exemplify the combination of desirable attributes for the family. Love is conceived in the family context, especially toward children, then toward parents, brothers, and friends who are incorporated into the family (Diaz-Guerrero & Szalay, 1993). Within marriage, there are strong gender differences in expectancies and roles, and commitment is the main determinant in the development and maintenance of "successful marriages" (Diaz-Loving, 1996). In the United States, affect, love, and marriage are associated with the satisfaction of personal needs through a mutually satisfactory relationship with another individual, allowing both of them to reach happiness. As a consequence, subjects think about sex and feelings in regard to a chosen specific other who satisfies their expectations, individual needs and desires (Diaz-Guerrero & Szalay, 1993). In societies such as the United States that emphasize individual well-being and hedonism as the guiding life values, the stability of marriage is based on romantic love, with people remaining together for as long as they feel satisfied, but without the social responsibility or commitment to stay married when things do not work out as romantically expected (Diaz-Loving, 1996).

Community, Society, and Religion

Mexicans experience a strong identification with groups that provide affiliative ties between individuals. Society is conceived of a grand union of interdependent people linked by positive interpersonal cooperation, and approximating brotherhood. This idealistic perception of society produces expectations and goals directed toward positive human values such as morality, equality, justice, and development, which stands in contrast to a mushrooming practice of corruption, egotism, and injustice. This discrepancy provokes high levels of frustration that is expressed through disillusionment (Diaz-Guerrero & Szalay, 1993).

Society for North Americans is made up of a set of individuals who for fortuitous reasons are living in the same place, at the same time, and who thereby share some common concerns and interests, a group of individuals whose liberty is subject to specific necessary restrictions that are imposed by large collectives of human beings. Grand social units are perceived with skepticism that is overcome only by a pragmatic orientation toward solving problems, such as safeguarding human rights, overcoming economic difficulties, reducing unemployment, and others. This pragmatic orientation is built on an unconditional faith in legal and constitutional processes and on an emphasis on law and rights. This outlook is congruent with the tendency to think about isolated individuals more than about great collectives, and about processes of problem solving rather than about social or philosophic principles (Diaz Guerrero & Szalay, 1993).

Integrated into the conceptualization of society are moral and religious sentiments. Mexicans see Catholicism as an all-encompassing faith, which evokes social attitudes of love, compassionate morality, affect, and understanding. God is a supreme being with unquestioned absolute power who looks over His flock like an understanding and loving parent; in the same manner a father should shelter and protect his family, according to the Mexican sociocultural premises. Because morality is divinely specified and dictated, it is understandable that values are presented as ideal, positive, and virtuous. God has sent His commandments and humans should show an immediate willingness to accept, pursue, and abide by these ideals. Obedience to this "loving father" has interpersonal and social implications that are contingent on future reinforcement or punishment (Diaz-Guerrero, 1994). North Americans see religion as a matter of faith and belief based on personal choice and moral autonomy. Individuality and autonomy prescribe a highly personal, but less emotional, relationship with God. Morality in turn represents choosing between correct (good), and incorrect (bad), rational premises. Subjects center their attention on specific contexts and practical problems such as sex, everyday life, drugs, and so forth. Morality is a personal choice based on personal conscience and subjected to individual autonomy (Diaz-Guerrero & Szalay, 1993).

Education and Economy. In Mexico, education overlaps with the role of the family, individual goals, and the adequate behavior of students. The aim is to achieve social goals (progress and development), with emphasis on the social and interpersonal impact of the formal and informal educational process, all of it orchestrated to develop children who conform to the moral ideals and social norms of interdependence. In the United States, education is a process of acquiring knowledge and aptitudes with practical and applicable value. The role of schools is to prepare individuals for a productive and happy life. There is a strong preoccupation with the possession of specific knowledge; a wide variety of schools exist where knowledge can be acquired depending on personal preference (Diaz-Guerrero & Szalay, 1993).

Living in a rapidly, though unevenly, changing developing country, Mexicans see economy as a major national problem, deeply entrenched in politics and government, confronting basic needs of development and progress against poverty and crisis (clothing, housing, transportation, and food). In the United States, the economy is related to business and personal finances in a market controlled by the process of supply and demand, with uncertainty and preoccupation about unpredictable highs and lows, such as inflation, recession, or depression (Diaz-Guerrero & Szalay, 1993).

Work and Politics. Mexicans see jobs as a necessary obligation, a means for obtaining bare necessities, a way of earning a living. Work, which is embedded in effort, becomes an instrument for ensuring certain family, social, and national goals, such as economic development and social progress. Work is thus a socially directed responsibility, with particular attention given to its impact on the economic progress of family and country. North Americans center their lives on the completion of job and work. Hard work is a virtue that gives a sense of achievement and accomplishment, a goal in itself; it is the basis of personal pride, success, and satisfaction. Responsibility at work is a personal attribute, like maturity and loyalty (Diaz-Guerrero & Szalay, 1993). In the individualistic perspective, progress is especially closely linked to science and technology (Triandis, 1992).

Mexicans have tended to pay relatively little attention to the political process. People are worried about their well-being and the future of the nation and are skeptical about politics as a means for solving these problems. North Americans interpret politics as a process of change through campaigns, competition, and majority rule based on elections (Diaz-Guerrero & Szalay, 1993).

PERSONALITY CHARACTERISTICS OF THE MEXICAN POPULATION

Personality develops in a process of constant interaction between the individual's bio-psychic needs and the historic sociocultural premises and norms of adequate and desirable behavior for a particular culture (Diaz-Guerrero, 1994). Personality psychologists have identified a long list of traits, which partially determine the constant and systematic behavior of particular subjects across situations. Cross-situational consistency is most evident and profound in the self-concept, a core dimension within the personality structure. To go back to William James' (1891/1952) classical definition, the self-concept is the perception that a person has of him- or herself, and all that he or she can call his or her own, including one's body, family, friends, possessions, beliefs, values, and so on. These attributes are distributed across several interrelated dimensions that reflect the personal sociocultural experiences of each individual (LaRosa & Diaz-Loving, 1988, 1991).

To identify the basic categories that reflect and compose the self-concept of Mexican subjects, LaRosa and Diaz-Loving (1991) interviewed 24 groups of high school and college students. Five categories of the self-concept were investigated, as follows:

- Physical, which refers to bodily attributes, such as attractive and healthy, as well as to physical abilities, physical characteristics, and physical functioning.
- Social, which includes the perception of styles and contents of interpersonal relationships and the degree of satisfaction produced by them.
- Emotional, which gives a picture of the sentiments and emotions experienced in daily life, as a consequence of social interactions and their perceived success or failure.

- Occupational-educational, which refers to work and school activities, as well as the level of success obtained.
- Ethical-moral, which includes personal and cultural values and social norms.

The next step involved obtaining an ethnopsychologically sensitive operationalization of these dimensions of self; 800 students generated adjectives that described each dimension. Those with the highest frequency for the physical dimension were: tall, thin, short, fat, ugly, and so forth; for social: happy, sad, sentimental, aggressive, loving, sensible; for emotional: amiable, sociable, amicable, shy, introverted, sympathetic; for occupational-educational: hardworking, lazy, intelligent, active, responsible, capable; and for ethical or moral: honest, good, responsible, bad, corrupt. Another sample of 800 students gave antonyms for the most frequent descriptors. Pairs of bipolar adjectives were then set on a semantic differential with "I am" as the stimuli. Exploratory factor analysis was followed by recomposition and new fieldwork with over 3,000 subjects from the general population. Confirmatory factor analysis yielded four general categories with factor loadings over .50 and eight values over 2 (LaRosa & Diaz-Loving, 1991).

SOCIAL SELF-CONCEPT DIMENSIONS

The social self describes the degree of emphasis on an individual's closeness or interdependence with other people. Markus and Kitayama (1991) saw the interdependent self as part of a social fabric, where belonging, fitting in, maintaining harmony, being empathic, self-modifying, and promoting other persons' well-being become important values and cherished personal goals. In Mexico, affiliative sociability includes being respectful, amiable, decent, friendly, pleasant, desirable, modest, polite, courteous, and considerate. On the negative side the descriptions are: disrespectful, rude, indecent, hostile, offensive, undesirable, stuck-up, impolite, uncourteous, and inconsiderate.

This dimension is highly congruent with the revised Mexican historic sociocultural premises, the philosophy of life, and the interpretation of concepts within the language. A basic attribute of the population is the ability and need to get along with others in a smooth and not confrontational and self-modifying style. These characteristics allow Mexican individuals to have considerate and constructive interpersonal relationships. Diaz-

Guerrero (1992) described Mexican adolescents as generally pleasant, courteous, socially sensitive, agreeable, and intent on producing a good impression, and behaving as they are "supposed to behave in all situations." The emphasis is clear: Being sensitive, courteous, and interested in having smooth social interaction is highly valued. This first factor extracted by Diaz-Guerrero from the self-descriptions of adolescents reflects the concept described by Triandis, Marin, and Betancourt (1984) as *"simpatia,"* a cultural Hispanic script, featuring emphasis on positive behavior in agreeable situations, and on avoidance of interpersonal conflict and negative behaviors. *Simpatia* dictates the need to be polite and respectful and discourages criticism and confrontation with others.

The second factor, expressive sociability, refers to the expressive and communication tendencies. Mexicans place themselves on an axis bounded by sociability and loneliness. At one extreme, this dimension is exemplified by using such terms as extraverted, communicative, fun, outgoing, free, expressive, friendly, and sociable, and at the opposite end of the continuum by descriptors such as introverted, quiet, boring, timid, inhibited, reserved, lonely, and unsociable. This scale measures a tendency toward interacting and having fun with others, and spending a substantial part of one's life in experiencing the pleasures of human interaction.

EMOTIONAL SELF-CONCEPT DIMENSIONS

After the construction of the interactional and interdependent social selves, the emotional dimensions constitute the most prominent aspect of the Mexican self. The emotional self includes three subcategories. First, there are "mood states," characterized by being animated, feeling happy, optimistic, glad, joyful, and interestingly enough, feeling fulfilled and successful. Negative mood is present when people are frustrated, discouraged, sad, embittered, pessimistic, depressed, unsuccessful, and melancholic. The fact is that within the Mexican culture, those who have positive moods are considered to be fulfilled and successful, which indicates how, in a culture where personal relationships are paramount, being happy and achieving gratifying affective relationships is enough to succeed in life (Diaz-Guerrero, 1984). By contrast, in individualistically oriented cultures people define themselves in terms of their activity and productivity, and their sense of fulfillment and success is derived from instrumental personal achievements (Triandis, 1995).

The second emotional scale overlaps with the social self in that it considers the emotions that are evoked in interaction with others. These forms of expressing feelings are a result of a socialization process that reinforces individuals who receive and give love, and punishes those who experience rejection and communicate hostility. These interpersonal emotions and sentiments include loving, affectionate, caring, tender, romantic, and sentimental; their antonyms: hateful, hard, cold, rude, indifferent, and insensitive. The integration of social and emotional concerns indicates the importance of positive social relationships based on courteousness, education, and amiability, the happiness and joy in which they are embedded, the closeness and friendship brought to relationships, and the behaviors needed to show caring, affect, and love (LaRosa & Diaz-Loving, 1991).

In the United States, Hispanics (who include a high percentage of people of Mexican descent) have been shown to prefer interpersonal relationships in their ingroups that are nurturing, loving, intimate, and respectful, whereas non-Hispanic Whites have a greater degree of preference for confrontational and superordinate relationships (Triandis, Marin, Hui, Lisansky, & Ottani, 1984; see also chap. 12 in this volume, by Ottati, Triandis, and Hui).

The last emotional self-concept scale refers to the ways of responding to the problems and stresses of everyday living. This dimension of emotional health shows the importance of coping with life and interpersonal relationships in a peaceful, serene, calm, and tranquil way, as exemplified by such terms as reflecting and thinking things over, being reflective, not getting easily upset about things, maintaining stability, trying to get along with others, being generous and noble. In contrast, scorned within the Mexican culture is a person who is not able to negotiate or conciliate in a constructive and positive way, and thus becomes resentful of others, is voluble and temperamental, is unable to cope with stress and frustration, gets nervous and anxious, tends to bother other people, is aggressive, consistently attacks, has conflicts and problems with others, is self-centered and egotistical (LaRosa & Diaz-Loving, 1991). Such individuals find themselves constantly at odds with the contemplative Mexican majority. By contrast, in the United States the preferred style of coping with life is competitive, active, and instrumental (Diaz-Guerrero, 1979).

EDUCATIONAL AND OCCUPATIONAL
SELF-CONCEPT

The educational and occupational dimension reflects the necessary characteristics for the efficient development of the multiple phases related to work and education. In industrialized cultures these attributes provide the principal sources of satisfaction and personal realization. The characteristics necessary to be successful at work are reliable, hardworking, studious, capable, responsible, reliable, efficient, punctual, and intelligent. This occupational Mexican category, which looks like a page torn out of a manual from an instrumental individualistic society, can be interpreted in indigenous terms. The semantics of intelligence for the Mexican culture show that parents believe the most intelligent children are obedient and conforming, which could explain the choice of such words as hardworking, studious, responsible, and reliable, all characteristics expected from "good children" (Torquemada Gonzalez, Elizalde Lora, Moreno Martinez, & Perez López, 1994). In addition, the perception of time is different from one culture to another. Research done with children shows that Mexicans believe that time goes by more slowly than do North American children (Holtzman et al., 1975). They also place a greater value on event time (quality of interpersonal relationships) than on clock time (length of interaction).

The 20th century has witnessed a proliferation of cross-cultural communication, acculturation and migration, all of which have closed the gap between cultures in a constant process toward globalization. The rules of international commerce make it necessary for traditional cultures to become competitive if they are to survive. Thus, their members will have to change by increasing their orientation toward work and competition. However, interdependent and sociocentric attributes have proven to be highly desirable for prosocial behaviors, mental health, and interpersonal relationships. It is therefore important to facilitate in this process of change, the development of truly advanced traditional human beings, and to promote becoming more instrumental in order to adequately contend with professional activities, yet without losing the positive attributes necessary to engage in peaceful, constructive, and satisfying personal relationships.

ETHICAL SELF-CONCEPT

Humans are axiological beings and they constitute the source of values and evaluative activity for themselves, and others, through action as well as through ideals and attachments. To a certain extent, happiness depends on achieving values and ideals that maintain a harmonious relationship with the physical and social environment. For Mexicans, the more representative aspects of morality are: loyalty applied to standards of family, work, and interpersonal relationships; honesty with money and feelings; sincerity and honor. Immorality is centered on corruption, which dishonors one's family and society (LaRosa & Diaz Loving, 1991). Given the importance of honesty, sincerity, and loyalty as key Mexican values, it is necessary to promote the adherence to them in actual real-life situations.

INTERIM EVALUATION

It is apparent that the empirical investigation of the links between culture and personality in Mexico has made tremendous progress over the span of the last four decades. Forty years ago, the field was dominated by intuitive pronouncements by perceptive and sophisticated observers (e.g., Chavez, 1901; León de Garay, 1956; Ramos, 1938). By this time, some of these preempirical formulations have been validated by means of contemporary, flexible, and complex research designs, whereas others await systematic and quantitative scrutiny. In the process, a substantial body of objective and factual research data has come into being. What information can be derived from these accumulated findings? What questions remain unanswered?

1. Perhaps the most solid conclusion that can be drawn on the basis of the available data pertains to the importance of primary interpersonal ties for the typical Mexican man or woman. Mexicans do not experience themselves as isolated social atoms; they primarily define themselves in reference to the lifelong, intense, and sometimes ambivalent, relationships to their family members, neighbors and fellow residents, and their fellow citizens. The desire to seek social acceptance and approval is strong and helps subordinate disagreements, confrontations, and conflicts to the need for amity and harmony.
2. To this end, many Mexicans are prepared to modify or even accommodate their behavior and even their selves to the requirements of the social situation. Their interpersonal style then tends to be autoplastic or self-modifying.
3. In the course of socialization, compliance, respect, and obedience prevail over self-expression, self-assertion, and self-actualization. The power distance (Hofstede, 1980) between fathers and children is, as a rule, great, but is in part mitigated by a closer and more intimate tie to the mother.
4. Traditionally, there has been a pronounced difference between male and female gender roles, and especially so within the family. The

objectives and ideals of socialization for sons and daughters have been clearly different; similarly, the expectations for fathers' and mothers' behaviors are unambiguously defined and quite divergent.

5. A potentially important, but as yet incompletely investigated sociocultural premise pertains to coping with stress. Historically, Mexicans have tended to be socialized to endure stress stoically, patiently, even gracefully; North Americans have been typically brought up to cope with stress actively, energetically, aggressively, even heroically. However, as yet the scope of this promising sociocultural premise is not specifically determined nor is the extent of its modification through modernization clear.

6. Factor analytic studies have clarified the nature of the dimensions of the Mexican self-concept and have shed light on their hierarchical interrelationship. They confirm the prominence of *simpatia,* imperfectly translated as likableness or geniality, in Mexican self-perception and social behavior and bring to the fore the importance of expressive sociability, positive mood states, affectionate social interaction, and reflective, serene, calm, and tranquil attitudes.

At the same time, it must be recognized that the research enterprise on personality in Mexican culture is continuously in progress and remains incomplete. Here are some of the questions that await systematic empirically based answers:

1. Emphasis in cross-cultural research, reflected in this chapter, has been upon the comparison of Mexicans with their neighbors in the United States. What we as yet do not know is whether the various cultural differences obtained are specific to Mexico or whether they reflect more generic contrasts between Hispanic and English-speaking countries in the Western Hemisphere and beyond it. Early replications of Diaz-Guerrero's (1967a, 1967b) work in Puerto Rico (Maldonado Sierra, Trent, & Fernandez Marina, 1960) reflect a high degree of similarity with Mexican findings. However, they also point to some differences between Puerto Rican and Mexican results which, as yet, have not been further pursued.

2. Given the multimodal nature of personality characteristics in culture (Wallace, 1970, also see chap. 1 of this volume), greater emphasis should be accorded to comparison of groups in Mexico, across genders, regions, educational levels, and socioeconomic states. Some

work along these lines has been performed and is reported elsewhere in this chapter. Further and more rigorous pursuit of such research is all the more desirable because a lopsided emphasis upon comparing Mexicans with non-Mexicans may engender the impression of uniformity and may inadvertently foster stereotypes.

3. Along similar lines, thought should be given to developing approaches for the investigation of intraindividual variation in various culturally influenced dimensions of behavior and experience. Under what circumstances, for example, will the expression of *simpatia* give way to manifestations of hostility and expressions of aggression? And when, if ever, is sociability transformed into misanthropy? Answers to these questions would help move the field of personality in culture beyond a static profile of traits to the investigation of functional relationships between characteristic behaviors and their situational and personal antecedents.

4. Upon reviewing the research results pertaining to personality in Mexico, we are struck by the preponderance of investigations based on supposedly culturally universal or *etic* concepts. With the exception of Diaz-Guerrero's introduction and exploration of Mexican sociocultural premises, concepts rooted in Mexican culture have seen little systematic study. As research is diversified, we are looking forward to a greater number of quantitative and systematic projects focused on such culturally indigenous or *emic* notions as *simpatia, respeto, amor propio, tristeza*, and others.

5. Finally, we note that the bulk of recent, methodologically sophisticated research has been done by means of self-descriptive paper-and-pencil instruments. Would our present picture of the Mexican personality characteristics be different if, for example, choices and dilemmas were investigated or if thematic and other projective techniques were more prominently employed? The very eagerness of the Mexicans to please their partners in dialogues and other interactions may possibly increase their chances of giving positive, morally and socially desirable responses. Of course, at this point what we can offer is only speculation. However, there is no arguing against a multimethod approach to investigation, such as was implemented in part by Holtzman et al. (1975), which is bound to enrich our store of knowledge with a more differentiated and complex body of results.

CONCLUSIONS

Mexico and the United States have evolved in different geographical, social, cultural, economic, and political circumstances. Their respective sociocultural ecosystems have shaped the characteristics, beliefs, attitudes, values, and behaviors of the individuals and groups that compose these two societies. Cultural and individual diversity and similarity derived from these processes make up integral components of the quality of intercultural and interpersonal relationships. In these encounters, diversity can lead to creativity and high-quality decisions (e.g. McGrath, 1984), whereas similarity can increase cohesion and attraction (e.g., Byrne, 1971) and reduce conflict (e.g., Jackson, 1991). Relating to ethnic entities, these considerations apply to intergroup relationships that focus attention on group membership and emphasize stereotypes, and interpersonal relations, based on the individual's attributes and personality. In fostering constructive relations, in both instances, special care should be taken to avoid the basic attribution error committed when mere categorization and stereotypes result in negative oversimplifications of the link between the ethnic category and the personal attributes assigned to an individual.

The subjective evaluation of perceived distance and similarity, in interacting with members of different cultures, can lead to integration and problem resolution, or to a sense of helplessness when someone cannot understand the new culture, or feels confused by the actions of persons within it (e.g., Oberg, 1960).

In considering possible difficulties in intercultural relations, it is clear that the objective assessment of cultural distance (compounded of diversity and similarity) between North American and Mexican people, is a necessary precursor to more adaptive, comfortable, and productive interpersonal relationships. In other words, we should know more about the real and perceived self-descriptions and characteristics of both the ingroup and the outgroup, understand why the members of one culture act toward the other the way they do, why they categorize experience they way they do, and in short, comprehend the implicit assumptions and the observable practices in the other culture.

Cross-cultural and ethnopsychological research has shown the aversive consequences of cultural distance and culture shock. However, intercultural and interpersonal relationships can be enhanced through adequate preparation. Reduction in social distance is possible to achieve by means of techniques that allow individuals to culturally adjust and cope with the new culture. Another way is to develop cultural competence, which includes learning the necessary skills to have creative, amiable, and constructive encounters. For example, Triandis (1994) recommended empathy, interest in the host culture, openness to different points of view, readiness to socialize, and a critical attitude toward stereotypes.

In the specific context of the Mexican culture, the recommendations would include recognizing the central role of family, amiability, courteousness, happiness, respect, serenity, and the self-modifying or autoplastic coping style prevalent in the culture. Of course, learning the local language also helps on the road to a sense of being in control and at home in a new culture. However, the most important component requires immersing oneself, as much as possible, in the host culture. We sincerely hope that the information on the culture, meaning, and personality of Mexicans and North Americans presented in this chapter will result in more realistic mutual perceptions of these two cultures and that it will promote an inquiring, skeptical, yet open-minded, orientation toward the understanding of the other culture and accepting, and interacting with, its members.

REFERENCES

Andrade Palos, P. (1987). Relación padres–hijos y locus de control: El caso de México [Relationship between parents' and children's locus of control: The case of Mexico]. *Revista de Psicología Social y Personalidad, 3*(2), 39–49.

Andrade Palos, P. (1996). Siginificado de papa y mama en adolescentes [Meaning of father and mother in adolescents]. In F. Obregon Salido, I. Reyes Lagunes, & R. Diaz-Loving (Eds.), *La psicología social en México* (Vol. VI, pp. 337–342). Mexico City: Trillas.

Aronson, E. (1995). *The social animal.* (7th ed.). San Francisco, W. H. Freeman & Co.

Avendano Sandoval, R., & Diaz-Guerrero, R. (1990). El desarrollo de una escala de abnegación para los mexicanos [The development of an abnegation scale for Mexicans]. In R. Diaz-Loving & P. Andrade Palos (Eds.), *La psicología social en México*, (Vol. III, pp. 9–14). Mexico: AMEPSO.

Bem, D. (1970). *Beliefs, attitudes and human affairs.* Belmont, CA: Brooks/Cole.

Berry, J. W., Poortinga, Y., Segall, M., & Dasen, P. (1992). *Cross-cultural psychology.* New York: Cambridge University Press.

Bruner, J. (1990). *Acts of meaning.* Cambridge, MA: Harvard University Press.

Byrne, D. (1971). *The attraction paradigm.* New York: Academic Press.

Chavez, E. (1901). Ensayo sobre los rasgos distintivos de la personalidad como factor del carácter del mexicano [Essay on the distinctive personality traits as a factor of the character of the Mexican]. *Revista Positiva, 3,* 84–89.

Diaz-Guerrero, R. (1967a). The active and the passive syndromes. *Revista Interamericana de Psicologia, 1,* 263–272.

Diaz-Guerrero, R. (1967b). Sociocultural premises, attitudes and cross–cultural research. *International Journal of Psychology, 2*(2), 79–87.

Diaz-Guerrero, R. (1979). The development of coping style. *Human Development, 22,* 320–331.

Diaz-Guerrero, R. (1982). The psychology of the historic-socio-cultural premises. *Spanish Language Psychology, 2,* 383–410.

Diaz-Guerrero, R. (1984). Tristeza y psicopatología en Mexico [Sadness and psychopathology in Mexico]. *Salud Mental, 7*(2), 3–9.

Diaz-Guerrero, R. (1986). Historio-sociocultura y personalidad. Definición y caracteristicas de los factores en la familia Mexicana [History, socioculture and personality. Definition and characteristics of the Mexican family features]. *Revista de Psicologia Social y Personalidad, 2*(1), 15–42.

Diaz-Guerrero, R. (1991, February). Mexican ethnopsychology. Paper presented at the Society for Cross-Cultural Research, San Juan, Puerto, Rico.

Diaz-Guerrero, R. (1994). *Psicologia del mexicano: Descubrimiento de la etnopsicología* [Psychology of the Mexican: The discovery of ethnopsychology]. (6th ed.). Mexico City: Trillas.

Diaz-Guerrero, R., & Peck, R. F. (1963). Respeto y posición social en dos culturas (Respect and social status in two cultures). Paper presented at the Seventh Interamerican Congress of Psychology, Mexico City.

Diaz-Guerrero, R., & Szalay, L. B. (1993). *El mundo subjetivo de mexicanos y norteamericanos* [The subjective world of Mexicans and North Americans]. Mexico City: Trillas.

Diaz-Loving, R. (1996). Una teoria bio-psico-sociocultural de la relación de pareja [A bio-psycho-sociocultural theory of dyadic relations]. *Revista Interamericana de Psicologia, 19*(1), 18–29.

Diaz-Loving, R., & Andrade Palos, P. (1984). Una escala de Locus de Control para niños mexicanos [A locus of control scale for Mexican children]. *Revista Interamericana de Psicología, 19*(1–2), 21–33.

Draguns, J. G. (1979). Cultura y personalidad [Culture and personality]. In J. O. Whittaker (Ed.), *La psicología social en el mundo de hoy* (pp. 287–319). Mexico City: Trillas.

Herskovits, M. (1955). *Cultural anthropology*. New York: Knopf.

Hofstede, G. (1980). *Culture's consequences: International differences in work-related values*. Beverly Hills, CA: Sage.

Holtzman, W., Diaz-Guerrero, R., & Schwartz, J. (1975). *Personality development in two cultures*. Austin: University of Texas Press.

Hovland, C. I., Janis, I. L., & Kelly, H. H. (1953). *Communication and persuasion*. New Haven, CT: Yale University Press.

Hui, C. H. (1990). Work attitudes, leadership styles and managerial behaviors in different cultures. In R. Brislin (Ed.), *Applied cross-cultural psychology* (pp. 186–208). Thousand Oaks, CA: Sage.

Jackson, S. E. (1991). *Diversity in the workplace: Human resources initiatives*. New York: Guilford.

James, W. (1952). *The principles of psychology*. Chicago: Encyclopedia Brittanica. (Original work published 1891).

La Rosa, J., & Diaz-Loving, R. (1988). Diferencial semántico del autoconcepto en estudiantes (Semantic differential of students' self-concepts) *Revista de Psicologia Social y Personalidad, 4*, 39–58.

LaRosa, J., & Diaz Loving, R. (1991). Evaluación del autoconcepto: Una escala multidimensional [Evaluation of self concept: A multidimensional scale]. *Revista Latinoamericana de Psicología, 23*(1), 15–34.

León de Garay, A. (1956). *Una aproximación a la psicología del mexicano* [A sketch of the psychology of the Mexican]. Mexico: Panoramas.

Lewin, K. (1936). Some social psychological differences between the United States and Germany. *Character and Personality, 4*, 265–293.

Maldonado Sierra, E. D., Trent, R. D., & Fernandez Marina, R. (1960). Neurosis and traditional family beliefs in Puerto Rico. *International Journal of Social Psychiatry, 6*, 237–246.

Marin, G., & Triandis, H. C. (1984, August). El alocentrismo como una caracteristica importante de la conducta de los Latinos y Latinoamericanos [Allocentrism as an important characteristic in the behavior of Latins and Latin Americans]. Paper presented at the XXIII International Congress of Psychology, Acapulco, Mexico.

Markus, H., & Kitayama, S. (1991). Culture and self: Implications for cognition, emotion and motivation. *Psychological Review, 98*, 224–253.

Matsumoto, D. (1994). *People: Psychology from a cultural perspective*. Pacific Grove, CA: Brooks/Cole.

McGrath, J. (1984). *Groups: Interaction and performance*. Englewood Cliffs, NJ: Prentice-Hall.

Oberg, K. (1960). Culture shock: Adjustment to new cultural environments. *Practical Anthropology, 7*, 177–182.

Ramos, S. (1938). *El perfil del hombre y la cultura en México* [The profile of person and culture in Mexico]. Mexico City: Pedro Robledo.

Ross, W. D. (1924). *The works of Aristotle*. Oxford, England: Oxford University Press.

Smith, P., & Bond, M. (1994). *Social psychology across cultures: Analysis and perspectives*. Boston: Allyn & Bacon.

Torquemada Gonzalez, A. D., Elizalde Lora, L., Moreno Martinez, A., & Perez López, C. (1994). Realización de conductas responsables en niños urbanos y rurales [Responsible behaviors in rural and urban children]. In I. Reyes Lagunes & R. Diaz Loving (Eds.), *La psicología social en México*, (Vol. V, pp. 387–393). Mexico: AMEPSO.

Triandis, H. C. (1992). Cross-cultural research in social psychology. In D. Granberg & G. Sarup (Eds.), *Social judgement and intergroup relations: Essays in honor of Muzafer Sherif* (pp. 229–244). New York: Springer Verlag.

Triandis, H. C. (1994). *Culture and social behavior*. New York: McGraw-Hill.

Triandis, H. C. (1995). *Individualism and collectivism*. Boulder, CO: Westview.

Triandis, H., Marin, G., & Betancourt, H. (1984). Simpatia as a cultural script of Hispanics. *Journal of Personality and Social Psychology, 47*, 1363–1375.

Triandis, H. C., Marin, G., Betancourt, H., & Chang, B. (1982). Acculturation, biculturalism, and familism among Hispanic and mainstream Navy recruits. Technical Report No. 15. Champaign, IL: University of Illinois Department of Psychology.

Triandis, H., Marin, G., Hui, C. H., Lisansky, J., & Ottani, V. (1984). Role perceptions of Hispanic young adults. *Journal of Cross-Cultural Psychology, 15*, 297–320.

Tylor, E. B. (1877). *Primitive culture. Researches into the development of mythologies, philosophy, religion, language, art and customs*. New York: Holt.

Vexliard, A. (1968). Tempérement et modalités d'adaptation [Temperament and modes of adaptation]. *Bulletin de Psychologie, 21*, 1–15.

Wallace, A. F. C. (1970). *Culture and personalilty* (2nd ed.). New York: Random House.

7

Chinese-American Differences: A Chinese View

Kan Zhang
Chinese Academy of Sciences, Beijing, China

Yueh-Ting Lee
Westfield State College

Yanfang Liu
Chinese Academy of Sciences, Beijing, China

Clark McCauley
Bryn Mawr College

Thus it is said that if you know others and yourself, you will not lose in every battle; if you do not know others but yourself, you win one and lose one; if you do not know others and do not know yourself, you will lose in every battle. —Sun Tzu, *The Art of War* (540 B.C.)

Although most psychologists do not seek understanding of self and others in order to win battles, perhaps we can follow Sun Tzu toward more effective business and cultural interaction between nations. One of the purposes of this chapter is to help Americans, especially American businesspeople, to understand how Chinese see themselves in relation to Americans. Americans may thereby take a step toward better understanding of one fourth of the world's people. Another purpose is to provide an example of the kind of research that can reveal the dimensions of national comparisons, that is, the dimensions of national stereotyping.

PERSONALITY AND CULTURE IN THE UNITED
STATES AND CHINA

Is there any basic difference between Chinese and American personalities or behavioral patterns? Perhaps the answer is yes, despite considerable evidence of cross-cultural generality in personological constructs and determinants (e.g., Brown, 1991; Buss, 1991; Eaves, Eysenck, & Martin, 1989; Y-T. Lee & Seligman, 1997; Linton, 1945; Pepitone & Triandis, 1987). Consider how Chinese and Americans approach giving a speech. What behavior and personality do we expect a typical American speaker to display at the beginning of a formal speech or an academic colloquium? What behavior and personality do we expect a typical Chinese speaker to display at the beginning of a formal speech or an academic colloquium? The answers to these questions may have much to do with what is required for effective self-presentation by Eastern and Western people.

For example, in the European and Northern American communities (especially in the United States), a popular speaker should include a few jokes that can make audiences laugh. In their political campaigns, American politicians usually have (or at least try to exhibit) a sense of humor so as to be favored by their audiences and voters. In China, a good speaker tends to begin with apologies by saying "Thank you for taking the time and trouble to come. You know much more about the subject matters than I do." These apologies suggest that you are very modest and humble. If you display a modest personality in China or other Asian countries, people may like you and think you are a good public speaker. In short, people in the United States try to display a humorous personality, whereas people in China try to be modest and humble. This difference may go deeper than display rules; people from different cultures may have different interior lives (e.g., associations, expectations, thinking style).

Research on Cultural Differences Between the United States and China

Francis L. K. Hsu, a native Chinese and a student of Bronislaw Malinowski, described Chinese and American differences in a variety of ways—for example, modal culture or "basicity" of culture, national or "social character," "themes of cultures," "ethos" or "philosophy of life" (see Hsu, 1981, p. 6). An anthropologist of high stature, Hsu (1953, 1954, 1972) performed the most significant research of his era on personality and behavior in Sino-American culture. Scientifically, he was probably the first anthropologist to focus directly on differences between Chinese and American culture, and an overview of his work can be found in his well-articulated and widely cited book:

> A majority of Chinese in China can deal with each other better than they can with the inhabitants of the United States, while a majority of Americans can do the same better with their own countrymen than with the Chinese in China. They may not approve of or understand all that their respective fellow countrymen do, but in the normal course of events they are less likely than foreigners to be surprised by them. For each people share a large body of basic, common ideas, attitudes, and expectations which provide the average man with his bearings in dealing with his fellow countrymen and which hold the society together, contemporaneously and over time. (Hsu, 1981, p. 3)

To Hsu, the basic norms and the common ideas, attitudes, and stereotypes that are shared within a culture are the content of modal personality, social character, and ethos of the culture. About 50 years ago, Hsu (1948) wrote the first book on personality in culture from a Chinese perspective, and his later books (1963, 1983) developed further the differences between Chinese and American personalities (or behavioral patterns). For example, one of the basic personality differences Hsu made salient is that Americans are individual centered, whereas Chinese are situation centered (Hsu, 1981).

In addition to Hsu's aforementioned anthropological research, other social scientists (e.g., Fairbank, 1987; Gao, Ting-Toomey, & Gudykunst, 1996; Pye, 1992; Solomon, 1972; Sun, 1983; Tu, 1991) have studied personality differences between Chinese and Americans in negotiation, communication, and political behavior. In particular, psychologists approached personality in Sino-American culture in terms of a variety of issues, such as values and beliefs (e.g., Bond, 1986, 1996; Leung, 1996; Ralston, Gustafson, Elsass, Cheung, & Terpstra, 1992; Yang & Bond, 1990), emotional expression (Klineberg, 1938; Russell & Yik, 1996), social motivation and perception or attributional judgment (Crittenden, 1996; Y-T. Lee, 1993a, 1995; Y-T. Lee & Ottati, 1995; Lee, Pepitone, & Albright, 1997; Morris & Peng, 1994; Roseman et al., 1995; Stevenson, 1992; Triandis, 1994), personality structure (McCrae, Costa, & Yik, 1996), social interaction and face (e.g., Gabrenya & Hwang, 1996), leadership and decision making (Chen, 1995; Smith & Wang, 1996; Yates & J. W. Lee, 1996), and attitude toward euthanasia and abortion (Y-T. Lee, Kleinbach, Hu, Peng, & Chen, 1996). Taken together, this literature strongly suggests a difference between Chinese and American behavioral patterns and personalities.

Converging Perceptions as Evidence of Cultural Differences

Judgment of cultural differences in personality may have some veridicality (Hall & Hall, 1990; Y-T. Lee, 1994; Y-T. Lee & Duenas, 1995; Y-T. Lee, Jussim, & McCauley, 1995). That is to say, the basic (or modal) social personalities of Chinese and Americans may in fact differ between the two cultures. In a notable study, Bond (1986) examined the mutual stereotypes of two interacting groups at the Chinese University of Hong Kong. American exchange students and local Chinese undergraduates were asked to rate a typical ingroup member (auto-stereotype) and a typical outgroup member (hetero-stereotype) on 30 bipolar trait scales. In his findings, both groups agreed that, in terms of personality, the typical Chinese student was more emotionally controlled but less open and extroverted than the typical American exchange student. According to Chinese Confucianism, intro- vertedness or inhibitedness is actually a virtue and a good personality (see Peabody, chap. 4 of this volume, on the "tight–loose" dimension of cultural difference). The agreement between American and Chinese views of their differences is an important kind of convergent validation of the reality of these differences.

Similarly, Y-T. Lee and Ottati (1993) have proposed that Chinese people are, objectively speaking, more similar to one another than U.S. people are similar to one another. Consistent with this hypothesis, both Chinese and American subjects perceived Chinese people to be more homogeneous than Americans. Again, this convergence of report is evidence that objectively, Americans may be more heterogeneous, independent, and individualistic, whereas Chinese are perhaps homogeneous and dependent. The finding, which was confirmed in other studies (see Y-T. Lee, 1995; Triandis, 1994; also see Hsu, 1981, 1983), implies that if cultures are objectively different, human judgment or cognition may accurately capture or encode this differ- ence. That is, people may be perceptually sensitive to real cultural differ- ences in modal personality.

AMERICANS AND CHINESE IN CHINESE EYES

As noted earlier, there is a broad literature dealing with Sino-American differences in behavior and personality. The focus of the current chapter is on how the Chinese people in the People's Republic of China see Americans and see Chinese themselves. Although limited to a one-way view of Chinese-American differences, we believe this view is important and relatively little studied. It addresses an aspect of an important issue that this book undertakes to address, "What do Americans have to be prepared to know when they go to another culture?" (see Lee, McCauley, & Draguns, chap. 1 of this volume). As Kenny (1994; Kenny, Bond, Mohr, & Horn, 1996) has pointed out, successful interaction often depends on knowing "how Person X thinks of me."

A better knowledge of Chinese perceptions may also be important for Americans and others who will never visit China. In addition to its long history, resourceful culture, and economic/political influence, China is a great nation in terms of its population and area. Psychologists and social scientists concerned for the generality of their theories have suffered in the past and continue to suffer from inadequate representation of a significant fraction of the world's people. Particularly rare are studies of mainland Chinese in their own culture (see Lee, McCauley, & Draguns, chap. 1 of this volume).

Although some Americans and many other Western scholars (e.g., Blowers, 1996; Bond, 1986, 1996; Crittenden, 1996; Fairbank, 1987; Pye, 1992; Stevenson, 1992) have expressed their keen interest in the Chinese people and in Chinese thinking style or behavioral patterns, their research has primarily dealt either with Chinese outside mainland China or with mainland Chinese in the past. Therefore this chapter aims to report on and analyze how Chinese college students see Americans and themselves in regard to personality traits and social perceptions in the 1990s, as China's recent economic development has led more and more Americans interact with Chinese in one way or another (see Landis & Bhagat, 1996).

Chinese Students' Views of Chinese-American Differences

Based on a previous Chinese inventory of Sino-American personality traits (Y-T. Lee & Ottati, 1993), a questionnaire of 15 bipolar personality-trait items was designed for this investigation. Chinese respondents used these 15 items to describe typical Chinese and, a few pages later in an omnibus survey, used the same 15 items to describe typical Americans. Each item was represented as a 9-point scale (4 3 2 1 0 1 2 3 4): friendly–unfriendly, selfish–altruistic, emotional–rational, sports loving–not sports loving, hardworking–not hardworking, religious–not religious, similar to me–not similar to me, attractive–unattractive, trustworthy–not trustworthy, easy to understand–not easy to understand, stingy–generous, cooperative–not cooperative, group oriented–individual oriented, disobedient–obedient, competitive–not competitive.

A total of 500 copies of the questionnaire were distributed to college students at three universities in Beijing where students come from all parts of China: 99 students from the Chinese Agriculture Engineering University, 196 from the People's University of China (liberal arts and social sciences), 197 from Qinghua University (engineering and polytech). Eight questionnaires were not returned, leaving 492 questionnaires for analysis (return rate 98%).

How Do Chinese Students See Chinese and Americans?

Item responses were transformed into a 1–9 scale, and items were reversed as necessary so that scores above 5 indicated that the target group had more of the positive traits listed in Table 7.1. Analyses of results by respondent age, gender, and university found only few and small differences; results are presented for all respondents together.

TABLE 7.1
Chinese Students' Stereotypes of "Typical Chinese" and "Typical Americans"

Trait	Target				Stereotype (American- Chinese)
	Chinese		American		
	M	SD	M	SD	
1. Friendly	4.2	2.2	3.1	1.9	−1.1*
2. Altruistic	6.4	2.0	5.8	2.0	−0.6*
3. Rational	6.0	2.5	5.5	2.5	−0.6*
4. Sports loving	2.1	1.7	5.2	2.0	+3.1*
5. Hardworking	4.0	2.3	2.8	2.1	−1.2*
6. Religious	3.1	2.1	5.9	2.2	+2.8*
7. Similar to me	6.2	2.2	4.1	2.2	−2.1*
8. Attractive	4.1	2.0	4.2	1.9	+0.1
9. Trustworthy	5.2	2.2	4.2	2.0	−1.0*
10. Easy to understand	4.7	2.2	5.2	2.3	+0.5*
11. Generous	5.4	2.0	4.9	2.0	−0.5*
12. Cooperative	4.2	2.4	4.8	2.4	+0.6*
13. Collectivist	6.2	2.5	3.9	2.2	−2.3*
14. Obedient	7.2	1.7	3.9	2.2	−3.4*
15. Competitive	2.0	1.6	4.5	2.4	+2.5*

Note. The higher the mean rating on a 1–9 scale,, the more likely it is that Chinese subjects perceived people in a target group to have a particular personality trait. Asterisks indicate a significant stereotype,, that is,, mean difference between typical Chinese and typical American is significant at $p < .01$,, two-tailed by t test for correlated samples.

Table 7.1 shows that Chinese students see the typical American as more sports loving, more religious, and more competitive than the typical Chinese. The typical American is also seen as less friendly, less hardworking, less similar, less trustworthy, less collectivist, and less obedient than the typical Chinese. Some of these perceived differences are of considerable size, amounting to 2–3 points mean difference on a 9-point scale.

Dimensions of Chinese-American Differences

Each student on each trait rating was given a difference score, trait rating of typical American *minus* trait rating of typical Chinese, in order to provide an individual-difference measure of stereotyping. These individual stereotype measures were subjected to Statistical Package for Social Sciences (SPSS) principal components analysis and four components were obtained with eigenvalues greater than 1.0: eigenvalues of 3.0 (20% of variance), 1.8 (12% of variance), 1.3 (9% of variance), 1.2 (8% of variance). Varimax rotation led to an interpretable solution with three factors. Factor 1 was identified with agreeableness on the basis of factor loadings ranging from .72 to .55 for (in order of loading) friendly, trustworthy, altruistic, attractive, and generous. Factor 2 was identified as assertiveness on the basis of factor loadings ranging from .68 to .47 for (in order of loading) sports loving, disobedient, competitive, and religious. Factor 3 was identified as conscientiousness on the basis of factor loadings ranging from .63 to .52 for (in order of loading) hardworking, collectivist, cooperative, and rational.

Agreeableness, assertiveness, and conscientiousness are the "Big Three" of the "Big Five" dimensions identified in Western personality research (the remaining two are emotional stability and intellect; see Peabody, chap. 4 of this volume). Thus the three dimensions recovered from our Chinese raters offer a striking correspondence with the dimensions recovered from American trait ratings of both self and others.

It is important to be clear about the meaning of our three dimensions. The three factors emerge from the intercorrelations of perceived trait differences. Chinese students vary in seeing Americans more or less like themselves in agreeableness, assertiveness, and conscientiousness. That is, these are the dimensions on which Chinese differ in the strength of their stereotyping of Chinese-American differences.

These three dimensions can be used to describe where Chinese students see the greatest differences between themselves and Americans. It is interesting to note that the biggest stereotype involves assertiveness, where Americans are seen as much more sports-minded, disobedient, competitive, and religious than Chinese. The stereotype for conscientiousness is less consistent; Americans are seen as less hardworking and collectivist, but about as cooperative and rational as Chinese. The stereotype for agreeableness is even less consistent; Americans are seen as less friendly, less similar, and less trustworthy, but about as altruistic, attractive, understandable, and generous as Chinese. Thus the three dimensions of perceived differences bring order to the description of the typical Chinese student's stereotyping, as well as describing the differences among Chinese students in the strength of stereotyping.

Accuracy of the Observed Stereotypes

Is there a kernel of truth in the stereotypes held by our Chinese students? With regard to some traits, perhaps the answer is yes. Certain judgments of Sino-American trait differences in Table 7.1 are consistent with results of other researchers. For example, Americans may in fact be more sports loving (or athletic) than Chinese. According to Betty Lee Sung (1992), development of the mental faculties was more important than development of the physique in the traditional Chinese way of thinking: "In the mind of many Chinese, sports are viewed as frivolous play and a waste of time and energy" (Sung, 1992, p. 222). In China, participation in games that require brute strength, such as football and boxing, is seldom encouraged, although "Kung fu or other disciplines of the martial arts did not call for physical strength as much as concentration, skill, and agility" (Sung, 1992, p. 222). This may help us to understand the accuracy of the stereotypes about Asian Americans who perform academically well at schools and about African or White Americans who perform athletically well in sports (Ottati & Y-T. Lee, 1995).

Are Americans more religious than Chinese? According to Lee, Pepitone, and Albright (1997), most Chinese believe in fate, not in God. Not many people go to churches in China. On the other hand, the polling results (Gallup, 1996) show that 58% of Americans go to church very often, that 96% of Americans believe in God, and that 88% of Americans think religion is fairly or very important to their own life. Thus the perception that Americans are more religious than Chinese is not without foundation.

Personality Judgments and Ingroup Favoritism

Do the results in Table 7.1 suggest an ingroup favoritism? As described by Brewer (1979) and Y-T. Lee (1993b), ingroup favoritism means ingroup members see themselves (e.g, Chinese) as more favorable and better than outgroup members (e.g., Americans). Some support for ingroup favoritism emerges from focusing on just those traits in Table 7.1 where a substantial difference (mean difference of a scale unit or more) was perceived between Chinese and Americans. Six of these most stereotyped traits show Americans less friendly, less hardworking, less similar, less trustworthy, less collectivist, and less obedient than Chinese. From a Chinese point of view, all of these traits are positive and Americans are seen as having less of these traits. Only three of the most stereotyped traits show positive differences, where Americans are seen as more sports loving, more religious, and more competitive than Chinese. These three traits, from a Chinese point of view, are only weakly positive and might even be negative for many Chinese raters. In the absence of independent evidence of the value of these traits to our Chinese students, we suggest then that our results do show ingroup favoritism.

As Peabody (chap. 4 of this volume) describes, it should be possible in future research to get at the descriptive component of national stereotypes in a way unconfounded with the evaluative component. Here we would like only to point out, as a limitation of the present results, that it seems to us that our first factor, agreeableness, is particularly loaded with evaluation.

SUMMARY AND CONCLUSIONS

In this chapter, we reviewed some of the basic research on the differences in Sino-American personality and behavioral pattern. Previous studies in anthropology, psychology, and other social sciences suggested that Chinese are more situation or group-oriented, whereas Americans are more individual oriented. Consistent with previous research, the results of our survey of 500 Chinese university students showed that they see themselves as substantially different from Americans on many traits. Specifically, our factor analysis revealed three underlying dimensions of perceived differences that we identified with three of the Big Five dimensions—agreeableness, assertiveness, and conscientiousness. Americans are seen as much more assertive but only somewhat less extroverted and conscientious than Chinese.

So far as we know, this is the first study of the dimensions of cultural difference that has used perceived difference scores from individual subjects as the basic datum. The usual approach (see Peabody, 1985, and chap. 4 of this volume) is to have one or more groups of judges rate two or more target nations on a common list of traits. Then the investigator factor analyzes a data file in which the rows are nations, the columns are traits, and the data in each row are the mean ratings of one target nation on the different traits. The resulting factors, drawn from intercorrelations of traits over nations, are the dimensions of trait scales applied to individual nations.

Our approach, in contrast, was to create a difference score (rating of Americans *minus* rating of Chinese) on each trait for each of our Chinese raters. Thus our factors are dimensions of trait scales applied to perceived national differences, that is, the dimensions of national stereotyping. We did try a more conventional factor analysis of trait ratings of Chinese as target, and separately of Americans as target (results not detailed here). The two separate analyses produced dissimilar factors, and neither set of factors was as clearly interpretable as the factors from our analysis of perceived differences.

The greater clarity of the factors derived from perceived differences may derive from the elimination of nuisance variance associated with individual differences in use of the trait scales (e.g., some raters avoiding extremes on every scale, rater disagreement about the evaluation of different traits). Or it may be that the structure of perceived differences—of national stereo-types—is different from the structure of traits applied to one nation at a time. If either of these interpretations can be supported in future research, then our direct analysis of rater stereotypes may prove a useful innovation for future research on the structure of national and cultural differences.

Our results are also interesting in supporting the relevance of individual personality research to cross-cultural personality research. The Big Five personality dimensions emerged from analysis of individual differences within cultures, mostly Western cultures, and it is possible that further work might show that the dimensions of within-cultural differentiation are not the same as the dimensions of cross-cultural differences, real or perceived. Nevertheless, the results presented in this chapter do suggest a surprising convergence in which the Big Five appear to be as useful in comparing cultures as they have become in comparing individuals within Western culture. Sojourners in another culture may join personality re-searchers (Peabody, chap. 4 of this volume) in finding that agreeableness, assertiveness, and conscientiousness are key dimensions for understanding cultural differences.

ACKNOWLEDGMENTS

Thanks are extended to Linda Albright, Ryan Kane, and Dean Peabody for offering helpful criticisms and comments on this chapter, and to Jiancheng Zhuan for assisting in some data analysis.

REFERENCES

Blowers, G. (1996). The prospects for a Chinese psychology. In M. Bond (Ed.), *The handbook of Chinese psychology* (pp. 1–14). Hong Kong: Oxford University Press.

Bond, M. H. (1986). *The psychology of the Chinese people*. London: Oxford University Press.

Bond, M. (1996). Chinese values. In M. Bond (Ed.), *The handbook of Chinese psychology* (pp. 208–226). Hong Kong: Oxford University Press.

Brewer, M. (1979). Ingroup bias in the minimal intergroup situation: A cognitive-motivational analysis. *Psychological Bulletin, 86,* 307–324.

Brown, D. E. (1991). *Human universals*. New York: McGraw-Hill.

Buss, D. M. (1991). Evolutionary personality theory. *Annual Review of Psychology, 12,* 1–49.

Chen, C. C. (1995). New trends in rewards allocation preferences: A Sino-U.S. comparison. *Academy of Management Journal, 38,* 408–428.

Crittenden, K. (1996). Causal attribution processes among the Chinese. In M. Bond (Ed.), *The handbook of Chinese psychology* (pp. 263–279). Hong Kong: Oxford University Press.

Eaves, L. J., Eysenck, H. J., & Martin, N. G. (1989). *Genes, culture and personality: An empirical approach*. New York: Academic Press.

Fairbank, J. K. (1987). *China watch*. Cambridge, MA: Harvard University Press.

Gabrenya, W. K., & Hwang, K. K. (1996). Chinese social interaction: Harmony and hierarchy on the Good Earth. In M. Bond (Ed.), *The handbook of Chinese psychology* (pp. 309–321). Hong Kong: Oxford University Press.

Gallup, G. (1996). *The Gallup poll: Public opinion 1995*. Wilmington, DE: Scholarly Resources Inc.

Gao, G., Ting-Toomey, S., & Gudykunst, W. (1996). Chinese communication processes. In M. H. Bond (Ed.), *The handbook of Chinese psychology* (pp. 280–293). Hong Kong: Oxford University Press.

Hall, E., & Hall, M. (1990). *Understanding cultural differences*. Yarmouth, ME: International Press.

Hsu, F. L. K. (1948). *Under the ancestor's shadow: Chinese culture and personality*. New York: Columbia University Press.

Hsu, F. L. K. (1953). *American and Chinese: Two ways of life*. New York: Schuman.

Hsu, F. L. K. (1954). *Aspects of culture and personality*. New York: Abelard-Schuman.

Hsu, F. L. K. (1963). *Clan, caste and club*. Princeton, NJ: Van Nostrand.

Hsu, F. L. K. (1972). *Psychological anthropology*. Cambridge, MA: Schenkman Publishing Co.

Hsu, F. L. K. (1981). *Americans and Chinese: Passage to differences*. Honolulu: University Press of Hawaii.

Hsu, F. L. K. (1983). *Rugged individualism reconsidered*. Knoxville: University of Tennessee Press.

Kenny, D. (1994). *Interpersonal perception: A social relations analysis*. New York: Guilford.

Kenny, D., Bond, C., Mohr, C., & Horn, E. (1996). Do we know how much people like one another? *Journal of Personality and Social Psychology, 71,* 928–936.

Klineberg, O. (1938). Emotional expression in Chinese literature. *Journal of Abnormal and Social Psychology, 33,* 517–520.

Landis, D., & Bhagat, R. (1996). *Handbook of intercultural training* (2nd ed.). Thousands Oaks, CA: Sage.

Lee, Y-T. (1993a). Cultural sensitivity and psychological open-mindedness: Understanding ourselves in the global village. *Contemporary Psychology, 38,* 794–795.

Lee, Y-T. (1993b). Ingroup favoritism and homogeneity among African and Chinese American students. *Journal of Social Psychology, 133,* 225–235.

Lee, Y-T. (1994). Why does psychology have cultural limitations? *American Psychologist, 49,* 524–525.

Lee, Y-T. (1995). A comparison of politics and personality in China and in the U. S.: Testing a "kernel of truth" hypothesis. *The Journal of Contemporary China, 9,* 56–68.

Lee, Y-T., & Duenas, G. (1995). Stereotype accuracy in multicultural business. In Y-T. Lee, L. Jussim, & C. McCauley (Eds.), *Stereotype accuracy: Toward appreciating group differences* (pp. 157–186). Washington, DC: American Psychological Association.

Lee, Y-T., Jussim, L., & McCauley, C. (Eds.). (1995). *Stereotype accuracy: Toward appreciating group differences*. Washington, DC: American Psychological Association.

Lee, Y-T., Kleinbach, R., Hu, P., Peng, Z. Z., & Chen, X. Y. (1996). Cross-cultural research on euthanasia and abortion. *The Journal of Social Issues, 52*(2), 131–148.

Lee, Y-T., & Ottati, V. (1993). Determinants of ingroup and outgroup perception of heterogeneity: An investigation of Chinese-American stereotypes. *Journal of Cross-Cultural Psychology, 24,* 298–318.

Lee, Y-T., & Ottati, V. (1995). Perceived group homogeneity as a function of group membership salience and stereotype threats. *Personality and Social Psychology Bulletin, 21*(6), 612–621.

Lee, Y-T., Pepitone, A., & Albright, L. (1997). Descriptive and prescriptive beliefs about justice: A Sino-U.S. comparison. *Cross-Cultural Research, 31,* 99–11.

Lee, Y-T., & Seligman, M. E. P. (1997). Are Americans more optimistic than the Chinese? *Personality and Social Psychology Bulletin, 23*(1), 32–40.

Leung, K. (1996). The role of beliefs in Chinese culture. In M. H. Bond (Ed.), *The handbook of Chinese psychology* (pp. 247–262). Hong Kong: Oxford University Press.

Linton, R. (1945). *The cultural background of personality.* New York: Appleton–Century–Crofts.

McCrae, R. R., Costa, P. T., & Yik, M. S. (1996). Universal aspects of Chinese personality structure. In M. Bond (Ed.), *The handbook of Chinese psychology* (pp. 189–207). Hong Kong: Oxford University Press.

Morris, M. W., & Peng, K. (1994). Culture and cause: American and Chinese attributions for social and physical events. *Journal of Personality and Social Psychology, 67,* 949–971.

Ottati, V., & Lee, Y-T., (1995). Accuracy: A neglected component of stereotype research. In Y-T. Lee, L. Jussim, & C. R. McCauley (Eds.), *Stereotype accuracy: Toward appreciating group differences* (pp. 29–59). Washington, DC: American Psychological Association.

Peabody, D. (1985). *National characteristics.* New York: Cambridge University Press.

Pepitone, A., & Triandis, H. (1987). On the universality of social psychological theories. *Journal of Cross-Cultural Psychology, 18,* 471–498.

Pye, L. W. (1992). *Chinese negotiation style: Commercial approaches and cultural principles.* New York: Quorum Books.

Ralston, D. A., Gustafson, D. J., Elsass, P. M., Cheung, F., & Terpstra, R. H. (1992). Eastern values: A comparison of managers in the United States, Hong Kong, and the People's Republic of China. *Journal of Applied Psychology, 77,* 664–671.

Roseman, I. J., Dhawan, N., Rettek, S. I., Naidu, R. K. et al. (1995). Cultural differences and cross-cultural similarities in appraisals and emotional responses. *Journal of Cross-Cultural Psychology, 26,* 23–48.

Russell, J. A., & Yik, M. S. M. (1996). Emotion among Chinese. In M. H. Bond (Ed.), *The handbook of Chinese psychology* (pp. 166–188). Hong Kong: Oxford University Press.

Smith, P. B., & Wang, Z. M. (1996). Chinese leadership and organizational structure. In M. H. Bond (Ed.), *The handbook of Chinese psychology.* Hong Kong: Oxford University Press.

Solomon, R. (1972). *Mao's revolution and the Chinese political culture.* Berkeley, CA: University of California Press.

Stevenson, H. W. (1992). Learning from Asian schools. *Scientific American, 267,* 70–76.

Sun, L. K. (1983). *The "deep structure" of Chinese culture* (in Chinese). Hong Kong: Yishan, passim.

Sung, B. L. (1992). Bicultural conflict. In E. Angeloni (Ed.), *Anthropology* (Vol. 92/93, pp. 220–227). Guilford, CT: The Dushkin Publishing Group.

Triandis, H. (1994). *Culture and social behavior.* New York: McGraw-Hill.

Tu, W. M. (1991). Cultural China: The periphery as the center. *Daedalus: Journal of the American Academy of Arts and Sciences, 120,* 1–32.

Yang, K. S., & Bond, M. (1990). Exploring implicit personality theories with indigenous or imported constructs: The Chinese case. *Journal of Personality and Social Psychology, 58,* 1087–1095.

Yates, J. F., & Lee, J. W. (1996). Chinese decision-making. In M. H. Bond (Ed.), *The handbook of Chinese psychology* (pp. 338–351). Hong Kong: Oxford University Press.

8

Culture, Self, and Personality in Africa

Barnabas I. Okeke
Office of Mental Health/Retardation, Philadelphia

Juris G. Draguns
The Pennsylvania State University

Ben Sheku
Winston Allen
Office of Mental Health/Retardation, Philadelphia

Over several centuries, European explorers, settlers, sojourners, and investigators encountered in Africa a social reality that diverged markedly from their accumulated social experience and knowledge. Their contemporary successors, be they cultural anthropologists, cross-cultural psychologists, or other social scientists, are still involved in grappling with the mixed legacy of observations, preconceptions, and misunderstandings that have accumulated over the long history of contact between Europe and Africa. On the one hand, the idealized image of the noble savage originated in part in the African context. On the other hand, the pejorative stereotype of the primitive, childlike, and immature African arose who, from the ethnocentric Western point of view, was even less than fully human. As an elaboration of this prejudice, indigenous cultures and the behavior of the people within them were dismissed as being barely worthy of study or, at best, condescendingly relegated to the status of stunned and vestigial remnants from Africa's nebulous past. Against the background of these distorted stereotypes, another trend gradually appeared and started gathering momentum. Cultural anthropologists concentrated their sights on the small-scale, traditional, tribal groups and began investigating their ways of life. This approach preserved valuable information and yielded promising and seminal insights. However, it contributed to yet another misunderstanding. The collective picture that emerged from these ethnographies of African cultures was that of slowly changing, rural, and small cultural groups untouched by the worldwide social, political, economic, and technological transformations of the 20th century. Yet, the typical contemporary African is more likely to be the resident of the urban conglomerates in and around Accra, Dakar, Johannesburg, Kinshasa, Lagos, and Nairobi. Such a person may share neighborhoods and work environments with members of several different ethnicities and is forced to communicate in the prevailing lingua franca of the region such as English, French, Portuguese, or Swahili. Although the objective world of natural phenomena and human-made objects has been changing gradually, virtually a kaleidoscopic change has been experienced at the social level. This discrepancy has contributed to the disorientation and confusion of individuals, approximating to the condition of alienation or anomie (Davol & Reimanis, 1959; Merton, 1957). Yet, their socialization, experience, and outlook are to varying degrees shaped by the historically transmitted African way of life. What are then its features and, above all, its reflections in the characteristic patterns of behavior and subjective experience, that is, in personality? In this chapter, we endeavor to provide answers to these questions. As we embark upon this task, we are impressed by its tremendous complexity. Africa is home to a multitude of distinct ethnic or cultural groups, most of them with their own distinct language as well as worldview, philosophy of life, values, beliefs, and customs. Still, there are certain converging trends that may variously stem from Africa's shared history and experience. Thus, African cultures may be intrinsically characterized by closer bonds within the family and the community. They are also marked by the trauma of several centuries of European colonization and the enforced social change that was brought about by this experience of outside domination. Politically liberated, Africans are now challenged by the opportunities and risks of modern technology and, above all, by the fast pace of worldwide transformation and change.

In geographic terms, we restrict our coverage to Africa south of the Sahara and thereby exclude the countries on the shores of the Mediterranean and the Red Sea. These regions have experienced the impact of Arab culture which, like the more recent European influences, originated outside of the African continent.

Against this historical background, the general objectives of this chapter are threefold. We start out by introducing the Triple Reality Model that has guided us in conceptualizing and integrating the empirical findings contained in this chapter. Our second task is to provide a concise review of the procedures and results of the empirical research on psychology in Africa, especially as it pertains to personality. Third, we extract a limited number of conclusions from this accumulation of research-based information; we append our assessment of this as yet incomplete enterprise of investigation.

TRIPLE REALITY MODEL

The Triple Reality Model is an interdisciplinary theoretical development that attempts to deal with issues of different disciplines by using the interaction of several, simultaneously experienced, distinct realities. It deals with the complexities of behavior and its interrelationship with environment. A set of concepts from the social psychological (Kleiner & Okeke, 1991; Lewin, 1966; Okeke, 1987; Parker & Kleiner, 1966) and the social structural (Merton, 1957; Okeke, 1987) levels of analysis is used to predict behavior and its impact in any culture, both on the individual or the group.

For discussion purposes, we define the Triple Reality Model as the set of interactions between the three types of realities: namely, objective, social, and subjective/psychological realities.

Objective reality refers to the structure of a situation as it actually exists. For example, Merton's (1957) concept of anomie is defined as a property of the social system and not as a property of individuals. Specifically, it has to do with the degree to which the socially defined means to achievement actually lead to the socially prescribed indicators of achievement. We may add at this point, that these are American/Western socially defined means and indexes of achievement, that is, a status-striving motivation (status-driven opportunity structure). But in other economic security structures different motives may be playing a stronger role (Okeke, 1987). Anomie is the degree to which the opportunity structure (or status structure) is closed. It is defined in Merton's terms as the relationship between the goals and the means of achieving them in the society, education, and income. Thus, a person is said to experience a high degree of anomie when a pronounced discrepancy exists between the widely shared social goals, for example, prosperity or financial independence, and the means for their attainment, for example, opportunity for obtaining a job with a good income. Economic security is thought of as the harmony between internal needs and the availability of the means for their satisfaction. In some sense, it means looking at the material aspects of life, for example, food, shelter, clothing, health, and so forth. Measured empirically, it is based on the cumulative index of such variables as unemployment, morbidity, mortality, and so on, that collectively constitute a set of indicators of the economic base for survival.

Social reality refers to the structure of a situation as it is perceived by a collective or group of interacting individuals. The interaction may be principally behavioral or predominantly symbolic interaction. For example, it might involve the collective evaluation of the opportunity structure by a 'social network" made up of members of a given culture. A possible instance may be the emergence of consensus among the participants in a social network about the meaning of a shared experience, such as the merits of the program of a political party, even when no objective basis exists for this judgment.

Subjective reality is the property of a situation as perceived by an individual. In this example, this would refer to the individual's own evaluation of the opportunity structure or his or her opinion about some issue. Perception of opportunity structure is one person's estimate of the opportunity structure, that is, one's reading of how open or closed the opportunity structure is, or how anomic or integrated the whole system appears to the individual. Perception of economic structure is the person's own estimate of how secure or insecure the system is.

These three types of reality coexist and interact with each other. There is no necessary congruence or agreement between them. That is to say, any two realities may agree completely, disagree completely, or overlap to varying degrees. The last is the most likely state of affairs. It then becomes necessary to measure the different realities by methods appropriate for each type, because there is no way of determining at a glance the degree of congruence between the realities being considered. By independently measuring these realities, we can evaluate their interrelationships, as well as the effects of their interaction. It is only in rare situations that the three realities coincide. In some cases, especially in survey research, an individual can be correct about the reality. For example, take the answer to the question, "What is your occupation?" If the individual says, "I'm an engineer," the immediate social group recognizes him as an engineer, and he actually is an engineer, then the congruence of the three realities is complete.

The Triple Reality Model has points of contact with another tripartite division of experiences that was proposed by the Swiss pioneer of existential analysis, Ludwig Binswanger (1958). According to this formulation, all humans live and operate in three worlds, *Umwelt,* which can be equated with the palpable, physical environment; *Mitwelt,* which constitutes the arena of interaction with other human beings and their myriad perceptions, conceptions, and expectations; and *Eigenwelt,* which represents the experience within their own selves and minds, in all of its subtlety and complexity. In contrast with the conceptualization proposed previously, Binswanger's orientation was more retrospective than prospective. He aimed to capture an individual's experience in all of its richness in order to understand its roots and ramifications in psychotherapy. Our objective is different. We seek to disentangle these three distinct threads in order to specify the determinants of personal choices and actions in the present, predict the future behavior, and explain the impact of the past experience upon present conduct.

EMPIRICAL FINDINGS: A VARIETY OF APPROACHES, A FEW EMERGING TRENDS

Sources of Data

In general, modern scientific psychologists have three options in gathering information about a phenomenon hitherto not yet investigated:

1. They can observe the phenomenon in question, record their observations, and take special precautions in order to separate their observations—that which they have perceived—from preconceptions, biases, inferences, and subjective impressions. This is the naturalistic method, prominently employed by clinical observers within our own culture and extended across culture lines by ethnographers, cultural anthropologists, and other social scientists. In the form of the time-sampling technique, for example (Whiting & Whiting, 1975), the naturalistic approach has achieved a high degree of objectivity and precision.
2. They can standardize their techniques of gathering information and then quantify and compare in some manner the results obtained. This approach constitutes the gist of the survey method, perhaps best known throughout the modern world in the form of opinion polls. The burden is upon the survey researcher to demonstrate the representativeness of the samples used and the generalizability of the results obtained. Moreover, he or she must show that the results obtained have not been distorted by the attitudes, values, expectations,

or prejudices of the researcher and that the respondent has not been swayed by the wording and format of the questions. Great progress has been achieved in purifying the data collection process from these distortions and in applying sophisticated statistical techniques for the analysis of data obtained.

3. Finally, the investigator may impose controls, create a miniature, time-limited replica of reality in which only one or few conditions are allowed to vary. He or she can then observe, in specific and quantitative terms, the impact of this variation upon one or several indicators of a specified performance. In other words, the researcher can conduct an experiment. Experiments are generally regarded as the most rigorous and conclusive variant of the scientific method. However, experiments are exceedingly difficult to design and to conduct, and especially so when the experiment is transplanted to a new and different cultural milieu. It is therefore not surprising that the yield of experimentation in Africa is as yet relatively modest. This conclusion may be subject to revision, perhaps even in the relatively near future. The development of psychology within Africa is proceeding apace, despite formidable obstacles (Nsamenang, 1995).

At this time it must be admitted that, in research on personality in Africa, qualitative methods prevail over quantitative ones. Within the Triple Reality Model, both qualitative and quantitative data are considered. Qualitative data (pertaining to such concepts as anomie and insecurity) often describe the general conditions in which more specific variables can be quantified and measured (such as subjective dissatisfaction or social disorganization). Much of what we know about personality in Africa comes from naturalistically collected data. For over a hundred years, numerous anthropologists, more recently followed by increasing numbers of sociologists, psychiatrists, psychologists, and psychoanalysts, have come to Africa from Europe and North America, in order to explore, by a combination of interviews and observations, the behavior and experience of peoples living in very different cultures. In the last few decades, French (e.g., Ortigues & Ortigues, 1973) and Swiss (e.g., Parin, Morgenthaler, & Parin-Mathèy, 1963, 1980) investigators have gone so far as to conduct an approximation of psychoanalysis with sizable numbers of West Africans. Specifically, they have attempted to elicit a flow of free associations from African subjects who, however, more often were paid volunteers rather than help-seeking clients. A lot of perceptive observations about the subjective world of Africans were contributed while providing psychotherapy or other clinical services to African clients, either within Africa (e.g., Peltzer, 1995) or outside of it (Nathan, 1994; Nwachuku & Ivey, 1991). Some glimpses into the personal experience within African cultures were obtained by means of thematic projective techniques, specifically developed within the African continent (Ombredane, 1954). Within the context of providing developmental aid in a medical setting, Staewen (1991) described numerous instances of characteristic patterns of interaction between Westerners and Africans as well as the problems encountered and resolved in the course of these contacts. Increasingly, the participant observations of anthropologists are being supplemented by the accounts of experiences of educators, physicians, developmental helpers, and others. Collectively, these reports constitute the "raw material" of which the African composite of triple realities is constructed. Stimulating and provocative as all of these extensions of the naturalistic method are, they are of limited help in disentangling the causal nexus that connects past circumstances and present characteristics. The unique value of these data is in providing a panoramic view of individual behavior and experience in the context of their occurrence. Within the Triple Realities framework, the focus of these studies is on the subjective level of experience; their connections with the social and objective aspects of reality remain tenuous.

Three additional limitations must be kept in mind while sifting and evaluating the accumulation of findings pertinent to human behavior and experience in Africa. First, it should not be forgotten that most of the observers in these studies were outsiders and not Africans. Their reports and conclusions then are susceptible to misconstructions and misunderstandings that often occur as human beings try to comprehend what is to them a new and unfamiliar social reality. Many of these non-African sojourners may to different degrees have been aware of these potential distortions and some of them have worked hard in order to forestall or overcome them.

Some of the early writers, however, succumbed to the tendency of judging African phenomena through the prism of their culture-bound Western experience. Whatever appeared different or novel to them ran the risk of being deemed primitive, inferior, immature, or incompetent (e.g., Carothers, 1953; Ritchie, 1944). More recently, warnings have been sounded against equating cultural differences with social or cultural deficiencies (Draguns, 1996, 1997). Social scientists (e.g., Cole & Bruner, 1971) have also inveighed against trying to explain cultural differences in cognitive, social, or other performance on the basis of any alleged deficits embedded in the persons' cultural experience or milieu. The so-called deficit hypothesis that attempts to do just that has been generally rejected by modern cross-cultural psychologists (Segall, Dasen, Berry, & Poortinga, 1990).

In any case, it is undeniable that what we know about personality in Africa is traceable to perceptions by non-Africans viewing the objects of their investigation from their own extraneous perspectives; African psychologists are by this time a growing contingent of the investigators engaged in this enterprise. With time, the limitations inherent in the study of African phenomena by non-African observers will disappear. As yet, however, the stamp of an external frame of reference in observers, methods, theories, and concepts is still with us, and so are the pitfalls that this anomalous situation brings with it.

The second source of complexity concerns the gathering and comparison of psychological data across cultures. In particular, the equivalence of stimuli, procedures, and settings has proved to be extremely difficult to achieve, especially when the differences between cultures are major. Volumes (e.g., Brislin, Lonner, & Thorndike, 1973; Irvine & Berry, 1983) have been written about this problem and great strides have been made toward resolving it. Yet, a subtle, but pervasive aspect of this issue continues to bedevil the cross-cultural research enterprise. In research about Africa, the flow of conceptualization has been one way: exclusively from Europe and North America to Africa. This circumstance has resulted in a paradoxical dichotomy: The phenomena investigated are African; the explanations and concepts imposed upon them are Euro-American. The challenge for the future is to reinterpret these data from the African point of view and then integrate the extraneous and indigenous explanations on a more universal plane.

Finally, the third complication pertains to the variations within the contemporary African population. Peltzer (1995) has identified the following three distinctive components of the people inhabiting present-day Africa: (a) traditional persons who are as yet little affected by modernization and who are functioning within the established and seemingly timeless framework of their culture, (b) transitional persons, often living in, and shuttling between, the two cultures in the course of their daily round of activities, for example, between work and home or between the temporary urban living dwelling and the ancestral traditional village where their extended family continues to reside, and (c) modern individuals, participating fully in the activities of the contemporary, industrial or postindustrial, world. As yet, these important distinctions have not been taken into account in most empirical studies of personality in Africa. If it is assumed that this trichotomy is relevant to personal experience and functioning, its disregard may then have contributed to the error variance in the studies extant and may have distorted the resulting findings. In the case of the transitional person especially, overlooking these distinctions may have increased the share of unaccounted intraindividual variation and thereby complicated and misshaped the results obtained.

RESULTS AND TRENDS: THEIR AMBIGUITIES AND COMPLEXITIES

Despite these difficulties, it is possible to identify some promising and convergent trends that have emerged from several decades of personality-oriented research. In presenting these tentative conclusions, we are painfully aware of the risk of succumbing to stereotypes and glossing over the heterogeneity and complexity of psychological phenomena in Africa. To counteract this danger, we advance the following three precautions. First, we are mindful of the great diversity among African cultures. No generalization applies to all of them and allowances must be explicitly made for multiplicity of trends, atypical features, and exceptional instances. Second, within any culture the general expectation is for a multimodal distribution of all or most personality characteristics, as Wallace (1970) empirically demonstrated even for small-scale tribal societies. Third, within a specific individual we make a provision for the coexistence of several, sometimes apparently incompatible or even mutually exclusive trends. Thus, a pronounced sociocentric orientation does not preclude the existence of individual striving. These considerations are articulated here to nip in the bud any speculations on a uniform African personality or, worse still, on a specifically or exclusively African personality type.

Within the Triple Reality Model, the studies presented refer primarily to the social reality experienced by Africans. To the extent that this social reality corresponds to the objective reality, stability and security are enhanced at the subjective level. However, as gaps and inconsistencies are encountered between the objective and social levels, confusion, uncertainty, and helplessness set in. Subjectively, threat and insecurity are felt and the individual experiences conflict with his or her social network or reference group.

Empirical Findings

With the aforementioned caveats, we introduce the following tentative generalizations, as a way of summarizing the results extant and of providing guidelines for future investigation:

1. Perhaps the most substantial finding so far obtained pertains to the sociocentric orientation that is prevalent or is strongly represented in most African cultures. A set of findings from a variety of sources, obtained by means of diverse methods, bolsters this general conclusion. It can be said, on the basis of empirical data, that, in Africa, many persons experience themselves as being "from birth onward integrated into strong, cohesive ingroups, which throughout people's lifetime continue to protect them in exchange for unquestioning loyalty" (Hofstede, 1991, p. 51). This enduring bond reverberates within the person and shapes his or her self-experience. The self of a sociocentric person constitutes an aggregate of a person's social relationships and attachments and of their reflection within the person. The self-boundaries are permeable and loose, and the self serves as a bridge that connects the person to other human beings rather than as a wall that separates him or her from other individuals (Chang, 1988; Landrine, 1992). From a global bird's eye point of view, these trends were noted in both West and East African samples by Hofstede (1984) in his worldwide investigation of work-related attitudes. Admittedly, these samples were neither representative nor random, but were based on availability and convenience. Nonetheless, the finding of sociocentric orientation among Africans has received corroboration from a variety of perspectives, methods, and instruments, with populations from all regions of the continent.

   Anthropologists and other participant observers of various African cultures (e.g., Guerry, 1971; Knapen, 1970; R. A. LeVine & S. E. LeVine, 1988; R. A. LeVine et al., 1994; R. L. Munroe, R. H. Munroe, & R. A. LeVine, 1972; Peltzer, 1995; Staewen, 1991; Tavares, 1973; Whiting & Whiting, 1975) are in agreement that the African infant and child develops in the context of constant presence of and interaction with other human beings. Growing Africans have little chance to feel lonely because they are rarely left alone. In a comparison of infants in Scotland and Nigeria, Agiobu-Kemmer (1984) found that Nigerian children spent more time with human beings than with physical objects. The reverse was true with Scottish children who spent more time with physical objects than with human beings. The sphere of private experience, fostered and cultivated in the individualistic cultures of Europe and America, is not explicitly heeded in daily interactions in many parts of Africa. In any case, the boundaries between public and private domains are porous and easily penetrated. Among the Baoule of Ivory Coast, as Guerry (1971) reported, "everything is so much shared that no room is left for personal life. Nothing is hidden; anybody can come into your house and look around everywhere. Personal questions are asked unselfconsciously, without intrusive intent" (p. 31). As Guerry put it: "Not to ask them would be a sign of indifference and contempt"[1] (p. 32).

These observations are supplemented by the intensive data gathered in the course of psychoanalytically oriented interviews by Parin et al. (1963, 1980) and Ortigues and Ortigues (1973) among several ethnic groups in West Africa. These data were integrated with systematic observations of child–parent interaction and of parents' socialization practices. Ortigues and Ortigues concluded that the Oedipal rivalry between father and son, considered by classical psychoanalysts to be the fountainhead of masculine identification, is displaced in Senegal to a rivalry with brothers and other male peers. Once this dynamic is resolved, it constitutes a major vehicle for the promotion of solidarity with male peers. As such, it fosters a sense of belonging. However, Ortigues and Ortigues also pointed out that Senegalese young men remain highly vulnerable to separation anxiety when removed from their extended family and community. Their functioning is easily disrupted by rejection by their reference group. Self-esteem is crucially dependent on group approval, and shame more than guilt regulates behavior and experience.

On the basis of their intensive ethnopsychoanalytic observations of the Anyi (also called Agni) of Ivory Coast and the Dogon of Mali (Parin et al., 1963, 1980), Parin and Parin-Mathèy (1964) proposed that African social behavior is moderated by a group ego that guides individuals effectively within their cultural milieu, but leaves them defenseless and disoriented in unfamiliar environments. Detailed case studies of both normal and psychiatrically disabled individuals at the Fann Hospital Center in Dakar, Senegal (Collomb, 1965, 1973) confirm the central importance of a sense of belonging for the personal

---

[1]Translated from French.

adaptation of many Africans. In intercultural encounters between Africans and Europeans, a great many misinterpretations and misunderstandings are traceable to the African group-centered orientation that is all too often overlooked or disregarded by the individualistically inclined Westerners (Staewen, 1991). On the basis of extensive and intensive clinical experience in seven African countries, Peltzer (1995) has been able to confirm the earlier formulations by Parin et al. and Ortigues and Ortigues on the importance of the group ego in the traditional African pattern of adaptation. Peltzer, however, has also noted a shift in the experience of many contemporary transitional Africans toward a more personal integration and control of behavior, away from the unquestioning internalization of group practices. In this respect as well as many others, Africans of this day and age find themselves in transition. Social change reverberates within their personal experience and affects their personalities.

The concept of locus of control (Rotter, 1966) has also been studied in Africa. It taps an individual's conviction or belief of the extent to which the events of his or her life are determined by personal effort or by uncontrollable external (and often social) influences. Consistent with other findings, African samples have generally tended toward external attributions on standardized scales of locus of control (Smith, Trompenaars, & Dungan, 1995), although there are a few exceptions to this trend (e.g., Maqsud, 1981). A major study of this variable among the Yoruba of Nigeria (Dada & Aweritefe, 1988) both exemplifies and substantiates this trend. An earlier study by Reimanis and Posen (1980) contributed a more complex pattern of findings. Reimanis and Posen demonstrated that only the personal control subscale of the locus of control measure clearly differentiated African from Euro-American subjects. Personal control refers to the degree to which the person experiences being in control of his or her destiny. By contrast, two other components of the internality–externality construct, systems control (to what extent can a person influence the political process?) and control ideology (general belief in the importance of external vs. internal factors in determining outcomes), were found to be determined by more recent economic and political events. Specifically, Reimanis and Posen found significant differences between Nigerians, who had enjoyed independence for close to 20 years and Zimbabweans, then still under White rule. The impact of anomie on locus of control was also demonstrated among the Zulu farmers of

South Africa (Magwaza & Bhana, 1991). The pattern of findings was complex, but in general confirmed the greater externality of migratory rather than sedentary groups; external locus of control was also positively related to coercive or involuntary migration. Thus, locus of control appears to be a complex, probably multidimensional, variable that is codetermined by both cultural and situational factors. Another source of variation is internalized social change. Peltzer (1995) pooled his own extensive clinical observations with recent trends in research findings and concluded that, for the contemporary African involved in transition toward modernization "internalization and the internal locus of control become more relevant than they used to be, while the external locus of control becomes less relevant" (p. 17).

Social emphasis is also highlighted in the employment setting. Earley (1984) compared industrial workers in Ghana, England, and the United States. There was more social interaction at work in Ghana than in the other two countries. Similarly, in two self-report studies of managers in Nigeria (Eze, 1985) and Zimbabwe (Wilson, Sibanda, & Torres, 1991) social goals were found to prevail over self-oriented and material ones, although this pattern of results was not entirely clear-cut. Carr, McLachlan, Zimba, and Bowa (1995) in Malawi introduced the concept of motivational gravity, a form of social pressure toward conformity and against self-advancement. Motivational gravity was demonstrated to operate in social interactions both between peers and between superiors and subordinates. In a mental hospital setting, McLachlan, Nyirenda, and Nyando (1995) reported a greater emphasis on violations of social propriety and decorum in attributions for admissions to a psychiatric hospital in Malawi than appears to be the case elsewhere.

African conceptions of intelligence are interlaced with notions of social appropriateness and competence. Serpell (1989) discovered that the a-Chewa of Zambia consider cooperation and obedience to be the central components of intelligence. Remarkably, similar conceptions have been found to prevail across the continent, among the Baoulé of Ivory Coast where the indigenous notion of intelligence features such traits as responsibility, politeness, obedience, and respect (Dasen et al., 1985). Thus, social smoothness, conformity, and sophistication are so highly valued, at least in some African cultures, as to constitute the keystones of culturally defined cognitive ability and skill.

The positive consequences of this social orientation are readily apparent. They include a high level of social sophistication in interacting with others, usually within one's ingroup, personal sensitivity, ease of social interaction, at least within one's familiar social milieu, and freedom from disruptive social anxiety or social inhibition, for example, in the form of shyness (e.g., Parin et al., 1980). Moreover, sociocentric or collectivistic cultures cushion their members against disruptive and violent expressions of aggression, by others or themselves, and prevent destructive behavior against self and others. A great deal of personal security is thus inculcated, and intense and painful intrapsychic conflicts are averted.

However, like any other psychological characteristic, sociocentric orientation has its shadow or negative side. As Corin and Murphy (1979) have noted, sociocentric individuals are susceptible to the experience of confusion, helplessness, and even panic when they are separated from their customary sources of support within the family, community, or tribal group. Such as a situation comes about through migration or displacement that may be forced or involuntary. The effect of such experiences is especially disruptive when the host culture fails to mitigate the culture shock by sensitivity to and understanding of the displaced person's needs. These are situations in which social reality is at variance with objective reality. Nathan (1994), a Parisian psychoanalyst with an extensive African clientele, has observed social disorientation reactions to this kind of brutal cultural transplantation that, at their extreme, mimicked autistic symptoms. Moreover, another critical situation for persons securely integrated into as a stable social structure comes during unplanned, unexpected, and abrupt social change. At such a time, a person with a pronounced sociocentric outlook is likely to experience severe disruption and discomfort, perhaps in the form of free-floating or displaced anxiety. Anxious feelings were also documented in an intensive study, based on interview and observational data, by Staewen and Schönberg (1970) among the Yoruba of Nigeria shortly after the country's declaration of independence. However, the number of subjects in this study was small and there were no provisions for comparing them with members of other groups or with their own baseline prior to major social and political change.

Even in situations governed by distrust and hostility, African orientation has not been geared to withdrawal from contact with and avoidance of ideation about the social source of anxiety and threat (e.g., Parin et al., 1980). Social discomfort results in fears of persecution that appear to be less abnormal and paranoid in the African context than they are in the West (e.g., Sow, 1980) as they are embedded in cultural beliefs of powerful magical malevolent influence. Thus, friends as well as foes are constantly featured in African thought and are never far from their consciousness.

2. The socialization experience that promotes orientation toward social harmony and integration appears to be compounded of six essential elements: (a) close bodily contact with the mother during infancy and prompt relief of hunger and physical discomfort during this stage of development (Guerry, 1971; Knapen, 1970; LeVine & LeVine, 1988; Nsamenang, 1992; Peltzer, 1995; Staewen, 1991, Tavares, 1973), (b) mothering by several adults during infancy and early childhood (Knapen, 1970; LeVine et al., 1994; Nsamenang, 1992; Peltzer, 1995; Tavares, 1973), (c) systematic inculcation of respect and obedience toward parents, elders, and other adults (Knapen, 1970; LeVine et al., 1994; Monroe & Monroe, 1972; Tavares, 1973) beginning shortly after weaning and continuing through early and middle childhood, (d) rather relaxed and unpressured training toward bodily self-control (Knapen, 1970; LeVine et al., 1994; Nsamenang, 1992; Peltzer, 1995; Tavares, 1973), (e) providing a rather wide scope for exploration of the physical and social environment early in life and tolerating, if not actively encouraging, a great deal of elbow room as soon as the child becomes fully mobile (Knapen, 1970; LeVine et al., 1994; Peltzer, 1995; Tavares, 1973), and (f) peer groups of children of the same age and gender assuming importance as agents of socialization, providers of security and acceptance, and sources of self-esteem (Knapen, 1970; Peltzer, 1995; Tavares, 1973). On the basis of extensive and thorough observations of mother–child interaction among the Gusii of Kenya, LeVine et al. concluded that the objectives of socialization within that group include comfort and conformity, but do not prominently feature exploration and self-assertion. As yet, there is little basis for generalizing these specific observations to all of Africa, but it would appear that, with some exceptions, the combination of the six socialization experiences specified previously is characteristic in diverse regions of Africa. From the psychoanalytic point of view, this conjunction of developmental features is likely to result in pronounced oral fixations (Parin & Parin-Mathèy, 1964), in the form of spontaneity, generosity,

sociability, dependence, and also, susceptibility to separation anxiety. By contrast, anal fixations, with emphasis on neatness, overcontrol, and inhibition of spontaneity, are relatively rarely encountered in Africa. The American developmental theorist, Bronfenbrenner (1994), concluded that African socialization as described earlier imbues a growing human being with a sense of coherence and stability that, in contemporary North America, is constantly at risk and under threat. The Belgian anthropologist Knapen (1970) considered that the African pattern of socially structured developmental experiences is effectively geared toward lifelong integration into an extended family, a clan, a closely integrated family. It equips the person poorly for the anonymity and impersonality of modern existence in huge and fast changing urban conglomerates and it prepares such an individual inadequately for the experience of solitude and separation.

3. The cognitive style prevalent in Africa is oriented toward synthesis rather than analysis. Africans are more inclined to integrate or fuse their experiences into an inclusive whole. They are less disposed toward extricating a component or an element from a pattern of stimuli into which it is embedded. Thus, global, holistic, intuitive, and expressive cognitive operations prevail over fragmentary, isolated, or detail-oriented mental activities. To many Africans, such a mode of reasoning appears more "natural" than its opposite, with its emphasis upon elements, components, and distinctions. Thus, it would appear that the cognitive style of field dependence (Witkin & Berry, 1975) would be more congenial to many Africans than field independence. In perceptual operations, field-dependent persons experience difficulty in extricating a figure from a complex pattern into which it is embedded. Field-independent persons excel in such operations. Field-dependent style indeed has been found to be pronounced in some African cultures (e.g., Berry, 1967), but instances of high degrees of field independence have also been documented (Dawson, 1967; Wober, 1975). Moreover, it is not quite clear whether the dimension of field dependence–field independence measures the same psychological properties in North America and in Africa (Wober, 1975), even though the hypothesized and partially corroborated correlates of field dependence are prominently represented in Africa. They include social perceptiveness, readiness to accommodate to group's preferences, demands, and standards, and generally subordinating one's own perspective to that of the group. Thus, the cognitive style of field

independence may represent the stylistic correlate of the generalized emphasis upon susceptibility to social influence by the ingroups that is inculcated through African socialization. Such emphasis is represented in a variety of domains of experience and behavior throughout the life cycle. Nothing, however, in the available store of findings indicates that the characteristic cognitive orientation in Africa is expressive of, or associated with, lesser cognitive proficiency or lower cognitive maturity. As Cole, Gay, Glick, and Sharp (1971) have demonstrated with the Kpelle of Liberia, African subjects are entirely capable of complex, mathematically correct, and logically justified mental operations, provided that they are performed with familiar stimulus materials that matter to them in their daily lives. Thus, the conclusions of an earlier era, for example, Lévy-Bruhl's (1928) early speculations about the alleged predominance of "magical thinking" in Africa, can be laid to rest once and for all.

The penchant toward synthesis rather than analysis among Africans may be related to a greater acceptance of intuition in reasoning and a more active emotional involvement in cognitive operations. The Senegalese poet and the founding president of his country, Leopold Senghor (cited in Wober, 1975), once said that emotions are as African as reason is Greek. Unfortunately, this characteristic has not yet received the attention from researchers that it deserves, even though fragments of evidence from a variety of sources appear to corroborate its prominence in African experience. Wober (1975) regretfully noted that "the great skill in Africa of artistic and cognitive achievement in sculpture and music and the cognitive areas of parable and public administration ('lore and law') have escaped qualitative study and certainly quantitative measurement by psychologists. Yet we surely know enough to realize that traditional systems, before it is too late to study them, offered plenty of challenges to such investigation" (p. 118). Another promising idea is that the African sensotype emphasizes auditory and kinesthetic experience in contrast to the dominance of visual modality that is allegedly prevalent in Euro-American culture (Wober, 1966). Unfortunately, this intriguing formulation has not received rigorous empirical scrutiny though systematic cross-cultural comparisons.

Along somewhat similar lines, a wise Dogon elder (in Mali) observed: "The whites, they think too much and then they make many things, and the more things they make, the more they think. And then they earn a lot of money and then they may lose all their money and may have nothing left. Then they think still more and make even more money; there is never enough of it for them. Thus they become upset. And so it comes that they are unhappy"[2] (Parin et al., 1963).

4. The holistic orientation that is prevalent in Africa tends to deemphasize or even break down the boundaries between somatic and psychological components of experience (Le Guerinel, 1971; Peltzer, 1995). In a similar manner, the prevalent holistic emphasis lowers barriers between the material and the spiritual and between the natural and the supernatural. According to the African law of opposites (Okeke & Sheku, 1997), consideration of reality compels that the opposite of reality also be taken into account. Thus, dealing with an issue at the programmatic reality level leads to the consideration of supernatural and visionary dreams and opens the door to communing with all unnatural and natural spirits, without the experience of incongruity or dissonance. Moreover, psychological distress readily provokes physical discomfort, stress triggers a gamut of both bodily and psychic reactions, and the experience of physical malaise easily spills over into a negative psychological state. Conversely, Africans may experience a greater degree of bodily self-awareness and may be more in touch with their somatic and proprioceptive sensations. Leff (1977) noted a tendency among Nigerian psychiatric patients to fuse their negative emotional states, such as aggression, anxiety, and depression, into a global experience of acute and intense discomfort. Similarly, experiences in dreams or trance states are fitted together, seemingly in a spontaneous and effortless fashion, with concrete events of everyday life, and the presence and participation of ancestral sprits in the mundane social interactions in the person's immediately environment is widely accepted. This blurring of boundaries that are deeply ingrained in the Western psyche is relevant to the Triple Reality Model espoused in this chapter. The point needs to be emphasized that although the divisions separating the three domains of reality remain real in Africa as well as in Euro-America, they are more easily bridged or transcended in Africa then elsewhere.

5. The socialization toward harmony and integration serves well most Africans in protecting them from the experience of intrapsychic

---

[2]Translated from German.

conflict, and from anxiety, as well as from depression that may follow these conflicts. Guilt is less prominent as a means of social control than it is in the West (Ortigues & Ortigues, 1973; Parin et al., 1980; Peltzer, 1995). In general, African individuals, as observed by psychodynamically oriented clinicians, are less tormented by internalized psychic discomfort. Prototypically, the African process of socialization serves a person well. It equips him or her with a flexible adaptive structure, an adequate degree of self-acceptance, and a variety of workable and acceptable outlets of emotional expression. It also provides for lifelong sources of social support that may not be unconditionally available, but tend to be readily provided to anyone who does not violate the explicit or implicit rules of group living. The previous statement is, of course, an approximation and, in reference to specific ethnic entities, it is contradicted by socially disorganized ethnic groups such as the Ik of East Africa as described by Turnbull (1972). It should, moreover, be kept in mind that the extreme social disintegration recorded by Turnbull was the result of forcible removal of the Ik from their traditional sources of sustenance. Apart from this highly atypical instance, the generalization holds that in most African cultures individuals are thoroughly integrated into their families, clans, and communities whereby both interpersonal strife and intrapsychic conflict are reduced.

6. Despite the positive tone of the preceding point, psychological distress in its manifold forms exists in Africa as it does elsewhere. It may be instructive to highlight some of its typical manifestations. Early reports about the virtual absence of depression in Africa (Carothers, 1953) have given way to the recognition that it exists, although it is expressed and experienced differently than in the Euro-American West. In terms of its manifestations, self-blame and self-rejection are rarely its prominent components and quite often they are altogether absent. The paradox from the point of view of Western observers is the existence of depression without guilt. Moreover, careful phenomenological analyses (Prince, 1968; Zeldine et al., 1975) have revealed that it is experienced in a somewhat different form from the West. Masked depression is characteristic in the form of somatic symptoms, ideas of possession, and delusions of persecution. An important antecedent of depression in Africa is the experience of object loss, at least in some cultures (Krauss, 1968), which engenders a pronounced sense of uselessness and dramatically lowers self-esteem.

CONCLUSIONS

We have seen that the African experience is different in degree, though not in kind, from the experiences of human beings in other parts of the world. In presenting these findings, we have tried to steer clear of either idealizing or denigrating the African mode of coping. Rather, we have emphasized the interplay of advantages and disadvantages and have tried to convey the distinctive flavor and style of African adaptation. It is now time to proceed toward formulating conclusions. We have summarized the findings that we have surveyed under six headings. On the basis of the research extant, there is a pronounced tendency toward sociocentric adaptation in most African cultures. Its goal is harmony and integration within the concentric circles of family, clan, community, and tribe. It does not explicitly promote the development of individual uniqueness and does not provide, let alone guarantee, an inviolate zone of privacy. This formula of adaptation is facilitated by a mode of socialization that fosters security, provides room for independence, but is, at the same time, geared toward conformity and obedience rather than self-expression and social innovation and change. The African mode of thinking is inclusive rather than fragmentary and the lines between bodily and mental experience and between the spiritual and material are easily crossed. This pattern of adaptive characteristics produces a mixture of positive and negative results: smooth social relations and relative freedom from intrapsychic conflict, yet susceptibility to helplessness, panic, and disorientation when removed from one's social frame of reference.

There is so much that as yet we do not know. Many problems have not yet been investigated, on some issues no firm conclusions have emerged, and on many points findings are inconsistent and contradictory. The empirical investigation of personality in Africa is then an enterprise in process that, moreover, unfolds in a continent that for the past several decades has been battered by winds of change. All too often, investigators have attempted to capture psychological characteristics in Africa at a frozen moment. The Triple Reality Model that we have introduced has the capacity of generating and testing predictions in societies in the process of change. As Guthrie and Tanco (1980) have demonstrated, not all social transformations are productive of negative consequences. The Triple Reality Model may enable researchers to pinpoint the conditions that are associated with negative or positive consequences of social change. Moreover, it may be possible to identify those social and cultural conditions that could avert personal dysfunction and social disorganization. Over and above this general expectation, we propose that the investigation of personality in Africa proceed in the following three directions. First, there is a great need of investigating the transitional personality (Peltzer, 1995) found in a great many contemporary African cultures. In the process, an unknown share of findings we have reviewed, based as they are on the behavior of traditional Africans, will be called into question. Second, we emphasize the need for studying variation within Africa, both between cultures and within cultures. The former objective is anticipated by the classical comparisons in field dependence–field independence between the Temne and Mende of Sierra Leone by Dawson (1967). Another example of a meaningful intra-African comparison is provided by Boski's (1983) research on person perception among the three major ethnic components of Nigeria's population: the Hausa, the Ibo, and the Yoruba. Third, increased attention should be directed toward the intrapersonal organization and interrelationship of psychological characteristics. How does individuality come to be expressed in a social context that does not accentuate it? How are the inconsistencies between laissez faire upbringing and rigorous obedience training reconciled? How is parental and filial affection experienced in a society that places a premium on security and acceptance, but is undemonstrative in expressions of warmth and praise? Africa remains a goldmine of psychological information that has been scarcely tapped. It will continue to enrich and make more complex our understanding of the multiple human mechanisms of fulfilling one's needs and attaining one's goals in an intricate, partially gratifying, and partially frustrating environment.

REFERENCES

Agiobu-Kemmer, I. (1984). Cognitive aspects of infant development. In H. V. Curran (Ed.), *Nigerian children: Developmental perspectives* (pp. 74–117). London: Routledge Kegan Paul.

Berry, J. W. (1967). Independence and conformity in subsistence-level societies. *Journal of Personality and Social Psychology, 7,* 415–418.

Binswanger, L. (1958). The existential analysis school of thought. In R. May (Ed.), *Existence: A new dimension in psychiatry and psychology* (pp. 214–236). New York: Basic Books.

Boski, P. (1983). A study of person perception in Nigeria. Ethnicity and self versus other attributions for achievement-related outcomes. *Journal of Cross-Cultural Psychology, 14,* 85–108.

Brislin, R. W., Lonner, W. J., & Thorndike, R. M. (1973). *Cross-cultural research methods.* New York: Wiley.

Bronfenbrenner, U. (1994). Foreword. In R. A. LeVine et al. (Eds.), *Child care and culture: Lessons from Africa* (pp. xi–xvii). New York: Cambridge University Press.

Carothers, J. C. (1953). *The African mind in health and disease: A study in ethnopsychiatry.* Geneva: World Health Organization.

Carr, S. C., McLachlan, M., Zimba, C. G., & Bowa, M. (1995). Managing motivational gravity in Malawi. *Journal of Social Psychology, 135,* 659–662.

Chang, S. C. (1988). The nature of self: A transcultural view: Part I. Theoretical aspects. *Transcultural Psychiatric Research Review, 25*(3), 169–204.

Cole, M., & Bruner, J. S. (1971). Cultural differences and inferences about psychological processes. *American Psychologist, 26,* 867–876.

Cole, M., Gay, J., Glick, J. A., & Sharp, D. W. (1971). *The cultural context of learning and thinking: An exploration in experimental anthropology.* New York: Basic Books.

Collomb, H. (1965). Assistance psychiatrique en Afrique: Expérience sénégalaise [Psychiatric services in Africa: Experience in Senegal]. *Psychopathologie Africaine, 1,* 167–239.

Collomb, H. (1973). Rencontre des deux systemes de soin. A propos de thérapeutiques des malades mentales en Afrique [The encounter of two systems of care: Concerning therapies for the mentally ill in Africa]. *Social Science and Medicine, 7,* 623–633.

Corin, E., & Murphy, H. B. M. (1979). Psychiatric perspectives in Africa: The Western viewpoint. *Transcultural Psychiatric Research Review, 16,* 147–178.

Dada, M. K., & Awaritefe, A. (1988). Locus of control concept in the Nigerian culture. *Nigerian Journal of Psychiatry, 1,* 172–180.

Dasen, P. R., Dembele, B., Ettien, K., Kabran, K., Kamagate, D., Koffi, D. A., & N'Guessan, A. (1985). N'gouèlé, l'intelligence chez les Baoulé [N'guèlé: The concept of intelligence of the Baoulé]. *Archives de Psychologie, 53,* 293–324.

Davol, S. H., & Reimanis, G. (1959). The role of anomie as a psychological concept. *Journal of Individual Psychology, 15,* 215–225.

Dawson, J. L. M. (1967). Cultural and psychological influences upon spatial-perceptual processes in West Africa (Parts I and II). *International Journal of Psychology, 2,* 115–125, 171–185.

Draguns, J. G. (1996). Humanly universal and culturally distinctive: Charting the course of cultural counseling. In P. B. Pedersen, J. G. Draguns, W. J. Lonner, & J. E. Trimble (Eds.), *Counseling across cultures* (4th ed., pp. 1–20). Thousand Oaks, CA: Sage.

Draguns, J. G. (1997). Abnormal behavior patterns across cultures: Implications for counseling and psychotherapy. *International Journal of Intercultural Relations, 21,* 213–248.

Earley, P. C. (1984). Social interaction: The frequency of use and valuation in the United States, England and Ghana. *Journal of Cross-Cultural Psychology, 15,* 477–485.

Eze, N. (1985). Sources of motivation among Nigerian managers. *Journal of Social Psychology, 125,* 341–345.

Guerry, V. (1971). *La vie quotidienne dans un village baoulé* [Everyday life in a Baoulé village]. Abidjan, Ivory Coast: INADES.

Guthrie, G. M., & Tanco, P. P. (1980). Alienation. In H. C. Triandis & J. G. Draguns (Eds.), *Handbook of cross-cultural psychology. Psychopathology* (Vol. 6, pp. 9–60). Boston: Allyn & Bacon.

Hofstede, G. (1984). *Culture's consequences: International differences in work related values.* Beverly Hills, CA: Sage.

Hofstede, G. (1991). *Cultures and organizations: Software of the mind.* London: McGraw-Hill.

Irvine, S. H., & Berry, J. W. (Eds.). (1983). *Human assessment and cultural factors.* New York: Plenum.

Kleiner, R. J., & Okeke, B. I. (1991). Advances in field theory: New approaches and methods in cross-cultural research. *Journal of Cross-Cultural Psychology, 22,* 509–524.

Knapen, M. T. (1970). *L'enfant Mukongo. Orientations de base du système educatif et développement de personalité* [The Mukongo child. Foundations of upbringing and personality development]. Louvain, Belgium: Nauwelaerts.

Krauss, R. (1968). Cross-cultural validation of psychoanalytic theories of depression *Pennsylvania Psychiatric Quarterly, 8,* 24–33.

Landrine, H. (1992). Clinical implications of cultural differences: The referential versus the indexical self. *Clinical Psychology Review, 12,* 401–415.

Leff, J. (1977). *Psychiatry around the globe: A transcultural view.* New York: Marcel Dekker.

Le Guerinel, N. (1971). Le langage du corps chez l'Africain [The language of the body in Africans]. *Psychopathologie Africaine, 7,* 13–56.

LeVine, R. A., Dixon, S., LeVine, S., Richman, A., Leiderman, P. H., Keefer, C. H., & Brazelton, T. B. (1994). *Child care and culture: Lessons from Africa.* New York: Cambridge University Press.

LeVine, R. A., & LeVine, S. E. (1988). Parental strategies among the Gusii of Kenya. In R. A. LeVine, P. M. Miller, & M. M. West (Eds.), *Parental behavior in diverse societies* (pp. 27–36). San Francisco: Jossey-Bass.

Lévy-Bruhl, L. (1928). *How natives think.* London: Allen & Kenwin.

Lewin, K. (1966). *Principles of topological psychology.* New York: McGraw-Hill.

Magwaza, A. S., & Bhana, K. (1991). Stress, locus of control, and psychological states in Black South African migrants. *Journal of Social Psychology, 131,* 157–164.

Maqsud, M. (1981). Locus of control in Nigerian adolescents and their ethnic membership. *Journal of Social Psychology, 113,* 13–19.

McLachlan, M., Nyirenda, T., & Nyando, M. C. (1995). Attribution for admission to Zomba mental hospital: Implications for the development of mental health services in Malawi. *International Journal of Social Psychiatry, 41,* 79–87.

Merton, R. K. (1957). *Social theory and social structure* (Rev. ed.). Glencoe, IL: The Free Press.

Munroe, R. H., & Munroe, R. L. (1972). Obedience among children in an East African society. *Journal of Cross-Cultural Psychology, 3,* 395–399.

Munroe, R. L., Munroe, R. H., & LeVine, R. A. (1972). Africa. In F. L. K. Hsu (Ed.), *Psychological anthropology* (pp. 71–120). Cambridge, MA: Schenkman.

Nathan, T. (1994). *L'influence qui guérit* [The healing influence]. Paris: Editions Odile Jacob.

Nsamenang, A. B. (1992). *Human development in cultural context: A Third World perspective.* Newbury Park, CA: Sage.

Nsamenang, A. B. (1995). Factors influencing the development of psychology in sub-Saharan Africa. *International Journal of Psychology, 30,* 729–740.

Nwachuku, U. T., & Ivey, A. E. (1991). Culture-specific counseling: An alternative training model. *Journal of Counseling and Development, 70,* 106–115.

Okeke, B. I. (1987). *Towards the verification of an interdisciplinary theory of migration: The Nigerian and Israeli contexts.* Unpublished doctoral dissertation, Temple University, Philadelphia.

Okeke, B. I., & Sheku, B. (1997). African law of opposites and the field theory. *Newsletter of the Society for the Advancement of Field Theory, 13*(No. 1).

Ombredane, A. (1954). *L'exploration de la mentalité des Noirs congolais au moyen d'une épreuve projective. Le Congo T. A. T.* [Exploration of the mentality of Congolese Blacks by means of a projective test: The Congo TAT]. Brussels: Institut Royal Colonial Belge.

Ortigues, M. C., & Ortigues, E. (1973). *Oedipe africain* [African Oedipus]. (2nd ed.). Paris: Plon.

Parin, P., Morgenthaler, F. & Parin-Matthèy, G. (1963). *Die Weissen denken zuviel: Psychoanalytische Untersuchungen bei den Dogon in Westafrika.* [The Whites think too much. Psychoanalytic investigations among the Dogon in West Africa]. Zurich: Atlantis Verlag.

Parin, P., Morgenthaler, F., & Parin-Matthèy, G. (1980). *Fear thy neighbor as thyself* (P. Klamerth, Trans.). Chicago: University of Chicago Press.

Parin, P., & Parin-Matthèy, G. (1964). Ego and orality in the analysis of West Africans. *Psychoanalytic Study of Society, 3,* 197–203.

Parker, S., & Kleiner, R. J. (1966). *Mental illness in the urban Negroe community.* Glencoe, IL: The Free Press.

Peltzer, K. (1995). *Psychology and health in African cultures: Examples of ethnopsychotherapeutic practice.* Frankfurt/Main: IKO-Verlag für interkulturelle Kommunikation.

Prince, R. (1968). The changing picture of depressive syndromes in Africa: Is it fact or diagnostic fashion? *Canadian Journal of African Studies, 1,* 117–129.

Reimanis, G., & Posen, C. F. (1980). Locus of control and anomie in Western and African cultures. *Journal of Social Psychology, 112,* 181–189.

Ritchie, J. F. (1944). The African as a grown up nursling. *Rhodes-Livingstone Institute Journal, 1,* 55–60. (Cited in Wober, 1975)

Rotter, J. B. (1966). Generalized expectancies for internal versus external control of reinforcement. *Psychological Monographs, 80,* (Whole No. 609).

Segall, M. H., Dasen, P. R., Berry, P. R., & Poortinga, Y. P. (1990). *Human behavior in global perspective: An introduction to cross-cultural psychology.* New York: Pergamon.

Serpell, R. (1989). Dimensions endogènes de l'intelligence chez les a-Chewa et autres peuples africains [The indigenous dimensions of intelligence among the a-Chewa and other African ethnic groups]. In J. Retschitzky, M. Bossell-Lago, & P.Dasen (Eds.), *La recherche interculturelle: Tome 2* (pp. 164–182). Paris: L'Harmattan.

Smith, P. B., Trompenaars, F., & Dugan, S. (1995). The Rotter locus of control scale in 43 countries: A test of cultural relativity. *International Journal of Psychology, 30,* 377–400.

Sow, I. (1980). *Anthropological structures of madness in Africa.* New York: International Universities Press.

Staewen, C. (1991). *Kulturelle und psychologische Bedingungen der Zusammenarbeit mit Afrikanern* [Cultural and psychological preconditions for cooperation with Africans]. Munich: Weltforum Verlag.

Staewen, C., & Schönberg, F. (1970). *Kulturwandel und Angstentwicklung bei den Yoruba Westafrikas.* [Cultural change and the development of anxiety among the Yoruba of West Africa]. Munich: Weltforum-Verlag.

Tavares, A. M. (1973). *Reflexões sobre problemas de infância africana* [Reflections about the problems of African childhood]. Luanda: Instituto de Investigacaõ de Angola.

Turnbull, C. M. (1972). *The mountain people.* New York: Simon & Schuster.

Wallace, A. F. C. (1970). *Culture and personality* (2nd ed.). New York: Random House.

Whiting, B. B., & Whiting, J. W. M. (1975). *Children of six cultures: A psycho-cultural analysis.* Cambridge, MA: Harvard University Press.

Wilson, D., Sibanda, P., & Torres, C. (1991). Values of Zimbabwean and United States students. *Journal of Social Psychology, 131,* 443–445.

Witkin, H. A., & Berry, J. W. (1975). Psychological differentiation in cross-cultural perspectiove. *Journal of Cross-Cultural Psychology, 6,* 4–87.

Wober, M. (1966). Sensotypes. *Journal of Social Psychology, 70,* 181–189.

Wober, M. (1975). *Psychology in Africa.* London: International African Institute.

Zeldine, G., Ahvi, R., Leuckx, R., Boussat, M., Saibou, A., Haanck, C., Collignon, R., Touranne, G., & Collomb, H. (1975). A propos de l'utilisation d'une échelle d'évaluation en psychiatrie transculturelle [Use of a rating scale in transcultural psychiatry]. *Encéphale, 1,* 133–145.

9

Where Political System Meets Culture: Effects on Efficacy Appraisal

Gabriele Oettingen
Heiner Maier
Max Planck Institute for Human Development and Education

The present chapter focuses on the question: To what extent do political systems and other cultural factors concur in their influence on psychological processes? More specifically, it is asked how they work together in shaping people's efficacy expectations, as these have been identified as one of the most powerful predictors of motivation and successful performance. The chapter has three parts. First, the relevance of political system factors for efficacy appraisal is investigated by taking advantage of an experiment of culture, East and West Berlin before unification. Second, we examine the role of cultural factors independent of political system factors by comparing children's efficacy expectations in different cultures adhering to corresponding political systems: East Berlin versus Moscow and West Berlin versus Los Angeles. Third, we underline the prominent role of the combined working of political system and other cultural factors for efficacy appraisal by considering the value systems (see Smith, Dugan, & Trompenaars, 1996) and children's efficacy beliefs in three former Eastern bloc countries (Czechoslovakia, German Democratic Republic [GDR], Poland) and the Union of Soviet Socialist Republics (USSR). Finally, we suggest future research that could clarify the specific processes involved in efficacy appraisal across cultures.

THE BENEFITS OF A STRONG SENSE OF EFFICACY

Under the influence of the neo-behaviorist tradition following the approach of Edward Chace Tolman (1932/1967), the concept of expectation has been

163

the most powerful cognitive variable predicting motivation and performance to date. Expectations, that is, subjective judgments about how likely
it will be that certain future events will occur or not, are based on past
experience and thus reflect a person's performance history (for a review of
the history of the concepts of expectations, see Oettingen, 1997b). No matter
how expectancy judgments are assessed—as self-efficacy expectations (or
sense of efficacy) that is, expectations as to whether a person can execute
a certain behavior relevant for a desired outcome; as outcome expectations,
that is, expectations as to whether a certain behavior leads to a desired
outcome (Bandura, 1986, 1997); or as generalized expectations, that is,
expectations as to whether a certain desired outcome will occur—evidence
is mounting that optimistic, positive expectations of success foster effort
and persistence and eventually successful performance as well. Findings on
the beneficial effects of optimistic expectations emerge in various life
domains, for example, in the school, work, and sports domain, in the
interpersonal domain, and in the domain of physical and mental health (for
summaries, see Bandura, 1997; Oettingen, 1997b; Scheier & Carver, 1992;
Seligman, 1991; Taylor & J. D. Brown, 1988, 1994).

Because expectations and in particular self-efficacy expectations are
powerful predictors of successful performance, the question of how expectations, and more specifically self-efficacy expectations develop is an important research topic. Two factors are relevant here: first, the cognitive
maturity of a child (Ruble, 1983) and second, the social environment in
which the person is embedded (Bandura, 1986). Whereas cognitive maturity
guarantees the cognitive tools necessary for the child to appraise self-efficacy
expectations, the social environment provides the information that a child
can use for self-efficacy appraisal. If the social environment is an important
factor in determining the emergence of one's sense of efficacy, the sociocultural background of a person should also play a crucial role therein.

POLITICAL SYSTEM AND EFFICACY APPRAISAL

East and West Berlin: An Experiment of Culture

Can political system variables affect the development of self-efficacy, that
is, one's judgment of the extent to which one can carry out the behavior
necessary for a desired outcome? East and West Berlin before unification
was an ideal setting to address this question. Over centuries East and West

Berlin shared a cultural and historical background including one political system. Between 1945 and 1990 East and West Berliners, however, lived under different political systems, communism versus social-capitalism. Possible differences between East and West Berlin can therefore be readily interpreted as stemming from these political system differences and their consequences, for example, their economic, social-structural, and educational consequences.

The consequences of political system differences on the educational context should be of particular relevance for children's sense of efficacy in the achievement domain, that is, whether children believe that they can successfully execute the behavior leading to achieving success and avoiding failure. Which factors of the educational context are critical? To answer this question, it is necessary to consider the information sources that are relevant for efficacy appraisal.

Information Sources of Efficacy Appraisal

Bandura (1986) specified four information sources that people use in forming their subjective efficacy. The principal source is *performance experience*. Successful performances foster a strong sense of efficacy, in particular when achieved in the face of adversity. Failures promote a weak sense of efficacy, especially when experienced early and frequently and if they cannot be discounted as due to lack of effort or unfavorable circumstances. Failures are less harmful if people have already attained an optimistic sense of efficacy through initial frequent successes. The second source of efficacy appraisal is *vicarious experience*. Here the attainments achieved by similar other persons who serve as models are observed. Successes of similar others raise a person's sense of efficacy, whereas failures diminish it (Bandura, 1986). However, the achievements of similar others might also serve as the basis of social comparison. They influence self-efficacy appraisal by providing a standard of comparison against which one's abilities can be judged. Most achievements such as school grades are judged relatively, and one's own capability is inferred by comparing one's attainments to those of one's peers (Festinger, 1954). Third, performance evaluations by other persons can influence one's sense of efficacy. Such active attempts of *verbal persuasion* are particularly effective when the communicator is endowed with competence and authority. A fourth information source results from the *physiological reactions* that a person experiences when confronted with difficult performance situations. For example, feeling one's heart beating during an important test would indicate a low level of efficacy, whereas "staying cool" would be a sign of high self-efficacy.

Efficacy Appraisal in East and West Berlin

Information Sources in the School Context. Considering these four sources of efficacy appraisal, it comes as no surprise that children entering school begin to lose the naive performance optimism that they had maintained until then (Stipek, 1988). In school for the first time students' performance histories are laid bare (performance experience), children have plenty of opportunities to compare themselves with similar others (vicarious experience and social comparison), they are evaluated by authorities (verbal persuasion), and they find themselves in challenging academic situations (physiological reactions). The loss of naive optimism through the school experience should be especially pronounced in educational settings that focus on precise and unambiguous performance feedback, on public evaluation and social comparison, on the authority of the ingroup and the teachers, and on real challenges.

The East and West Berlin School Contexts. East and West Berlin school contexts before unification differed precisely in the factors just reported. In East Berlin differentiated performance feedback was given to each child by the teacher and by the "class collective" from first grade on. Further, performance evaluations were publicized and the child was asked to critically evaluate him or herself in front of the whole class. Moreover, in former East Germany a strictly unidimensional style of teaching (Rosenholtz & Rosenholtz, 1981) was practiced, where children in a given grade level were confronted with the exact same materials, tasks, and tests and were bound to the same pacing, irrespective of their potential or interests. This, too, facilitated differential evaluation by the teachers and the class collective. Finally, the school and leisure domain overlapped considerably (i.e., children from one classroom used to meet again in the same constellation in the afternoon). Thus, the child's performance rank in class was observed by the child herself and all her peers and became a social reality that could hardly be changed.

In contrast, the West Berlin school context favored comparatively more vague and private performance evaluations starting as early as the second school grade, as well as more individualized and multidimensional teaching styles. In addition, the school and leisure context were less likely to overlap in West Berlin. Thus, these children were given more interpretative leeway in forming their subjective sense of efficacy. Because it favored public performance evaluations and standardized teaching strategies, the East Berlin school context should have fostered children's precise estimation of their potential and discouraged self-serving, overly positive self-evaluations to a greater extent than the West Berlin school context.

These differences in educational practices were partly due to diverging educational policies between East and West Berlin. In East Berlin, but not in West Berlin, the educational program, guided by official party doctrine, aimed to develop harmonious socialistic personalities by teaching all students to evaluate themselves "adequately," that is, consistent with the authorities' (i.e., teachers' and class collective's) evaluations of their competence and personal attributes (Franz, 1987; Waterkamp, 1990).

East and West Berlin: A Cross-Sectional Study.   In June 1990, before unification of the two Germanies, we assessed the self-efficacy beliefs and recorded the math and verbal grades of more than 300 East Berlin children from two schools, Grades 2 to 6 (Oettingen, Little, Lindenberger, & Baltes, 1994). We compared the data to a matched study in West Berlin conducted in 1991, involving over 500 children. Children's sense of academic efficacy was operationalized as their judgments pertaining to whether they thought they could try hard, be smart, or have luck when it came to their school performance (see the Control, Agency, Means–Ends Instrument by Skinner, Chapman, & Baltes, 1988).

East Berlin children had a lower sense of academic efficacy than West Berlin children. That is, in comparison to West Berlin children they had less confidence in their ability to exert effort in school, they considered themselves to be less smart, and they thought they would attract less luck. The differences began in the third grade, and were pervasive for the rest of the school years. At the same time, East Berlin children conformed more readily with their teachers' performance evaluations than West Berlin children as indicated by stronger correlations between their efficacy beliefs and the course grades they received from their teachers (Oettingen et al., 1994).

The Role of Intelligence.   In 1991, 1 year after the first assessment, but still before the East Berlin school system adopted the West Berlin educational policies, we returned to our East Berlin schools and replicated our findings (Oettingen & Little, 1993). At this point in time, we also administered the Raven Progressive Matrices Test to measure children's intelligence. We suspected that the observed differences between East and West Berlin children's efficacy beliefs and conformity were due to the scores of less intelligent children, because when entering school less intelligent children are more frequently confronted with negative performance feedback that contradicts their naive optimism. Therefore the less intelligent children may need to revise their initial naive performance optimism to a greater extent than intelligent children. Moreover, because of the initial negative performance feedback they should more readily accept future failure feedback than intelligent children. Most important, this effect should be particularly pronounced in school systems aiming at "adequate" self-evaluation, that is, more in East than in West Berlin.

The differential mean levels between East and West Berlin children's sense of efficacy were due to the scores of children of lower intelligence: Differences emerged in the low- and middle-intelligent children, but not in the intelligent children (Oettingen & Little, 1993). Similarly, East and West Berlin children's differences in readiness to conform to their teachers' evaluations were moderated by their intelligence. For East Berlin children who ranked in the lower third of intelligence, more than 80% of the variance of self-efficacy beliefs were explained by course grades, 40% more than in the respective West Berlin group. For the middle group the difference in explained variance between East and West Berlin children was 16%; no difference in explained variance was observed for the high-intelligent group.

We next considered the correlations within East and West Berlin. In West Berlin, correlations increased with intelligence and were in accordance with a well-known finding: Positive performance feedback is more readily embraced than negative performance feedback. In East Berlin, however, where adequate self-evaluation was the explicit educational goal, less intelligent children accepted their negative reality more readily than more intelligent children accepted their positive reality. Less intelligent children in East Berlin, having received accurate and thus negative feedback from the beginning of school, were not sheltered by a robust sense of efficacy and thus readily accepted the teachers' pessimistic performance evaluations.

Implications for East and West Berlin Children. As mentioned earlier, a growing body of literature suggests that a strong sense of efficacy promotes effortful action and persistence, cognitive and self-regulatory learning skills, reduces fear of failure, and raises standards and aspirations (for a summary, see Bandura, 1997). Accordingly, East Berlin's less intelligent children should have suffered more from the motivational and affective problems linked to a weak sense of efficacy than the West Berlin comparison group. The .90 correlations between children's self-perceptions and teachers' performance evaluations in East Berlin also imply negative consequences for the less intelligent East Berlin children. They reflect the children's ready acceptance of the teachers' pessimistic performance prognosis, which should have considerably narrowed their developmental plasticity (cf. Baltes, Lindenberger, & Staudinger, 1998). In summary, then, our findings suggest that the East Berlin educational background was of disadvantage for the less intelligent children, those children who would have benefited most from the motivational advantages of a strong sense of efficacy.

East Berlin in Transition: A Longitudinal Study. Our hypothesis that the political system and the respective educational goals and practices influenced the development of children's sense of efficacy would be further supported if, after East Berlin adopted the West Berlin school system in fall 1991, the East Berlin data pattern assimilated to that of West Berlin. Indeed, in the spring of 1992, after East Berlin children had been taught according to the West Berlin educational model, the East Berlin children's level of agreement between their perceived self-efficacy and their teachers' performance evaluations decreased to that in West Berlin (Little, Lopez, Oettingen, & Baltes, 1997). It seems, then, that the giving up of the educational goal adequate self-evaluation lessened East Berlin children's agreement with the teachers' performance judgments. In contrast, the level of self-efficacy beliefs did not change. After 1 year of being taught under the West Berlin educational model, East Berlin children still believed less in their capability to exert effort, to be smart, and to have luck in school than their West Berlin counterparts.

In sum, with the advent of the West Berlin school system, agreement between student self-efficacy perceptions and teacher evaluations decreased in East Berlin, whereas the mean levels still did not change. It seems that with the introduction of more privacy in performance feedback and a comparatively more multidimensional teaching style in East Berlin, conformity faded. It might also be, however, that a diminished respect for the authorities' evaluations lessened children's readiness to give in to the teachers' evaluations. Unlike conformity, the level of self-efficacy beliefs does not depend only on the teachers' performance evaluations, but also on the other three information sources of efficacy appraisal. This might be an explanation for why the level of efficacy beliefs did not increase to the West

Berlin level at the same time. However, we expect that in the years or decades to come the level of East Berlin children's efficacy beliefs will eventually parallel those in West Berlin.

Supportive Evidence. How well do the differences in the political systems and their consequences serve as an explanation for the observed differences in East and West Berlin children's sense of efficacy and in students' conformity with the teacher evaluations? We found similar patterns of results from studies that were conducted by other researchers, with different subjects, in different places, and with different instruments. A couple of such studies are reviewed briefly in the following section.

Adolescents with low academic performance from various schools in East Germany were less convinced of their academic potential than their counterpart comparison group from West Germany, whereas there was no difference among students with strong academic performance (Hannover, 1995). Also, the East German youngsters conformed more readily with their teachers' evaluations than did their West German peers. A further study demonstrates the assimilation of East Berlin children's conformity to the West Berlin level after the introduction of the West Berlin school system in East Berlin: East and West German adolescents who were tested in 1993 (i.e., after the East Germans had been taught according to the West German model for 2 years) did not show any differences in conformity anymore. However, as we observed in our sample of younger children, the East German adolescents continued to evince a lower sense of efficacy than the West German comparison group (Ettrich, Krause, Hofer, & Wild, 1996). Taken together, the findings suggest that the educational goal of adequate self-evaluation that was fostered by the policies of former East Germany was effectively implemented: Children and adolescents believed less in their self-efficacy in the eastern than in the western part of Germany. At the same time, students in East Germany conformed more readily with their teachers' evaluations of their performance, a finding that was very sensitive to the changes in the educational context. As the educational goal of adequate self-evaluation was abandoned, East German children became more independent from their authorities' opinions.

More pessimism in subjective efficacy is not only observed in East when compared to West German children and adolescents but also in East versus West German adults. For example, a representative sample of adults in Dresden (East Germany) scored lower in work-related efficacy expectations than a matched sample from Mainz (West Germany; Frese, Kring,

Soose, & Zempel, 1996). Further, higher levels of pessimism in the Eastern part of Germany is not a new phenomenon and thus cannot be attributed to the political changes immediately before the fall of the wall. As early as in the mid-1980s we assessed pessimistic versus optimistic expectations in East versus West Berlin: Explanatory style was extracted from newspaper reports of the 1984 Olympic Games. Despite having more Olympic victories to report, East Berlin newspaper accounts were more pessimistic than West Berlin reports (Oettingen & Seligman, 1990). Finally, pessimism in East Germany is not restricted to the cognitive side of expectations. A study in the mid-1980s pertaining to the affective components of pessimism yielded corroborative evidence: Bar patrons in East Berlin demonstrated more behavior consistent with depressive affect (i.e., turned-down mouths, hunched posture, sheltered bodies, as well as lack of expressive behavior and lack of smiles and laughs) than those in West Berlin (Oettingen & Seligman, 1990). Seven years later, in 1991, the research team returned to the bars. With the changing political system in East Germany fewer turned-down mouths, fewer hunched and sheltered postures, as well as more expressive behavior and more frequent smiles and laughs were observed in the East Berlin bars. In other words, with the fall of the wall the behavior consistent with depressive affect had waned in East Berlin to the level of West Berlin (in 1991 the differences between East and West Berlin patrons were restricted to a higher frequency of expressive behavior in East Berlin; see Oettingen, 1995b). In sum, the political system influences seem to be pervasive: They extend from childhood to adulthood, they endure over time, and they pertain to the cognitive as well as to the affective side of a person's outlook.

CULTURE AND EFFICACY APPRAISAL

Thus far we have been looking for the causes of the observed results in the differences between the two political systems and their effects on educational policies and school environments. However, the political systems of East and West Germany should have affected the educational contexts not only directly via the educational policies, but also indirectly via differential effects on existing cultural values. That is, over the years the two political systems should have positively and negatively reinforced traditional cultural values in unique ways. Indeed, in East and West Germany of the early 1990s had evolved specific cultural values, which by being reflected in the educational context, further influenced the development of children's self-efficacy beliefs. These considerations also imply that the influences on self-efficacy appraisal can be looked upon at three different levels: on the distal level of political system and culture (e.g., norms, values), on the middle level of the societal contexts (e.g., educational, economic), and on the proximal level of psychological processes (e.g., efficacy appraisal; see Fig. 9.1).

Dimensions of Cultural Values: Individualism and Power Distance

The observed differences in children's self-efficacy beliefs were congruent not only with the educational practices but also with the differences between East and West Berlin's cultural values as they existed before the fall of the wall. To illustrate this, we use two prominent dimensions on which societal or cultural values can vary, namely individualism versus collectivism and small versus large power distance (Hofstede, 1991; Triandis, 1995, 1996; see also Laungani, chap. 10 of this volume; McCauley, Ottati, & Lee, chap. 5 of this volume; Peabody, chap. 4 of this volume).

Individualism Versus Collectivism.   Thirty years ago Hofstede conducted a study on work-related values in members of a multinational company that included samples of over 40 cultures. He identified a first

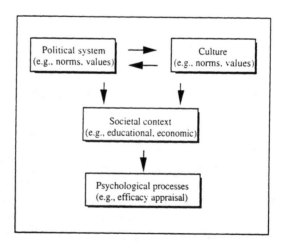

FIG. 9.1. Political system and culture influence societal context and psychological processes.

dimension, which he called individualism versus collectivism. People in individualist cultures value personal goals and are concerned primarily with their own well-being and that of their immediate family. They can be also characterized by a more independent rather than interdependent definition of the self (see Markus & Kitayama, 1994). In contrast, collectivist cultures foster the pursuit of ingroup goals and demand lasting loyalty from the members of the ingroup.

Small Versus Large Power Distance. People in cultures with a small power distance value a comparatively more equal distribution of power and positions of high status are believed to be potentially reachable for the powerless. In contrast, cultures with a large power distance value hierarchical structures and the inequality of status is readily accepted by the powerless. In general, power distance and individualism/collectivism dimensions are correlated, with small power distance being associated with a more individualist orientation.

Cultural Values Translated in the Educational Context

How are the two dimensions of cultural values, individualism versus collectivism and small versus large power distance, reflected in the educational systems? Schools in individualist cultures foster performance feedback and teaching strategies that serve the fulfilment of individual needs and personal potentials and children are expected to learn how to learn. In contrast, the educational context in collectivist cultures promotes goal striving in the service of the ingroup (e.g., the classroom, working group, family) and children are expected to learn how to perform in order to fulfill their role in the ingroup (for a related analysis pertaining to the influence of cultural values on psychotherapy interventions, see Draguns, 1995). Therefore children in individualist cultures should base their self-appraisals of efficacy on information concerning their personal performance (Rosenholtz & Rosenholtz, 1981). In contrast, in collectivist cultures, children should evaluate their self-efficacy in accord with the ingroup members.

In cultures with a small power distance, school is child centered (Stipek, 1991) and students are expected to freely interact with their peers and teachers. They are encouraged to speak up and even to contradict the words of the authorities. Parents are expected to be loyal to their children rather than to the teachers. Appraisal of children's academic efficacy in cultures with a small power distance are therefore more likely to be based on the child's own creation of his or her self-initiated performance history (e.g., outcomes of projects initiated and implemented independently of their teachers' influence) and teachers' evaluations are not given undue weight. In contrast, in cultures with a large power distance, education is teacher centered. Children accept the teacher to be the initiator of all activities and take him or her as the irrefutable and competent authority. Parents are to side with the teachers. In cultures with a large power distance, efficacy appraisal is more likely to be based on a performance history largely guided by the doings of the teachers (e.g., they select the topics and form of studying) and the teachers' verbal evaluations and nonverbal behaviors are heavily weighted in the children's self-efficacy appraisal. In sum, in cultures with a small power differential children are allowed to operate more as origins than as pawns (Ryan & Stiller, 1991).

What do these considerations imply for the observed differences between the East and West Berlin children? Speculating that the political system in East Berlin reinforced comparatively stronger values of collectivism and perhaps even of large power distance, we postulate *indirect effects* of the newly emerged cultural values on the educational system that converge with the *direct* effects of the political systems on the educational context. Interestingly, the direct (explicit rules and regulations) and the indirect (reinforcement of existing cultural values) effects of the political system in East Berlin seem to point in the same direction. Both promote group- and teacher-centered evaluative feedback and teaching styles. This in turn should facilitate children basing their self-efficacy appraisal on unambiguous performance evaluations by the group and the teacher. Our findings of both a comparatively weaker sense of efficacy and higher conformity among East Berlin children when compared to West Berlin children are congruent with these postulations.

Cultural Values Independent of Political System: East Berlin Versus Moscow and West Berlin Versus Los Angeles

If one wants to examine the effects of cultural values independent of the political system, one has to extend the previous research design and add comparisons of *different* cultures with *similar* political systems. We therefore assessed efficacy beliefs in children who were embedded in cultures whose political systems resembled either East Berlin or West Berlin: We compared East Berlin with Moscow and West Berlin with Los Angeles (both the East Berlin and the Moscow samples were tested in 1990, after democratic reforms began, but while Mikhail Gorbachev was still president of the Soviet Union). We chose Moscow and Los Angeles as the two cities of comparison, because they are major cities in the countries with the strongest political influence on East and West Germany, respectively.

Children's sense of efficacy was weaker in East Berlin than in Moscow (N over 500) and in West Berlin than in Los Angeles (N over 600). At the same time, when making their efficacy appraisals, the East Berlin children weighted the evaluations of their teachers more strongly than the Moscow children, and the West Berlin children more strongly than the Los Angeles children (Little, Oettingen, Stetsenko, & Baltes, 1995; Oettingen, 1995a; Stetsenko, Little, Oettingen, & Baltes, 1995). In other words, the children in both parts of Berlin evidenced a lower sense of efficacy and showed higher conformity with the teacher evaluations than the children of the comparison East and West cultures.

Cultural Values in East Berlin and Moscow.   How can we explain these results? We want to consider first the differences in cultural values and educational background between East Berlin and Moscow. Despite the fact that East Berlin adopted the educational goals, regulations, and curricula directly from the political authorities in Moscow, there were large differences between East Berlin and Moscow educational settings with respect to how the demands of the political regime were actually implemented. In the 1980s, Russian politicians and educational scientists complained extensively about the disrespect for authorities (e.g., teachers, political personnel) and the problem of insufficient adherence to educational and political regulations and goals among students. In daily school life these regulations were simply disregarded, merely adopted formally, or taken as a showcase (Ligachev, 1989). In line with these complaints are reports of adolescents deploring the "lack of independence and the excessive petty tutelage by their teachers" (Kon, 1989, p. 60). Furthermore, youngsters disregarded school regulations and enjoyed making fun of teachers (Elkonin & Dragunova, 1967). Overall, this description of everyday school life corresponded to the disrespect for authorities and the disobedience of rules expressed in Russian cultural products such as fairy tales, novels, and proverbs (see e.g., "the sky is high and the tsar is far"). These reports are corroborated by recent findings from a survey (conducted in 1991) which revealed less authoritarianism in Moscow residents than in a corresponding American sample (McFarland, Ageyev, & Abalakina-Paap, 1992).

It seems, then, that in Moscow the rules and regulations of the political system, which emphasized the importance of the ingroup (e.g., class collective) and the authority (e.g., teacher), competed with the traditional values of respecting authorities as mere "showcase," that is, for utilitarian reasons. The discordance between the demands of the political system and the traditional cultural values seems to have resulted in a loose implementation of the political rules and regulations. However, if the rules and regulations mandated by the official party line are only haphazardly followed, the respective group- and teacher-centered educational strategies should be weakened. Thus, self-efficacy appraisal should be largely based on the child's own creation of his or her self-initiated performance history and less so on the evaluations of authority figures. This implies that there is interpretative latitude for the children's subjective efficacy in an optimistic, positive direction.

East Germans, on the contrary, are not known to have rebelled against the rules and regulations imposed by the communist regime. East Germany was one of the last countries of the Eastern bloc to try out new political, societal, and economical developments. Only when they were given allowance by the Soviet regime, did they loosen their political rules and become open to societal change. Then, however, they readily accepted the West German mandates and regulations. In particular, in East Berlin, with its Prussian tradition of dealing submissively with authorities, people did not resist the rules imposed by the communist political system. Because the communist regime also valued loyalty to the ingroup and the authorities, it found in Berlin an opportune context to flourish. If the rules and regulations superimposed by the official party line were meticulously followed, the group- and teacher-centered educational strategies unfolded their full effects on the children's efficacy beliefs. No room for a self-serving, positive interpretation of one's efficacy was left and self-judgments were based completely on the ingroup's and the teachers' evaluations.

To summarize, in East Berlin the political goal of building harmoniously developed socialistic personalities by teaching adequate self-evaluations was diligently observed, whereas in Moscow the respective group- and teacher-centered educational goals and regulations were only haphazardly implemented. These interpretations are consistent with our findings of children's weaker self-efficacy beliefs and higher conformity with the teachers' evaluations in East Berlin when compared to Moscow.

Cultural Values in West Berlin and Los Angeles.   Whereas the observed differences between East Berlin and Moscow seem to be largely due to a differential implementation of the educational rules imposed by the common political doctrine, the differences between West Berlin and Los Angeles can be traced to different educational philosophies in West Germany and the United States. For several decades, *educational philosophies* in the United States have strongly suggested the development and expression of children's personal interests and potentials (see Ames, 1992; Stipek, 1991). Therefore, child-centered and multidimensional teaching styles have been widely introduced. The individual child (and not the group or the teacher) can choose from an array of subjects (e.g., math, art, language) and from a host of tasks (e.g., algebra, geometry). Moreover, the student can determine how he or she wants to go about solving the tasks (e.g., alone, in groups, in school, at home) and at what pace to proceed. Such individualized and multidimensional teaching strategies lead to self-efficacy appraisal based on child-initiated performance, that is, on his or her strengths irrespective of any groups' or authorities' demands. Moreover, such individualized education makes clear, unambiguous performance ranking of students difficult, not only for the teachers, but also for the child herself and for her peers. Finally, privacy as to where a child stands in relation to her classmates is seen as a truism in the United States. Accordingly, children have plenty of interpretative leeway for appraising their efficacy in the positive direction.

Multidimensional teaching styles are largely unknown in West Germany. Rather, the rule is a unidimensional teaching form with the same materials and tests offered to all children in a given classroom. In West Berlin (in contrast to former East Berlin with its strictly unidimensional teaching style; see previous discussion) the teacher has some freedom for individualization (e.g., to form working groups from time to time, to choose learning materials, to create tests). Moreover, in West Berlin privacy of performance feedback has been proposed but not guaranteed in daily school pursuits. Taken together, comparatively more teacher-centered and unidimensional teaching style and comparatively less respect for an individual's privacy in West Berlin is consonant with the observed lower sense of efficacy and higher conformity in West Berlin than in Los Angeles.

How do the observed differences in children's efficacy beliefs between West Berlin and Los Angeles and the corresponding differences in the educational systems relate to the respective cultural values of West Germany and the United States? Hofstede (1991) indeed found less individualism in West Germany than in the United States. Our comparison between West Berlin and Los Angeles, then, suggests again that cultures with collectivist values promote a less optimistic sense of self-efficacy and more conformity than cultures with comparatively more individualist values. Interestingly, a meta-analysis on the relation between efficacy beliefs and academic performance shows that a relatively weak link between efficacy and performance (rs .30–.40) is not only found in Los Angeles but also in other parts of the United States (Multon, Brown, & Lent, 1991).

The observed differences between West Berlin and Los Angeles may also stem from variations in cultural values with respect to power distance. First, in the United States there are recent complaints about an overemphasis on laissez-faire teaching and a lack of authority orientation in the educational practices. Second, although Hofstede viewed both West Germany and the United States as adhering to relatively low power distance, it might well be that in the West German *educational system* the values of large power distance are still more prominent than in the American educational system. At the least, the German academic domain has remained highly traditional despite many attempts to change its hierarchical structure and autocratic student–teacher relationship. German subjects in Hofstede's study were employed in a multinational company that was owned by American entrepreneurs. Such a company might have been less conservative with respect to hierarchy and authority focus than the German educational system.

In sum, in West Berlin, with its relatively collectivistic values, the educational policies were more group and teacher centered than in Los Angeles, where individualist values prevailed and the educational policies fostered individualized and child-centered educational practices. These observations are consistent with a lower sense of efficacy and higher conformity in West Berlin than in Los Angeles.

POLITICAL SYSTEM AND CULTURAL VALUES CONCUR IN INFLUENCING EFFICACY APPRAISAL: SUPPORTIVE EVIDENCE FROM EASTERN EUROPE

Where Political System Matches Culture: East Berlin and Los Angeles

The East Berlin children held an extreme position in our comparative research. Of all samples they were least convinced of their potential and they conformed most readily with the authorities' evaluations. It seems, then, that the political system and other cultural factors there worked together, so that in East Berlin the children's subjective potential was most effectively weakened and their conformity most effectively strengthened.

Children from Los Angeles were also an extreme case. They estimated their potential highest and their self-perceptions were influenced least by the authorities' opinions. As in East Berlin, in Los Angeles the political system and the cultural factors concurred—but in the direction of individualism and low power distance—so that children's subjective efficacy was most successfully strengthened and their conformity most efficiently weakened.

Where Political System Contradicts Culture: West Berlin and Moscow

In West Berlin and in Moscow the political system factors opposed the existing cultural values. We speculate that in West Berlin the democratic political system, which aimed at individualist values and low power distance, collided with the traditional values of collectivism and high power distance. Conversely, in Moscow values of collectivism and large power distance introduced by the communist regime collided with values of individualism and the underlying resistance to authority of traditional Russia. Admittedly, these considerations are speculative, especially considering the fact that Hofstede included in his sample (of over 40 cultures) neither the G.D.R. (or East Germany) nor the U.S.S.R. We therefore do not know where East Berlin and Moscow would range with respect to their values of individualism and power distance.

Dimensions of Cultural Values: Conservatism and Loyalty

Recent findings, however, speak to the question of cultural values in the former USSR and the GDR (or East Germany). Smith et al. (1996) analyzed a large data set assessing cultural values in almost 9,000 employees of business organizations from 43 nations (Trompenaars, 1985). The study, which was carried out in the beginning of the 1980s, goes beyond Hofstede's survey in that it includes nine countries of the former Eastern bloc, including the former USSR and GDR or East Germany. Using multidimensional scaling analyses Smith et al. extracted two central dimensions of cultural values, conservatism and loyal involvement.

Conservatism. The dimension of *egalitarian commitment versus conservatism* embraces three value systems. The first was *achievement versus ascription,* that is, whether status can be effortfully achieved or is ascribed.

An example item would be "the respect a person gets is highly dependent on the family into which he or she is born," to which subjects responded by strongly agreeing or strongly disagreeing. The second value system was *universalism versus particularism,* which referred to whether societal obligations (i.e., to tell the truth, be responsible) or relational obligations (i.e., networking, obligations to a friend) are more highly valued. Moral dilemmas were presented in which the subject had to decide whether, for example, he or she would lie when a sworn witness in order to rescue a friend from being fined. The third value system referred to *self-responsibility versus paternalism,* thematizing whether employers should stay out of their employees' private lives or whether they should get involved in various life domains of their employees (housing, celebration of marriages, etc.).

Loyalty.   The dimension *utilitarian versus loyal involvement* consisted principally of items that were supposed to measure the concept of individualism-collectivism (Smith et al., 1996; Trompenaars, 1985). They were presented in the form of dilemmas about whether involvement in a group is based on utilitarian considerations or loyalty. For example, subjects were asked who should be held responsible for failure—the group member who made the mistake or the whole group? Or subjects were confronted with the dilemma of what children should do with the family business after the father's death—sell it and divide the profit or carry on and improve it?

Relevant for the present context is that both dimensions—egalitarian commitment versus conservatism, and utilitarian versus loyal involvement—correlated substantially with Hofstede's (1991) dimensions of individualism versus collectivism. The more conservative and the more loyal countries' values were, the more collectivist. The dimensions extracted by Smith et al. (1996) also related moderately to Hofstede's dimension of power distance, with higher values on conservatism and loyal involvement corresponding to larger power differentials.

Conservatism and Loyalty in Former Eastern Bloc Countries

Smith and colleages' (1996) discovery that the dimensions of cultural values in former Eastern bloc countries were related to Hofstede's dimensions of individualism and power distance could shed more light on our hypotheses that the concurrence of political systems' and other cultural values play a dominant role in shaping the appraisal of a person's efficacy.

First, their findings support our assumption that cultural values of East Germany in the 1980s were comparatively more collectivist and showed a larger power differential than those of West Germany. Subjects from the former GDR (or East Germany) scored higher on conservatism and on loyalty than those from the former Federal Republic of Germany (FRG or West Germany). Both dimensions are consistent with high collectivism and large power distance. In other words, the communist and the social-capitalist political systems differentially reinforced cultural values in the two Germanies, so that values related to collectivism and large power distance emerged in East Germany to a stronger degree than in West Germany. Thus the Smith et al. (1996) findings support our assumptions about greater collectivist values and focus on group- and teacher-focused education in East versus West Berlin and the resulting lower sense of efficacy and higher conformity in the Eastern part of the city.

Second, the reported analyses by Smith et al. (1996) support our assumption of more individualism and less power distance in Moscow than in East Berlin. The former USSR showed considerably higher values on utilitarian (vs. loyal) involvement than the former GDR. This was precisely the dimension that paralleled the dimension of individualism versus collectivism, and also correlated with small versus large power distance. Thus, our findings of higher efficacy and lower conformity in Moscow than in East Berlin, as well as the description of the highly individual and independent handling of the political and educational regulations in Moscow versus the authority-focused and dependent dealings in East Berlin, seem to be well supported by the corresponding findings of Smith et al. on the level of cultural values.

However, one might argue that the higher sense of efficacy and the lower conformity observed in Moscow and Los Angeles were simply due to the fact that the Moscow and Los Angeles children were growing up in countries that were the world's leading powers. The children's personal efficacy may have been strengthened by their identification with their country's role of power broker or through modeling of the high efficacy and independence of the representatives in their power-maintaining countries. According to Kipnis (1972) power corrupts in the sense that feelings of power go along with illusory positive expectations of success and self-serving attributions. The argument that the differences in geopolitical power of the USSR and East Germany are one of the origins of the observed differences in children's efficacy appraisal would be strengthened if we observed in other Eastern bloc countries of inferior political power, such as

Czechoslovakia and Poland, a sense of efficacy and conformity similar to East Germany, but weaker than in the USSR.

In light of this argument, can we still support our hypothesis that the differences in efficacy appraisal between East Berlin and Moscow are based on the respective differences in cultural values? Again, the analyses by Smith et al. (1996) are informative here. They included former Czechoslovakia and Poland in their study and showed that the cultural values of these two countries resembled those of the U.S.S.R. but distinctly differed from East Germany. Like the USSR, both countries scored higher on individualism than East Germany. More specifically, all communist countries included in the analyses (i.e., Bulgaria, China, Czechoslovakia, East Germany, Hungary, Poland, Rumania, Russia, Yugoslavia) scored moderately on conservatism (i.e., they valued ascription, networking, and paternalism to a moderate degree), but all, including Czechoslovakia, Poland, and the USSR, scored much higher on utilitarian (and lower on loyal) involvement than East Germany.

Subjects from the three former communist countries—USSR, Czechoslovakia, and Poland—valued utilitarian involvement or individualism more than those from the former GDR, who were committed to loyal involvement or collectivism. Thus, in the school contexts of Prague, Warsaw, and Moscow alike, we would expect the educational and political rules to be implemented with less diligence than in East Berlin. This would leave more interpretative latitude for the children's efficacy appraisal, which in turn would foster a stronger, more positive sense of efficacy and encourage less conformity. In summary, if identification with the country's political status in the world plays a dominant role in affecting children's efficacy appraisal, we should find a pattern of efficacy in Prague, Warsaw, and East Berlin that differs from that in Moscow; if the influence of cultural values is critical, we should find similar high levels of self-efficacy beliefs in Prague, Warsaw, and Moscow that would differ from East Berlin.

Efficacy Appraisal in East Berlin, Moscow, Prague, and Warsaw

In spring 1991, shortly after Vá Havel and Lech Walesa were elected presidents of Czechoslovakia and Poland, respectively, we assessed efficacy beliefs in more than 700 children from Prague and almost 200 from Warsaw and compared the data with those of our East Berlin and Moscow samples (Oettingen, Maier, Kotaskova, Smolenska, & Stetsenko, 1997).

The findings yielded support for the dominant role of cultural values for efficacy appraisal. As in Moscow, children in Prague and Warsaw had a stronger sense of efficacy than East Berlin students. At the same time, they conformed less readily with the teachers' evaluations than the children in East Berlin. It seems, then, that countries ranking high on utilitarian involvement foster a stronger sense of efficacy and lower conformity than countries characterized by values of loyal involvement.

Interestingly, the Moscow, Prague, and Warsaw children differed in the means they thought were especially effective for being a good student. Whereas Moscow children thought they were particularly smart, Prague children believed that exerting effort was their strength, and the Warsaw children thought they had luck on their side. East Berlin children, in contrast, had a lower sense of efficacy on all three achievement-related means than the children from the other Eastern European countries. Only in perceived access to ability did they not differ from the children of Prague.

These findings are consistent with our assumption that the communist political system has been confronted with more individualist values in Czechoslovakia, Poland, and the Soviet Union than in Germany. The hypothesis that the communist political system in Germany matched the existing cultural values of relatively high collectivism and large power distance is further supported by Smith et al.'s (1996) findings that West Germany, although not having been ruled by the communist political system, also ranked higher on loyal involvement or collectivism than the USSR, Czechoslovakia, and Poland. In sum, the combined working of the political system and the traditional values of collectivism and large power distance in East Germany seem to be at the core of the East German students' uniquely weak sense of efficacy and high conformity with the teachers' evaluations. As early as the second-grade level, the connection between self-and teacher- evaluations was very strong among the East Berlin children ($r = .79$).

In the beginning of the 1990s it was suggested that communism in cultures characterized by an individualist orientation should be met with more and earlier resistance than in cultures characterized by a collectivist orientation (Pecjak, 1990). It was further suggested that collectivist economic practices should flourish less in traditionally individualist cultures than in collectivist cultures (Draguns, 1996). Our findings suggest that the concurrence of political system and culture does indeed reinforce the existing cultural values and the cultural context in a distinct way, which then impacts on individual functioning. Moreover, they point to efficacy and conformity as possible mediators between cultural context and political resistance. It may well be that in East Germany, where communism met collectivism, the lower sense of efficacy and the higher conformity additionally deterred people from joining the Perestroika movement. In other Eastern European countries, meanwhile, where communism met individualism, relatively high efficacy and low conformity fostered early engagement in political resistance.

IMPLICATIONS FOR INTERPERSONAL RELATIONSHIPS IN ACHIEVEMENT CONTEXTS

Overall, the reported findings suggest that the political system reinforced not only the existing values of the various cultures in a distinct way, but that the differential reinforcement of the existing cultural values affected the development of individuals' efficacy beliefs and their conformity with the evaluations of others. This consideration implies that people in these different cultures may, when they communicate, be confronted with misunderstandings caused by differences in subjective efficacy and conformity.

First, we want to consider problems that might arise in the communication between East and West Germans who shared a cultural tradition but were raised under different political systems. We want to consider two scenarios: first, competition between East and West Germans in achievement situations, and second, social interactions during collaboration. East Germans forced to compete with West Germans may suffer from a motivational disadvantage. When confronted with challenges and difficulties, West Germans may be less likely to forgo their positive self-view than their East German competitors. In the context of a difficult labor market, East Germans might give up earlier and thus suffer on a long-term basis from their weaker sense of efficacy.

Further implications arise for social interactions in achievement situations. For example, when East and West Germans collaborate, the strong sense of efficacy of the West Germans could be considered by East Germans as arrogant and their relatively low conformity as impudent. Conversely, the weak sense of efficacy among East Germans could be thought of as overly pessimistic by West Germans. They might even interpret this as laziness and lack of interest. Further, high conformity with authorities among the East Germans could lead to misunderstandings insofar as they might be scolded as spineless and dependent by West Germans.

That the observed differences in subjective efficacy and conformity are indeed reflected in East and West Germans' stereotypes is supported by a study that showed that both East Germans and West Germans postreunification labeled East Germans as having lower self-efficacy and demonstrating less initiative and more dependence than West Germans (Harenberg, 1991). Thus, our observations support the notion by Lee and Duenas (1995) that in stereotypes can be found a "kernel of truth."

Misunderstandings might arise when East Germans interact not only with West Germans but also with members of other cultures: Of all our samples, the East Berlin children had by far the weakest sense of efficacy and the highest conformity. However, there is reason to be optimistic, at least from an ethnocentric view (the two authors are West Germans). Our data show that it takes explicit educational efforts to make children believe in their failures. As soon as one stops these efforts, and this happened when East Germany adopted the West German school system, students' high conformity with the teachers' evaluations decreased. We do not know, however, how long it will take to strengthen the East German children's self-efficacy.

Interactions between members of the other cultures investigated, may suffer from similar communication problems. For example, the stronger self-efficacy and lower conformity found among the Los Angeles students when compared with the Moscow children (Little et al., 1995) implies that when interacting with Russians, Americans might be tempted to view them as too pessimistic, unmotivated, and dependent. Conversely, Americans could be perceived by Russian partners as unrealistically optimistic, superficial, and resistent to reality feedback. Knowing about such possible misunderstandings is likely to be an important first step to overcoming problems in communication between members of different cultures (Ottati & Lee, 1995).

PSYCHOLOGICAL PROCESSES IN THE CONTEXT OF CULTURE

The findings reported in the present chapter point to the relevance that cross-cultural research has for the psychology of action (see also Oettingen, 1997a). For example, the results from East Berlin suggest that the assumed moderate relationship between subjective efficacy and performance evaluations (Multon, S. D. Brown, & Lent, 1991; Stipek, 1988) does not generalize across cultures, although we observed it in the Los Angeles sample as well. With particular educational practices, children's self-evaluations correspond almost perfectly to the evaluations of their teachers and they do so even when children are as young as second grade.

Triandis (1996) has recently postulated a universal psychology composed of various indigenous psychologies (Kim & Berry, 1993). According to Triandis, the contemporary psychological literature can be seen as a Western indigenous contribution to this universal psychology. Our findings support this notion and further suggest that even seemingly short-lived influences such as political system variables, in combination with existing cultural factors, can substantially affect psychological functioning.

Much cross-cultural research to date is outcome research in the sense that it focuses on whether cultures differ in specific variables of interest, such as structure of personality (Paunonen et al., 1996), emotional expression (Stephan, Stephan, & Cabezas de Vargas, 1996), behavioral problems (Lambert, Knight, Taylor, & Achenbach, 1996), sense of self (Markus & Kitayama, 1994), explanatory style (Lee & Seligman, 1997; Oettingen, 1995a; Oettingen & Seligman, 1990), or self-efficacy beliefs (Little et al., 1995; Oettingen et al., 1994). Specific processes, for example, how self-efficacy is appraised or how self-efficacy influences action, are barely analyzed across cultures. This may be because the implicit assumption in the field holds that these processes are universal. If, however, we take the thesis of a universal psychology built from many indigenous psychologies seriously, we need to examine whether these processes also depend on cultural influences.

Our previous work on action control focused on self-efficacy appraisal as an outcome. Taking a process perspective on self-efficacy appraisal raises at least two new questions. The first question pertains to how sociocultural factors relate to the processes of efficacy appraisal. The second question pertains to how sociocultural factors relate to the processes mediating the relation between self-efficacy and behavior. These issues are briefly outlined next.

The first question is based on the assumption that sociocultural factors should not only influence the frequency, form, and value of the information sources of efficacy appraisal, but also the extent to which the available sources are taken as valid and reliable information for efficacy appraisal. In other words, to what extent do sociocultural factors influence whether people attend to the four information sources of efficacy appraisal, how they weight them, and eventually how they integrate them in their self-efficacy judgments?

The second question relates to cultural influences on the processes by which efficacy beliefs influence thinking, feeling, and acting. Cultures might vary, for example, with respect to whether and how affective variables mediate the relation between efficacy beliefs and action. For example, a strong sense of efficacy in a highly individualist culture is likely to foster pride, whereas in a collectivist culture, it could signal personal responsibility for the ingroup or it might even cause fear of being excluded by the community. Accordingly, when people from collectivist cultures are confronted with new or complex tasks, where arousal and fear are a hindrance, a strong sense of efficacy could be a drawback. For tasks that demand flexibility and complex thinking, the classic motivational benefits of a high sense of efficacy might thus be diminished or even reversed.

CONCLUSION

Political system factors can influence children's academic self-efficacy beliefs in two ways, by direct influence on educational goals and regulations and by selective reinforcement of existing cultural values. Our first study on children's sense of efficacy and their conformity with the teachers' evaluations sought to identify the impact of political system factors on efficacy appraisal by comparing children living in the same culture but under a different political system (East and West Berlin). The differential effects of cultural values independent of political system were examined by a comparative study of children who lived in different cultures that had similar political systems (East Berlin vs. Moscow and West Berlin vs. Los Angeles). The combined effects of political system and cultural values on the development of efficacy beliefs became apparent when two more samples of former Eastern bloc countries were integrated in our comparative research (Prague and Warsaw). Like their peers in Moscow—but not in East Berlin—children from Prague and Warsaw maintained a robust sense of efficacy and strong independence from the authorities in spite of the ingroup- and authority-focused values and goals of the former communist regimes.

ACKNOWLEDGMENTS

Part of the research reported in this chapter was supported by the Max Planck Institute for Human Development. We thank Paul B. Baltes and Todd D. Little for valuable discussions, and Jane R. Brown and Peter M. Gollwitzer for helpful comments on an earlier version of this manuscript.

REFERENCES

Ames, C. (1992). Classrooms: Goals, structures, and student motivation. *Journal of Educational Psychology, 84,* 261–271.

Baltes, P. B., Lindenberger, U., & Staudinger, U. M. (1998). Life span theory in developmental psychology. In W. Damon (Series Ed.) & R. M. Lerner (Vol. Ed.), *Handbook of child psychology: Vol. 1. Theoretical model of human development* (pp. 1029–1143). New York: Wiley.

Bandura, A. (1986). *Social foundations of thought and action: A social cognitive theory.* Englewood Cliffs, NJ: Prentice-Hall.

Bandura, A. (1997). *Self-efficacy: The exercise of control.* New York: Freeman.

Draguns, J. G. (1995). Cultural influences upon psychopathology: Clinical and practical implications. *Journal of Social Distress and the Homeless, 4,* 79–103.

Draguns, J. G. (1996, August). *Freedom: A neglected variable in psychology.* Keynote Address at the Second International Baltic Psychology Conference, Tallinn, Estonia.

Elkonin, D., & Dragunova, T. (1967). *Age-related and individual characteristics of early adolescents.* Moscow: Prosveshenije.

Ettrich, K. U., Krause, R., Hofer, M., & Wild, E. (1996). Der Einflu_. familienbezogener Merkmale auf die Schulleistungen ost-und westdeutscher Jugendlicher [The influence of family-related characteristics on the achievement of young people in East and West Germany]. *Unterrichtswissenschaft, 24,* 106–127.

Festinger, L. (1954). A theory of social comparison processes. *Human Relations, 7,* 117–140.

Franz, S. (1987). *Unsere Schüler zur Selbsteinschätzung befähigen* [Teaching self-evaluation to our students]. Berlin: Volk und Wissen.

Frese, M., Kring, W., Soose, A., & Zempel, J. (1996). Personal initiative at work: Differences between East and West Germany. *Academy of Management Journal, 39,* 37–63.

Hannover, B. (1995). Self-serving biases and self-satisfaction in East versus West German students. *Journal of Cross-Cultural Psychology, 26,* 176–188.

Harenberg, W. (1991). Vereint und verschieden [United and different]. *Der Spiegel, 1,* 10–23.

Hofstede, G. (1991). *Cultures and organizations: Software of the mind.* London: McGraw-Hill.

Kim, U., & Berry, J. W. (Eds.). (1993). *Indigenous psychologies.* Newbury Park, CA: Sage.

Kipnis, D. (1972). Does power corrupt? *Journal of Personality and Social Psychology, 24,* 33–41.

Kon, I. S. (1989). The psychology of independence. *Soviet Education, 31*(9), 57–64.

Lambert, M. C., Knight, F. H., Taylor, R., & Achenbach, T. M. (1996). Comparisons of behavioral and emotional problems among children of Jamaica and the United States: Teacher reports for ages 6–11. *Journal of Cross-Cultural Psychology, 27,* 82–97.

Lee, Y.-T., & Duenas, G. (1995). Stereotype accuracy in multicultural business. In Y.-T. Lee, L. Jussim, & C. McCauley (Eds.), *Stereotype accuracy: Toward appreciating group differences* (pp. 157–186). Washington, DC: American Psychological Association.

Lee, Y.-T., & Seligman, M. E. P. (1997). Are Americans more optimistic than the Chinese? *Personality and Social Psychology Bulletin, 23,* 32–40.

Ligachev, E. (1989). On the course of restructuring the education system and the party's tasks in carrying it out. *Soviet Education, 31*(4), 6–68.

Little, T. D., Lopez, D. F., Oettingen, G., & Baltes, P. B. (1997). *A comparative-longitudinal study of action-control beliefs and school performance: On the role of context.* Berlin: Max Planck Institute for Human Development and Education.

Little, T. D., Oettingen, G., Stetsenko, A., & Baltes, P. B. (1995). Children's action-control beliefs about school performance: How do American children compare with German and Russian children? *Journal of Personality and Social Psychology, 69,* 686–700.

Markus, H. R., & Kitayama, S. (1994). A collective fear of the collective: Implications for selves and theories of selves. *Personality and Social Psychology Bulletin, 20,* 568–579.

McFarland, S. G., Ageyev, V. S., & Abalakina-Paap, M. A. (1992). Authoritarianism in the former Soviet Union. *Journal of Personality and Social Psychology, 63,* 1004–1010.

Multon, K. D., Brown, S. D., & Lent, R. W. (1991). Relation of self-efficacy beliefs to academic outcomes: A meta-analytic investigation. *Journal of Counseling Psychology, 38,* 30–38.

Oettingen, G. (1995a). Cross-cultural perspectives on self-efficacy. In A. Bandura (Ed.), *Self-efficacy in changing societies* (pp. 149–176). New York: Cambridge University Press.

Oettingen, G. (1995b). Explanatory style in the context of culture. In G. M. Buchanan & M. E. P. Seligman (Eds.), *Explanatory style* (pp. 209–224). Hillsdale, NJ: Lawrence Erlbaum Associates.

Oettingen, G. (1997a). Culture and future thought. *Culture & Psychology, 3*, 353–381.

Oettingen, G. (1997b). *Psychologie des Zukunftsdenkens* [Thinking about the future]. Göttingen, Germany: Hogrefe.

Oettingen, G., & Little, T. D. (1993). Intelligenz und Selbstwirksamkeitsurteile bei Ost- und Westberliner Schulkindern [Intelligence and performance-related self-efficacy beliefs in East and West Berlin children]. *Zeitschrift für Sozialpsychologie, 24*, 186–197.

Oettingen, G., Little, T. D., Lindenberger, U., & Baltes, P. B. (1994). Causality, agency, and control beliefs in East versus West Berlin children: A natural experiment on the role of context. *Journal of Personality and Social Psychology, 66*, 579–595.

Oettingen, G., Maier, H., Kotaskova, J., Smolenska, S., & Stetsenko, A. (1997). *The development of control beliefs in children from four Eastern European capitals.* Berlin: Max Planck Institute for Human Development and Education.

Oettingen, G., & Seligman, M. E. P. (1990). Pessimism and behavioural signs of depression in East versus West Berlin. *European Journal of Social Psychology, 20*, 207–220.

Ottati, V., & Lee, Y.-T. (1995). Accuracy: A neglected component of stereotype research. In Y.-T. Lee, L. Jussim, & C. McCauley (Eds.), *Stereotype accuracy: Toward appreciating group differences* (pp. 29–59). Washington, DC: American Psychological Association.

Paunonen, S. V., Keinonen, M., Trzebinski, J., Försterling, F., Grishenko-Roze, N., Kouznetsova, L., & Chan, D. W. (1996). The structure of personality in six cultures. *Journal of Cross-Cultural Psychology, 27*, 339–353.

Pecjak, V. (1990). *Kako se je podrl komunizem. Psihosocialna analiza dogodkov v nekdanjih in sedanjih socialisti cnih de zelah* [How communism collapsed. Psychosocial analysis of events in socialist countries]. Ljubljana, Yugoslavia: Samozolo zba.

Rosenholtz, S. J., & Rosenholtz, S. H. (1981). Classroom organization and the perception of ability. *Sociology of Education, 54*, 132–140.

Ruble, D. (1983). The development of social-comparison processes and their role in achievement-related self-socialization. In E. T. Higgins, D. Ruble, & W. W. Hartup (Eds.), *Social cognition and social development* (pp. 134–157). New York: Cambridge University Press.

Ryan, R. M., & Stiller, J. (1991). The social contexts of internalization: Parent and teacher influences on autonomy, motivation, and learning. In M. L. Maehr & P. R. Pintrich (Eds.), *Advances in motivation and achievement* (Vol. 7, pp. 115–149). Greenwich, CT: JAI.

Scheier, M. F., & Carver, C. S. (1992). Effects of optimism on psychological and physical well-being: Theoretical overview and empirical update. *Cognitive Therapy and Research, 16*, 201–228.

Seligman, M. E. P. (1991). *Learned optimism.* New York: Knopf.

Skinner, E. A., Chapman, M., & Baltes, P. B. (1988). Control, means-ends, and agency beliefs: A new conceptualization and its measurement during childhood. *Journal of Personality and Social Psychology, 54*, 117–133.

Smith, P. B., Dugan, S., & Trompenaars, F. (1996). National culture and the values of organizational employees: A dimensional analysis across 43 nations. *Journal of Cross-Cultural Psychology, 27*, 231–264.

Stephan, W. G., Stephan, C. W., & Cabezas de Vargas, M. (1996). Emotional expression in Costa Rica and the United States. *Journal of Cross-Cultural Psychology, 27*, 147–160.

Stetsenko, A., Little, T. D., Oettingen, G., & Baltes, P. B. (1995). Agency, control, and means–ends beliefs about school performance in Moscow children: How similar are they to beliefs of Western children. *Developmental Psychology, 31*, 285–299.

Stipek, D. J. (1988). *Motivation to learn: From theory to practice.* Englewood Cliffs, NJ: Prentice-Hall.

Stipek, D. J. (1991). Characterizing early childhood education programs. *New Directions for Child Development, 53*, 47–55.

Taylor, S. E., & Brown, J. D. (1988). Illusion and well-being: A social psychological perspective on mental health. *Psychological Bulletin, 103*, 193–210.

Taylor, S. E., & Brown, J. D. (1994). Positive illusions and well-being revisited: Separating fact from fiction. *Psychological Bulletin, 116*, 21–27.

Tolman, E. C. (1967). *Purposive behavior in animals and men.* New York: Appleton–Century–Crofts. (Original work published 1932)

Triandis, H. C. (1995). *Individualism and collectivism.* Boulder, CO: Westview.

Triandis, H. C. (1996). The psychological measurement of cultural syndromes. *American Psychologist,* *51,* 407–415.

Trompenaars, F. (1985). *The organisation of meaning and the meaning of organisation: A comparitive study on the conceptions of organisational structure in different cultures.* Unpublished doctoral dissertation, University of Pennsylvania, Philadelphia.

Waterkamp, D. (1990). Erziehung in der Schule [Education in the school]. In Bundesministerium für innerdeutsche Beziehungen (Ed.), *Vergleich von Bildung und Erziehung in der Bundesrepublik Deutschland und in der Deutschen Demokratischen Republik* (pp. 261–277). Köln, Germany: Wissenschaft und Politik.

10

Cultural Influences on Identity and Behavior: India and Britain

Pittu Laungani
South Bank University

Even a cursory observation reveals that cultures vary in terms of their political, social, economic, and physical environments. For instance, the life experiences and the social arrangements of people living in Baffin Island, where temperatures are often known to drop to 40°C, are likely to be very different from those living in Cheerapunji, where it rains over 400 in. a year! Studies have also shown that there are differences in levels of independence and conformity between the food-gathering communities and the food-hunting communities (Berry, 1967). In addition to physical and geographical differences, it is clear that cultures also vary with respect to their value systems.

The existing value systems have a significant bearing on the religious and social beliefs, the rites and rituals, the kinship patterns, and the social arrangements of the people of that culture and on the development of individual and social identities (Kakar, 1979/1992; Roland, 1988). Values are best defined *as the currently held normative expectations underlying individual and social conduct* (Laungani, 1995). Values have also been defined as universalistic statements about what we think is desirable or attractive (Smith & Bond, 1993). This, however, is a narrow definition because it overlooks the fact that values are both positive and negative. They guide us in terms of actions (behaviors) to be pursued and emulated, and actions to be avoided and discarded. The ethical components of values define for us appropriate and inappropriate behaviors.

Our salient belief systems concerning right and wrong, good and bad, normal and abnormal, appropriate and inappropriate, proper and improper, and the like, are to a large measure influenced by the values operative in our culture. When pressed, why we hold such and such a belief, why this is

191

important and that less so, we may be unable to offer plausible explanations. We might even be mystified as to why we hold certain beliefs dearly.

Yet values, like air, pervade our cultural atmosphere, and we imbibe them often without a conscious awareness of their origins. Values form the bases of social, political, and religious order. They are often the result of past legacies: religious, political, and philosophical. Because these beliefs are passed on over centuries, their roots get deeper and deeper and are not easily severed. Values become an integral part of our psychological and existential being. We carry them as securely as a tortoise its shell. To a large extent, values remain stable over time. However, values may change. Several factors, for example, migration from one culture to another, political, religious, scientific, and technological upheavals, war, insurrection, devastating epidemics, may bring about dramatic changes in our value systems, forcing us to reexamine our evaluations of ourselves, our beliefs, our behaviors, often in unpredictable ways, as Durkheim demonstrated in his classic studies on suicide.

Given the cultural specificity of certain values, it follows that many of our salient beliefs, attitudes, and behaviors, both private and public, are likely to be culture specific. Thus one would expect to find both within and between cultures, differences in the manner in which a variety of problems such as health, illness, mental illness, grief, bereavement, stress, child abuse, work, relationships, and so forth, are defined, conceptualized, and acted upon by peoples of those cultures.

CONCEPTUAL MODEL OF CULTURAL DIFFERENCES

Because private and social behaviors, to a large extent, are influenced by a set of core values operative in a given culture, it would help to posit a theoretical model that would articulate clearly the similarities and differences between different cultural groups, in particular, between Eastern and Western cultures. A theoretical model proposed by Laungani (1990, 1991a, 1991b, 1991c, 1992, 1995, 1996, 1997b) argues that there are four interrelated *core values* or *factors* that distinguish Western cultures from Eastern cultures, and more specifically British culture from Indian culture in terms of their salient value systems.The proposed four theoretical constructs are:

INDIVIDUALISM ... ... COMMUNALISM (COLLECTIVISM)
COGNITIVISM ... ... EMOTIONALISM
FREE WILL ... ... DETERMINISM
MATERIALISM ... ... SPIRITUALISM

It should be noted that the two concepts underlying each factor are not dichotomous. They are to be understood as extending along a *continuum*, starting at, say, *individualism*, at one end, and extending into communalism at the other. A dichotomous approach, however, tends to classify people in "either–or" terms. Such an approach is limited in its usefulness. An acceptance of the dichotmous approach, as Schwartz (1990) in his critique of individualism-collectivism, postulated "that individualist and collectivist values form two coherent syndromes that are in polar opposition" (p. 140). People seldom fit into neat theoretically formulated and/or empirically derived categories. The sheer complexity and variability of human behaviors and responses preclude serious attempts at such categorical classifications.

A dimensional approach on the other hand takes account of human variability. It has the advantage of allowing us to measure salient attitudes and behaviors at any given point in time and over time. It also enables us to hypothesize expected theoretical and empirical shifts in positions along the continuum both within and between cultural groups. Each of the hypothesized dimensions subsumes within it a variety of attitudes and behaviors that to a large extent are influenced by the norms and values operative within that culture. The theoretical bases of these factors have been described at length elsewhere (see Laungani, 1990b, 1991a, 1991b, 1991c; 1992; 1995, 1996, 1997b). Sachdev, has provided an empirical validation of the four factors. In her research study, Sachdev, by means of specifically designed questionnaires, compared the beliefs and values of the British-born Indian schoolchildren with those of the White schoolchildren in West London. The two groups of children—although both born and socialized in a predominantly Western culture—showed marked preferences in terms of their favored value systems. Her research also enabled her to predict the sets of conditions under which an individual's position is likely to shift —*in either direction*— along each continuum. Several sets of related hypotheses have also been subjected to rigorous empirical tests in India (Sachdev, 1992). The analyses of the data lend further support to the aforementioned model.

Further empirical validation of the theoretical model has also been provided by Sookhoo (1995), and Laungani, (1997a, in press-a). In their studies on coronary heart patients suffering from myocardial infarction, a set of questionnaires was administered to the two sample groups, one of which consisted of Asian (males and females of Indian origin) patients and the other of White patients. The patients for the study were randomly drawn from the cardiology department of a medical ward in a hospital in East

London. The analyses of the questionnaires revealed that the two groups showed significant preferences for their favored value systems. In-depth, one-to-one interviews with each of the subjects revealed that the Asian subjects, to a large extent, conceptualized their myocardial infacrtion, its onset, etiology, course of treatment, and eventual prognosis in terms of the determinism and spiritualism, whereas the White subjects saw their infarction in terms of free will. The close-knit family structures of the Asian subjects also enabled them to seek the comfort and security that they believed would assist them in the process of recovery. The White groups, on the other hand, either did not have the close-knit family structures, or preferred not to show any dependence on their family members.

Before discussing each factor it needs to be pointed out that the concepts to the left of each factor are applicable more to the British and to Western cultures in general, and those on the right to the Indians and to Eastern cultures in general. Let us now examine each concept briefly, and trace its relationship to the acquisition of identity and behaviors.

INDIVIDUALISM ... ... COMMUNALISM (COLLECTIVISM)

Over the years, much has been written on the concept of individualism and collectivism (Hofstede, 1980, 1991; Hui & Triandis, 1986; Kim, Triandis, & Yoon, 1992; Matsumoto, 1996; Triandis, 1994), and they have come to mean different things to different people. Many authors have construed the concepts in dichotomus terms, arguing that the sets of values related to each concept are in polar oppostion (Schwartz, 1990).

In so far as the concept collectivism is concerned, the author prefers the word communalism. The arguments for the retention of the word communalism instead of collectivism have been discussed elsewhere (Laungani, in press). Suffice it to say that in employing the term collectivism there is the unvoiced danger of reintroducing the old notions of "group mind," which were abandoned several decades ago. Although the term collectivism appears neutral in its connotation, it does convey a vague impression of large, amorphous crowds of people gathered together, responding to collectivist values.

One of the distinguishing features of Western society is its increasing emphasis on individualism. At an abstract level the concept itself has come to acquire several different meanings: an ability to exercise a degree of control over one's life, the ability to cope with one's problems, an ability to change for the better, reliance upon oneself, being responsible for one's actions, self-fulfilment and self-realization of one's internal resources. As Triandis (1994) pointed out, individualism, in essence, is concerned with giving priority to one's personal goals over the goals of one's ingroup. Individualism has also been the subject of considerable debate among Western thinkers (Bellah, 1985; Lukes, 1973; Matsumoto, 1996; Riesman, 1954; Schwartz, 1990; Spence, 1985; Triandis, 1994; Waterman, 1981). Some writers have argued that the notions of individualism are incompatible, even antithetical with communal and collective interests. The "dog-eat-dog" philosophy is seen as being divisive, inimical in terms of the promotion of communal goals, and in the long run, it alienates fellow beings from one another. However, there are others—among them, Sampson (1977) being the more outspoken of the defenders of individualism—who extol its virtues. Individualism, it is argued, is in keeping with the philosophy of humanism, which emphasizes, among other things, the notion of "dignity of man," its disentanglement from theology and religion, and its espousal of scientific enterprise as the fundamental bases for understanding the universe (Cooper, 1996). In recent years, the increasing popularity of individualism, as Sampson argued, can also be attributed to the Weberian spirit of capitalism and free enterprise. Sampson saw no reason why the philosophy of individualism should not also nurture a spirit of cooperation and coexistence.

How does the notion of individualism affect our understanding of differences in social behaviors?

1. The philosophy of individualism has a strong bearing on the notion of identity. Identity, in Western society, is construed by psychologists and psychiatrists of virtually all theoretical persuasions, in developmental terms, which starts from infancy. And in the process of development, one's identity—according to received wisdom—passes through several critical stages in adolescence, into adulthood. To acquire an appropriate identity that asserts one's strengths, is located in reality, separates the individual from others and is thereby kept distinct from those of others, reflects one's true inner being and leads to the fulfillment or the realization of one's potential, is by no means easy. It often results in conflict, which if unresolved leads to severe stress, and in extreme cases to an identity crisis (Erikson, 1963; Maslow, 1970).

2. Individualism tends to create conditions *that do not permit an easy sharing of one's problems and worries with others.* As Albert Camus

(1955) pointed out several years ago, individualism creates in people an *existential loneliness*, compounded by a sense of the absurd. The emphasis upon self-reliance, the inability to merge one's identity into those of others—familial or social, the expectation of being able to cope with one's problems, imposes severe stress upon the individual and may make the search for one's "true" identity a lifelong quest.

3. One of the dominant features of individualism is its recognition of and respect for an individual's physical and psychological space. People do not normally touch one another, for that is seen as an encroachment of one's physically defined boundaries. Second, physical contact, particularly between two men—an innocent holding of hands in public—may also be misconstrued; it arouses connotations of homosexuality. The taboos related to physical touch are so strong that, even in times of grief, they are not easily violated. Even eye-to-eye contacts between two people are normally avoided. Several studies have shown that the effects of violating another person's physical space lead to severe stress and, in extreme cases, to neurosis (Greenberg & Firestone, 1977; Rohner, 1974).

4. Closely related to the concept of physical space is that of "psychological space". This is concerned with defining boundaries that separate the psychological self from others. It is an idea of immense value in the West, respected in all social situations. It comes into play in all social encounters, from the most casual to the most intimate. One hears of people feeling "threatened," "upset," "angry," "awkward," "confused," and so on, when they feel that their subjectively defined space is invaded. For instance, bereavement in the family is perceived largely as an individual problem, of sole concern to the affected family. One does not intrude, for fear of invading the other person's psychological space. As has been pointed out elsewhere (Laungani, 1992) the notion of physical and psychological space is intertwined with the concept of *privacy*. Privacy implies a recognition of and respect for another person's individuality. Even the most casual encounters between people, in both social and familial situations, are dictated by a tacit recognition and acceptance of the other person's privacy. Several studies have demonstrated that the invasion of privacy leads to severe stress (Spielberger, 1979).

5. At a social level, individualism has also had an effect on the size of the British family structure, which from the postwar period onward has undergone a dramatic change (Eversley & Bonnnerjea, 1982).

Although the nuclear family is still seen as the norm, it is by no means clear how a "typical" British family shall be defined. With the gradual increase in one-parent families—at present around 14%—combined with the fact that just under 25% of the population live alone, the present nuclear family structure, is likely to change even more dramatically. The changes in the size and the structure of families, combined with high levels of social and occupational mobility, may have "destabilized" society, creating a sense of loss of community life, particularly in the urban metropolitan cities.

Communalism (or Collectivism)

Indian society, on the other hand, has been and continues to be community oriented (Kakar, 1981; Koller, 1982; Lannoy, 1976; Laungani, 1989; Mandelbaum, 1972; Sinari, 1984). Most Indians grow up and live in *extended-family* networks. The structural and functional aspects of the extended family, the social and psychological consequences of living within it, have been discussed elsewhere (Laungani, 1989). Suffice it to say that Indian society cannot be seen than other in familial and communal terms. It is and has been for centuries a family-oriented and community-based society. In an Indian family life, one's individuality is subordinated to collective solidarity, and one's ego is submerged into the collective ego of the family and one's community. It may be of passing interest to note here that Indians often use the collective pronoun *we* in their everyday speech. The use of the pronoun we or *hum* (in Hindi) signifies the suppression of one's individual ego into the collective ego of one's family and community. Thus one speaks with the collective voice of others, and in so doing gains their approval. When a problem—financial, medical, psychiatric, or whatever—affects an individual, it affects the entire family. The problem becomes one of concern for the whole family. The problems are discussed within the interlocking network of familial (hierarchical) relationships, and attempts are made to find a feasible solution.

A community in India is not just a collection of individuals gathered together for a common purpose. A community in the sense in which it is understood in India has several common features. People within a group are united by a common caste rank, or *jati,* religious grouping, and linguistic and geographical boundaries. The members within a community generally operate on a ranking or a hierarchical system. (A microcosm of such a ranking or hierarchical system may also be found within each extended-family network.) Elders are accorded special status within the community and their important role is very clearly recognized. Elders, whether they come from rural areas or from large metropolitan cities, are generally deferred to. On important issues, the members of a community may meet and confer with one another, and any decisions taken are often binding on the rest of the members within the community.

However, it needs to be emphasized that for an individual to stay as an integral part of the family and of the community, it is expected that the individual will submit to familial and communal norms, and will not deviate to an extent where it becomes necessary for severe sanctions to be imposed on the deviant or, as an extreme measure, for the deviant to be ostracized. The pressure to conform to family norms and expectations can and does cause acute stress in individual members in the family, leading, in some instances, to psychotic disorders and hysteria (Channabasavanna & Bhatti, 1982; Sethi & Manchanda, 1978).

Identity in India, to a large extent, is *ascribed* and not *achieved*. By virtue of being born into a given caste (this applies mainly to the Hindus who comprise over 82% of the total population of India), one's identity is ascribed at birth. There are advantages and disadvantages in such a traditional arrangement. On the one hand, the individual in an Indian family setup does not have to pass through the critical stages in the process of developing an identity—as is normally the case with children within individualistic cultures. On the other hand, an ascribed identity tends to restrict the choices open to the individual. Although personal choice is central to an individualistic society, it is seen as an exception in a communalistic society. Occupations are largely caste dependent, and caste, of course, is hierarchical and determined by birth. Although movement from the lower caste into a higher caste is virtually impossible, it is, of course, possible (as a result of certain "caste-polluting" actions) to lose one's caste and drop from a higher into a lower caste. Although the pattern of caste-related occupations is beginning to undergo a transformation in the urban areas of India, there is little evidence of such changes in the rural areas of the country, which are inhabited by nearly 80% of the Indian population. One has little choice even in terms of one's marriage partner. Marriages are arranged by the parents of the prospective spouses. Although the "style" of arranged marriages has undergone a modest change within Indian society—particularly among the affluent members of society in the urban sectors of the country—they are still the norm.

One is born into a given caste and is destined to remain in it until death. One's friends too are an integral part of one's extended family network; pressures from the elders and threats of ostracism ensure that one stays within the confines of one's caste and community and seldom or never strays away from it. The major features of individualism and communalism may be summarized as in Table 10.1.

With the exception of the caste system, which is a singularly unique feature of Indian society, other collectivist cultures, including China, Taiwan, Korea, Hong Kong, Philippines, Thailand, Nepal, Pakistan, Iran, Turkey, Portugal, Mexico, Peru, Venezuela, and Colombia, also share most of the features described previously (Cheng, 1996; Gulerce, 1996; Hofstede, 1980; Jing & Wan, 1997; Kim, 1997; Matsumoto, 1996; Sinha, Mishra, & Berry, 1996; Ward & Kennedy, 1996; Yang, 1997). For instance, Yang, in his excellent analyses of the traditional Chinese personality, referred to the tight, close-knit bond between the individual and his or her family. He points out that "Chinese familism disposes the Chinese to subordinate their personal interests, goals, glory, and welfare to their family's interests, goals, glory, and welfare to the extent that the family is primary and its members secondary" (p. 245). Further, in order to attain harmony within the family, it is essential for the individual to "surrender or merge into his or her family, and as a result, lose his or her individuality and idiosyncrasies as an independent actor" (p. 245).

COGNITIVISM ... ... EMOTIONALISM

This is concerned with the way in which the British (the English in particular) construe their private and social worlds and the ways in which they form and sustain social relationships. In broad terms it has been

TABLE 10.1
Major Features of Individualism...Communalism

Individualism	Communalism
Emphasis on high degree of self-control	Such emphasis unnecessary
Emphasis on personal responsibility	Emphasis on collective responsibility
Emphasis on self-achievement	Emphasis on collective achievement
Identity achieved	Identity ascribed
Anxiety is related to the *acquisition* of identity	Anxiety may be related to the "imposition" of a familial and caste-related identity
Emphasis on nuclear families	Emphasis on extended families

suggested by Pande (1968) that *British society is a work and activity-cen-tered* society and, in contradistinction, Indian society is relationship cen-tred. It should be emphasized that these different constructions of their social worlds are not accidental cultural developments. They stem from their inheritance of their different philosophical legacies.

In a *work and activity-centered* society, people are more likely to operate on a *cognitive* mode, where the emphasis is on *rationality, logic, and control.* Public expression of feelings and emotions—particularly among the middle classes in England—is often frowned upon. The expression of negative feelings causes mutual embarrassment and is often construed as being vulgar. Negative feelings and emotions, when they are expressed, are done so in a subtle and oblique manner.

In such a society, relationships are formed on the basis of *shared commonalities.* One is expected to "work at a relationship"—in a marriage, in a family situation, with friends, with colleagues at work, and even with one's children. In a work and activity-oriented society, one's identity, self-image, and self-esteem grow out of one's work and one's attitude to work. Work defines one's sense of worth.

However, work and its relation to self-esteem acquire meaning only when seen against the background of time. Our conception of time is both objective and subjective. At an objective level time is seen in terms of an Einsteinian dimension, where each hour is divided into fixed moments of minutes, seconds, and milliseconds. Each moment (at least on earth) expires at the same speed—an hour passes not a moment sooner, not a moment later. At a subjective level, however, there are variations in our perceptions of time. In a work- and activity-centered society, one's working life, including one's private life, is organized around time. To ensure the judicious use of time, one resorts to keeping appointment books, calenders, computer-assisted diaries; one works to fixed time schedules; one sets deadlines; one tries to keep within one's time limits. One is constantly aware of the swift passage of time, and to fritter it away is often construed as an act of criminality. Time therefore comes to acquire a significant meaning in a work- and activity-centered society. McClelland (1961) has shown that people in general, and high achievers in particular, use metaphors such as "a dashing waterfall," "a speeding train," and so on, to describe time. The fear of running out of time, the fear of not being able to accomplish one's short-term and long-term goals on time, is seen as one of the greatest stressors in Western society. Even casual encounters between friends or between colleagues at work operate on covert agendas. Meeting people is seldom construed as an end in itself; it is a means to an end, with time playing a significant role.

This is not the case in non-Western societies in general, and in Indian society in particular. Although at an objective level, time is construed in virtually the same way as it is in the West, at a subjective level, time in India is seen in *more flexible and even relaxed terms*. Time, in Indian metaphysics, is not conceptualized in linear terms. A linear model of time signifies a beginning, a middle, and an end, or, in other words, a past, a present, and a future. Time, in Indian philosophy, is conceptualized in circular terms, which means that time has no beginning (or its beginning remains unknown), no middle, and no end. These differential conceptualizations have serious implications for our understanding the nature of private and social behaviors.

For instance, at a day-to-day observational level, one does not notice among Indians the same sense of urgency that appears to have become the hallmark of Western society. Time in India is often viewed as "a quiet, motionless ocean," "a vast expanse of sky." It therefore comes as no surprise to learn that in Hindi there is only one word—*kal*—that stands both for yesterday and tomorrow. One gleans the meaning of the word from its context. The only exceptions to this flexible construction of time are to be found in those situations that are considered auspicious: undertaking an important journey, fixing the time of christening, betrothals, weddings, and funerals, and the like. In these situations one is expected to consult the family Brahmin priest, who then consults an almanac from which he (Brahmin priests are male) calculates the most auspicious time for the commencement of that particular activity. Such events, because of their religious significance, are seldom left to chance; one seeks divine guidance in their planning and execution.

The close physical proximity in which people continuously live and share their lives with one another forces a *relationship-centered society* to operate on an *emotional* mode. In such a society, feelings and emotions are not easily repressed, and their expression in general is not frowned upon. Crying, dependence on others, excessive emotionality, volatility, and verbal hostility, both in men and women, are not in anyway considered as signs of weakness or ill-breeding. Because feelings and emotions—both positive and negative—are expressed easily, there is little danger of treading incautiously on others' sensibilities and vulnerabilities, such as might be the case in work-and activity-centered societies. Given the extended-family structure of relationships, emotional outbursts are, as it were, "taken on board" by the family members. Quite often the emotional outbursts are of a symbolic nature—even highly stylized and ritualistic. Given the extreme closeness of life, the paucity of amenities, the absence of privacy, the inertia evoked by the overpowering heat and dust, the awesome feeling of claustrophobia, it is not at all surprising that families do often quarrel, fight, and swear at one another and from time to time assault one another too. But their quarrels and outbursts are often of a symbolic nature—for otherwise such quarrels would lead to a permanent rift, the consequences of which would be far more traumatic than those of living together. There is in such outbursts a surrealistic quality: At one level they are alarmingly real—the words and abuses hurled at one another, vicious and hurtful—yet at another, bewilderingly unreal. They serve no function other than the relief that such "cathartic" outbursts bring. But in a hierarchical family structure, each member within the family soon becomes aware of his or her own position within the hierarchy, and in the process of familial adjustment, learns the normative expressions of emotionality permissible to the person concerned. Even in such emotionally charged situations, the internalized familial norms often prevent the younger members of the family from openly expressing negative emotions toward their elders.

However, in a relationship-centered society, one is forced into relationships from which one cannot or is unable to opt out without severe sanctions being imposed upon the individual. Several studies have shown that one's inability to sever enforced relationships based on birth and caste often leads to severe stress and neurosis (Channabasavanna, & Bhatti, 1982).

The major features of cognitivism and emotionalism, and the relative differences, are summarized in Table 10.2.

FREE WILL ... ... DETERMINISM

There does not appear to be a satisfactory end in sight to the philosophical and scientific wrangles concerning the nature of free will, predestination,

TABLE 10.2
Major Features of Cognitivism...Emotionalism

Cognitivism	Emotionalism
Emphasis on rationality and logic	Emphasis on feelings and intuition
Feelings and emotions kept in check	Feelings and emotions expressed freely
Relations based on shared interests	Relations caste and family based
Relationships often seen as a means to an end	Relationships seen as er ds in themselves
Emphasis on work and activity	Emphasis on relation ships

determinism, and indeterminism. The Aristotelian legacy, although it has undergone several transformations, has remained with us for over 2,000 years (Flew, 1989). Prior to Newton's spectacular achievements, determinism was entangled in its theistic and metaphysical connotations. But after the publication of Newton's *Principia* in 1687, the concept of determinism was partially freed from its theistic connotations, and a nontheistic and mechanistic view of determinism in science, and indeed in the universe, gained prominence. A scientific notion of determinism, with its emphasis on causality, or conversely, its denial of noncausal events, found favor among the rationalist philosophers, who embraced it with great fervor (Popper, 1972). However, it was not until the emergence of quantum mechanics in the early 20th century that determinism in science, if not in human affairs, once again came to be seriously questioned. In keeping with his own views on the subject, Popper (1988) avoided the terms determinism and free will altogether and proposed the term *indeterminism*, which he argued is not the opposite of determinism nor is it the same as free will.

Notwithstanding the unresolved debates in philosophy on the subject, there is a peculiar dualism in Western thinking concerning free will and determinism. Scientific research in medicine, psychiatry, biology, and other related disciplines, including psychology, is based on the acceptance of a deterministic framework—hence the concern with seeking causal explanations, and with predictability in accordance with rational, scientific procedures of prediction. Yet, at a social, psychological, and commonsense level, there is a strong belief in the notion of free will, which manifests itself in the constant proverbs, homilies, poems, and popular advice offered freely to children and adults—often by the very people who adopt a deterministic model in the course of their professional and scientific work (Laungani, 1992).

What do we mean by free will? Free will might be defined as a *noncausal, voluntary action.* However, at a commonsense level it is defined as exercising voluntary control over one's actions. Thus, free will allows an individual to do what he or she wills, and in so doing, take "credit" for his or her successes, and accept blame for his or her failures and mishaps. As a result, one is locked into the consequences of one's own actions. One is entrapped into one's own existential predicament, from which there does not appear to be an easy way out.

Indians, by virtue of subscribing to a deterministic view of life, in a teleological sense at least, are prevented from taking final responsibility for their own actions. The notion of determinism plays an extremely crucial role in Indian thinking. The *law of karma,* which involves determinism and fatalism, has shaped the Indian view of life over centuries (Chapple, 1986; O'Flaherty, 1976, 1980; Reichenbach, 1990; Sinari, 1984; Weber, 1963). In its simplest form, the law of karma states that happiness or sorrow is the predetermined effect of actions committed by the person either in his or her present life or in one of his or her numerous past lives. Things do not happen because *we* make them happen. Things happen because they were *destined* to happen. If one's present life is determined by one's actions in one's previous life, it follows that any problem that affects an individual was destined to happen. Reichenbach (1990) pointed out that the law of karma is not concerned with the *general* relation between actions and their consequences. It is usually held to apply to the moral sphere and is concerned with the moral quality of actions and their consequences. Thus, according to the law of karma we receive the results of our own actions and not another's. The sins of our fathers are not visited upon us. As von-Furer-Haimendorf (1974) pointed out, the theory of karma rests on the idea that the individual has the moral responsibility for each of his or her actions, and hence the freedom of moral choice.

One can see how the law of karma is invoked to explain not only the onset of mental illness, but all sorts of misfortunes that may befall an individual. If one's present life is determined by one's actions in one's previous life, it follows that any illness—mental or physical—that strikes an individual in a family was destined to happen. This idea is not as strange as it might appear at first sight. For in the West too, it is not uncommon to attribute the causes of psychiatric disorders to the patient's past experiences (viz., infantile traumatic episodes, faulty or maladaptive learning, hereditary predispositions, genetic abnormalities, chemical imbalances, etc.). However, in India, the notion of past is carried into one's previous life or lives. Pandey, Srinivas, and Murlidhar (1980), in a study of informants of psychiatric patients in India, found that the most commonly stated causes of psychotic disorders were attributed to physical causes and sins and wrong deeds in their previous and present life. These findings have been corroborated by Srinivas and Trivedi (1982), who, in their study of 266 respondents selected from three villages in South India, attributed, among other factors, "God's curse" (or "the will of Allah" among the Muslims) as one of the most common causes of mental disorders.

The attribution of one's actions in one's previous birth to psychotic disorders takes away the sting and the stigma from suffering. No blame is apportioned to the afflicted individual; it was his or her karma. It was destined to happen. Determinism thus engenders in the Indian psyche a spirit of passive, if not resigned, acceptance. This prevents a person from plunging into an abyss of despair—a state from which the British, and indeed all individualistic societies, because of their fundamental belief in the doctrine of free will, cannot be protected. The main disadvantage of determinism lies in the fact that it often leads to a state of existential, and in certain instances, moral resignation, compounded by a profound sense of *inertia*. One takes no proactive measures; one merely accepts the vicissitudes of life without qualm. Although this may prevent a person from experiencing anxiety, it also prevents the person from overcoming the distressing condition.

The major features of free will and determinism are summarized in Table 10.3.

MATERIALISM ... ... SPIRITUALISM

Materialism refers to a belief in the existence of a material world, or a world composed of matter. What constitutes matter is itself debatable; the question has never been satisfactorily answered (Trefil, 1980). If matter consists of atoms, it appears that atoms are made of nuclei and electrons. Nuceli in turn are made up of protons and neutrons. What are protons and neutrons made of? Gell-Mann (see Davies, 1990) coined the word *quarks*. But quarks, it appears, have their own quirks. In other words, the assumed solidity of matter may indeed turn out to be a myth (Davies, 1990).

The notion of the solidity of matter was robustly debated in 1927 by Heisenberg, in his now famous research paper on indeterminacy in quantum theory (Heisenberg, 1930). Such debates, however, are confined to journals

TABLE 10.3
Major Features of Free Will...Determinism

Free Will	Determinism
Emphasis on freedom of choice	Freedom of choice limited
Proactive	Reactive
Free will is relevant only to one's present life	Determinism affects one's past, present, and future lives
Success or failure due largely to individual effort	Although effort is important, success or failure is related to one's *karma*
Self-blame or guilt is a residual consequence of failure	No guilt is attached to failure
Failure may lead to victim blaming	No blame is attached to victim

of philosophy and science. At a practical, day-to-day level, however, aided by empiricism, one accepts the assumed solidity of the world that one inhabits—but not without paying a heavy price, for such an acceptance gives rise to the popular myth that all explanations of phenomena, ranging from lunar cycles to lunacy, need to be sought within the (assumed) materialist framework. This is evidenced by the profound reluctance among psychiatrists, medical practitioners, and psychologists in general to entertain any explanations that are of a nonmaterial or supernatural nature. Nonmaterial explanations are treated at best with skepticism, and at worst with scorn.

A materialist philosophy also tends to engender in its subscribers the belief that our knowledge of the world is external to ourselves; reality is, as it were, "out there," and it is only through objective scientific enterprise that one will acquire an understanding of the external world and, with it, an understanding of "reality."

The few psychiatrists and psychologists who have steered away from materialistic explanations, or have shown the willingness to consider alternative nonmaterial explanations, comprise a very small minority. Most of them are only too aware that anyone offering such explanations of phenomena is in danger of incurring the wrath of the scientific community. Nonmaterial explanations fall within the purview of the prescientific communities, or in other words, superstitious and backward societies, to be found mainly in underdeveloped countries (and by subtle implication, in collectivist societies).

Let us consider an example to illustrate such forms of thinking in Western society. For over 2,000 years, yogis in India have made claims about their abilities to alter their states of consciousness at will, thereby bringing their autonomic nervous states under voluntary control (Radhakrishnan, 1923/1989). In the *hathayoga*, yogic exercises—or *asanas* as they are called—were claimed to have therapeutic effects for a variety of physical and psychological disorders. Such claims were seldom taken seriously by Western scientists. They were dismissed as unsubstantiated exaggerations. It was not until 1969, when Neal Miller successfully trained his laboratory rats to lower and raise their blood-pressure by selective reinforcement that there began to dawn on the Western mind that there might after all be some substance in the claims made by yoga. Using a similar selective reinforcement strategy, Miller found that he could train his students to exercise voluntary control over their autonomic responses. Suddenly the claims made by the yogis began to acquire credibility.

Miller's performing rats did the trick! Miller's findings opened the doors to yoga in American universities, and research into altered states of consciousness, followed by its applications into techniques of biofeedback, became respectable. The importance given to yogic asanas in a variety of stress management exercises designed by Western experts, then, is therefore hardly an accident.

In Indian thinking, the notion of materialism is a relatively unimportant concept. The external world to Indians is *not* composed of matter. It is seen as being *illusory*. It is *maya*. The concept of *maya*, as Zimmer (1951/1989) pointed out, "holds a key position in Vedantic thought and teaching" (p. 19). Because the external world is illusory, reality, or its perception, lies within the individual, and not, as Westerners believe, outside the individual. This, according to Zimmer, tends to make Indians more *inward looking* and Westerners more *outward looking*. Also, given the illusory nature of the external world, the Indian mind remains unfettered by materialistic boundaries. It resorts to explanations where material and spiritual, physical and metaphysical, natural and supernatural explanations of phenomena coexist with one another. What to a Western mind, weaned on Aristotelian logic, nourished on a scientific diet, socialized on materialism, empiricism, and positivism might seem an irreconcilable contradiction, leaves an Indian mind relatively unperturbed. To a Westerner if A is A, A cannot then be not-A. If dysentery is caused by certain forms of bacteria, it cannot then be due to the influence of the "evil-eye." The two are logically and empirically incompatible. But contradictions to Indians are a way of life. A is not only A, but under certain conditions, A may be not-A. One of the most interesting and differences between Indian thinking and Western thinking is this: Indians believe intuitively the external world to be illusory without actually "knowing" it; the Westerners "know" it to be illusory, without actually believing it. This differential construction of one's physical world has an important bearing on the patterns of their social relationships.

Indian beliefs and values revolve round the notion of spiritualism. The ultimate purpose of human existence is to transcend one's illusory physical existence, renounce the world of material aspirations, and attain a heightened state of spiritual awareness (Radhakrishnan, 1923/1989; Zimmer, 1951/1989). Any activity—particularly yoga—that is likely to promote such a state is to be encouraged.

The major features of materialism and spiritualism are shown in Table 10.4.

CONCLUSION

All cultures, as we have seen, exercise a powerful influence on the development of our identities and in initiating, sustaining, and controlling behaviors. Behaviors that fall outside the established conventional norms may be seen as deviations, and depending on the importance and the functional value of the behavior concerned, pressures—from mild to severe—may be brought to bear upon the individual to conform to the norms. And when that fails, sanctions may be imposed upon the deviant individual, ranging from confinement or incarceration, to ostracism, and so on. Certain forms of deviations in certain instances may be construed as forms of mental aberrations and, once identified, are dealt with in culturally appropriate ways., for example, confinement, medication, exorcism, and so forth, by a culturally accepted "expert" who is trained in such practices.

Thus, each culture devises its own internally consistent sets of rules. To understand a given pattern of behavior in another culture, it is necessary to understand the system of rules and the assumptions that guide the private and social behaviors of people in that culture.

This suggests an adoption of a relativistic position. It is often assumed that the adoption of a relativistic position would put an end to any form of pejorative (or racist) judgments of other cultures—because one is attempting to understand a culture from within the culture's own consistent system of rules (emic perspectives) and not from the investigator's cultural standpoint (etic perspectives). Thus, there would be no need to "order" cultures on a measurable scale of superiority or inferiority, civilized or primitive, and so on. Such an approach would also help to dilute, if not dissolve altogether, the oft-voiced accusations of scientific, educational, and economic imperialism that have been leveled against Western countries by the developing countries.

But the acceptance of relativistic doctrines creates its own peculiar problems. How does one make sense of the internal rules of another culture?

TABLE 10.4
Major Features of Materialism…Spiritualism

Materialism	Spiritualism
The world is solid, "real" physical	The world is illusory—it is *maya*
Rejection of contradictory explanations of phenomena	Coexistence of contradictory explanations of phenomena
Reality is external to the individual	Reality is internal to the individual
People in general tend to be outward looking	People in general tend to be inward looking
Reality perceived through scientific enterprise	Reality perceived through contemplation and inner reflection

One might learn the language in order to learn the rules of the cultural system, but that alone is not enough to guarantee a clear understanding of the principles underlying the rules of the culture. One of the main weaknesses of the relativistic principle, as Doyal and Harris (1986) pointed out, lies in the fact that in an attempt to understand the rules of the culture through translations, one would have to suspend judgments concerning whether a given rule was true or false, rational or irrational. If, for instance, one were to be told that the reason why a woman who had just delivered a baby was depressed (assuming one was able to understand the nuances of meanings associated with the word *depression* and find parallels to one's own understanding of depression in general and postnatal depression in particular) was because of the angry fluttering of birds in her stomach during her pregnancy, one would be totally bewildered by such information. It is obvious, therefore, that if the rules of the language of another culture do not have built into them canons of formal logic and conceptions of rationality, it becomes difficult, if not impossible, to interpret behaviors in any meaningful manner. No judgments of behaviors would ever be possible.

Although one can see the value of adopting a relativistic position, it does not lend itself to a ready acceptance. Relativism as a valid explanatory concept has come to be seriously questioned by several authors, including Gelner (1985). It has also been argued that relativism in recent years has come to acquire a variety of ideological connotations, and is often used as a gag to stifle any recognition of genuine differences in opinions, beliefs, values, and behaviors. In that sense, therefore, it is potentially dangerous. Its blanket acceptance has no room in it for any genuine understanding of cross-cultural differences in a variety of fields. The uncritical acceptance of relativism, as Popper (1963) has demonstrated, leads to an epistemological cul-de-sac. It does not permit one to transcend one's cultural boundaries. One is forever doomed to languish within the narrowly defined boundaries of one's culture.

However, to question relativism does not necessarily mean that there are no behaviors that are not culture specific. Some obviously are, and have been specifically recognized as such. Clear catalogues of culture-specific behaviors—particularly in the field of mental disturbances—have been examined by various authors working in this area (Draguns, 1981, 1990; Verma, 1988). It therefore seems reasonable to assume that some behaviors are culture specific and some universalistic.

The chapter highlighted the salient value systems of people in India and in England. Although India and England were singled out for a closer examination, it is clear that to a large measure the value systems described in this chapter are also applicable to other individualist and collectivist cultures. The chapter also examined the influence of cultural values on a variety of private and public behaviors of the peoples of the two cultures.

The postulated conceptual model allowed us to describe each of the dominant value systems as extending along a continuum, thus *suggesting that the perceived differences in the behaviors of people may, more often than not, be a matter of degree and not of kind.* Such a formulation has one or two distinct advantages over a dichotomous formulation. First, it enables one to measure any changes in value systems that may occur in an individual due to migration from one culture to another (e.g., a person moving from a collectivist to a individualistic culture, and vice versa). Second, it enables one to measure the influence of acculturation of second-generation children of parents who have emigrated to another culture. To what extent do children imbibe the values of the new culture into which they are born, and to what extent do they internalize the values of the parents' culture? Third, it enables one to hypothesize the source and types of variations in attitudes, values, and behaviors that are more likely to be influenced by those living in another culture.

Cultures shape us, and we, in turn, shape our cultures.

REFERENCES

Bellah, R. N. (1985). *Habits of the heart: Individuation and commitment in American life.* Berkeley: University of California Press.

Berry, J. W. (1967). Independence and conformity in subsistence-level societies. *Journal of Personality and Social Psychology, 7,* 415–418.

Camus, A. (1955). *The myth of Sisyphus.* London: Hamish Hamilton.

Channabasavanna, S. M., & Bhatti, R. S. (1982). A study on interactional patterns and family typologies in families of mental patients. In A. Kiev & A. V. Rao (Eds.), *Readings in transcultural psychiatry* (pp. 149–161;. Madras, India: Higginbothams.

Chapple, C. (1986). *Karma and creativity.* Albany: State University of New York Press.

Cheng, C. H. K. (1996). Towards a culturally relevant model of self-concept for the Hong Kong Chinese. In J. Pandey, D. Sinha, & D. P. S. Bhawuk (Eds.), *Asian contributions to cross-cultural psychology* (pp. 235–254). New Delhi: Sage.

Cooper, D. E. (1996). *World philosophies: An historical introduction.* Oxford, England: Blackwell.

Davies, P. (1990). *God and the new physics.* London: Penguin.

Doyal, L., & Harris, R. (1986). *Empiricism, explanation and rationality: An introduction to the philosophy of the social sciences.* London: Routledge.

Draguns, J. G. (1981). Psychological disorders of clinical severity. In H. C. Triandis & W. R. Brislin (Eds.), *Handbook of cross-cultural psychology* (Vol. 5). Boston: Allyn & Bacon.

Draguns, J. G. (1990). Culture and Psychopathology: Toward specifying the nature of the relationship. In J. J. Berman (Ed.), *Nebraska symposium on motivation, 1989* (pp. 235–277). Lincoln: Nebraska University Press.

Erikson, E. (1963). *Childhood and society,* London: Penguin.

Eversley, D., & Bonnerjea, L. (1982). Social change and indicators of diversity. In R. N. Rapaport, M. P. Fogarty, & R. Rapaport, (Eds.), *Families in Britain, 75–94.* London: Routledge & Kegan Paul.

Flew, A. (1989). *An introduction to Western philosophy* (Rev. ed.). German Democratic Republic: Thames and Hudson.

Gelner, E. (1985). *Relativism and the social sciences.* Cambridge, England: Cambridge Universty Press.

Greenberg, C. I., & Firestone, I. J. (1977). Compensatory response to crowding: Effects of personal space and privacy reduction. *Journal of Personality and Social Psychology, 35*(9), 637–644.

Gulerce, A. (1996). A family structure assessment device for Turkey. In J. Pandey, D. Sinha, & D. P. S. Bhawuk (Eds.), *Asian contributions to cross-cultural psychology* (pp. 108–118). New Delhi: Sage.

Heisenberg, W. (1930). *The physical principles of the quantum theory.* Berkeley: California University Press.

Hofstede, G. (1980). *Culture's consequencs: International differences in work-related values.* Beverly Hills, CA: Sage.

Hofstede, G. (1991). *Cultures and organizations: Software of the mind.* London: McGraw-Hill.

Hui, C. H., & Triandis, H. C. (1986). Individualism-collectivism: A study of cross-cultural researchers. *Journal of Cross-Cultural Psychology, 17,* 222–248.

Jing, Q., & Wan, C. (1997). Socialization of Chinese children. In H. S. R. Kao & D. Sinha (Eds.), *Asian perspectives on psychology* (pp. 25–39). New Delhi: Sage.

Kakar, S. (Ed.) (1992). *Identity and adulthood.* Delhi: Oxford India Paperbacks. (Original work published 1979)

Kakar, S. (1981). *The inner world—A psychoanalytic study of children and society in India.* Delhi: Oxford University Press.

Kim, U. (1997). Asian collectivism: An indigenous perspective. In H. S. R. Kao & D. Sinha (Eds.), *Asian perspectives on psychology* (pp. 147–163). New Delhi: Sage.

Kim, U., Triandis, H. C., & Yoon, G. (Eds.). (1992). *Individualism and collectivisim: Theoretical and methodological issues.* Newbury Park, CA: Sage.

Koller, J. M. (1982). *The Indian way: Asian perspectives.* London: Collier Macmillan.

Lannoy, R. (1976). *The speaking tree.* Oxford, England: Oxford University Press.

Laungani, P. (1989, October 28). Cultural influences on mental illness. *Political & Economic Weekly,* pp. 2427–2430.

Laungani, P. (1990). Turning eastward—An Asian view on child abuse. *Health & Hygiene, 11*(1), 26–29.

Laungani, P. (1991a, July). *The nature and experience of learning. Cross-cultural perspectives.* Paper read at a conference on experiential learning, University of Surrey, Guildford, England.

Laungani, P. (1991b, June). *Preventing child abuse and promoting child health across cultures.* Paper presented at The United Nations Conference on Action for Public Health, Sundsvall, Sweden.

Laungani, P. (1991c, July). *Stress across cultures: A theoretical analysis.* Paper presented at the conference of The Society of Public Health on Stress and the Health Services, London.

Laungani, P. (1992). Assessing child abuse through interviews of children and parents of children at risk, *Children and Society, 6*(1), 3–11.

Laungani, P. (1995). Stress in Eastern and Western cultures. In J. Brebner, E. Greenglass, P. Laungani, & A. O'Roark (Eds), *Stress and emotion* (Vol. 15, pp. 265–280). Washington, DC: Taylor & Francis.

Laungani, P. (1996). Research in cross-cultural settings: Ethical considerations. In E. Miao (Ed.), *Cross-cultural encounters. Proceedings of the 53rd annual convention of International Council of Psychologists* (pp. 107–136). Taipei, Taiwan: General Innovation Service.

Laungani, P. (1997a). Cross-cultural investigations of stress, anger, and coronary heart disease. In *Rage and stress: Proceedings of the national 1996 conference of the International Stress Management Association* (pp. 16–50). London: ISMA Publications.

Laungani, P. (1997b). Patterns of bereavement in Indian and English society. In J. D. Morgan (Ed.), *Readings in thanatology* (pp. 67–76). Amityville: Baywood Publishing.

Laungani, P. (in press). Coronary heart disease in India and England: Conceptual considerations. *International Journal of Health Management.*

Lukes, S. (1973). *Individualism.* Oxford, England: Basil Blackwell.

Mandelbaum, D. G. (1972). *Society in India* (Vol. 2). Berkeley: University of California Press.

Maslow, A. (1970). *Motivation and personality* (2nd ed.) New York: Harper & Row.

Matsumoto, D. (1996). *Culture and psychology.* Monterey, CA: Brooks/Cole.

McClelland, D. C. (1961). *The achieving society.* Princeton, NJ: Van Nostrand.

Miller, N. E. (1969). Learning of visceral and glandular responses. *Science, 163,*(3866), 434–435.

O'Flaherty, W. D. (1976). *The origins of evil in Hindu mythology.* Berkeley: University of California Press.

O'Flaherty, W. D. (1980). *Karma and rebirth in classical Indian traditions.* Berkeley: University of California Press.

Pande, S. (1968). The mystique of "Western" psychotherapy: An Eastern interpretation. *The Journal of Nervous and Mental Disease, 146,* 425–432.

Pandey, R. S., Srinivas, K. N., & Muralidhar, D. (1980). Socio-cultural beliefs and treatment acceptance. *Indian Journal of Psychiatry, 22,* 161–166.

Popper, K. (1963). *Conjectures and refutations.* London: Routledge & Kegan Paul.

Popper, K. (1972). *Objective knowledge: An evolutionary approach.* Oxford, England: Clarendon.

Popper, K. (1988). *The open universe: An argument for indeterminism.* London: Hutchinson.

Radhakrishnan, S. (1989). *Indian philosophy* (Vol. 2, centenary ed.). Delhi: Oxford University Press. (Original work published 1923)

Reichenbach, B. R. (1990). *The law of Karma: A philosophical study.* Honolulu: University of Hawaii Press.

Riesman, D. (1954). *Individualism reconsidered.* New York: Doubleday Anchor.

Rohner, R. P. (1974). Proxemics and stress: An empirical study of the relationship between space and roommate turnover. *Human Relations, 27*(7), 697–702.

Roland, A. (1988). *In search of self in India and Japan.* Princeton, NJ: Princeton University Press.

Sachdev, D. (1992).*Effects of psychocultural factors on the socialisation of British born Indian children and indigenous British children living in England.* Unpublished doctoral dissertation, South Bank University, London.

Sampson, E. E. (1977). *Psychology and the American ideal. Journal of Personality and Social Psychology, 15,* 189–194.

Schwartz, S. H. (1990). Individualism-collectivism: Critique and proposed refinements. *Journal of Cross-Cultural Psychology, 21,*(2), 139–157.

Sethi, B. B., & Manchanda, R. (1978). Family structure and psychiatric disorders. *Indian Journal of Psychiatry, 20,* 283–288.

Sinari, R. A. (1984). *The structure of Indian thought.* Delhi: Oxford University Press.

Sinha, D., Mishra, R. C., & Berry, J. W. (1996). Some eco-cultural and acculturational factors in intermodal perception. In: J. Pandey, D. Sinha, & D. P. S. Bhawuk (Eds.), *Asian contributions to cross-cultural psychology* (pp. 151–164). New Delhi: Sage.

Smith, P. B., & Bond, M. H. (1993). *Social psychology across cultures: Analysis and perspectives.* Hemel Hempstead, England: Harvester Wheatsheaf.

Sookhoo, D. (1995, August). *A comparative study of the health beliefs and health practices of British Whites and Asian adults with and without myocardial infarction.* Paper read at the 53rd annual convention of the International Council of Psychologists, Taipei, Taiwan.

Spence, J. T. (1985). Achievement American style: The rewards and costs of individualism. *American Psychologist, 40,* 1285–1295.

Spielberger, C. D. (1979). *Understanding stress and anxiety.* London: Harper & Row.

Srinivas, D. K., & Trivedi, S. (1982). Knowledge and attitude of mental diseases in a rural community of South India. *Social Science Medicine, 16,* 1635–1639.

Trefil, J. (1980). *From atoms to quarks: An introduction to the strange world of particle physics.* New York: Scribner's.

Triandis, H. C. (1994). *Culture and social behaviour.* New York: McGraw-Hill.

Verma, S. K. (1988). Mental illness and treatment. In J. Pandey (Ed.) *Psychology in India: The state-of-the-art,* (Vol. 3, pp. 289–337). New Delhi: Sage.

von-Furer-Haimendorf, C. (1974). The sense of sin in cross-cultural perspective. *Man, 9,* 539–556.

Ward, C. A., & Kennedy, A. (1996). Crossing cultures: The relationship between psychological and socio-cultural dimensions of cross-cultural adjustment. In J. Pandey, D. Sinha, & D. P. S. Bhawuk (Eds.), *Asian contributions to cross-cultural psychology* (pp. 289–306). New Delhi: Sage.

Waterman, A. A. (1981). Individualism and interdependence. *American Psychologist, 36,* 762–773.

Weber, M. (1963). *The sociology of religion* (4th ed). London: Allen & Unwin.

Yang, K. S. (1997). Theories and research in Chinese personality: An indigenous approach. In: H. S. R. Kao & D. Sinha (Eds.), *Asian perspectives on psychology* (pp. 236–264). New Delhi: Sage.

Zimmer, H. (1989). Philosophies of India (Bollingen Series XXVI). Princeton, NJ: Princeton University Press. (Original work published 1951)

11

Stereotype Legacy: Culture and Person in Japanese/American Business Interactions

Laura Miller
Loyola University

Within cross-cultural psychology there is a welcome growth in research on international differences in personality found in business or organizational settings. It is particularly noteworthy that so much of this work relates to Japanese business, including leadership (Misumi, 1985; Schmidt & Yeh, 1992; Smith, Misumi, Tayeb, Peterson, & Bond, 1989), worker motivation (Schwalb, Schwalb, Harnisch, Maehr, & Akabane, 1992), conflict (Sethi, 1975), salespeople (Dubinsky, Michaels, Kotabe, Lim, & Moon, 1992), and negotiation (Adler & Graham, 1989; Goldman, 1994). In addition to these general topics, we find specialized studies of preferred managerial types using the Myers–Briggs Type Indicator (Reynierse, 1995), gender-role and managerial stereotypes (Powell & Kido, 1994; Schein, Mueller, Lituchy, & Liu, 1996), and women's personality traits and career attitudes (Matsui, Ohsawa, & Onglatco, 1991).

Some scholars are particularly interested in understanding cross-cultural encounters (Brislin, 1981; Brislin, Cushner, Cherrie, & Yong, 1986; Gudykunst & Nishida, 1994; Moghaddam, Taylor, & Wright, 1993). Weisz, Rothbaum, and Blackburn (1984) examined Japanese and American differences in attribution and found that tendencies toward either internal attribution or external attribution may be linked to people's relationship with the environment. In the Japanese case, according to the researchers, control over the environment is accomplished through accommodation, whereas in the American case it is gained through direct action. They inferred that

213

in interethnic settings, these differences in attributional styles and methods for control of the environment will yield negative interethnic perceptions.

A popular paradigm seen in much of this literature is that Japanese individuals have a proclivity toward collectivism whereas Americans place an extreme emphasis on *individualism* (Bond & Forgas, 1984; Hofstede, 1980; Yamaguchi, 1994). This paradigm may be useful as a starting point for identifying potentially sweeping differences, as a type of first approximation prior to actual analysis. Nevertheless, there is a danger in using it exclusively as the primary explanatory framework. Social theorists have pointed out that cultural propensities are often tied to historical or economic processes. Riesman, Glazer, and Denney (1950) and Bell (1976) linked social values of individualism or collectivism to economic trends, noting that during periods of economic affluence societies promote greater individualism, whereas economic stagnation results in a focus on community and social problems. Using the categories of individualism and collectivism in an uncontexted, ahistorical manner may lead to the assumption that these proclivities are timeless traits that are somehow inherent to particular populations.

In addition, although a characterization of Japanese as predominantly group oriented might have been true in the immediate postwar period, it does not seem to capture the current behavior and values of the majority of Japanese under the age of 40. One outcome of economic prosperity during the last few decades has been the erosion of adherence to a collectivist ideology by the Japanese themselves, and more emphasis on individualism (Sengoku, 1991; Shimizu, 1987). A term currently popular in Japan to describe this cohort, who are represented in media as individualistic, hedonistic, materialistic, lacking in commitment, and selfish, is *shinjinrui*, "new human beings." In recent opinion polls, Japanese between the ages of 16 and 39 express attitudes that stress individual needs and desires over community or workplace (Nihon Keizai Shimbunsha, 1997). This group is much more willing to change jobs and is less interested in the benefits afforded from corporate loyalty. Also exemplary of the new generation's quest for individuality is the popularity of diverse personality prototypes and typologies in young women's magazines (Miller, 1997).

Unlike the perspective of most scholars in the field of psychology, where culture is treated as merely a mediating influence, anthropologists who study personality believe that perception of self and others is primarily the product of culturally contexted identities. The anthropological challenge to categories of personality that are posited as universal is best seen in the work of Shweder and D'Andrade (1980), who questioned whether or not linguistic labels for personality traits represent behavioral validity. Shweder (1979a, 1979b) reviewed some of the assumptions found in culture and personality literature, and noted that cross-cultural research depends on a simplification and essentialization of traits without regard for indigenous models of personality. Thus, interest shifted to native understandings of these indigenous models rather than reliance on experimental methods for generating cross-cultural comparisons.

Following a brief review of anthropological research on Japanese conceptions of self, I discuss a few of the personality stereotypes Japanese and Americans in business settings have about each other. Inferences based on differences in cultural assumptions and communicative phenomena that might underlie a few of these stereotypes are then suggested.

THE JAPANESE SELF

Because of a long history of anthropological interest in Japan, there is considerable work in a variety of specialized subfields, including the psychological anthropology of Japan and the anthropology of Japanese business (for a review of this literature see Kelly, 1991). Included among the early studies of "national characteristics and modal personality" (in which predominant personality traits were attached to entire national groups) is Benedict's (1946) famous book *The Chrysanthemum and the Sword*. Benedict tried to explain contradictory traits in the Japanese character through a discussion of how both indulgence and discipline contribute to their formation. Contemporary anthropologists view Benedict's work with mixed feelings and are divided over its merits: Despite numerous factual errors many still hold glimmers of admiration for the psychological insights she provided. The book's controversial status is party due to its pedigree, because it was commissioned in 1944 by the Foreign Morale Analysis Division of the War Office's Information Department to help explain wartime actions and to provide counsel for occupation policy. Although the book is now regarded as a dusty classic in the United States, where it only sold around 30,000 copies, it is still avidly read and admired in Japan. The Japanese version has gone through around 139 printings, sold 2.3 million copies, and is now in its eighth edition (Befu, 1996).

Critics point out that many of Benedict's (1946) posited personality traits were part of American wartime stereotyping of the Japanese: brutal and sadistic samurai who may also be gentle and aesthetic, people who are brave yet timid, insolent but polite. Johnson's (1988) study of how Americans have viewed the Japanese over time illustrates how either positive or negative versions of the Japanese character depend on historical and economic circumstances. For example, after the war "deviousness" became "quietness," and "cruelty" turned into "stoicism." Johnson cautioned that we use grand characterizations carefully, taking into account their impermanence and possible multiplicity. These days few anthropologists have confidence in studies of national characteristics and modal personality. The idea that entire ethnic groups can be described and compared with lists of linguistic labels is now widely regarded as too simplistic. Even in the early days of the popularity of such studies they were viewed as problematic. Wallace (1952) found that only between 28% and 37% of the adult population in his study possessed the modal personalities (based on 21 features) of their group.

Other early studies of Japanese cultural psychology were carried out by DeVos (1973, 1985), who relied on projective testing and surveys to illuminate issues of infant socialization, individual achievement motivation, social deviancy, and dependency orientation. By the 1970s, however, the focus of interest shifted from "traits" that could be used as labels for entire populations to description of the dominant cultural themes and values expressed in individual behavior and the life trajectory (Lebra, 1976; Plath, 1980).

Anthropologists also began to attend to the role of cultural models in the creation and maintenance of ethnic characterization. Several scholars approached this issue through an examination of publicly expressed ideologies of Japanese identity contrasted with actual practice and observed behavior (Goodman & Refsing, 1992; Sugimoto & Mouer, 1989). Of particular interest has been the development of reified cultural constructions of Japaneseness seen in the phenomenon of *nihonjinron*, "theories of the Japanese" (Befu & Manabe, 1990; Dale, 1986; Sugimoto & Mouer, 1989). This dominant ideology submerges class, regional identity, gender, ethnicity, and other Japanese social diversity in a rhetoric of homogeneity. A folk model of "typical" life involving collectivism, self-effacement, and harmonious, family-based corporate life is accepted not simply as a description of the values found among male workers of elite firms—it is commonly and routinely taken as the embodiment of the basic Japanese personality, regardless of social status, ethnicity, gender, and other diversity (Kelly, 1986; Miller, 1995a). Nevertheless, although the folk model and its consequent depictions of ethnic personality traits is largely erroneous (Japan is much more heterogenous than commonly recognized, and these are idealized traits based on less than one third of the population), it still has great power and meaning in everyday Japanese mental representations of themselves. The sociologist Merton (cf. 1968) stressed this many years ago in the Thomas Theorem: "If men define situations as real, they are real in their consequences" (p. 475). Despite the empirical status of Japanese diversity, the folk model will exert influence on popular representations of Japanese modal personality, and will also effect Japanese and American interethnic interactions, a point to which I return later.

More recent anthropological studies have turned to subjective views of the self—how people think of themselves as individuals—rather than idealized personality traits or cultural themes. This interest in indigenous modes for locating the self has been labeled *ethnopsychologies* (White, 1992; White & Kikpatrick, 1985). Kondo (1990), drawing on feminist theories, saw the Japanese self as changing and "crafted" into multiple identities in the course of ongoing interaction. Based on her experience working in a small confectionery shop in Tokyo, she found meanings of self constantly created and repositioned among the male artisans and female part-time subordinates who were her coworkers. Bachnik (1992a,1992b, 1994a, 1994b) examined the organization of the self through the paired concepts of *uchi/soto* (inside/outside). Using both linguistic material and ethnographic observations, Bachnik also uncovered shifting constructions of the self. Similarly, contributors to the edited book entitled *Japanese Sense of Self* (Rosenberger, 1992) explicated how the Japanese define themselves with particular attention to situated inside–outside and public–private dimensions. These dimensions in turn influence the degree of formality and verbosity we find. As Neustupný (1987) noted, Japanese conversation is not easily initiated with outgroup members. Anthropological descriptions of the Japanese self are similar to the social psychological notion of a relational self or an interdependent self, which is thought to be characteristic of collectivist societies (Markus & Kitayama, 1991; Misumi, 1985; Yamaguchi, 1994).

Perhaps more than any other model of Japanese personality, this focus on situated context allows for a less simplistic and one-dimensional view. Kelly (1991) noted that although there is wide disagreement about concepts of Japanese selfhood, the most successful theories and models are those in which the role of ideology and context are taken into consideration, whereas merely ahistorical generalizations have proven less serviceable. For example, a common characterization of Japanese as "hierarchical" (and Americans as "egalitarian") fails to take into account how status differences are not *things*, but processes created during interaction. Japanese businesspeople do not continuously, or exclusively, orient to each other as representatives of preassigned social categories or statuses, so hierarchical status between any two people will not necessarily be expressed the same way, or even appear in every interaction. Videotaped and audiotaped instances of naturally occurring Japanese workplace interaction (Miller, 1996) demonstrates that workers do not always manifest hierarchical relationships linguistically, even though, if asked, they claim it is obligatory behavior that is always present. Behavior toward a boss in one setting, in which hierarchy and formality may be exhibited, might be quite different in another setting, where intimacy is fostered through informality and egalitarian speech patterns. There are two points to learn from this. First, although acknowledging the power and role of ideology in social life, we should not confound it with empirical description. Second, rather than simply relying on over-generalized, all-encompassing descriptors, we should focus on how the expression of particular personality traits or behaviors, such as formality or informality, might correlate with specific settings or with categories of interactants, and how these contrast with American counterparts.

An upsurge of interest in Japan during the 1970s and 1980s led to further research and writing that often synthesized findings from both the psychological and anthropological literature. This is an extensive genre in which we find many worthwhile books (e.g., Hall & Hall, 1987), in addition to many that are just plain awful (e.g., DeMente, 1981).

JAPANESE AND AMERICANS IN BUSINESS INTERACTIONS

The reality of the global business environment created a new readership for the Japan book trade. What once were mainly Japan buffs and specialists became a markedly different audience. The new market reflected the fact that many people read about Japan because they believed it was essential in order to do well in business. Most of the inaugural books and articles in this genre, which appeared on the scene with surprising briskness, were not much more than travel guides dressed up with superficial descriptions of Japanese culture (for a review of this literature, see Miller, 1987). In other cases authors took existing social science concepts about personality and intercultural communication from academic literature and applied them to hypothetical Japanese-American business interactions. For instance, Alston (1985), March (1982), Moran (1981, 1985), Norbury and Bownas (1980), and Pascale and Athos (1981) all cited the prior research of social psychologist Barnlund (1974, 1975), psychiatrist and psychoanalyst Doi (1973, 1974), and anthropologist Lebra (1976) as evidence to support their explanations for problems in Japanese and American business interactions.

A second wave of writing, although still frankly pragmatic in orientation, included several books that focused on the interactions that occur, or are likely to occur, between Japanese and those of other cultural backgrounds (usually Americans). Most of this literature presented qualitatively analyzed case studies or "critical incidents" as a method for describing the sort of sticky patch one should expect to encounter (Gercik, 1992; Hall & Hall, 1987; Kataoka, 1991; March, 1992; for a review see Miller, 1994d). After the saturation of the market by first-wave books that were generally shallow, there was a demand for books such as these that were not only deliberately useful, but descriptively or analytically rich as well (Heidkamp, 1992; Nashima, 1990). What characterizes this literature overall was the attempt to incorporate psychological characteristics and cultural values into descriptions of differences between Japanese and Americans in business settings.

Although useful in alerting the grossly uninformed about basic differences in cultural assumptions and practice, these studies often hinged on previous generalizations as established facts (rather than ideological constructs) that could "explain" interethnic problems. The result is that, without attempting to locate other possible causes of misunderstanding and misinterpretation, researchers relied exclusively on unquestioned "national" personality stereotypes to unpack or explicate the data they gathered from interviews, questionnaires, surveys, personal impressions, and anecdotal stories. Although able to account for some interethnic problems, this approach often neglected critical cultural or linguistic differences that are below a level of conscious awareness, thus beyond the range of data collected through these self-report methods.

MUTUAL STEREOTYPES

The stereotypes and perceptions that Americans hold about Japanese are not much different from the stereotypes Japanese hold of themselves, and vice versa. These shared stereotypes frequently form complementary or mirror images of each other. There are numerous instances of other groups who hold mutual stereotypes arising from interethnic contact. Both Basso (1970) and R. Scollon and S. Scollon (1981) described the interlocking images of the silent, taciturn Athabascan or Western Apache speaker, and the boastful, loquacious Anglo. In many instances these stereotypes derive from differences in contrasting norms for when silence or volubility are considered appropriate for each group (a situation similar to the Japanese and American case). For Western Apache or Athabascans, volubility is related to intimacy, and individuals feel uncomfortable talking much until they know the other person well. On the other hand, American English speakers view "chatting someone up" as an appropriate method for getting to know them better. Yet rather than viewing this as a product of situated difference in cultural rules for conduct, participants on both sides point to stereotypical ethnic characterizations as explanation. Americans and Japanese likewise have many sets of parallel portraits of themselves and each other. Thirty years ago Abate and Berrien (1967) described analogous stereotypes of deference and affiliation for Japanese and dominance and autonomy for Americans. In later decades macrolevel differences between Japanese and Americans that are thought to contribute to interethnic difficulties continue to be presented as oppositions, such as the ones listed in Table 11.1.

Barnlund's research (1974, 1975) on differences between Japanese and American communication, described as a "classic" work by Ramsey and Birk (1983, p. 238), is based on mutual beliefs about differences that are said to exist in areas such as topics for conversation, favorite forms of interaction, self-disclosure, and tactility. The American and Japanese student respondents to his questionnaire described Americans as self-assertive, frank, and informal, whereas Japanese were characterized by both groups as reserved, formal, and evasive. Based on these traits, Barnlund inferred that Americans will prefer spontaneous forms of conversation, and enjoy talking to a broad range of people. On the other hand, Japanese will value regulated and prescribed forms of interaction, and will be more discriminating in who they select as interactants. Given these tendencies, Barnlund proposed the types of problems these differences may create. He concluded that the Japanese might feel communicatively invaded, whereas Americans will be annoyed at formalities. Furthermore, Japanese will view Americans as flippant about formality, insensitive to status, too tactile, and overly hasty

TABLE 11.1

Studies of the Stereotypes of Japanese and Americans

Study	Japanese	American
Doi (1974)	nonverbal, indirect	verbal, direct
Condon (1974)	subjective, indirect, idealistic	objective, direct, realistic
Barnlund (1975)	low tactility, selective	high tactility, nonselective
Gibney (1979)	indirect, cooperative	direct, competitive
Pascale & Athos (1981)	indirect, cooperative	direct, competitive
March (1982)	indirect, cooperative	direct, competitive
Ramsey & Birk (1983)	nonverbal, indirect, holistic, harmonizing	verbal, direct, quantitative, persuasive
Okabe (1983)	synthetic, relativism, groupism, idealism	analytical, absolutism, individualism, realism
Graham & Herberger (1983)	indirect, cooperative	direct, competitive
Graham & Sato (1984)	cooperative, implicit	competitive, explicit
Alston (1985)	indirect, cooperative	direct, competitive
Young (1985)	dualism, formalism, honor/obligation	unitarianism, pragmatic, contract
Hall & Hall (1987)	high context, indirect	low context, direct
Linowes (1993)	indirect	direct

in decision making. Americans in turn will view Japanese as overly ritualistic, distant, evasive, and two-faced.

Studies conducted in Japan on the communication perceptions of Japanese and foreigners (Naotsuka et al., 1985) contrasted informants' views on a variety of hypothetical interethnic interactions. Problem areas investigated included verbal directness, degree of formality, privacy, arrogance, decision making, and individual or group orientation. The researchers concluded that a lack of awareness of different attitudes about each of these areas resulted in negative judgments by each group of the others' behavior. For example, they found that foreigners are often embarrassed or angered by the quantity and nature of personal questions posed by their Japanese acquaintances. These questions are intended by Japanese to learn information about someone in order to establish them as members of their *uchi* or inside circle. When American recipients of such questions evade them or provide ambiguous answers, Japanese view it as a refusal to share oneself and a rebuffing of friendship.

Doi (1962, 1973, 1974) coined the popular concept of *amae* (from the verb *amaeru*) to refer to Japanese interdependence and the desire to be indulged. In the context of Japanese and American encounters, Doi believed that *amae* leads to a distinct emphasis on nonverbal and passive communication for Japanese, which will diverge from the verbal emphasis of Americans. Doi (1974) also noted that the Japanese concepts of *tatemae* (public self) and *honne* (private self) will result in communicative misinterpretation when Americans decode this duality as two-facedness or insincerity (see Pervin, chap. 2 of this volume).

Numerous other researchers have carried on this legacy of contrasting stereotypical traits in an effort to show how awareness and understanding of them may benefit interethnic business. Ramsey and Birk (1983), and Okabe (1983) provided overviews of the literature on complementary Japanese and American personality traits and communicative styles, offering them as candidates for why misunderstanding occurs. Loveday (1986) discussed differences in the prosody of Japanese and English speakers, and suggested that these differences may result in difficulties in interethnic interactions. He claimed that when Japanese speak slowly it indicates thoughtfulness, yet this pace elicits impatience and frustration on the part of Westerners. March (1982) examined negotiation styles and the cultural and psychological information he saw as necessary for doing business. Focusing on a few actual case studies, he suggested that negotiations may go astray due to differences in posited communicative styles.

Moran (1985) used published materials, interviews with Japanese and American businesspeople, and case studies to illustrate the cultural assumptions relevant to business interactions. Although occasionally drawing from the storehouse of stereotypes, he also linked many misunderstandings to differences in business practice rather than going back to these tired platitudes. For example, in his discussion of the Japanese consensus system, he correctly presented it as a pragmatic and down-to-earth process rather than some sort of mystical, spontaneous product of group consciousness and harmony, as others such as Arggle (1982) and Kerlinger (1951) have done. Graham (1983) also looked at Japanese and American communicative styles in business. Using videotapes of simulations and content analysis, he found that Japanese and Americans are much nearer each other in number of conversational overlaps and silences than either group is to Brazilians.

Hall and Hall (1987) have written a book that explores contrasts in Japanese and American culture, behavior, and personality characteristics based on case studies and interviews. Drawing from earlier research on concepts of time and space, they posited some American and Japanese differences in these areas. They also provided concrete recommendations for how Americans can avoid misunderstandings, often in the form of "checklists" that offer admonitions such as "be patient," "take the long-term view," and "be prepared." Their most helpful advice concerns American expectations of privacy and personal space, and how these contrast with Japanese assumptions.

With at least two decades of intense scholarship behind us, an enormous literature on this subject has accumulated. Despite the wonderful insights and powerful findings it provides, there are still some troubling issues that need to be considered. First, in most cases the etic perspectives of researchers means that native ethnopsychologies are rarely considered. What we find instead are reductionist approaches in which researchers posit some selected personality traits, and then look for them in interviews, questionnaires, simulated interactions, and remembered encounters.

Second, there is a tendency to view personality and behavioral features as inherent aspects of "cultures." Yet as Moerman (1988) cogently illustrated, culture is not a uniformly owned property, but is created, negotiated, and contested during the course of interaction. This narrow focus on two cultural groups and lists of polarized traits neglects social variables such as class, gender, education, regional difference, and other possible intraindividual variation.

Finally, there is often an uncritical acceptance of consciously reported accounts of difference as constituting the core of the problem in interethnic encounters. Most research is either cross-cultural, in which information about two cultures is compared and potential problems are hypothesized, or else is based on reconstructed memories of interethnic encounters. We might, therefore, legitimately ask whether or not our reliance on crude personality stereotypes of ethnic groups as the primary explanation for difficulty has prevented us from locating other, locally contexted and specific causes for misunderstanding. Only recently have some researchers begun to use tape recordings of naturally occurring encounters between Japanese and Americans as the unit of study (Iino, 1996; Miller, 1991a, 1991b, 1994a, 1994b, 1994c, 1995b, 1996). Perhaps microanalysis of what happens in these taped encounters will aid our understanding of the nature of Japanese and American interaction.

REAL PEOPLE AND ACTUAL ENCOUNTERS

Scholars in the field of sociolinguistics have determined that many misunderstandings occur at a level of unconscious awareness (Basso, 1970;

Gumperz, 1982a, 1982b; R. Scollon & S. Scollon, 1981). People frequently make situated judgments based on unconscious expectations, yet analyze any resulting problems as personality traits, or as common characteristics of particular ethnic groups, thus contributing to ethnic stereotyping. For example, R. Scollon (1981) found that negative stereotypes are attributed to English speakers who take long pauses during conversation. Scherer (1972) noted that English speakers with louder voices are often considered confident and assertive. Tannen (1981a, 1981b) located aspects of conversational style that underlie stereotypes of New York Jewish speakers. Using taped data from naturally occurring conversation, she found that these speakers employ fast, overlapping talk to indicate involvement and interest. She asserted that the personality stereotype of the "pushy" New Yorker derives in part from this culturally different communicative pattern.

The mutual stereotypes that Japanese and Americans have about each other may likewise be based on interpretations of other phenomena besides personality. One difference relates to culturally based styles of speaking. For instance, an aspect of communicative style that is often overlooked is how listeners in a conversation attend to a speaker's talk. Miller (1991b, 1994a) claimed that Japanese and American listening styles are unconscious features of communication that are often carried over into interethnic conversations. When Americans do not listen Japanese-style, they are viewed by their Japanese interlocutors as having personalities that lack empathy, and as cold or analytical types. This contributes to the stereotype of Americans as "logical" and "individualistic." Americans, in turn, are apt to misinterpret Japanese listening as excessive agreement and compliance, thereby buttressing the stereotype of Japanese as lacking individuality.

Occasionally, the Japanese perception of Americans as "direct," "forthright," and "straightforward," or the American perception of Japanese as "evasive" or "indirect," relates to linguistic factors rather than to personality characteristics (Miller, 1994b). The syntactic and discourse structures of Japanese allows for constructions in which information that is obligatory in English grammar may be omitted. An example is the second- and first-person pronouns, essential in English but often implicit in Japanese. Americans who overuse pronouns when speaking Japanese frequently sound excessively direct, even rude, to native speakers. In other cases, speakers of one language do not always notice or identify the formulaic expressions and prefacing words that are used to buffer negative responses (Miller, 1994b). One consequence is that, using the grammar and norms of their respective languages, Japanese interpret Americans as outspoken and brash, whereas Americans see Japanese as ambiguous and formal.

There may also be different assumptions about the nature of the interaction, expectations about business procedure, and culturally specific criteria for identifying and conducting communicative tasks such as explaining, giving directions, or complaining (Miller, 1994b). Something as seemingly straightforward as differences between what Japanese and Americans view as the purpose of business meetings may lead to misinterpretations (Miller, 1994c). The American assumption that meetings are about problem solving, conflict resolution, and other active, participatory behavior contrasts with Japanese expectations. In many cases, much of what Americans do in what they consider a "proper" meeting is done by Japanese prior to such a formal event in premeeting interactions. Japanese meetings often are nothing more than ritual events to publicly express decisions after the problem solving, conflict resolution, and other participatory work has already been negotiated in private. The result is that, even when empirically both Japanese and Americans afterwards can see on videotapes that neither of these traits are being manifested, during the interaction itself Americans who are trying to quickly schedule meetings are characterized by Japanese as pushy, whereas Japanese reluctance to do so until after private negotiation is viewed by Americans as evasiveness. In other words, a difference in business procedure gets translated into personality stereotypes.

Perhaps the most important distinction in Japanese and American encounters will be the nature of the social relationships of the speakers. The crucial dimension of *uchi/soto* (inside/outside) defines those aspects of one's personality that will be evident during conversation. In presenting the public or outside self to strangers or outgroup members, and in certain culturally specific settings (such as ritual events), Japanese will tend to display deferential, hierarchical, self-effacing conduct. The private personality, in which an individual may display confidence, assertiveness, and directness, will be reserved for interactions with coworkers, friends, and family. Most Americans only meet the public selves of Japan, and interpret these as the "true" personality. The withholding of the personal self in public settings, including a college class when answering a questionnaire, produces a skewed portrait. (When viewing American public behavior, Japanese in turn see it as deficient in restraint and sensitivity.) Thus, the social relationship of speakers embedded in a situation will modify expectations of appropriate reserve and volubility. Because first encounters with others create lasting impressions, perhaps this difference in appropriate verbal behavior accounts for some common stereotypes.

In those cases where the characterization is not negative, and is accurate most of the time, what could be wrong in maintaining and buttressing these ethnic stereotypes? Lee (1997) proposed that accurate stereotypes "tell us something about the modal personality, that is, the *predominant* characteristics of a given population. Stereotypes allow us to see the forest before we focus on the trees." One problem with his premise is that traits that may be "predominant" in one setting, or when speaking to one type of individual or interlocutor, will be radically different in another setting, or with other categories of participant. (An American's indirectness and reserve when speaking to a widow at a funeral would be different than when speaking to a child at her birthday party.) The uncritical acceptance of stereotypes, regardless of their nature or accuracy, might therefore contribute to the misinterpretation and misunderstanding of situated motives, actions, and behavior. (This was also illustrated in the earlier example concerning differences in listening behavior.) The following example relates to another prevalent stereotype. Descriptions of Japanese as reserved and nonverbal, which mainly characterize interactions with strangers, or *soto* "outside" settings, are probably not effective for understanding behavior in closer relationships, including those between coworkers in business environments. These are social situations in which a high incidence of joking, complaining, and the sharing of what Americans might regard as private information of the "none-of-your-business" variety are typical Japanese methods for forging group solidarity (Miller, 1991a, 1994a). Americans who work in Japanese offices occasionally have difficulty with this behavior, which is viewed as "unprofessional" in the American corporate world. Their refusal to engage in what they see as trivial chit-chat with coworkers brands them as cold, distant, and lacking in empathy by their Japanese colleagues. In addition, armed with a belief that Japanese are always polite and indirect, Americans who gradually begin to form friendships with them are often shocked and put off by the abundance of probing or personal questions. Because this behavior doesn't fit the stereotype, Japanese attempting to form closer relationships with Americans are often viewed as aberrant, impertinent, and intrusive. Every year groups of high school teachers visiting from Japan have home-stay experiences in the United States, a setting that falls into the *uchi* or inside, private category. I have been told by numerous American home-stay families of their astonishment, and discomfort, when their new Japanese acquaintances ask them why they don't have children, or what their annual salaries are! The Japanese teachers, in turn, tell me how these Americans seem unwilling to engage in the true sharing of self that is important for creating the bonds of friendship. Because they hold a strong stereotype of Americans as forthright and open, this reluctance to share certain types of information is construed as deliberate unfriendliness. Rather than invoke common stereotypes, we should instead learn to identify those cultural and social *situations* in which particular personality traits or communicative styles are seen as desirable.

In addition to the underlying cultural and sociolinguistic frames used in interethnic encounters, we also need to acknowledge the power of the cultural convictions we carry. Despite the fact that Americans can, and frequently are, evasive, cooperative, and self-effacing in business, highly valued individualism will overshadow actual behavior in participants' minds. One outcome is that stereotypes of American managerial style as direct, outspoken, and confrontational is often more ideological than actual. Wasson's (1996) study of everyday talk in an American corporation, based on videotapes of naturally occurring talk, demonstrates that workers shift from presenting selves that are independent and commanding to selves that are cooperative and group oriented. Yet when asked to describe these conversations, the workers remember only the behaviors that resemble the stereotype of the competitive, direct, and therefore "good" manager. An important task, therefore, is understanding the distinction between reified cultural values that generate stereotypes, and actual ongoing, culturally contexted behavior in the real world.

My perspective here is not that stereotypes are unhelpful because of the reasons Jussim, McCauley, and Lee (1995) posited for why many social scientists have disdained them: that stereotypes are "irrational," "illogical," or "negative," or that they are not "100% generalizations." Rather, my uneasiness with the prevailing enshrinement of these traits, even when these are positive or do not appear to evoke negative evaluations, is that: (a) They are based on limited interactions with a very narrow class of people (male workers in elite firms who are strangers) and are therefore not representative of most of the population most of the time, (b) they are based on consciously remembered behavior, ignoring the differences in either linguistic or unconscious behavior that actually creates and fuels them, and (c) they are often reified images that are part of cultural ideology, and are thus folk models that may have political functions that change dramatically over time.

In some cases stereotypes function as guideposts that identify differences in values and assumptions, as Lee and Duenas have suggested (1995). In the Japanese and American case, stereotypes may be useful only if we are careful to first determine the nature of the setting and the social relationships of those involved. From that starting point we may then point to stereotypical traits and behaviors that are believed by each society, respectively, to be appropriate to those specific settings and types of encounters. Unfortunately, in the literature as it presently exists, stereotypes are not usually presented as ideological constructs that will enable us to pinpoint areas of cultural focus and meaning, but rather are given as empirical facts that can be used to "explain" misunderstandings. In addition, continual focus on a set of posited traits, even where these can be proven to be true, may funnel our attention to phenomena that may not, after all, emerge or prove to be relevant to interethnic interaction. Rather than assume that certain qualities will automatically materialize and have an impact on such encounters, we need to begin with the specific social settings involved and to learn about the cultural meanings and expectations that adhere to them. What is my expected role, and what is the culturally preferred "presentation of self" (Goffman, 1959) for this particular occasion of talk? Is this social situation one that demands reserve and formality in this culture? Or is this a time to display openness and spontaneity? Recognizing that all social actors, regardless of their ethnic affiliation, engage in numerous and varied sociocultural settings, each requiring a different yet culturally appropriate social persona, will serve us better in our pursuit of interethnic understanding.

REFERENCES

Abate, M., & Berrien, F. (1967). Validation of stereotype: Japanese versus American students. *Journal of Personality & Social Psychology, 7,* 435–438.

Adler, N. J, & Graham, J. L. (1989). Cross-cultural comparison: The international comparison fallacy. *Journal of International Business Studies, 20,* 515–538.

Alston, J. P. (1985). *The American samurai: Blending American and Japanese managerial practices.* New York: Walter de Gruyter.

Arggle, M. (1982). Inter-cultural communication. In S. Bochner (Ed.), *Cultures in contact: Studies in cross-cultural interaction* (pp. 61–79). Oxford, England: Pergamon.

Bachnik, J. M. (1992a). *Kejime:* Indexing self and social life in Japan. In N. Rosenberger (Ed.), *Japanese sense of self* (pp. 152–172). Cambridge, England: Cambridge University Press.

Bachnik, J. M. (1992b). The "two faces" of self in society in Japan. *Ethos, 20,* 3–32.

Bachnik, J. M. (1994a). Introduction: *Uchi/soto:* Challenging our conceptions of self, social order, and language. In J. M. Bachnik & C. J. Quinn (Eds.), *Situated meaning: Inside and outside in Japanese self, society, and language* (pp. 4–37). Princeton, NJ: Princeton University Press.

Bachnik, J. M. (1994b). *Uchi/Soto:* Authority and intimacy, hierarchy and solidarity in Japan. In J. M. Bachnik & C. J. Quinn (Eds.), *Situated meaning: Inside and outside in Japanese self, society, and language* (pp. 221–243). Princeton, NJ: Princeton University Press.

Barnlund, D. (1974). The public self and the private self in Japan and the United States. In J. Condon & M. Saito (Eds.), *Intercultural encounters with Japan: Communication—contact and conflict* (pp. 27–96). Tokyo: The Simul Press.

Barnlund, D. (1975). *Public self and private self in Japan and the United States: Communicative styles in two cultures*. Tokyo: The Simul Press.

Basso, K. (1970). "To give up on words": Silence in Western Apache culture. *Southwestern Journal of Anthropology, 26*, 211–230.

Befu, H. (1996, April). Discussant's comments. Round Table on *The Chrysanthemum and the Sword* at Fifty, Association for Asian Studies, Honolulu.

Befu, H., & Manabe, K. (1990). Empirical status of *nihonjinron*: How real is the myth? In A. Bascaro, F. Gatti, & M. Raveri (Eds.), *Rethinking Japan: Social sciences, ideology and thought* (Vol. 2, pp. 124–133). New York: St. Martin's Press.

Bell, D. (1976). *The cultural constructions of capitalism*. New York: Basic Books.

Benedict, R. (1946). *The chrysanthemum and the sword*. Boston: Houghton Mifflin.

Bond, M. H., & Forgas, J. P. (1984). Linking person perception to behavioral intention across cultures: The role of cultural collectivism. *Journal of Cross-Cultural Psychology, 15*, 337–352.

Brislin, R. W. (1981). *Cross-cultural encounter: Face-to-face interaction*. New York: Pergamon.

Brislin, R. W., Cushner, K., Cherrie, C., & Yong, M. (1986). *Intercultural interaction: A practical guide*. Newbury Park, CA: Sage.

Condon, J. C. (1974). The values approach to cultural patterns of communication. In J. Condon & M. Saito (Eds.), *Intercultural encounters with Japan: Communication—contact and conflict* (pp. 132–152). Tokyo: The Simul Press.

Dale, P. (1986). *The myth of Japanese uniqueness*. New York: St. Martin's Press.

DeMente, B. (1981). *The Japanese way of doing business: The psychology of management in Japan*. Englewood Cliffs, NJ: Prentice-Hall.

DeVos, G. A. (1973). *Socialization for achievement: Essays on the cultural psychology of the Japanese*. Berkeley: University of California Press.

DeVos, G. A. (1985). Dimensions of the self in Japanese culture. In A. J. Marsella, G. A. DeVos, & F. L. K. Hsu (Eds.), *Culture and self: Asian and Western perspectives* (pp. 141–184). New York: Tavistock.

Doi, T. (1962). *Amae*: A key concept for understanding Japanese personality structure. In R. Smith & R. K. Beardsley (Eds.), *Japanese culture: Its development and characteristics* (pp. 132–139). Chicago: Aldine.

Doi, T. (1973). *The anatomy of dependence* (J. Bester, Trans.). Tokyo: Kodansha.

Doi, T. (1974). Some psychological themes in Japanese human relationships. In J. Condon & M. Saito (Eds.), *Intercultural encounters with Japan: Communication—contact and conflict* (pp. 17–26). Tokyo: The Simul Press.

Dubinsky, A., Michaels, R. E., Kotabe, M., Lim, C. U., & Moon, H. C. (1992). Influence of role stress on industrial salespeople's work outcomes in the United States, Japan and Korea. *Journal of International Business Studies, 23*, 77–99.

Gercik, P. (1992). *On track with the Japanese: A case-by-case approach to building successful relationships*. New York: Kodansha International.

Gibney, F. (1979). *Japan: The Fragile superpower*. Tokyo: Charles E. Tuttle.

Goffman, E. (1959). *The presentation of self in everyday life*. Garden City, NY: Doubleday.

Goldman, A. (1994). The centrality of *"ningensei"* to Japanese negotiating and interpersonal relationships: Implications for US-Japanese communication. *International Journal of Intercultural Relations, 18*, 29–54.

Goodman, R., & Refsing, K. (Eds.). (1992). *Ideology and practice in modern Japan*. London: Routledge.

Graham, J. (1983). Brazilian, Japanese and American business negotiations. *Journal of International Business Studies*, Spring/Summer, 47–59.

Graham, J., & Herberger, R. (1983). Negotiations abroad—Don't shoot from the hip. *Harvard Business Review, 61*, 160–168.

Graham, J., & Sato, Y. (1984). *Smart bargaining: Doing business with the Japanese*. Cambridge, MA: Ballinger.

Gudykunst, W., & Nishida, T. (1994). *Bridging Japanese/North American differences*. Thousand Oaks, CA: Sage.

Gumperz, J. (1982a). *Discourse strategies*. Cambridge, England: Cambridge University Press.

Gumperz, J. (Ed.). (1982b). *Language and social identity.* Cambridge, England: Cambridge University Press.

Hall, E. T., & Hall, M. R. (1987). *Hidden differences: Doing business with the Japanese.* Garden City, NY: Anchor Press/Doubleday.

Heidkamp, M. (1992, July 27). Selling books on Japan. *Publisher's Weekly,* pp. 18–20.

Hofstede, G. (1980). *Culture's consequences: International differences in work-related values.* Beverly Hills, CA: Sage

Iino, M. (1996). *Excellent foreigner: Gaijinization of Japanese language and culture in contact situations.* Unpublished doctoral dissertation, University of Pennsylvania, Philadelphia.

Johnson, S. (1988). *The Japanese through American eyes.* Stanford, CA: Stanford University Press.

Jussim, L., McCauley, C., & Lee, Y-T. (1995). Why study stereotype accuracy and inaccuracy? In Y-T. Lee, C. McCauley, & L. Jussim (Eds.), *Stereotype accuracy: Towards appreciating group differences* (pp. 3–27). Washington DC: American Psychological Association.

Kataoka, H. (1991). *Japanese cultural encounters and how to handle them.* Lincolnwood, IL: Passport Books.

Kelly, W. (1986). Rationalization and nostalgia: Cultural dynamics of new middle class Japan. *American Ethnologist, 13,* 603–618.

Kelly, W. (1991). Directions in the anthropology of contemporary Japan. *Annual Review of Anthropology, 20,* 395–931.

Kerlinger, F. N. (1951). Decision-making in Japan. *Social Forces, 30,* 36–41.

Kondo, D. (1990). *Crafting selves: Power, gender, and discourses of identity in a Japanese workplace.* Chicago: University of Chicago Press.

Lebra, T. S. (1976). *Japanese patterns of behavior.* Honolulu: University Press of Hawaii.

Lee, Y-T. (1997, November 3). Stereotypes allow us to see the forest before we focus on the trees. *Executive Memo, Vol. XVII.*

Lee, Y-T., & Duenas, G. (1995). Stereotype accuracy in multicultural business. In Y-T. Lee, C. McCauley, & L. Jussim (Eds.), *Stereotype accuracy: Towards appreciating group differences* (pp. 157–186). Washington DC: American Psychological Association.

Linowes, R. G. (1993). The Japanese manager's traumatic entry into the United States: Understanding the American-Japanese cultural divide. *Academy of Management Executives, 7,* 21–37.

Loveday, L. (1986). *Explorations in Japanese sociolinguistics.* Amsterdam: John Benjamins.

March, R. M. (1982). Business negotiations as cross-cultural communication: The Japanese-Western case. *Cross Currents, 9,* 55–65.

March, R. M. (1992). *Working for a Japanese company: Insights into the multicultural workplace.* Tokyo: Kodansha.

Markus, H. R., & Kitayama, S. (1991). Culture and the self: Implications for cognition, emotion and motivation. *Psychological Review, 98,* 224–253.

Matsui, T., Ohsawa, T., & Onglatco, M. L. (1991). Personality and career commitment among Japanese female clerical employees. *Journal of Vocational Behavior, 38,* 351–360.

Merton, R. K. (1968). *Social theory and social structure.* New York: The Free Press.

Miller, L. (1987). Doing business with the Japanese: A review of recent "how to" books. *Journal of Asian Culture, 11,* 155–162.

Miller, L. (1991a). Consequences of Japanese and American business conversation. *Intercultural Communication Studies, 1,* 95–103.

Miller, L. (1991b). Verbal listening behavior in conversations between Japanese and Americans. In J. Blommaert & J. Verschueren (Eds.), *The pragmatics of intercultural and international communication* (pp. 110–130). Amsterdam: John Benjamins.

Miller, L. (1994a). Giving good listening: Interaction and identity in Japan's bicultural workplace. *The World & I, 9,* 221–229.

Miller, L. (1994b). Japanese and American indirectness. *Journal of Asian and Pacific Communication, 5,* 37–55.

Miller, L. (1994c). Japanese and American meetings and what goes on before them. *Pragmatics, 4,* 221–238.

Miller, L. (1994d). Tracking down recent insights into Japanese business. *The American Asian Review, 12,* 153–164.

Miller, L. (1995a). Introduction: Beyond the *sarariiman* folk model. *The American Asian Review, 3,* 19–27.

Miller, L. (1995b). Two aspects of Japanese and American co-worker interaction: Giving instruction and creating rapport. *Journal of Applied Behavioral Sciences, 31*, 141–161.

Miller, L. (1996, April). *Subversive subordinates or situated language use? A consideration of* keigo *ideology and sociolinguistic description.* Paper presented at a meeting of the Association for Asian Studies, Honolulu.

Miller, L. (1997). People types: Personality classification in Japanese women's magazines. *Journal of Popular Culture, 31*(2), 143–159.

Misumi, J. (1985). *The behavioral science of leadership: An interdisciplinary research program.* Ann Arbor: University of Michigan Press.

Moerman, M. (1988). *Talking culture: Ethnography and conversation analysis.* Philadelphia: University of Pennsylvania Press.

Moghaddam, F. M., Taylor, D. M., & Wright, S. C. (1993). *Social psychology in cross-cultural perspective.* New York: Freeman.

Moran, R. (1981). Learning cross-culturally: The case study of management. In G. Althen (Ed.), *Learning across cultures* (pp. 138–142). Washington DC: National Association for Foreign Student Affairs.

Moran, R. (1985). *Getting your yen's worth: How to negotiate with Japan, Inc.* Houston: Gulf Publishing Company.

Naotsuka, R., Sakamoto, N., Hirose, T., Hagihara, H., Ota, J., Maeda, S., Hara, T., & Iwasaki, K. (1985). *Mutual understanding of different cultures.* Tokyo: Taishukan.

Nashima, M. (1990, November 12–18). Supplies failing to meet demand: More books providing in-depth information are needed. *The Japan Times Weekly,* p. 14.

Neustupný, J. V. (1987). *Communicating with the Japanese.* Tokyo: The Japan Times.

Nihon Keizai Shimbunsha. (1997). *2020 nen kara keishô: Nihon ga kieru [Alarm bell for the year 2020: Japan will vanish].* Tokyo: Author.

Norbury, P., & Bownas, G. (Eds.). (1980). *Business in Japan: A guide to Japanese business practice and procedure.* Boulder, CO: Westview.

Okabe, R. (1983). Cultural assumptions East and West: Japan and the United States. In W. Gudykunst (Ed.), *Intercultural communication theory: Current perspectives* (pp. 21–44). Beverly Hills, CA: Sage.

Pascale, R. T., & Athos, A. (1981). *The art of Japanese management: Applications for American executives.* New York: Simon & Schuster.

Plath, D. (1980). *Long engagements: Maturity in modern Japan.* Stanford, CA: Stanford University Press.

Powell, G. N., & Kido, Y. (1994). Managerial stereotypes in a global economy: A comparative study of Japanese and American business students' perspectives. *Psychological Reports, 74,* 219–226.

Ramsey, S., & Birk, J. (1983). Preparation of North Americans for interactions with Japanese: Considerations of language and communication style. In D. Landis & R. Brislin (Eds.), *Handbook of intercultural training: Vol. 3. Area studies in intercultural training* (pp. 227–259). New York: Pergamon.

Reynierse, J. H. (1995). A comparative analysis of Japanese and American managerial types through organizational levels in business and industry. *Journal of Psychological Type, 33,* 19–32.

Riesman, D., Glazer, N., & Denney, R. (1950). *The lonely crowd.* New Haven, CT: Yale University Press.

Rosenberger, N. R. (Ed.). (1992). *Japanese sense of self.* Cambridge, England: Cambridge University Press.

Schein, V. E., Mueller, R., Lituchy, T., & Liu, J. (1996). Think manager—think male: A global phenomenon? *Journal of Organizational Behavior, 17,* 33–41.

Scherer, K. (1972). Judging personality from voice: A cross cultural approach to an old issue in interpersonal perception. *Journal of Personality & Social Psychology, 40,* 191–210.

Schmidt, S. M., & Yeh, R. S. (1992). The structure of leader influence: A cross-national comparison. *Journal of Cross-Cultural Psychology, 23,* 251–264.

Schwalb, D. W., Schwalb, B. J., Harnisch, D. L., Maehr, M. L., & Akabane, K. (1992). Personal investment in Japan and the USA: A study of worker motivation. *International Journal of Intercultural Relations, 16,* 107–124.

Scollon, R. (1981). The rhythmic integration of ordinary talk. In D. Tannen (Ed.), *Analyzing discourse: Text and talk* (pp. 335–349). Washington, DC: Georgetown University Press.

Scollon, R., & Scollon, S. (1981). *Narrative, literacy and face in interethnic communication*. Norwood, NJ: Ablex.

Sengoku, T. (1991). *Majime no hôkai: Heisei Nihon no wakamonotachi* [*The collapse of seriousness: Young people in Japan's heisei era*]. Tokyo: Saimaru Shuppankai.

Sethi, S. P. (1975). *Japanese business and social conflict: A comparative analysis of response patterns with American business*. Cambridge, MA: Ballinger.

Shimizu, K. (1987). *Bunka no henyô* [*The transformation of culture*]. Kyoto: Jibunshoin.

Shweder, R. A. (1979a). Rethinking culture and personality theory: Part I. A critical examination of two classical postulates. *Ethos, 7,* 255–278.

Shweder, R. A. (1979b). Rethinking culture and personality theory: Part II. A critical examination of two more classical postulates. *Ethos, 7,* 279–311.

Shweder, R. A., & D'Andrade, R. (1980). The systematic distortion hypothesis. In R. Shweder (Ed.), *Fallible judgment in behavioral research* (pp. 37–58). San Francisco: Jossey-Bass.

Smith, P. B., Misumi, J., Tayeb, M. H., Peterson, M. F., & Bond, M. H. (1989). On the generality of leadership styles across cultures. *Journal of Occupational Psychology, 62,* 97–110.

Sugimoto, Y., & Mouer, R. E. (Eds.). (1989). *Constructs for understanding Japan*. London: Kegan Paul.

Tannen, D. (1981a). The machine-gun question: An example of conversational style. *Journal of Pragmatics, 5,* 383–397.

Tannen, D. (1981b). New York Jewish conversational style. *International Journal of the Sociology of Language, 30,* 133–149.

Wallace, A. (1952). Individual differences and cultural uniformity. *American Sociological Review, 17,* 747–750.

Wasson, C. (1996, November). *Bring the body bag: American managers' language ideology of confrontation*. Paper presented at the annual meeting of the American Anthropological Association.

Weisz, J. R., Rothbaum, F. M., & Blackburn, T. C. (1984). Standing out and standing in: The psychology of control in America and Japan. *American Psychologist, 39,* 955–969.

White, G. M. (1992). Ethnopsychology. In T. S. Schwartz, G. M. White, & C. A. Lutz, (Eds.), *New directions in psychological anthropology* (pp. 21–46). Cambridge, England: Cambridge University Press.

White, G. M., & Kirkpatrick, J. (Eds). (1985). *Person, self and experience: Exploring Pacific ethnopsychologies*. Berkeley: University of California Press.

Yamaguchi, S. (1994). Collectivism among the Japanese: A perspective from the self. In U. Kim, H. C. Triandis, Ç. Kâ™itçibaÕi, S. Choi, & G. Yoon (Eds.), *Individualism and collectivism: Theory, methods, and applications* (pp. 175–188). Thousand Oaks, CA: Sage.

Young, C. (1985). *Nichibei bijinêsu komyunikêshon to sôgo rikai* [Japanese and American business communication and mutual understanding]. In M. Tokugawa (Ed.), *Nichibei komyunikêshon: Kotoba to bunka* (pp. 143–153). Tokyo: Minami Shoten.

IV

Implications of Studying Personality and Person Perception in Culture

Subjective Culture and the Workplace: Comparing Hispanic and Mainstream Naval Recruits

Victor Ottati
Purdue University and Loyola University, Chicago

Harry C. Triandis
University of Illinois at Champaign–Urbana

C. Harry Hui
University of Hong Kong

Hispanics have migrated across U.S. borders since the earliest stages of American history. This pattern of migration has, at various points in time, encountered considerable resistance. The 1994 passage of California Proposition 187 provides a recent historical example. This proposition is primarily directed toward illegal Mexican immigrants. It deprives illegal immigrants of welfare benefits, education, and all but emergency medical care. It also requires that teachers, police officers, and welfare workers report any knowledge of illegal immigrants to the Office of Immigration and Naturalization for purposes of deportation. Endorsement of California Proposition 187 may reflect American prejudice against Hispanics, or alternatively, an attempt to protect the United States against perceived economic threat (Lee, Ottati, & Hussain, 1997).

Despite resistance to Hispanic migration across American borders, Hispanics are becoming an increasingly visible segment of the U.S. population. Thus, it has become quite common for Hispanic and Mainstream Americans to work in close proximity within U.S. work organizations. A clear understanding of work values held by Hispanic and Mainstream Americans might enable U.S. work organizations to create a work environment that maximizes productivity and cooperation between these groups. Do Hispanic and Mainstream Americans bring similar or different values to the workplace? We explore this question by examining work-related values among Hispanic and Mainstream American recruits in the U.S. Navy. We also consider the extent to which these values are associated with corresponding differences in the way Hispanic and Mainstream recruits view supervisor–subordinate relations.

Four Work-Related Value Dimensions

Hofstede (1980) verified that four work-related value dimensions vary cross-culturally. In many cases, one or more of these dimensions has reemerged in replications and extensions of Hofstede's original work (e.g., Bochner & Hesketh, 1994; Chinese Culture Connection, 1987; Smith, Dugan, & Trompenaars, 1996). These dimensions can be labeled *individualism-collectivism, power distance, uncertainty avoidance,* and *masculinity,* respectively. We focus primarily on between-culture variation in these values. Yet, it should be noted that endorsement of these values also varies across individuals within a given culture (Leung & Bond, 1989; Triandis, 1994).

Individualism-Collectivism. Much research has focused on the individualism–collectivism value dimension. Within individualistic societies, (a) the goals and welfare of the individual have greater priority or salience than the goals and welfare of the ingroup (Bochner, 1994; Hofstede, 1980; Hui & Triandis, 1986; Leung & Bond, 1984), (b) individuals emphasize their personal beliefs and needs (Leung & Bond, 1984), and (c) individuals emphasize personal pleasure and enjoyment over social duty. Within collectivistic societies, (a) the goals and welfare of the ingroup have greater priority or salience than the goals and welfare of the individual (Bochner, 1994; Hofstede, 1980; Hui & Triandis, 1986), (b) individuals emphasize the views and needs of the ingroup (Leung & Bond, 1984), (c) individuals display a readiness to cooperate with members of the ingroup (Leung & Bond, 1984), and (d) individuals are willing to share material and nonmaterial benefits (Hui & Triandis, 1986).

Individualism-collectivism covaries with a variety of societal dimensions. Individualistic cultures tend to have high levels of gross national product (Hofstede, 1980), high levels of need for achievement (but see Hui

& Villareal, 1989), and greater reliance upon equity as a distributive rule of justice (Bond, Leung, & Wan, 1982). In collectivist cultures, individuals display greater cooperation in The Prisoner's Dilemma Task (Cox, Lobel, & McLeod, 1991), greater reliance upon equality as a distributive rule of justice (Bond et al., 1982), and a reduced likelihood of social loafing (Earley, 1993). Other linkages with the individualism–collectivism construct are more directly relevant to work-related behavior. For example, individuals from collectivist cultures have been shown to prefer greater social involvement with their company and closer supervisor–subordinate relationships (Smith et al., 1996). In contrast, people from individualistic cultures are more calculating or utilitarian in terms of their company involvement (Bochner & Hesketh, 1994).

Because Hispanics emphasize cooperativeness, gregariousness, and group orientation, most scholars characterize Hispanic culture as collectivistic (e.g., Mintz, 1966; Triandis, Marin, Hui, Lisansky, & Ottati, 1984; Wells, 1969). Indeed, a review of the literature led Turner (1980) to conclude that the major difference between Hispanics and Anglos is the group orientation that characterizes the former and the individualism that characterizes the latter. It should be noted, however, that collectivist tendencies are limited to the ingroup. Thus, Triandis et al. reported that Hispanics are high on parent, kin, and friend collectivism, but quite low on coworker collectivism.

Power Distance.   Highly correlated with individualism-collectivism is a second value dimension labeled power distance (Hofstede, 1980; Hofstede & Bond, 1984). Power distance refers to the importance a culture assigns to status differences. This includes differences in the relative status of both groups and individuals. Thus, power distance subsumes the concept of social class and other aspects of social stratification. Within a work organization context, it reflects the extent to which individuals expect and accept that power is distributed unequally (Hofstede & Bond, 1984). Important to note, power distance refers to a normative framework that the powerless as well as the powerful subscribe to (Bochner & Hesketh, 1994). In Hofstede's (1980) work, power distance contains two components. One reflects a tendency for subordinates to submissively avoid disagreements with their manager. A second involves a preference for more autocratic or paternalistic supervisors (high power distance) versus a preference for more participative or consultive supervisors (low power distance). Because power distance is positively correlated with collectivism, it predicts many cultural characteristics previously described as linked to individualism-collectivism. Hofstede (1991) has suggested that power distance has decreased worldwide throughout the past 30 years. Nevertheless, he contended that most countries have maintained the same rank order during this time period.

Hofstede (1980) reported that power distance reaches its highest levels in the Philippines and in Latin America. Other authors argue that contemporary Hispanics maintain rigid class distinctions that were in effect during the Spanish colonial period (e.g., Grebler, Moore, & Guzman, 1970; Wells, 1969). The notion that Hispanics accept a stratified and hierarchical society is also emphasized in anthropological descriptions of Mexican-American (Clark, 1959; Madsen, 1973), Puerto Rican (Mintz, 1966), and Cuban culture (Rogg, 1974). Power distance among Hispanics is, according to various authors, also exemplified by the use of honorific titles (Diaz-Royo, 1974), the distinctions between the uses of formal and informal pronouns (Diaz-Royo, 1974), and the stress on harmony and politeness among Mexican Americans (Burma, 1970; Madsen, 1973) and Puerto Ricans (Wagenheim, 1972).

Uncertainty Avoidance.   All societies have a need for certainty, security, rules, and norms. However, some societies manifest a greater need than others. Uncertainty avoidance reflects the degree to which a society develops beliefs and institutional structures designed to reduce threat and anxiety elicited by ambiguous life situations. High-uncertainty-avoidance societies possess a large generation gap and tend to endorse gerontocracy. In these societies, individuals possess strong superegos and prefer clearly delineated requirements and instructions. Although these individuals do not typically emphasize achievement, activation of this motive usually involves security-oriented goals rather than monetary or intellectual success. Within work organizations, uncertainty avoidance is highly associated with formalization. Ambiguous work roles may be especially stressful for individuals possessing high uncertainty avoidance (Nicholson, Nova, & Goh, 1983).

Hofstede (1980) obtained the highest uncertainty avoidance scores in Greece, Japan, and Latin America. Among Hispanics, the close relationship between parents and children may manifest uncertainty avoidance. Mexican-American parents restrict their children more than Anglo parents and Puerto Rican parents encourage dependency, obedience, and conformity among children (Mintz, 1966; Wells, 1969). Hispanics also avoid risky confrontations (Diaz-Royo, 1974; Mintz, 1966). These considerations suggest that Hispanic naval recruits may possess higher levels of uncertainty avoidance than Mainstream recruits.

Masculinity. According to Hofstede (1980), the masculinity value dimension is based on a universal tendency to dichotomize gender roles and the nearly universal association of assertiveness with men and nurturance with women. Societies high in masculinity tend to view work as a central value of life. The goal of work is generally viewed in terms of personal advancement and increased earnings. High-masculinity societies tend to define achievement in terms of recognition and wealth rather than lifestyle. Achievement motivation is high. People like to work long hours and are attracted to larger organizations. Men and women are valued differently for performing the same job and gender-role differences are pronounced. Societies that score low in masculinity do not view work as so central to their lives. There is more emphasis on the rendering of services and on having a congenial physical and social environment. Achievement is defined more in terms of human contact and lifestyle. People prefer shorter working hours to more pay and are attracted to smaller organizations where more rewarding human relationships can flourish. There are small value differences between men and women in the same job and less gender-role differentiation in general.

Hofstede (1980) obtained the highest masculinity scores in Japan, with Austria, Venezuela, Italy, Switzerland, Great Britain, and Mexico also being high. It is difficult to predict the relative standing of Hispanics more generally along this dimension. Work, although important, is not a central value among Hispanics. Work is not an end in itself but rather a means to an end, because the goal of work is to enjoy life (Szalay, Ruiz, Strohl, Lopez, & Turbyville, 1978). Furthermore, leisure is very highly valued in certain Hispanic cultures (Seda, 1973). On the other hand, evidence also suggests Hispanics prefer self-employment (Clark, 1959; Mead, 1953) and strongly differentiate between gender roles (Pescatello, 1973; but see Levine & West, 1979). Thus, the existing literature is equivocal regarding the propensity of Hispanics to embrace a masculine value system. An equally inconsistent picture emerges when one considers achievement motivation. Some authors have suggested that Mexican Americans lack achievement motivation whereas others argue that different measures of achievement should be used when evaluating Hispanics. Still others (e.g., Gil, 1976) argue that Mexican Americans and Anglo-Americans share similar levels of achievement motivation.

Ethnicity, Global Values, and Supervisor–Subordinate Relations: Hypotheses and Predictions

Our discussion thus far suggests Hispanic and Mainstream naval recruits will differ along Hofstede's four value dimensions. Relative to mainstream recruits, one can predict that Hispanic recruits will score higher on collectivism, power distance, and uncertainty avoidance. One can generate corresponding predictions when comparing Hispanic and Mainstream recruits with regard to supervisor–subordinate relations. For example, if Hispanic recruits are higher in collectivism, they might prefer supervisors who reward team output rather than individual output. If Hispanic recruits are higher in power distance, they may be more tolerant of supervisor behaviors that are authoritarian, and less concerned with participation in work-relevant decisions. If Hispanics are high in uncertainty avoidance, they might prefer supervisors who provide clear rules, close supervision, and definite goals. Lastly, if Hispanic and Mainstream recruits differ in masculinity, the less masculine group should be more likely to view work as a noncentral value, to emphasize service to others, to define achievement in term of human contacts, and to prefer small and interpersonally warm work organizations.

The Role of Acculturation and Occupational Culture: Further Hypotheses and Predictions

The hypotheses just outlined assume that Hispanic and Mainstream naval recruits possess different value systems that emerge from their distinct ethnic backgrounds. From this perspective, "subjective culture" arises from social identification with the ethnic ingroup. Yet, most individuals identify with multiple social groupings (e.g., ethnicity, citizenship, occupation) and membership in each of these groupings can activate different facets of self-construal (Brewer & Gardner, 1996). Thus, it seems unlikely that ethnicity will be the sole determinant of work-related values among naval recruits. Unlike traditional Hispanic populations, Hispanic naval recruits are U.S. citizens who may be acculturated to the Mainstream American value system (Triandis, Hui, Lisansky, & Marin, 1982; Wong-Reiger & Quintana, 1987; see also Holt & Keats, 1992; Lee & Larwood, 1983, for evidence of acculturation among non-Hispanic populations). Acculturation to the Mainstream value system is especially likely to occur within work contexts (Wong-Rieger & Quintana, 1987). If Hispanic naval recruits are acculturated, this should reduce or eliminate the previously hypothesized differences between Hispanic and Mainstream recruits. Furthermore, the tendency for Hispanics to resemble mainstream recruits should be especially pronounced for Hispanic scoring high in acculturation.

In addition to sharing American citizenship, Hispanic and Mainstream recruits share membership in a common "military culture" that possesses its own unique set of values. Members of the military may conform to this value system irrespective of their ethnic background. This might reduce or eliminate the previously hypothesized differences between Hispanic and Mainstream recruits. Furthermore, the military is an organization that emphasizes a hierarchical distribution of power. Thus, Hispanic and Mainstream recruits may both subscribe to a military culture that is high in power distance.

METHOD

Subjects

Seventy-three Hispanic and 81 Mainstream recruits responded to the questionnaire while being classified into navy jobs, as part of a larger study of the perceptions of the social environment by these recruits. In each of the three navy recruiting stations (Florida, California, and Illinois) when a Spanish-surname recruit was to be classified, the classification officer checked the recruit's self-identification on an application form on which "Hispanic" was one of the ways in which the applicant could describe himself. If the Spanish-surname recruit had selected the "Hispanic" self-identification label, he was asked to complete the questionnaire. At that time another recruit (with a non-Spanish surname) was randomly selected and given the same questionnaire. These other recruits are here referred to as "Mainstream" and will include both Whites and Blacks as well as Hispanics who did not identify themselves as "Hispanic."

Instrument

A questionnaire consisting of 159 items explored similarities and differences between Hispanics and Mainstream respondents. Most of the items were constructed to reflect Hofstede's (1980) four value dimensions. Some items matched Hofstede's items exactly. Furthermore, a number of supervisor–subordinate situations were constructed that included elements hypothesized to be relevant to the preferences of Hispanic and Mainstream individuals.

RESULTS

Effects of Ethnicity on Global Values

Item analysis yielded five items that were reliably related to the individu-alism–collectivism dimension. These items assessed the degree to which respondents value time for personal and family life, residing in a desirable location, freedom to adopt their own approach to their job, and self-reliance on the job (individualism items). A fifth item assessed the belief that an organization is responsible for the health and welfare of people who work in it (collectivism item, also relates to uncertainty avoidance). When summing these items (after reverse scoring the individualism items), a t test failed to yield a significant difference between the Mainstream and Hispanic recruits. On the other hand, an analysis of the percentages of the responses to the various categories suggested the Hispanic recruits were higher on collectivism in four of the five items. Thus, there is a weak trend coinciding with the expected difference on collectivism.

Ten items reliably measured power distance in both samples. One provided a description of four different types of managers possessing a decision-making style that ranged from autocratic (i.e., makes decisions promptly and communicates them to subordinates firmly) to consultive (i.e., calls meetings with subordinates when there is an important decision to be made). Responses to this item failed to differ when comparing the two samples. Modal responses to the remaining nine power distance items are presented in Table 12.1 for Mainstream and Hispanic recruits separately. One of these ("Employees lose respect for a supervisor who asks them for their advice before he makes a final decision") provided a significantly different distribution $\chi^2(4) = 17.1, p < .002$). Only 22.2% of the Mainstream recruits agreed with this statement, whereas 32.2% of the Hispanics agreed with it. Also, whereas 25.9% of the Mainstream recruits strongly disagreed, only 5.5% of the Hispanics chose that response. This item suggests that Hispanic recruits possess higher power distance. Although most of the remaining items did not reach statistical significance, 9 of the 10 power distance items were in the hypothesized direction. A binomial test indicates that such a distribution would occur by chance only once in 1,000 studies. In addition, the sum of the relevant items measuring power distance was compared across the ethnic groups by t test. The test was significant ($p < .02$). We can conclude then that the Hispanic recruits were higher on power distance than the Mainstream recruits.

TABLE 12.1

Modal Responses to Items Related to Power Distance

How frequently do the following events take place in the organizations you know something about?	Mainstream	Hispanics
(A = Very Frequently to E = Almost Never)		
1. Employees are afraid to express disagreement with their supervisors.	B+	C+
2. High-level people get involved in details of the job that should be left to lower level people.	C	C
3. Some groups of employees look down on other groups of employees.	C	B
4. Employees lose respect for a supervisor who asks them for their advice before he makes a final decision.	D $p < .002$	C
5. Employees in industry participate in decisions taken by management. (correlates negatively)	B	B
6. A company or organization's rules should not be broken even when the employee thinks it is in the organization's best interests (A = strongly agree to E = strongly disagree).	B	B+
7. How frequently in your work environment are subordinates afraid to express disagreement with their supervisors?	Sometimes	Frequently
Rate the jobs below as A = Excellent, B = Good, C = OK, D = Poor, or E = Refuse to do.		
8. Job 1. In this job people are required to work under strict rules and regulations. Individual accountability is emphasized.	C $p < .03$	B
9. Job 2. In this job a team of several individuals has to perform according to strict rules and regulation. Team accountability is emphasized.	C	C+

Modal responses to the nine items that reliably assessed uncertainty avoidance are presented in Table 12.2. One of these reached significance in the direction predicted, and seven out of nine provided data in this same direction. For example, when asked if it was important to have a job that has an element of variety and adventure (an idea that is the opposite of uncertainty avoidance), 35% of the Mainstream but only 14% of the Hispanic recruits indicated that it was of the utmost importance; furthermore, whereas 2% of the Mainstream recruits indicated it had little or no importance, 7% of the Hispanics gave that response ($\chi^2(4) = 10.0, p < .04$). A binomial test indicates that when seven out of nine items are in the same direction, this result has a probability of $p < .02$. In addition, the sum of the relevant items measuring uncertainty avoidance was compared across

TABLE 12.2

Modal Responses to Items Related to Uncertainty Avoidance

	Mainstream	Hispanic
How frequently do the following events take place in the *organizations you know about?(A = Very frequently to E = Almost* *never)*		
1. People are not sure what their duties and responsibilities really are.	C	C
2. Competition between employees usually does more harm than good.	C	B
3. How often do you feel nervous and tense at work?	C	C+
In choosing an ideal job, how important would it be to you to? *(A) of Utmost Importance, (B) Very Important, (C) of Moder* *ate (Importance,, (D) of Little Importance, (E) of Very Little* *or No Importance*		
4. Have an element of variety and adventure in the job (correlates negatively with uncertainty avoidance).	B+ $p < .04$	B
5. Be consulted by your direct supervisor in his decisions.	B	B+
6. Work in a well-defined job situation where the requirem ents are clear.	B-	B
7. In this job people are required to work under strict rules and regulations. Individual accountability is emphasized. (This item correlates with both power distance and uncer tainty avoidance.)	C $p < .03$	B
8. An organization has major responsibility for the health and welfare of the people who work in it, and also for their families. (A = Strongly Agree, B = Agree, C = Undecided)	,B	B
9. A large corporation is generally a more desirable place to work than a small company (A = Strongly Agree, B = Agree, C = Undecided)	B	B+

ethnic groups by *t* test, and the test was significant ($p < .02$). Thus, as predicted, the Hispanic recruits were higher on uncertainty avoidance.

Eight items were reliably related to the masculinity dimension. These items assessed the degree to which respondents value task challenges, making a real contribution to company success, and opportunity for advancement to a higher job level (positively related to masculinity). Other items assessed the degree to which respondents value good physical work conditions, secure employment, and opportunity to help others, as well as the degree to which they believe that some employees have an inherited aversion to work (negatively related to masculinity). An analysis of these items suggested the Mainstream recruits were higher than the Hispanic recruits on this dimension (binomial test, $p < .035$).

Effects of Ethnicity on Attitudes Toward
Supervisor–Subordinate Relations

The previous analyses revealed only a weak trend indicative of higher collectivism among Hispanic recruits. The evidence was equally uncompelling when considering supervisor–subordinate behavior relevant to this dimension. Specifically, two items assessed preference for collective work situations such as where a supervisor rewards the group rather than individuals. Neither item differed when comparing the Hispanic and Mainstream recruits.

The higher power distance scores obtained for Hispanic recruits should lead them to perceive nonparticipatory supervisors less negatively than do the Mainstream recruits. This hypothesis was supported by three items:

1. In this item two men were described discussing their relationship with their supervisor, and the subjects were invited to agree with the views of one of the men. One man argued that "The superior, by being the superior, is expected to order and the subordinate is expected to obey without questioning. No exemption or personal consideration should be made by the superior." The other man argued that a superior should pay attention to the subordinate's personal life. Only 24% of the Mainstream sample and 46% of the Hispanics agreed with the views of the man quoted first. This difference is significant ($\chi^2(4) = 7.72, p < .01$).

2. This item described three companies and asked subjects which company they would prefer to work for. Only 23% of the Mainstream sample wanted to work for Company B, whereas 36% of the Hispanics chose that company. The description of Company B was as follows: "In this company major decisions are taken after careful discussion between top union and top management leaders. Workers give their ideas to their union and this way their ideas sometimes make a difference in the decisions." The trend suggests that the Hispanics showed more tolerance for this situation than did the Mainstream recruits ($p < .10$).

3. This item described four managers and asked the subjects to indicate under whom they would prefer to work. Mainstream subjects favored a consultative manager, whereas Hispanics favored a manager who "Usually makes his or her decisions promptly, but before going ahead tries to explain them fully to his or her subordinates, gives the reasons

for the decisions and answers whatever questions they may have" (p < .24). The combined probability of these three independent events, by Stouffer's method, is p < .004. Thus, the greater power distance among the Hispanic than Mainstream recruits appears to translate into corresponding differences in their respective views of supervisor–subordinate relations.

The higher uncertainty avoidance scores obtained for Hispanic recruits should lead them to prefer supervisors who provide clear rules and goals more so than Mainstream recruits. This hypothesis was examined by comparing the preferences of the two samples for supervisors and jobs that require much traveling, variety, and adventure versus security. The two samples were not significantly different on this item, both preferring the former to the latter. We must remember, however, that the samples consist of navy recruits, who by virtue of joining the navy have indicated preferences for the former job type. Thus, it would appear that although Hispanics are higher in uncertainty avoidance, in the specific case of navy recruits, this does not translate into preferences for security over adventure in viewing jobs. Another item asked subjects to choose between two instructors. One was described as explaining facts very clearly, drilling his students, and lecturing them a lot; the other was more vague but stimulating. Thirty-one percent of the Hispanics liked the former, whereas only 23% of the Mainstream subjects did so. Both samples preferred the latter, but the relative preference was much clearer for the Mainstream recruits 23–77 than for the Hispanics 31–69 (p < .16). Thus, taken together the evidence is equivocal regarding whether differences in uncertainty avoidance translate into corresponding differences in the way these two groups view supervisor–subordinate relations.

It was also predicted that Hispanics would view achievement in terms of service to others rather than in terms of wealth. This hypothesis was tested with three items. The first item described three kinds of companies. The first company recruited people who could get along with each other, paid relatively low wages, and emphasized good interpersonal relationships. Only 2% of the Mainstream sample liked that company, whereas 10% of the Hispanics did; the second company emphasized compatibility but not as much as the first company, and provided average wages. The Mainstream and Hispanic approval rates were 47% and 36%, respectively. The last company emphasized the skills of the employees, paid no attention to compatibility, but had above-average wages. The Mainstream and Hispanic percentages were 51 and 54, respectively. Thus, both samples appear to be high in masculinity—emphasize wages over service to others.

The next item described three jobs. The first job included several of the subject's friends, but did not pay well; the second had two of the subject's acquaintances and average wage; and the third paid above average but included no acquaintances. In choosing among these three jobs, both the Mainstream and Hispanic samples overwhelmingly chose the latter job. Thus, again we find the Hispanics just as wage oriented as the Mainstream respondents and willing to sacrifice a friendly work environment for money.

The third item contrasted two organizations. The first was a small one with 50 employees, all of whom know each other, which does not pay as well as the average, whereas the second was a large organization of several thousand employees paying better than average. Again, both samples overwhelmingly chose pay over a friendly environment (the percentages were 69 and 76 for the Mainstream and Hispanic samples, respectively). Thus, the two groups did not differ in terms of their preference for masculine (vs. feminine) job scenarios.

Comparing Our Sample to Hofstede's Worldwide Sample

To compare our naval sample to Hofstede's (1980) worldwide sample of IBM employees, we restricted our attention to (a) items that perfectly matched Hofstede's items, and (b) items for which Hofstede provided worldwide information. This drastically reduced the number and reliability of items composing each scale, often eliminating the previously reported differences between Hispanic and Mainstream recruits. Nevertheless, because it is critical that one consider only identical items when making such comparisons, this was the only viable strategy.

For individualism-collectivism, only one item satisfied our selection criteria. On this item, Hofstede's civilian sample ranged from 3.16 (Great Britain, individualistic) to 3.89 (Brazil and Chile, collectivist). Hofstede's civilian U.S. sample scored at 3.22, which is quite individualistic. Both the Hispanic ($M = 3.22$) and Mainstream ($M = 3.27$) recruits matched the U.S. civilian sample on this item. This pattern is consistent with the acculturation hypothesis.

For power distance, three items satisfied our selection criteria. On these items, Hofstede's civilian sample yielded scores ranging from 11 (Austria, low power distance) to 94 (Philippines, high power distance). Hofstede's civilian U.S. sample scored at 40, which is relatively low. In contrast, both the Hispanic ($M = 114$) and Mainstream ($M = 117$) recruits scored much higher than any of the 40 countries in Hofstede's sample. This finding is particularly striking because, assuming that power distance has decreased worldwide over the past 30 years (Hofstede, 1991), it actually underestimates the relative extremity of the naval recruits along this dimension. This strongly suggests that the military constitutes a unique occupational subculture within the the United States that is very high on power distance.

For uncertainty avoidance, two items satisfied our selection criteria. The means for the Hispanic and Mainstream naval recruits fell in the low-middle range of Hofstede's worldwide civilian sample. On the item "Competition between employees usually does more harm than good," Hofstede's civilian sample ranged from those who most strongly disagreed ($M = 3.41$, New Zealand, low uncertainty avoidance) to those who most strongly agreed ($M = 2.31$, Portugal, high uncertainty avoidance). Hofstede's civilian U.S. sample scored at 3.29, reflecting low uncertainty avoidance. Both the Hispanic ($M = 2.82$) and Mainstream ($M = 3.00$) naval recruits were higher than Hofstede's civilian U.S. sample but lower than many Latin American countries on uncertainty avoidance. Thus, the U.S. Navy appears to function as a subculture, which falls between civilians in the United States and Latin America on uncertainty avoidance.

Relative to Hofstede's worldwide civilian sample, the Hispanic and Mainstream recruits were high on masculinity. On one item Hofstede's civilian sample ranged from 3.42 (Norway, low masculinity) to 2.36 (Colombia, high masculinity). Both the Hispanic ($M = 2.55$) and Mainstream ($M = 2.69$) naval recruits scored relatively high on this item, suggesting once again that the U.S. Navy constitutes a unique subculture. Perhaps high-masculinity individuals are attracted to the military.

We can conclude, then, that navy recruits, relative to Hofstede's industrial samples, tend to be extremely high on power distance, moderately high on uncertainty avoidance and masculinity, and close to the U.S. mean on individualism-collectivism.

Relationships Between Hofstede's Variables and Acculturation and Biculturalism

To examine the effects of acculturation and biculturalism on Hofstede's values within the Hispanic sample, we returned to our original indices of power distance, uncertainty avoidance, and masculinity containing 10, 9, and 8 items, respectively. Indices for each value dimension were correlated with the indices of acculturation and biculturalism described by Triandis et al. (1982). The correlations that reached significance indicated that acculturation is negatively related to power distance [acculturation index 1 (generational family history) correlated $r = -.22$, $p < .03$; index 2 (ideal ethnicity for social interactions) $r = -.28$, $p < .01$]. Thus the more acculturated Hispanic navy recruits scored lower on power distance. Because the Mainstream power distance is lower than that of Hispanics, this indicates that acculturation moves Hispanics closer to the Mainstream on power distance. In addition, biculturalism was negatively related to uncertainty avoidance among Hispanics ($r = -.25$, $p < .02$). Again, given the finding that the Hispanic sample is higher than the Mainstream sample on uncertainty avoidance, this indicates that biculturalism moves the Hispanics closer to the Mainstream on this dimension. These results are consistent with the idea that the more acculturated are the Hispanics the more they resemble the Mainstream respondents in terms of power distance and uncertainty avoidance.

DISCUSSION

A review of the literature suggested that Hispanics are higher than Mainstream American individuals on power distance (differentiation according to status, clear separation of people by status), uncertainty avoidance (preference for clear rules, certainty, fear of failure), and collectivism (goals and welfare of the group takes precedence over those of the individual). The existing literature was less clear regarding the relative ordering of Hispanics and Mainstream Americans along the dimension of masculinity. The present research considered the extent to which a similar pattern of differences emerges when comparing Hispanic and Mainstream recruits in the U.S. Navy. The degree to which corresponding differences emerge when assessing attitudes toward supervisor–subordinate relations was also investigated.

The expected differences in power distance and uncertainty avoidance were clearly obtained. On both dimensions, the Hispanic naval recruits scored higher than the Mainstream recruits. The expected difference for collectivism, although appearing as a trend, was less reliable. As for masculinity, it appears the Mainstream recruits scored higher than the Hispanic recruits along this dimension. Analyses within the Hispanic sample suggested that acculturation to Mainstream American cultural values played an important role within this group. Among Hispanic recruits, high scores on acculturation and biculturalism predicted greater similarity to the Mainstream recruits on power distance and uncertainty avoidance, respectively.

Comparison of the navy samples with worldwide norms on the same questionnaire items showed that the navy samples are extremely high on power distance, somewhat high on uncertainty avoidance and masculinity, and close to the U.S. mean on collectivism. This indicates that there is a distinct military culture that is very high on power distance, and perhaps somewhat high on uncertainty avoidance and masculinity.

Examination of Hispanic and Mainstream preferences for various kinds of supervisor–subordinate relationships showed that the Hispanics were more willing than the Mainstream recruits to tolerate a nonparticipatory (high power distance) supervisor. However, on the other dimensions clear differences were not found. Reactions to supervisors described as high or low in initiating structure (clear about goals, providing structured assignments and follow-up) and high or low on consideration (showing concern for personal problems of the people who work for them) indicated that both Hispanics and Mainstream recruits prefer supervisors who are high on both attributes, and reject supervisors who are low on both attributes. However, the Mainstream viewed supervisors high on initiating structure and low on consideration to be more acceptable than did the Hispanics. Also, the Hispanics found the supervisor low in initiating structure and high in consideration to be more acceptable than did the Mainstream subjects. Thus, although the navy recruits are extremely similar to each other, they do show some differences in preferences for supervisors. Hispanics may give more weight to interpersonal relationships than do the Mainstream recruits.

CONCLUSION

We have considered three determinants of work-related values held by Hispanic and Mainstream recruits. The first is ethnicity. From this perspective, contemporary Hispanic and Mainstream recruits should possess distinct work values that reflect long-standing differences in their ethnic background. A second determinant is acculturation to Mainstream American culture. To the degree this factor operates, Hispanic and Mainstream recruits should share similar work values that coincide with those held by Mainstream Americans more generally. A third determinant of work values is membership in the military culture. If this third factor predominates, Hispanic and Mainstream recruits should share a common system of work values that differs from the value system of most civilians in the world.

All three of these viewpoints received some support in our study. Ethnic differences were clearly obtained for certain value dimensions (e.g., power distance, uncertainty avoidance). Acculturation led Hispanic recruits to resemble Mainstream recruits along certain dimensions. Moreover, linkage to a common military culture led both groups to differ from most civilian populations in certain respects (e.g., power distance). Thus, it appears that ethnic tradition, acculturation to Mainstream values, and membership in a common military culture all combined to influence work-related values among Hispanic and Mainstream naval recruits.

Our findings regarding the role of ethnicity and acculturation as predictors of work-related values serve to replicate previous research in this domain. A more unique and striking aspect of our findings involves the importance of occupational subculture. For certain value dimensions, the effect of occupational subculture may be considerably greater than the effect of ethnicity. This appears to have been the case for power distance in the present study. Although Hispanic and Mainstream recruits differed in the predicted manner along this dimension, the most notable finding is that both of these groups scored much higher than any nation in Hofstede's (1980) international sample of IBM workers. Thus, in this particular case, occupation-related social identity appears to be a more salient determinant of work-related values than ethnic-based social identity (see Brewer & Gardner, 1996, for a related discussion). At the very least, this should alert researchers to the impact of selective occupational sampling in cross-cultural research. Cross-cultural findings that emerge for one occupational subculture may be quite different than those that emerge for other occupational groups.

REFERENCES

Bochner, S. (1994). Cross-cultural differences in the self-concept: A test of Hofstede's individualism/collectivism distinction. *Journal of Cross-Cultural Psychology, 25,* 273–283.

Bochner, S., & Hesketh, B. (1994). Power distance, individualism/collectivism, and job-related attitudes in a culturally diverse work group. *Journal of Cross-Cultural Psychology, 25,* 233–257.

Bond, M. H., Leung, K., & Wan, K. C. (1982). How does cultural collectivism operate? The impact of task and maintenence contribution on reward distribution. *Journal of Cross-Cultural Psychology, 13,* 186–200.

Brewer, M., & Gardner, W. (1996). Who is this "we"? Levels of collective identity and self representations. *Journal of Personality and Social Psychology, 71,* 83–93.

Burma, J. H. (1970). *Mexican-Americans in the United States: A reader*. Cambridge, MA: Schenkman.

Chinese Culture Connection. (1987). Chinese values and the search for culture free dimensions of culture. *Journal of Cross-Cultural Psychology, 18*, 143–164.

Clark, M. (1959). *Health in the Mexican-American culture: A community study*. Berkeley: University of California Press.

Cox, T. H., Lobel, S. A., & McLeod, P. L. (1991). Effects of ethnic group cultural differences on cooperative and competitive behavior on a group task. *Academy of Management Journal, 34*, 827–847.

Diaz-Royo, A. T. (1974). *The enculturation processes of Puerto Rican highland children*. Unpublished doctoral dissertation, University of Michigan, Ann Arbor.

Earley, P. C. (1993). East meets west meets mideast: Further explorations of collectivistic and individualistic work groups. *Academy of Management Journal, 36*, 319–348.

Gil, V. E. (1976). *The personal adjustment and acculturation of Cuban immigrants in Los Angeles*. Unpublished doctoral dissertation, University of Michigan, Ann Arbor.

Grebler, L., Moore, J. W., & Guzman, R. C. (1970). *The Mexican-American people: The nation's second largest minority*. New York: The Free Press.

Hofstede, G. (1980). *Culture's consequences: International differences in work-related values*. Beverly Hills, CA: Sage.

Hofstede, G. (1991). *Cultures and organizations: Software of the mind*. London: McGraw-Hill.

Hofstede, G., & Bond, M. H. (1984). Hofstede's culture dimensions: An independent validation using Rokeach's value survey. *Journal of Cross-Cultural Psychology, 15*, 417–433.

Holt, J., & Keats, D. M. (1992). Work cognitions in multicultural interaction. *Journal of Cross-Cultural Psychology, 22*, 421–443.

Hui, C. H., & Triandis, H. C. (1986). Individualism-collectivism: A study of cross-cultural researchers. *Journal of Cross-Cultural Psychology, 17*, 225–248.

Hui, C. H., & Villareal, M. J. (1989). Individualism-collectivism and psychological needs: Their relationship in two cultures. *Journal of Cross-Cultural Psychology, 20*, 310–323.

Lee, Y., & Larwood, L. (1983). The socialization of expatriate managers in multinational firms. *Academy of Management Journal, 26*, 657–665.

Lee, Y., Ottati, V., & Hussain, I. (1997). *California's Proposition 187: A case of cultural conflict or national economic concern?* Manuscript under review.

Leung, K., & Bond, M. H. (1984). The impact of cultural collectivism on reward allocation. *Journal of Personality and Social Psychology, 47*, 793–804.

Leung, K., & Bond, M. H. (1989). On the empirical identification of dimensions for cross cultural comparisons. *Journal of Cross-Cultural Psychology, 20*, 133–151.

Levine, R. V., & West, L. (1979). Attitudes toward women in the United States and Brazil. *Journal of Social Psychology, 108*, 265–266.

Madsen, W. (1973). *Mexican-Americans of South Texas*. New York: Holt, Rinehart & Winston.

Mead, M. (1953). *Cultural patterns and technical change*. Paris: United Nations Educational, Scientific and Cultural Organizations.

Mintz, S. W. (1966). Puerto Rico: An essay in the definition of a national culture. In *Status of Puerto Rico: Selected background studies* (for the U.S.-P.R. Commission on the Status of P.R.). Washington, DC: U.S. Government Printing Office.

Nicholson, P. J., Nova, S., & Goh, S. C. (1983). The relationship of organization structure and interpersonal attitudes to role conflict and ambiguity in different work environments. *Academy of Management Journal, 26*, 148–155.

Pescatello, A. (1973). *Female and male in Latin America*. Pittsburgh: University of Pittsburgh Press.

Rogg, E. (1974). *The assimilation of Cuban exiles*. New York: Aberdeen.

Seda, E. (1973). *Social change and personality in a Puerto Rican agrarian reform community*. Evanston, IL: Northwestern University Press.

Smith, P. B., Dugan, S., & Trompenaars, F. (1996). National culture and the values of organizational employees: A dimensional analysis across 43 nations. *Journal of Cross-Cultural Psychology, 27*, 231–264.

Szalay, L., Ruiz, P., Strohl, J., Lopez, R., & Turbyville, L. (1978). *The Hispanic-American cultural frame of reference*. Washington, DC: Institute of Comparative Social & Cultural Studies, Inc.

Triandis, H. C. (1994). Theoretical and methodological approaches to the study of collectivism and individualism. In U. Kim, H. C. Triandis, C. Kagitcibasi, S. C. Choi, & G. Yoon (Eds.), *Individualism and collectivism: Theory, method, and applications* (pp. 41–51). Thousand Oaks, CA: Sage.

Triandis, H. C., Hui, C. H., Lisansky, J., & Marin, G. (1982). *Acculturation and biculturalism among Hispanic navy recruits* (Tech. Rep. No. 6, ONR Contract). Champaign: University of Illinois, Department of Psychology.

Triandis, H. C., Marin, G., Hui, C. H., Lisansky, J., & Ottati, V. (1984). Role perceptions of Hispanic young adults. *Journal of Cross-Cultural Psychology, 15,* 297–320.

Turner, S. P. (1980). *A model to predict retention and attrition of Hispanic-Americans in the navy.* Arlington, VA: Office of Naval Research.

Wagenheim, K. (1972). *Puerto Rico, a profile.* New York: Praeger.

Wells, H. (1969). *The modernization of Puerto Rico.* Cambridge, MA: Harvard University Press.

Wong-Reiger, D., & Quintana, D. (1987). Comparative acculturation of Southeast Asian and Hispanic immigrants and sojourners. *Journal of Cross-Cultural Psychology, 18,* 345–362.

13

Communicating Information About Culture and Personality in Formal Cross-Cultural Training Programs

Richard Brislin
University of Hawaii

The following experiences have a number of issues in common:

1. Given that programs in their interest areas do not exist in their own countries, international students travel abroad to study for advanced degrees in an unfamiliar college or university.
2. Realizing the long-range benefits to their career development, businesspeople accept overseas assignments in the branch offices of their companies.
3. To jump-start their stalled careers, people seek out and accept Peace Corps assignments in areas that stretch their abilities.
4. In lieu of paying off student loans that put them through college, recent graduates accept positions on Native American reservation lands in Arizona.
5. Vaguely bored with their high school curriculum, students in their late teen years seek out junior-year-abroad experiences through organizations such as Youth For Understanding and AFS International.
6. Given recent migration patterns within their cities, high school teachers find themselves in front of classes where a majority of students do not have English as their native language.
7. As a result of independence movements within countries previously called "part of the Soviet bloc," governments find it necessary to

identify people for their diplomatic corps and to assign them to overseas posts.

8. As part of a careful effort to improve the economic circumstances of a family in a developing nation, the best educated person seeks immigration to a highly industrialized country. Later, the government is petitioned to allow other family members to immigrate under "family reunification" policies.

What do these experiences have in common? All involve (a) extensive contact among people from very different cultural backgrounds, but the people may be (b) unprepared for this contact and may experience considerable stress as a result. The term most frequently used for this type of contact is *intercultural interactions*. There is *not* the commonality that people are living in a country other than their own given that intercultural interactions can occur as part of overseas assignments or as a result of contact among culturally diverse groups within large and complex nations such as the United States, Canada, or China. Beyond the contact itself, another commonality is that people may have (c) unrealistic or faulty expectations concerning their upcoming experiences that have to be modified as part of their adjustment to the new demands in their lives. These expectations may include the belief among some Peace Corps volunteers that "American know-how" is what people in developing countries need. Or, the expectation may be that the extended family will surely resume its old and comfortable norms once all its members are resettled in the new country.

Another commonality is that cross-cultural training programs (also frequently called intercultural communication training: Brislin & Yoshida, 1994; Fowler & Mumford, 1995; Landis & Bhagat, 1996) have been offered to people *about to experience* these various forms of intercultural contact. In addition or as an alternative, programs have been offered to people *shortly after they have begun their experiences* and after they have encountered enough difficulties to convince themselves that participation in a training program may be worthwhile. Many times, the unrealistic and overly positive expectations people harbor must be challenged by their everyday experiences. Once expectations and reality come closer, people may become interested in a training program dealing with issues such as cross-cultural adjustment, cultural differences that affect everyday behaviors, and the advantages that stem from extensive intercultural contact (Adler, 1997; Allport, 1954; Kagitcibasi, 1978).

In this chapter, the structure, goals, and selected content areas of cross-cultural training programs are discussed. Further, some practical advice for administering programs and presenting material is offered, and this advice is based on the wisdom of experienced practitioners (Paige, 1996; Ptak, Cooper, & Brislin, 1995). In keeping with the theme of the entire book, the contributions of research in personality and individual differences are emphasized. As in any research area, cross-cultural training has benefited from accepted definitions of terms. *Sojourners* are people who live and work in cultures other than their own. This term is preferred to *expatriates* because use of sojourners connotes that people will most likely be returning to their own culture within some period of time, perhaps after several years. *Hosts* are members of the culture in which the sojourners are spending time.

CROSS-CULTURAL EXPERIENCES AND TRAINING PROGRAMS: KEY ELEMENTS

Most people begin their intercultural experiences, such as the eight types mentioned previously, without much formal preparation. International students, for example, obtain their visas, buy their airline tickets, arrive on campus in another country, register for courses during the same time as host country nationals, and begin their studies. Such an approach is often called "sink or swim." Some international students undoubtedly do well, but there is always the dread on the part of thoughtful university administrators that the percentage of students successfully completing their degree programs, without experiencing undue stress, could be increased (Westwood & Barker, 1990). "Culture shock" (Furnham & Bochner, 1986) is perhaps the best known term in the relevant literature and it refers to the stress, upheaval, frustration, and sense of helplessness that occurs when people experience serious difficulties when adjusting to life in another culture. In this chapter, examples are most frequently drawn from the experiences of people living in another country, such as overseas businesspeople, diplomats, or international students. Consequently, terms such as *adjusting to the pace of life in another country* are used. However, the same concepts can be used to discuss the experiences of people who have extensive intercultural contact within their own country. Examples are health care professionals from urban areas who take job assignments in rural areas where members of culturally diverse groups reside, or teachers from the suburbs who commute to their jobs in inner-city schools.

In sharp contrast to "sink or swim," many people are invited (or required by their organizations) to participate in a cross-cultural training program. These training programs are marked by features such as the following: They are planned, structured, have a budget, take place at a designated time and at a designated place, and are staffed by professionals who are knowledgeable about adjustment issues facing individuals about to interact extensively with people from other cultures. The general goal of these programs is to increase the likelihood that sojourners will encounter success in their work and a sense of satisfaction with their lives. A four-part criterion of cross-cultural success has been found useful by a number of researchers and training practitioners (Bhawuk, 1990; Brislin & Yoshida, 1994; Kealey, 1996), and knowledge of this multiple-part criterion can guide decisions in the planning of training program content and the choice of pedagogical approaches.

Criteria of Cross-Cultural Success. The four-part criterion begins with the assumption that sojourners (a) should experience a sense of fulfillment in the lives, should feel that they are making contributions in their work, and should have positive interpersonal relationships with hosts. Most often, these concepts will be assessed through self-reports or through the reports of others, such as spouses or superiors in the workplace. In addition to these self-reports, (b) hosts should report that the sojourners seem to be satisfied with their lives, are making contributions, and have positive interpersonal relations. Informally, hosts should be far more likely to report that "we are happy the sojourners are here" than they are to report that "we wish they had stayed in their own country." The third part is that (c) sojourners should accomplish their assigned tasks in a reasonable amount of time. Almost all sojourners have tasks associated with them: International students want to obtain degrees, overseas businesspeople want to establish joint trade agreements, and technical assistance advisors want to introduce new projects whose maintenance will continue after they return home. Keeping in mind reasonable adjustments in schedules given the pragmatics of working in another culture (e.g., second language, unfamiliar bureaucracies), task accomplishment should proceed in a timely manner.

The last part of the criterion (d) is that, after a predictable period of time during which they exerpience the psychological upheaval and anxiety stemming from culture shock, sojourners should experience no more stress than they would in their own culture. The time built for "the culture shock reaction" is an important caveat. Most sojourners experience culture shock, and the interesting speculation has been put forth that those sojourners who become most actively involved in the host culture experience the most culture shock. In contrast to people who remain in enclaves within the host culture (e.g., communities of fellow sojourners in Manila, Tokyo, or Paris), people who become extensively involved in host culture activities are more likely to encounter the misunderstandings, frustrations, and seemingly impenetrable bureaucracies that lead to culture shock. The informal wisdom of people who have studied intercultural contact (e.g., Bhawuk, 1990; Furnham & Bochner, 1986) is that superiors at work, friends, and hosts should be patient for about 6 months until sojourners deal with their culture shock and develop the cognitive and behavioral skills so that they are as effective as they would be in similar jobs in their own country.

Practical Issues in Organizing Training Programs. The piece of wisdom concerning patience for people undergoing culture shock is just one guideline shared by cross-cultural training's experienced practitioners. Whenever possible, trainers consult the published literature on cross-cultural experiences and training (e.g, the two editions of the relevant handbook edited by Landis & Brislin, 1983, and Landis & Bhagat, 1996), but not all aspects of training have been subjected to empirical scrutiny. This is especially true of the dynamic aspects of training involving change, reactions to trainee rigidity and other problems of program acceptance, and guidance through such trainee realizations that "I have indeed been guilty of ethnocentrism at times." Arguments concerning the suitability of reseach on these topics are similar to those in debates on the effectiveness of clinical interventions into people's mental health difficulties. Can the dynamic nature of patient-client interactions, as well as the complexities of potential changes, be captured in control-group studies (Beutler & Harwood, 1995; Rigazio-DiGilio, Goncalves, & Ivey, 1996) and will such studies lead to prescriptive guidelines?

Whether practitioners answer "yes" or "no" to a variant of this question applied to cross-cultural training, most researchers and trainers point out that there has not been enough research to provide solid prescriptions to all decisions concerning program content, structure, and goals. In the absence of research findings, trainers must trust their judgments (after consultations with colleagues) and make the best choices they can. The following thoughts combine the relevant literature on program evaluation as well as informal wisdom gathered from experienced practitioners (Paige, 1996; Ptak et al., 1995), as well as the author's own experiences. These thoughts also provide background for suggestions about integrating the results of cross-cultural personality research that are made later in this chapter.

In different organizations, cross-cultural training is either a responsibility of full-time employees (e.g., Peace Corps, international student offices on university campuses) or it is a service for which competitive bids are sought (most businesses). Cross-cultural training specialists must realize that they are not competing only among themselves for contracts. They are competing for the limited training budgets of organizations, budgets that might be invested in computer training, leadership development, sales force motivation, integrating robotics, and so forth. This list, with its connotation of "the business world," is no accident. To earn enough to make a living, or to "moonlight" from their regular jobs in a financially significant manner, trainers must appeal to the business world. Possible exceptions are the military and departments of education, but these important parts of society often have their own human relations specialists who offer training programs in addition to myriad other duties. When they do go outside for help from consultants, the fees are modest. Given the importance of acceptance by the business world, trainers must be very skilled at answering the question, "What is the benefit to our business, and our competitive advantage, to hire you and your services?" Trainers often wisely carry out a needs analysis of an organization prior to the introduction of their actual program, asking questions such as "What problems do you face that might be addressed in a training program?" At times, trainers will *not* be able to find exact answers in the published literature and must make judgments based on the best (but incomplete) information available. For people who are uncomfortable going beyond very solid, replicated findings that can be gathered from the literature, my reaction has to be that they will not find satisfaction as cross-cultural trainers.

Trainers have to keep in mind that any program must lead to immediate acceptance. In *every* training program in which I have participated, there has been a paper-and-pencil evaluation form distributed to participants after the last formal presentation or session. Trainees are asked questions such as, "Was the material interesting? Was it at the proper level given the background of participant? Was it useful for our organizational goals? Did the trainer maintain participant interest in the subject matter?" If trainers do not receive favorable ratings, they are not invited back for other sessions. Trainers might argue that their material is challenging and *useful in the long run*, that participants need time to absorb it, and that evaluations taken 6 months after training will be positive. Such comments will fall on deaf ears.

An organization's executives will rarely request long-range evaluations. It is far easier for them to make decisions based on end-of-program evaluations than to incur the additional expense of gathering information from scattered trainees some time after training. This state of affairs is similar to a practice that will be familiar to many readers. Lecturers are hired by a college to teach credit courses. If these lecturers do not receive favorable end-of-semester teacher evaluations from their students, their chances of being rehired for the next semester fall significantly. Appeals to chairs and deans that "my material was challenging, students worked hard and so didn't have enough 'fun' to give me great ratings, and we should wait to see how many are accepted by graduate schools" will not carry much weight.

A potential difficulty of cross-cultural training, shared by all programs that deal with human behavior, is that many potential customers and potential participants do not feel a pressing need for the changes implicit in the training goals. Many people feel that they are good leaders, are good communicators, and get along just fine with their coworkers and subordinates who come from different cultural backgrounds. At times, there is resistance if trainees feel that they are being undeservedly labeled *ethnocentric* or *culturally insensitive.* More complex resistance occurs when trainees, as a result of program content and exercises, come to recognize instances of insensitivity in their recent pasts. Rather than admitting this, however, they lash out at the program staff with comments such as "superficial materials" and "this money should have been spent on computer training!" The ability to deal with trainee resistance, and to avoid a "burnout" reaction after multiple encounters with hostile trainees, is an essential component of successful trainers.

The problem of hostile trainees cannot be solved by introducing bland materials that do not challenge program participants. The reaction will surely be, "We already know this stuff—we read newspapers and magazines that go beyond this material." Nor is a good approach to introduce materials so advanced that participants will be reminded of their most challenging college courses. The reaction will surely be, "This material is too academic and not at all practical—the program leader may be a great professor, but she or he is a terrible trainer." So what are participants looking for in their trainers? They are willing to work with challenging material, but it must be presented in a clear, perhaps even entertaining way. Trainees will have surely been members of audiences for exciting, dynamic, and motivating public speakers who command appearance fees of $5,000 and up for a 90-minute appearance. They will not expect the highest levels of excitement and inspiration of every trainer, but they clearly are looking for people who "know their stuff," are enthusiastic about their material, and can communicate it well. Trainees also want to feel comfortable during question-and-answer sessions and (especially) during one-on-one contacts during breaks and during lunch hours. The following comment about a trainer was interpreted as highly positive by an organization's executives who then invited the trainer back for other sessions: "This person is a psychologist but didn't make me feel uncomfortable and turn people off when he answered our questions."

One way to make trainees comfortable is to call upon one's sense of humor. Amusing stories that communicate important points are an extremely valuable tool. For intercultural training, this can be one of the easier pieces of advice to follow, because many cross-cultural encounters lead to misunderstandings that (at least retrospectively) are amusing. Skillful trainers can draw important concepts from these stories *without* casting aspersions on any of the cultures involved and *without* making goats of characters in the stories.

Trainers should also be prepared to answer questions about issues that are only tangentially related to the program content. In my experience, if the program has the terms *cross-cultural* or *diversity* in the title, participants will ask questions that might seem to be the products of free association. For example, questions about male–female interactions in the workplace, the glass ceiling facing women and minorities, the place of affirmative action, and even the generation gap separating older and younger workers often arise. Trainers must realize that if these are the issues that trouble participants, a response such as "these bring up topics beyond the scope of this program" will not yield appreciative responses.

TRAINING PROGRAM CONTENT: INTEGRATING RESEARCH ON PERSONALITY AND INDIVIDUAL DIFFERENCES

I have presented fairly lengthy background information about cross-cultural training programs because I believe it is necessary when making decisions about integrating *any* cross-cultural research reported in the field's books and journals. Any concepts drawn from research have to be seen as relevant to trainees' current and upcoming experiences, and they have to be seen as relevant to the organization's mission. The concepts have to be presented in a way that is neither too simplistic nor too complex, and they have to be seen as practical rather than as interesting academic notions of possible use sometime in the distant future. The concepts also have to be presented in an interesting way, because trainees do not want to be reminded of their most demanding but dry college courses.

Research findings from cross-cultural studies of personality can find a valued place in the content chosen for a training program. Choices of content, of course, always follow from prior choices concerning program goals. In the remainder of this chapter, I assume that a major goal of training is to prepare people to interact effectively with hosts, to make accurate attributions when encountering unfamiliar behaviors, to make decisions that downplay ethnocentric tendencies as much as possible, and to introduce new behaviors that can increase the chances of success in people's extensive intercultural interactions.

Drawing From Different Bodies of Research. I am aware of programs that have drawn from research areas such as the following.

1. *Concepts developed by Geert Hofstede (1980).* Perhaps the best known set of concepts to explain cross-cultural differences, especially for the world of work, was developed by Geert Hofstede. He argued convincingly that helpful advice can be offered to sojourners based on knowledge of a culture's level of individualism and collectivism; preferred *power distance* between superiors and subordinates; the emphasis placed on norms, rules, and regulations (called *uncertainty avoidance*); the amount of gender-role differentiation (called *masculinity-femininity*); and the emphasis placed on long-range planning (called *Confucian dynamism*: Hofstede & Bond, 1988). Although these concepts were developed to describe cultures, there are parallel analyses of concepts that are meant to describe differences among individuals. For example, individual differences in authoritarianism (Schultz, Stone, & Christie, 1997) can be included in the same training session that covers power distance, with the suggestion that people high in authoritarianism will find it easier to interact smoothly in high-power-distance cultures than will people low in authoritarianism.

2. *Individualism-collectivism and corresponding individual-differences concepts.* Individualism-collectivism has been extensively researched and used in training programs (e.g., Bhawuk, 1990; Brislin,

1993; Triandis, 1996) to the point where it deserves its own entry in a list such as the present one. Applications to training draw from extensive previous research on both subjective culture and culture assimilators as a specific training method (Triandis, 1972, 1994). Related research has investigated individual-differences *counterparts* of the cultural concept, such as the distinction between views of oneself as independent or interdependent (Markus & Kitayama, 1991; Singelis & Sharkey, 1995). This is one of the two approaches discussed in more detail in a subsequent section of this chapter.

3.   *Concepts based on evolutionary theory.* An increasingly active research tradition (e.g., Buss, 1996; see also Rushton, chap. 3 of this volume) has examined differences among people as they reflect adaptations that would have increased our distant ancestors' chances of survival. For example, trainees might be asked the question, "Is there a basic wariness when people interact with strangers who are physically different, with skin color being one very clear difference? Was this wariness functional for our distant ancestors because the strangers could be bringing danger? Is wariness in the company of physically different others, then, a result of our evolutionary past?" Returning to the theme of practical advice, I have to warn that drawing from evolutionary theory can be a tough sell. Many trainees have not thought extensively about the relation between biology and their behavior, preferring to believe that virtually all their decisions are the result of their free will. I have seen evolutionary theory successfully applied to the more specific goal of understanding male–female differences in the workplace, with evolutionary theory (Buss, 1996) providing a useful starting point for discussions of what men and women are looking for in relationships.

4.   *Using research on the "Big Five."* A great deal of research has been carried out examining the possible universality of five second-order personality traits (Paunonen et al., 1996; see also Lee, McCauley, & Draguns, chap. 1 of this volume; Pervin, chap. 2 of this volume; Peabody, chap. 4 of this volume) that have become known as the Big Five. Program content can link differences in the five personality traits to the criteria of cross-cultural success as reviewed previously. One active exercise would be to present information of the Big Five and the four-part criterion for cross-cultural success. Then, participants would be asked to relate the two bodies of research by making predictions concerning the relation between personality and

aspects of success. When I have administered this exercise, participants have suggested reasonable hypotheses such as the following: Individual differences in agreeableness will be related to the ease of developing positive interpersonal relations with hosts. Differences in conscientiousness will relate to success in task accomplishment. Sojourners high in openness to experience will be more likely to leave the confines of like-minded same-country friends and will instead seek out different experiences in the host culture. A more speculative possibility is that neuroticism will be related to the amount of debilitating culture shock people encounter, because sojourners high in this trait may overinterpret and internalize the inevitable difficulties that must be faced when living in another culture.

5. *Using research from the tradition known as* the indigenous approach. Another exciting body of research starts with the assumption that, as much as possible, research should start with concepts that are used by people within their own culture (Kim & Berry, 1993). Beginning steps include gathering answers to questions such as these: "What terms do people use to describe each other? What features of people are used to make predictions about their future behavior? How do people go about learning new material? How to they assure that children acquire the skills necessary to make contributions to society upon reaching adulthood?" When applied to intercultural contact, the key is to understand how hosts think about themselves and others because the behavior of sojourners will be examined through filters influenced by this thinking. Scholars who do research using the indigenous approach worry that if concepts developed in one culture are examined in another (e.g., intelligence as operationally defined by certain tests), results will be relatively meaningless and will represent a culturally insensitive imposition. The indigenous approach is covered later in this chapter when I discuss program content in more detail.

6. *Using the competencies approach.* Still another approach is to examine individual differences in the competencies people bring to and develop during their intercultural interactions (Dinges & Baldwin, 1996; Hammer, Nishida, & Wiseman, 1996). Although there is not a clear conceptual distinction between personality traits and individual competencies, the latter usually refer to aspects of people that (a) are visible in their overt behavior and that (b) involve skills that can develop with motivation and practice. For example, in a study of interactions between Americans and Japanese (see also Miller, chap.

11 of this volume), Hammer and his colleagues examined three competencies: understanding rules, according to Japanese norms, that apply in different social situations; displaying a knowledge of Japanese culture in general (e.g., food, gifts, sports); and displaying positive affect toward Japanese culture. Some competencies benefit from practice. Expanding on research he had published (Markus & Kitayama, 1991), Shinobu Kitayama once told me about a difficulty Japanese often have when interacting with Americans. After initial encounters with Americans, certain competencies are necessary if Japanese are to have continued interactions. One is that the individual Japanese person must communicate an independent self with opinions, interests, and a sense of humor. Such a view of oneself is not as essential in the collective society in which they were socialized. After arriving in the United States for graduate study, Dr. Kitayama would stand in front of a mirror practicing interactions with Americans and communicating a sense that "I am an interesting person with opinions and interests and you should include me when thinking of people to invite to various social occasions."

7.   *The predictors of intercultural success approach.* There is a scattered and loosely organized body of research that has attempted to answer the question, "Is there a measurable set of indicators that predict intercultural success?" At times, the answers to the question resemble personality traits, at other times they suggest competencies, and occasionally they refer to measurable, overt behaviors. Summarized by Kealey (1996), this theoretically loose list of predictors includes tolerance for ambiguity, stress tolerance, emotional maturity, political astuteness, perseverance, and self-confidence. This predictor approach has been used in very specific training programs for skilled professionals about to carry out tasks in a specific country.

For example, Kealey presented the outline of training materials for Canadian technical assistance advisers working in Egypt. Two predictors that would be covered are perseverance and "willingness to socialize with Egyptians on and off the job," and these would be related to the essential job skill of "never giving up on trying to help … Egyptian colleagues develop new skills and techniques (p. 91)."

8.   *The individual differences in intergroup relations approach.* Based on recent theoretical developments in the study of intergroup relations, this approach looks at the ways different people approach the task of interacting with people from other racial and cultural groups (Devine,

1995; Devine & Elliot, 1995; Lee, Jussim, & McCauley, 1995; Sidanius, Oratto, & Bobo, 1996). One difference between this and other approaches is that the *starting point* is the analysis of intergroup relations. This contrasts with research that examines existing concepts (e.g., the Big Five) for their *possible application* to understanding intergroup relations. For example, Devine examined the relation between prejudice and use of stereotypes. Her results indicate that people within a culture do not differ greatly in their knowledge of stereotypes. In fact, one indicator of membership in a culture is that people share stereotypes of diverse groups whose members have had a long presence within a country. However, there are individual differences in people's willingness to make decisions based on the stereotypes and to fight any tendency to treat culturally different people in a negative manner given the extensive of negative stereotypes. Another way to introduce stereotypes into training is to ask the same question posed by Lee and his colleagues: Do stereotypes summarize group characteristics as perceived by outsiders and are they a good starting point for analyzing cultural differences? My experience is that introducing stereotypes in training is often useful because it is a concept familiar to trainees. Trainees know what stereotypes are and their understanding of the term overlaps with that of behavioral and social scientists (more than many other concepts). Consequently, trainers find themselves taking advantage of the practical advice, "Start introducing material based on where trainees *are* in their thinking, not where the trainer thinks that their thinking should be."

Another part of the intergroup relations approach is to recognize that some people are simply not very skilled at interacting with people from different groups (Stephan, 1985). They become anxious during intercultural encounters and fumble in the demonstration of basic social skills such as making people feel welcome and finding mutually interesting topics for conversation. If they recognize their difficulties and are willing to change, such people can benefit from training that emphasizes practice in intergroup relations skills.

CONTENT FOR CROSS-CULTURAL TRAINING PROGRAMS: TWO EXAMPLES

Ways of integrating psychological research on individual differences into cross-cultural training programs become clearer through the analysis of more detailed examples. Two are presented here: using theoretical research on individualism and collectivism and using indigenous personality research. In both examples, various guidelines for program design are followed (e.g., summarized in Brislin & Yoshida, 1994; Gudykunst, Guzley, & Hammer, 1996). These include the practical issues described in the first part of this chapter as well as being sensitive to "where trainees are" at the start of a program and what sorts of contributions they can make, introducing a number of activities in which participants can become actively involved, introducing concepts that should be useful in a large number of specific social situations, and encouraging people to make attributions for behaviors that are similar to those hosts make about themselves.

A Program Using the Concepts Individualism and Collectivism.
Differences among people socialized into individualist versus collectivist cultures have important impacts when people move across cultural boundaries (Triandis, 1994, 1996). A training program might have four components: (a) a short lecture or formal presentation to introduce the concepts and their implications, (b) examples chosen because of their applicability to the participants' upcoming intercultural assignments, (c) analysis of critical incidents that require participants to analyze cultural misunderstandings not only from their own perspectives but also from the viewpoint of others, and (d) opportunities to apply the concepts to participants' own lives. To guide the choice of specific examples of concepts, it assumed that the audience consists of businesspeople about to undertake international assignments.

Any formal presentation would begin with major distinctions that distinguish individualist from collectivist cultures. In collective societies, there is one or more groups in people's lives *beyond the nuclear family* that are important in making decisions about one's life. The group might be one's extended family, organization, religious community, or any other group of people whose members are kept in mind when important decisions are made. In individualistic cultures, there is not such a group beyond the nuclear family. People have their nuclear family in mind when making decisions, but do not as frequently integrate the viewpoints of another group. This distinction is made admittedly more complex when we add individual differences into any analysis (Singelis & Sharkey, 1995). In both individualistic and collectivist cultures, there are differences among people in their thinking about others beyond the nuclear family. For example, in the individualistic United States there are people who are very concerned about the welfare of extended family members and who are so loyal to their organization that they would not leave if offered a better job elsewhere. In collectivist Japan, there are successful entrepreneurs who put their own profit motive above the concerns of any identifiable group. The existence of these *individual* differences do not call into question the existence of the *cultural* variables, just as the presence of people who want to silence their opponents does not eliminate the existence of free speech as a cultural value in many societies.

Four defining features of individualism versus collectivism have been identified (Bhawuk, 1995; Triandis, 1994), and all have implications for intercultural encounters. The first defining feature is whether people have an *independent* or an *interdependent* sense of self. Independent refers to a focus on one's own traits and skills, and interdependent refers to one's relations with others. When asked to describe themselves, people from collective cultures are more likely to discuss other people, whereas individualists are more likely to refer to features reminiscent of a personality test such as their ambition and willingness to work hard. The second feature deals with life's goals. Do people form their own goals with minimal reference to others, or do they carefully and consciously integrate the goals of others (again, beyond the nuclear family). Collectivists are more likely to participate in various arrangements that can be called "shared life goals." Many individualists, over the years, have commented on the willingness of married students from Asia to travel to other countries for their higher education while leaving young children behind. This violation of individualistic expectations is made more understandable when the concept of group goals is analyzed. Taking care of children is a goal of the international student parents, but it is also a goal of others: grandparents, aunts, uncles, and older cousins. The traveling parents know that their children will be in excellent hands.

The third defining feature deals with the distinction between attitudes and norms. Given their emphasis on the independent self, people socialized in individualistic cultures are comfortable with having large numbers of attitudes. They have attitudes toward such social phenomena as owning handguns, birth control, violence on television, and the attractiveness of various political candidates. Collectivists, on the other hand, are more likely to be influenced by group norms than by their individual attitudes. Given their sense of collective selves, it makes more sense for them to be attuned to norms shared by many people. It is more important to have a shared sense of the group concerning handgun ownership than it is for every individual to have a distinct attitude.

The fourth defining feature focuses on a distinction between relatedness and rationality in decision making. This distinction is at the core of many puzzling, frustrating, and hard-to-understand intercultural encounters. Given (again) a sense of self that involves others, people socialized in collective cultures often make decisions based on their relations with people. Individualists, on the other hand, are more likely to make decisions based on their analyses of rationality. This rationality often includes the element "we must treat people the same, no matter their relationship to us." This dilemma may capture the distinction. A professor has given significant help to a student on three separate occasions. The student sees the professor drinking heavily at a college reception, and later discovers that the professor was in a traffic accident. People at the reception are interviewed by the police. Does the student give answers based on her or his positive relation with the professor or based on a rational analysis such as "society can't tolerate the combination of drinking and driving."

Applications can then be made to the business world, and the trainer should follow the facial expressions and other body language communications of participants to determine if points are understood. The example of length of employment can often be clearly explained. If people have an independent sense of self, they will feel free to come and go from many organizations over a number of years. People with an interdependent self will be more likely to stay with the same organization because *that organization* may become part of the phenomenological self. The distinction between self-goals and group-goals can also be related to organizational tenure. In a collectivist culture, it makes more sense to invest in long training programs that teach complex skills. Not only will the skills be available to management in 10 years because the trainees will still be with the company, employees with the new skills will share them with coworkers given a sense of group goals in workplace.

People socialized in a collectivist culture will be more sensitive to group norms and will place these higher in their priorities than will individualists. Even though they do not want to socialize with coworkers during weekday evenings (their attitudes), they may go out to bars and restaurants if they feel that this is the expected norm. Relatedness will play a stronger role in decision making for collectivists than it will for individualists. Imagine two applicants for a position. One has a first-rate MBA degree and good job experience. The other dropped out of a bachelor's degree program and has never held a steady job, but is the boss's cousin. The emphasis on relatedness will play a more prominent role than the rationalist argument of "hire the best person" in a collectivist culture.

Now that trainees have been introduced to important concepts and have heard business examples, they can analyze critical incidents with the goal of identifying how cultural differences may be affecting people's interactions. There are several collections of these incidents (Bhawuk, 1995; Cushner & Brislin, 1996) that depict interactions among well-meaning people from different cultures. Despite people's good intentions, there is a misunderstanding based on unexpected and poorly understood cultural differences. The following incident is from a collection prepared by Bhawuk that was designed to demonstrate the application of the four defining features of individualism and collectivism to a wide variety of intercultural encounters. Trainees would read the incident, chose an alternative(s), and also explain the applicability of one or more of the defining features.

The Dynamic Leader

Brad had accepted the General Manager's position in Thailand for a Thai-U.S. joint venture company. His predecessor had prematurely returned to the United States for personal reasons. Because Brad had no family obligations and was not married, he didn't expect any problem in his own case.

On his arrival in Bangkok, he was accorded a warm welcome and he liked the spacious house provided by this company. He was quite excited to have a chauffeur, cook, and maids. He knew that he was going to get all these as perquisites, but to be using them was a different experience. He felt important and was very pleased.

At work, he proposed that all the key people meet once a week for a short period of time to take stock of the progress made and hoped that this would help them avoid communication gaps. His deputy, Mr. Thirayut, a U.S.-trained local manager, was not sure if they should do that, but Brad was ale to convince him that it was "good management" to do so.

In a few weeks Brad realized that people were quite shy in the meetings and Mr. Thirayut presented all the information. He suggested that this was a wasteful approach and emphatically demanded that everyone present his or her ideas in the meetings. No one said anything, but in the next meeting much less got done and everyone was unusually quiet.

How would you advise Brad?

1. Brad is trying to implement participative management which is alien to Thailand.

2. Brad is asserting himself which is not an acceptable behavior in Thailand.

3. Mr. Thirauyut is an autocratic person and other people are afraid of him.

4. The Thai managers want Brad to fail like his predecessor to that they can run the company the way they want.

After contemplating the various alternatives and making choices, participants would read that Item 2 is a good answer. People from individualist countries such as Brad are accustomed to speaking out and voicing their attitudes and opinions. This ability, carefully nurtured from the time of their childhood, reflects and reinforces a sense of independent self. On the other hand, "collectivists often are considerate of others' needs and may change their opinions and ideas to fit in with the group they care for (their ingroup)" (Bhawuk, 1995, p. 190).

If trainers are convinced that participants would enjoy becoming actively involved, they can ask participants to (a) think of incidents in their own lives that reflect the concepts covered in the program or (b) role play an incident from one of the published collections. Such active involvement will assist the trainees integrate and use their newly acquired knowledge.

A Program Using the Indigenous Approach. The indigenous approach begins with the assumption that there is a great deal to learn by analyzing how people describe, discuss, and analyze behavior *from their own perspectives.* Typical methods include listening to people describe themselves and others, asking them general questions such as "who is a good person," reading a culture's literature that has been popular for generations, studying indigenous dictionaries for terms that can be used to describe people, collecting proverbs handed down generation to generation, and so forth. When used in personality research, the goal is to identify dimensions on which people within a culture differ. I find the best examples of this approach very exciting because, for sojourners, information is available concerning what *hosts* look for when thinking about other people. Sojourners must realize that their personalities will be judged according to hosts' frameworks.

Aspects of Chinese personality have been identified using the indigenous approach by Cheung and her colleagues (1996). One example is a dimension called "Chinese tradition," and it distinguishes people who adhere to certain traditional practices from other Chinese who find modernity more attractive. One of the traditions should be clear from the previous discussion of collectivism: People should emphasize harmonious relations with others. Another is thrift, a familiar if old-fashioned concept that includes saving money, carefulness in spending, and a reticence to spend money on personal pleasures and entertainment. I have drawn from research on both of these concepts in my work with Asian businessmen who come from countries where a forward-thinking, dynamic Confucian philosophy has been influential. As documented by researchers known as the Chinese Culture Connection (1987), an emphasis on thrift has important implications. The rate of personal savings in some Asian countries (e.g., Japan, Korea, Taiwan) is higher than in the United States. This result of a value placed on thrift means that there will be money available for investments in various businesses.

A related concept investigated by researchers, more closely related to the practical world of business, concerns the nature and importance of *guanxi*. As analyzed by Luo and Chen (1996), "Guanxi is the word that describes the intricate, pervasive network of personal or business relations which Chinese cultivate energetically, subtly, and imaginatively. It refers to a relationship between two people or organizations containing implicit mutual obligation, assurance, and understanding and governs Chinese attitudes toward long-term social and business relationships" (pp. 293–294). The individual difference of interest to readers of this volume is that some people have more guanxi relationships than others and so have more access to resources to attain their goals.

Guanxi relationships involve exchanges of favors across various dimensions such as money, goods, information, and services, and the careful mental record keeping of these exchanges. To cut through complex bureaucracies and competing collectives, people engage in a web of favor giving and favor receiving. An important mark of one's status and even future prospects of success is access to people with favors to give, together with the realization that these favors must be returned. These "favor-giving and -receiving" networks can lead to charges by outsiders that decisions are based on favoritism and nepotism and that they come close to corrupt practices. There are many examples that can be shared with businesspeople in a training program. If a Chinese government bureaucrat gives extra time and attention to an American's or European's proposal for a joint venture, this is viewed as a favor and not part of the bureaucrat's job. The outsiders will be expected to return the favor, and this may take the form of hiring the bureaucrat's not very qualified relatives.

Recently, a collection of critical incidents has been completed for North Americans who want to work in China in business and educational settings (Wang, Williams, Wang, & Brislin, 1997). The following incident and alternatives would be presented to trainees.

The Request for a Price Concession

(The first part of this long incident describes how a woman from Evanston, Illinois, decided to contact companies in China to supply her home remodeling business with plumbing fixtures.) With the help of the Small Business Administration in nearby Chicago, Patricia began negotiations with manufacturing companies in Beijing. ... Her main contact person in Beijing was Yingjin Lei, an employee of one of the companies with which she was considering doing business. Lei had considerable English-language skills and was often asked by his company to be the liaison person when Americans, Australians, and Canadians began correspondence related to business matters.

Shortly after Patricia's arrival, Lei helped Patricia find an apartment. Later, he also introduced her to various government officials whose approval would eventually be necessary if business agreements were to be finalized. Lei also made arrangements for a dinner to which 12 people were invited, all of whom would be involved in the negotiations within his company.

During the first meeting at which actual business negotiations began, Patricia simply outlined the basics of her proposal. At the second meeting, Lei began acting as the spokesperson when Patricia presented her opinions about reasonable unit prices for various plumbing fixtures. Lei presented a counteroffer requesting a number of price concessions, and Patricia thought that some of the suggestions were unreasonable. She could recover her own costs and make a small profit given Lei's suggestions, she thought, but she certainly would never join the group whose members were known to "do well" in China. Patricia knew that the Chinese were good businesspeople and hard bargainers, but she suspected that there was something going on in these negotiations that was unfamiliar to her.

If Patricia asked you for your help in interpreting this incident, which of the following are reasonable replies you could make?

1. Patricia recognizes the favors Lei did for her, but her culture does not include the guidance that favors should be returned.
2. Lei feels that given the many favors he did for Patricia, she should

consider the possibility of returning the favors through the price concessions she requests.
3. Patricia is familiar with the concept of returning favors, but she may not know the magnitude of the favors that Lei has arranged for her.
4. Patricia's cultural background gives guidance to the practice of carefully returning each favor after a very short period from the time the favor was given.
5. Lei's cultural background guides him in the thought that returning favors is not important.

There are two correct answers, Items 2 and 3. Lei expects favors to be returned, and the return can be on business-related issues for which Patricia is unprepared. Patricia may know that favors should be returned from experiences in her own culture. But she (a) may not know that Lei has done a great deal for her compared to the treatment received by other Americans and that (b) Lei may be using his past favors as a bludgeon to obtain the price concession.

Other incidents in this package (Wang et al., 1997) deal with bureaucracies, developing interpersonal relations with Chinese, interpreting (what seem to be) ambiguous communications, examining different views of corruption and intellectual property rights, and dealing with status differences. As with all collections of critical incidents, groups of trainees can be asked to prepare role plays of interactions they find especially intriguing and present them to the rest of the participants.

CONCLUSIONS

Combining treatments of cultural differences and individual differences in the same program helps deal with another practical issue of the type covered earlier in this chapter. When presented with information on cultural differences, some sophisticated trainees will ask, "Aren't you saying all people in the other culture are pretty much the same, as in your discussion of collectivists, and aren't you just creating new stereotypes?" (Lee et al., 1995, also discussed ways of dealing effectively with this query). This question would probably not arise if individual differences are explicitly covered. But if the question does come up, the trainer could respond along the following lines. There are cultural differences such as individualism-collectivism and the importance of guanxi relationships, but we must always keep in mind the presence of individual differences. Within individualistic cultures, there will be people who are very close to their extended families and who view their jobs in a specific organization as permanent. In China, there are people who nurture guanxi relationships, but there are others who feel it is antiquated and interferes with opportunities for expansion into international business ventures. The existence of both cultural differences and individual differences must be constantly kept in mind. This combination admittedly makes analysis more difficult, but it provides a more realistic preparation for the complexities of adjusting to a culture other than one's own.

REFERENCES

Adler, N. (1997). *International dimensions of organizational behavior* (3rd ed.). Cincinatti, OH: South-Western.

Allport, G. (1954). *The nature of prejudice*. Reading, MA: Addison-Wesley.

Beutler, L., & Harwood, M. (1995). Prescriptive psychotherapies. *Applied & Preventive Psychology, 4,* 89–100.

Bhawuk, D. (1990). Cross-cultural orientation programs. In R. Brislin (Ed.), *Applied cross-cultural psychology* (pp. 325–346). Newbury Park, CA: Sage.

Bhawuk, D. (1995). *The role of culture theory in cross-cultural training: A comparative evaluation of culture-specific, culture-general, and theory-based assimilators.* Unpublished doctoral dissertation, University of Illinois, Urbana.

Brislin, R. (1993). *Understanding culture's influence on behavior.* Fort Worth, TX: Harcourt Brace.

Brislin, R., & Yoshida, T. (1994). *Intercultural communication training: An introduction.* Thousand Oaks, CA: Sage.

Buss, D. (1996). The evolutionary psychology of human social strategies. In E.T. Higgins & A. Kruglanski (Eds.), *Social psychology: Handbook of basic principles* (pp. 3–38). New York: Guilford.

Cheung, F., Leung, K., Fan, R., Song, W.-Z., Zhang, J.-X., & Zhang, J.-P. (1996). Development of the Chinese Personality Assessment Inventory. *Journal of Cross-Cultural Psychology, 27,* 181–199.

Chinese Culture Connection. (1987). Chinese values and the search for culture-free dimensions of culture. *Journal of Cross-Cultural Psychology, 18,* 143–164.

Cushner, K., & Brislin, R. (1996). *Intercultural interactions: A practical guide* (2nd ed.). Thousand Oaks, CA: Sage.

Devine, P. (1995). Getting hooked on research in social psychology: Examples from eyewitness identification and prejudice. In G. Brannigan & M. Merrens (Eds.), *The social psychologists: Research adventures* (pp. 161–184). New York: McGraw-Hill.

Devine, P., & Elliot, A. (1995). Are racial stereotypes *really* fading: The Princeton triology revisited. *Personality and Social Psychology Bulletin, 21,* 1139–1150.

Dinges, N., & Baldwin, K. (1996). Intercultural competence: A research perspective. In D. Landis & R. Bhagat (Eds.), *Handbook of intercultural training* (2nd ed., pp. 81–105). Thousand Oaks, CA: Sage.

Fowler, S., & Mumford, M. (1995). *Intercultural sourcebook: Cross-cultural training methods* (Vol. 1). Yarmouth, ME: Intercultural Press.

Furnham, A., & Bochner, S. (1986). *Culture shock: Psychological reactions to unfamiliar environments.* London: Methuen.

Gudykunst, W., Guzley, R., & Hammer, M. (1996). Designing intercultural training. In D. Landis & R. Bhagat (Eds.), *Handbook of intercultural training* (2nd ed., pp. 61–80). Thousand Oaks, CA: Sage.

Hammer, M., Nishida, H., & Wiseman, R. (1996). The influence of situational prototypes on dimensions of interrcultual communication competence. *Journal of Cross-Cultural Psychology, 27,* 267–282.

Hofstede, G. (1980). *Culture's consequences: International differences in work-related values*. Newbury Park, CA: Sage.

Hofstede, G., & Bond, M. (1988). Confucius & economic growth: New trends in culture's consequences. *Organizational Dynamics, 16*(4), 4–21.

Kagitcibasi, C. (1978). Cross-national encounters: Turkish students in the United States. *International Journal of Intercultural Relations, 2,* 141–160.

Kealey, D. (1996). The challenge of international personnel selection. In D. Landis & R. Bhagat (Eds.), *Handbook of intercultural training* (2nd ed., pp. 106–123). Thousand Oaks, CA: Sage.

Kim, U., & Berry, J. (Eds.). (1993). *Indigenous psychologies*. Newbury Park, CA: Sage.

Landis, D., & Bhagat, R. (Eds.). (1996). *Handbook of intercultural training* (2nd ed). Thousand Oaks, CA: Sage.

Landis, D., & Brislin, R. (Eds). (1983). *Handbook of intercultural training* (3 vols.). Elmsford, NY: Pergamon.

Lee, Y-T., Jussim, L., & McCauley, C. (Eds.). (1995). *Stereotype accuracy: Toward appreciating group differences*. Washington, DC: American Psychological Association.

Luo, Y., & Chen, M. (1996). Managerial implications of guanxi-based business strategies. *Journal of International Management, 2,* 293–316.

Markus, H., & Kitayama, S. (1991). Culture and the self: Implications for cognition, emotion, and motivation. *Psychological Review, 98,* 224–253.

Paige, R. (1996). Intercultural trainer competencies. In D. Landis & R. Bhagat (Eds.), *Handbook of intercultural training* (2nd ed., pp. 148–164). Thousand Oaks, CA: Sage.

Paunonen, S., Keinonen, M., Trzebinski, J., Forsterling, F., Grishenko-Roze, N., Kouznetsova, L., & Chan, D. (1996). The structure of personality in six cultures. *Journal of Cross-Cultural Psychology, 27,* 339–353.

Ptak, C., Cooper, J., & Brislin, R. (1995). Cross-cultural training programs: Advice and insights from experienced trainers. *International Journal of Intercultural Relations, 19*(3), 425–453.

Rigazio-DiGilio, S., Goncalves, O., & Ivey, A. (1996). From cultural to existential diversity: The impossibility of psychotherapy intergration within a traditional framework. *Applied & Preventive Psychology, 4,* 235–247.

Schultz, P., Stone. W., & Christie, R. (1997). Authoritarianism and mental rigidity: The einstellung problem revisited. *Personality and Social Psychology Bulletin, 23,* 3–9.

Sidanius, J., Oratto, F., & Bobo, L. (1996). Racism, conservatism, affirmative action, and intellectual sophistication: A matter of principled conservatism or group dominance? *Journal of Personality and Social Psychology, 70,* 476–490.

Singelis, T., & Sharkey, W. (1995). Culture, self-construal, & embarrassability. *Journal of Cross-Cultural Psychology, 26,* 622–644.

Stephan, W. (1985). Intergroup relations. In G. Lindzey & E. Aronson (Eds.), *Handbook of social psychology* (3rd. ed., Vol. 2, pp. 599–658). New York: Random House.

Triandis, H. (1972). *The analysis of subjective culture*. New York: Wiley.

Triandis, H. (1994). *Culture and social behavior*. New York: Mc-Graw Hill.

Triandis, H. (1996). The psychological measurement of cultural syndromes. *American Psychologist, 51,* 407–415.

Wang, M., Williams, D., Wang, L., & Brislin, R. (1997). *Critical incidents for mutual understanding among North Americans and Chinese*. Unpublished manuscript.

Westwood, M. & Barker, M. (1990). Academic achievement & social adaptation among international students: A comparison groups study of the peer-pairing program. *International Journal of Intercultural Relations, 14,* 251–263.

14

Person Perception Across Cultures

Clark McCauley
Bryn Mawr College

Juris Draguns
Pennsylvania State University

Yueh-Ting Lee
Westfield State College

This volume began as an effort to renew and extend the promise of Child's (1968) overview of personality in culture in the *Handbook of Personality Theory and Research*. We argued in the Introduction that growing awareness of issues in cross-cultural research has revived interest in Child's topic, after 30 years of relative neglect. In this concluding chapter, the editors look back at the contributions of the volume to give their own sense of the issues and directions of current research on personality in culture.

PERSONALITY IN CULTURE: THE STUDY OF HUMAN DIFFERENCES

Often overlooked in discussions of personality and culture is the fact that both of these constructs (i.e., personality and culture) are predicated upon comparisons. In personality, individuals are anxious, or extroverted, or open to new experience only in comparison with other individuals who are healthy-minded, introverted, or closed to new experience. An individual's "dynamic organization" (Allport, 1937) or "characteristic pattern" (Funder, 1997) cannot be understood absolutely but only by reference to others. Personality is a conception rooted in the observation of individual differences, especially differences in response to similar objective circumstances.

279

Similarly, the conception of culture is grounded in the observation of group differences, especially when these differences are observed against a background of similar objective circumstances (e.g., Hispanic and African-American subcultures within the United States). An anthropologist's description of a culture always implies a comparison with other cultures. At a minimum, the anthropological observer chooses what to report in relation to what is known about other cultures, particularly the anthropologist's native culture. To say that a culture is a "collectivist" culture would be meaningless without the implied comparison with an "individualist" culture (Markus & Kitayama, 1991; also see Lee & Seligman, 1997; Linton, 1945).

Basically then, studies of personality and studies of culture are studies of human differences. This perspective can usefully be amplified by attention to two distinctions made salient in Child's 1968 chapter.

A TYPOLOGY OF INDIVIDUAL-DIFFERENCES RESEARCH

Child's first distinction was between group differences and individual differences: the study of group character or of modal or typical group personality, as versus the study of personality structure and individual differences within a culture. This distinction recognizes that the structure and organization of individual differences within a culture need not be the same as the structure and organization of group differences. Child's second distinction separated perceived differences from actual differences: the study of what people believe about human differences, as versus the study of the facts of human differences (see similar discussion of Ichheiser, 1949, 1970).

The result of Child's two distinctions is a four-fold table of research interests: Both group differences and individual differences can be studied both in perception and in fact. The obvious importance of comparing perception and reality leads to two more kinds of research: the validity of perceived group differences and the validity of perceived individual differences within a group. Finally, an interest in the origins of the four kinds of differences—group and individual, perceived and actual—adds four more kinds of research.

Thus Child's distinctions lead to fully 10 different research issues concerned with personality in culture. Simply put, these are: perceived individual differences, perceived group differences, actual individual differences, actual group differences, validity of perceived individual differences, validity of perceived group differences, origin of perceived individual differences, origin of perceived group differences, origin of actual individual differences, and origin of actual group differences. These 10 research issues correspond to major subdivisions of psychology that are familiar under somewhat different designations. We consider each issue in turn, and relate each to the contributions to this volume.

RESEARCH ISSUES IN PERSONALITY AND CULTURE

Perceived Individual and Group Differences

The first issue corresponds to the study of *lay theory of personality* or *implicit personality theory* (e.g., Bruner & Tagiuri, 1954; Chiu, Hong, & Dweck, 1997; Dweck, Chiu, & Hong, 1995; Funder & West, 1993; Ichheiser, 1949, 1970; Mischel, 1984; Tagiuri & Petrullo, 1958). Implicit personality theory is the culturally shared network of inferences linking one personality characteristic with another; if we know that a person is friendly, for instance, we infer that he or she is likely to be helpful as well. This network is a powerful tool by which humans go beyond the given in person perception.

Study of lay personality theory did indeed begin with Asch's (1946) classic article on "impressions of personality" that relied exclusively on trait words such as *warm, cold, polite, blunt,* and so forth. But later research made clear that the network of inferences linking one trait word with another also links trait words with gender, clothing, physical appearance, social behaviors, personal preferences (food, music, sports), occupations, and more (Deaux & Lewis, 1984). For instance, college students whose favorite foods are fruit and tofu, compared with students whose favorite foods are hamburgers and chocolate shakes, are seen as more moral and more politically liberal (Stein & Nemeroff, 1995).

The second issue is the study of group stereotypes: culturally shared beliefs about probabilistic group differences (Lee, Jussim, & McCauley, 1995). Stereotypes are also networks of inferences; if we know that person is English, for instance, we infer that she is likely to be more reserved than an American (see Peabody, chap. 4 of this volume). The perceived links between group membership and personality traits have been given special attention as "stereotypes" (e.g., men more likely than women to be aggressive, business students more likely than arts and sciences students to be competitive), but stereotype inferences are not limited to traits (e.g., women more likely than men to be grade-school teachers, business students less likely than others to take a poetry course). In short, there is almost no piece of information about a person that does not give rise to inferences about what else is likely or unlikely to be true of that person.

These first two issues have a great deal in common. Group membership is, after all, a characteristic of individuals, just as personality traits are characteristics of individuals. Conversely, any individual characteristic or trait defines a group of persons who share that characteristic. It follows that an inference from one personality trait to another is formally the same as an inference from group membership to expectations about traits and behaviors. Thus we are inclined to see perceptions of individual differences and perception of group differences as part of one and the same implicit theory of personality. This theory is a culturally shared network of inferences linking together every kind of human attribute, characteristic, or product: traits, values, motives, behaviors, physical appearance, occupation, education, social status, and—not least—ethnic and national group membership.

Implicit Personality Theory in Relation to Academic Personality Theory

This enlarged view of implicit personality theory makes it more clearly and directly the layperson's counterpart of academic personality theory (see next section): Both extend far beyond the realm of trait adjectives. Just as lay personality theory links every kind of individual difference with many other differences, so does academic personality theory attempt to link self-reports or observer reports of individual difference with other kinds of observations. Academic personality theory is not just the study of the application and interrelation of personality trait words: *neurotic, extroverted, sensation seeking,* and so on. Rather, construct validation of personality scales always involves linking trait scores with as many as possible of the same kinds of individual-difference observations that appear in lay personality theory (group memberships, preferences, beliefs, behaviors).

Thus implicit personality theory, including perceptions of both individual and group differences, covers substantially the same ground as academic personality theory: Both are networks of probabilistic inferences linking many kinds of individual-difference characteristics with one another. The difference between the lay theory and the academic theory is a matter of evidence or accuracy, about which we say more later in considering the issues discussed in the section Validity of Perceived Individual and Group Differences.

Actual Individual Differences

The third issue, the study of actual individual differences, is, as already noted, the business of academic personality research, which has recently focused on the "Big Five" or "Five Factor Model" (FFM) as the structure best able to represent the interrelations of the many trait dimensions that have been used to assess individual differences within a group. The five-factor structure of personality self-reports (see Peabody, chap. 4. of this volume; Pervin, chap. 2 of this volume; Brislin, chap. 13 of this volume) seems to be recoverable as well from personality ratings by observers; that is, the subjective facts seem to match the lay perceptions (e.g., Goldberg, 1993; John, 1990; Magnusson & Torestad, 1993; McCrae & Costa, 1990).

Whether the Big Five model is applicable to personality differences outside of the Western nations in which it has arisen is still controversial. On the one hand, the results of several studies suggested that the Big Five factors were culturally general (e.g., Goldberg, 1993; John, 1990; McAdam, 1992; McCrae & Costa, 1990; also see Ozer & Reise, 1994, and Wiggins, in press, Wiggins & Pincus, 1992, for a review). On the other hand, evidence from other studies suggested that the Big Five or FFM was culturally specific (e.g., Almagor, Tellegen, & Waller, 1995; Benet & Waller, 1995; Diaz-Guerrero & Diaz Loving, 1994; Yang & Bond, 1990).

Although Pervin (chap. 2 of this volume) finds the cross-cultural replicability of factors in ratings and questionnaires "surprising and noteworthy," he raises two cautions about this research. The first caution is that this research is based on the "lexical hypothesis" (see also Peabody, chap. 4 of this volume) that the individual differences most important in a culture will come to be represented by single words in that culture's language. Pervin notes that few studies have started from an analysis of individual-difference words in non-Western cultures; the more usual approach is to start with Western personality words that are translated into the words of a different culture.

Pervin's second caution is that the lexical hypothesis is an assumption that may be better founded in Western than in non-Western cultures. The problem is that non-Westerners asked to describe an acquaintance may be relatively unlikely to use trait terms and more likely to offer a context-dependent description of behavior. Thus the FFM or any other result of personality research that starts from trait words may be less relevant to individual differences as perceived in non-Western cultures.

With regard to this second caution, we note that there is a tradition in Western individual-differences research that emphasizes context-dependent descriptions of behavior—the critical-incident technique used in industrial psychology (Flanagan, 1954). This technique is used both for evaluating job requirements and, in hiring or promotion interviews, to evaluate individuals in terms of job requirements. For assessing relations with superiors, for instance, an interviewer might ask, "Was there ever a time when you found yourself in serious disagreement with your superior about an important issue? How did you handle this situation?" It seems possible that individual-differences research based on the critical incident technique might be as useful in cross-cultural personality research as it has been in industrial psychology. Indeed the critical-incident technique is the backbone of cross-cultural training programs (Brislin, chap. 13 of this volume; see later discussion).

Actual Group Differences

The fourth issue, the study of actual group differences, is pursued in cross-cultural psychology and anthropology (e.g., Campbell, 1967; Lee & Ottati, 1993; Lynn, 1995; Whiting & Child, 1953). This kind of study seeks to determine the facts of group differences in one or more aspects of culture—values, schemas, beliefs, norms, rituals—and may go on to interpret the differences in terms of some model or structure of group functioning. Modal personality is only one aspect of cultural difference, but it is the aspect central to this volume.

Study of cultural differences in personality has taken the same direction as study of personality differences within a culture; the goal has been to identify a small number of dimensions that can structure the interrelations of the many trait dimensions that have been used to compare cultures. As Peabody (chap. 4 of this volume) describes, there are at this time two major approaches to assessing cultural differences in modal personality. A third approach in the work of Schwartz (1994) is promising, but has as yet not been exactly related to personality and is not well represented in this volume.

Hofstede and Bond. The first approach began with four dimensions based on Hofstede's (1980, 1991) study of work-related attitudes of IBM employees in many nations: individualism-collectivism, power distance, uncertainty avoidance, and masculinity. In the Chinese Value Survey (Chinese Culture Connection, 1987), Bond was able to identify four dimensions of value differences, and three of these dimensions corresponded with those established and named by Hofstede. However, in place of Hofstede's uncertainty avoidance, Bond found a dimension of Confucian dynamism (high value for thrift, perseverance, status ordering, sense of shame; low value for stability, "face," respect for tradition, reciprocating favors). Thus Hofstede and Bond together offered five dimensions for assessing cultural differences.

Ottati, Triandis, and Hui (chap. 12 of this volume) provide an example of the usefulness of the Hofstede dimensions for comparing Hispanic and Anglo recruits in the U.S. Navy. Hispanics were relatively higher than Anglos on power distance (preferring clear status differentiation) and uncertainty avoidance (preference for clear rules, certainty, fear of failure). Surprisingly, both Hispanic and Anglo recruits scored higher on power distance than the IBM employees of any nation studied by Hofstede. Ottati et al. suggest that a strong subculture, such as found in the military, can depart considerably from the modal personality of the larger culture in which it is embedded. This is a useful caution for researchers and for sojourners in foreign cultures.

Big Three and Top Two. The second approach comes from extending three of the Big Five dimensions from individual differences within a culture to differences between nations and cultures; the Big Three of the Big Five are assertiveness, agreeableness, and conscientiousness. Related to this approach is Peabody's (1985) research that wrings evaluation out of the Big Three to leave two more purely descriptive dimensions: tight-loose and assertive-unassertive. Thus the second approach also offers five possible dimensions for assessing cultural differences.

Peabody (chap. 4 of this volume) presents results indicating the usefulness of his two descriptive dimensions for assessing cultural differences. Similarly, extension of the Big Three to comparison of nations and cultures is supported by results reported in chapter 7 of this volume by Zhang, Lee, Liu, and McCauley. In this study, Chinese students rated the typical American and the typical Chinese on a number of scales, and each student's perceived difference between Chinese and Americans was calculated for each scale. Factor analysis of the intercorrelations of the scales led to three dimensions that could be identified with assertiveness, agreeableness, and conscientiousness. Chinese students saw Americans as much more assertive than Chinese, but only slightly less agreeable and conscientious.

The analysis employed by Zhang et al. was unusual in starting from a difference measure calculated at the level of the individual perceiver (McCauley, Stitt, & Segal, 1980). In this approach, the basic datum is the difference between one rater's ratings of two nations on one scale. In the usual approach, the basic datum is one rater's rating of one nation on one scale. The clarity of results obtained with the more direct measure of perceived difference suggests that this approach may be useful in future research.

Culture and Economics.   It seems likely that the Hofstede–Bond dimensions are not independent of the Big Three or Peabody's Top Two (our appellation, not Peabody's), and Peabody (chap. 4 of this volume) offers the beginnings of rapprochement in offering a number of hypotheses about possible relations between the various dimensions that have been offered. Taken together, these hypotheses represent a promising agenda for future research.

One of these hypotheses deserves particular attention. Peabody's dimension of tight-loose involves a combination of impulse control and conscientiousness with regard to task performance. This dimension thus seems very much related to Bond's Confucian dynamism dimension, which as noted earlier, involves high value on thrift and perseverance. The Confucian dynamism dimension has attracted a great deal of attention because national scores on the dimension are correlated with national differences in economic growth; in particular, the Asian Tigers (Taiwan, Hong Kong, Singapore, Korea, Japan) are relatively high on Confucian dynamism. Peabody suggests that the relation of tight-loose and Confucian dynamism to economic growth is a striking confirmation of Weber's (1904/1930) thesis that economic development is linked to a Protestant ethic of industry and thrift.

McCauley, Ottati, and Lee (chap. 5 of this volume) focus directly on Weber's thesis and its representation in research over the past 40 years. This history begins with McClelland's (1961) cross-cultural research in which achievement motivation was found to be correlated with economic growth. McClelland's principal approach to assessing achievement motivation was a content analysis of children's readers from the nations he studied. More recent research (Granato, Inglehart, & Leblang, 1996) has used cross-national polling data to construct an index of achievement motivation that assigns positive weight to thrift and determination and negative weight to obedience and religious faith. This index is substantially correlated, across nations, with differences in economic growth—again, a striking consonance with Weber's thesis.

In addition to achievement motivation, historical records of civic participation and public trust have also been shown to be related to cultural differences in economic development. The cultural differences of interest here were differences within one nation: Putnam (1993) has shown that civic traditions of different regions of Italy, assessed from records of the early 1900s, are powerfully related to regional differences in economic level assessed in 1977. This remarkable result offers two suggestions for future research. The more specific suggestion is that public records may be a fertile source of measures of cultural differences in future research. The more general suggestion is that the cultural differences important for economic development may have as much to do with social structure and social norms as with individual-level personality types.

In summing up this section, we may say that interest in cultural differences in economic success, starting with Weber, has been a major impetus to research on cultural differences. This impetus will likely continue as political scientists and economists become more aware of the economic significance of cultural differences.

Validity of Perceived Individual and Group Differences

The fifth issue involves a comparison of the results of the first and third types of research. That is, lay beliefs about how one personality characteristic is linked to another can be validated or corrected by the results of empirical research about the strength and direction of these linkages. Similarly, the sixth issue involves a comparison of the results of the second and fourth types of research, in which lay beliefs about group differences can be validated or corrected by the results of empirical research comparing these groups.

To our knowledge, there is relatively little concern about the validity of most implicit personality inferences. One can imagine research to determine whether red-haired people are more combative, people with glasses are more intelligent, or beer drinkers more friendly than wine drinkers. But one has to imagine such research without the help of exemplars. Even the "beautiful is good" stereotype, which has attracted considerable attention (Ashmore & Longo, 1995; Goldman & Lewis, 1977), has seldom been taken seriously as a testable proposition.

Inferences from certain kinds of group membership, however, are an exception to this lack of concern. Starting with Katz and Braly (1933), many have been concerned with the validity of stereotypes based on politically sensitive characteristics such as ethnicity, age, class, gender, or sexual preference. Even these inferences, however, have only recently moved from assumed invalidity to issues of empirical investigation (Lee et al., 1995; Lee & Ottati, 1993). Recent work on person perception (e.g., Funder, 1987; Funder & West, 1993; Kenny, 1994; Kenny & Albright, 1987) indicates that there are objective differences between individuals and between groups, and that social perceptions, including stereotypes, may accurately capture at least some of these differences (Jussim, Eccles, & Madon, 1996; McCauley, 1995; McCauley, Jussim, & Lee, 1995; Ottati & Lee, 1995).

In the absence of direct measures of real group differences, lay beliefs about these differences can at least be tested for reliability. If perceptions of group differences are consistent across different groups of observers, then these perceptions are more likely correct (see Peabody, chap. 4 of this volume). To the extent that different groups of observers disagree in their perceptions of group differences, the validity of these perceptions becomes more doubtful.

Okeke et al. (chap. 8 of this volume) employ just this logic in arguing against the validity of Western stereotypes of Africans. African perceptions of the differences between Africans and Westerners emphatically disagree with Western perceptions of these same differences. Here one sees the possibility of using Peabody's methods for separating evaluation from description in order to become clearer about the nature of the difference between ingroup and outgroup perceptions. Is the disagreement a matter of evaluation, or description, or both?

Similarly, Diaz Loving and Draguns (chap. 6 of this volume) examine the problematic nature of mutual stereotyping by nationals of Mexico and the United States. They show how Mexico and the United States have evolved different social, cultural, economic, and political circumstances, and that these circumstances must be appreciated in order to interpret individual differences in behavior. It is interesting to imagine the extent to which modal or typical personality may shift in the direction of the other group's norms, for members of either group who live and work for a long time in the other group's culture.

Finally, Laungani (chap. 10 of this volume) draws on research and his own cross-cultural experience to suggest four dimensions relevant to understanding personality and culture in Eastern India in comparison with

Great Britain. These dimensions are individualism versus communalism, cognitivism versus emotionalism, free will versus determinism, and materialism versus spiritualism; Indians tend to be more communal, emotional, determinist, and spiritual. The first of these dimensions, individualism versus communalism, is now familiar in cross-cultural research (see earlier discussion in the section Hofstede and Bond). The other three are relatively unfamiliar but offer considerable promise for future research on the relation of personality and culture.

A number of contributions to this volume emphasize the danger of employing overgeneralized expectations about group differences, even when these expectations have some empirical warrant. As already noted, Ottati, Triandis, and Hui warn that there may be powerful subcultures within a culture in which our expectations about the whole culture—even when based on research—will go awry. Similarly, Miller (chap. 11 of this volume) warns against incautious use of even accurate and positive generalizations about members of another culture. The accuracy may evaporate in particular situations, such as when a Japanese visitor to an American family understands the situation to require openness and intimacy building whereas Americans understand the same situation to require polite distance.

The issue that Miller raised is a serious problem for person perception across cultures. Along similar lines, Pervin (chap. 2 of this volume) has suggested that personality cannot be construed independently of a cultural definition of the situation in which behavior occurs. We think that this is essentially the same issue raised in the person-situation debate that started with Mischel's (1984) remarking on the weakness of cross-situational consistency in behavior. We think the resolution of all these issues is the same: an increased attention to the cultural definition of situations. There is often cultural variation in the understanding of what a given behavior means in a particular situation (this is the force of Miller's example about Japanese visiting Americans). It seems likely that all cultures may be alert to differences in assertiveness, agreeableness, and conscientiousness, but that cultures differ in their understanding of which situations are tests of these differences, and in their understanding of what behaviors in these situations are expressions of these differences.

The French social psychologist, Vexliard (1970), has conceptualized national character as a "structure in depth." Within this framework, national character is not expected to be revealed through surface personality traits. Rather, its expressions are to be found in the relationship between acts, behaviors, and decisions on the one hand, and core values, attitudes, and beliefs that are widely shared and even taken for granted within a national culture. Of necessity, the overt responses or self-reports would stand in a complex and ambiguous relationship to these basic, yet underlying, variables. So reformulated, national character has points of contact with the better known construct of subjective culture as proposed by Triandis (1972).

The importance of situational context in cross-cultural person perception is well represented in the procedures of cross-cultural training. Brislin (chap. 13 of this volume) reviews the circumstances for which such training is offered, and the research origins (including most of the research discussed previously) of the content of this training. But it is interesting to note that the preferred means of putting over this content is not just abstract representation of cultural differences in individualism-collectivism, or power distance, or the importance of agreeableness or conscientiousness for adjustment in the new culture. Rather research results—and professional judgment—about what is important for adjusting to the new culture are conveyed in critical-incident tests that are more like parables than research reports. On the conceptual plane, the critical-incident technique involves training in the interaction of individual differences with culturally defined situational differences. Here, it seems to us, practice has moved ahead of scholarly debates about whether cultural differences in personality can transcend cultural definitions of situations.

Origins of Perceptions of Individual and Group Differences

The seventh and eighth issues are part of social psychological research on social perception, social cognition, and social judgment. This research is well represented in the interface between cognitive psychology and social psychology that currently dominates mainline social psychology journals, along with issues of attribution, efficacy, and self-perception (see Introduction). In this literature, the origins of perceptions of individuals and groups are being sought in terms of the principles of human information processing—that is, within a model of man as all-too-fallible computer.

Cross-cultural comparisons from an information-processing perspective are so far relatively rare and this kind of research is not represented in the present volume. Nevertheless, we confidently predict a bright future for this kind of research. Information-processing measures of attitudes (Cacioppo, Gardner, & Berntson, 1997) and stereotypes (Linville, Fisher, & Salovey, 1989) are already in use with North American subjects; can comparative research be far behind? Particularly recommending this kind of research is the possibility that measures that depend on reaction time and procedural memory may circumvent some of the problems of translating measures across cultures (Pervin, chap. 2 of this volume; Miller, chap. 11 of this volume).

Origins of Individual and Group Differences

The 9th research issue is the study of nature and nurture in individual development (e.g., Eaves, Eysenck, & Martin, 1989; Eysenck, 1995; Loehlin, 1992), and the 10th is the study of cultural evolution (Brown, 1991; Buss, 1991; Pepitone & Triandis, 1987). Outside of this volume, developmental psychology is popular but there is relatively little research on cultural evolution. We are fortunate to have two contributions to this volume that focus on the origin of cultural differences.

Oettingen and Maier (chap. 9 of this volume) compare East and West Berlin and argue persuasively that greater acceptance of teacher authority and lower self-efficacy in East Berlin are the result of the differences between communist and capitalist ideologies applied to the two parts of one city. Their interpretation is strengthened by a creative measure of depression in the behavior of bar patrons in East and West Germany, a measure that indicated reduced depression after the Berlin Wall came down. The probability of such differences preexisting the division is vanishingly small and completely counterintuitive.

Also in this volume, Rushton (chap. 3) reviews evidence that there are biological differences in temperament that put European-origin people, on the average, between African-origin people and Asian-origin people on many different dimensions. The measures examined are varied indeed, including infant motor activity and crying, physical maturation rate, aggressiveness, crime rates, marital stability, sexual activity, hormone levels, intelligence, and self-esteem. Although politically controversial, this evidence has cumulated to the point where it can hardly be dismissed out of hand.

Whether or not one accepts Rushton's view of the genetic foundations of the measures he examines, these measures offer an interesting prospect for future research on personality in culture. Recent personality research is beginning to take seriously the idea that temperament differences in children contribute to later personality differences (Ekblad & Olweus, 1986; Kagan, Arcus, & Snidman, 1993; Revelle, 1995; Saklofske & Zeidner, 1995). If temperament differences are the foundation of personality differences, then Rushton's temperament measures should be related to more familiar personality dimensions.

Thus future research might examine whether the measures Rushton examines could be organized in terms of the Big Three personality dimensions of assertiveness, agreeableness, and conscientiousness (Peabody, chap. 4 of this volume). It might be possible to argue, for instance, that Asians are high on agreeableness and conscientiousness but low on assertiveness. Peabody's evaluation-free dimensions of tight-loose and assertive-unassertive might also be used to organize Rushton's results; it might be possible to argue that Asians are relatively tight and unassertive.

One value of this approach for cross-cultural study of personality is that at least the more biological of Rushton's temperament measures (activity level, maturation rate, hormone levels) are unlikely to be undermined by the kind of cultural relativity of meaning that can be advanced against more psychological measures (Pervin, chap. 2 of this volume).

This concludes our review of the contributions of this volume in relation to the typology of research issues in person perception that we drew from Child's 1968 chapter. This typology can also be useful in organizing the needs of the sojourner in another culture.

CONCLUSION: WHAT DOES THE SOJOURNER NEED TO KNOW?

Here we focus on what an American needs to know about culture and personality in order to visit or work with members of another culture. Although we adopt the perspective of a North American trying to prepare for interaction in another culture, we believe that the issues raised are relevant as well to individuals from other cultures seeking to interact with Americans. To personalize these issues, we ask the reader to identify him or herself with an American "I" (just as an example) in the following outline of four issues.

First, I need to recognize explicitly my own expectations of how the new group differs from my own; to the extent possible, I need also to evaluate the validity of these expectations. It is seldom that I meet a member of a group about which I have no preconceptions, and my preconceptions or stereotypes of group character are likely to color both my own initial behavior and my initial interpretation of the behavior of members of the new group. Even where data on the validity of my stereotype are lacking, it can be useful to recognize explicitly the strength of the stereotype that I bring to my interactions in the new group. These considerations correspond to issues 2, 4, and 6 in the aforementioned typology.

Second, I need to know the stereotypic expectations about my own group that I will be facing in dealing with members of the new group. Just as my preconceptions color my initial behaviors and interpretations, so will their preconceptions color their initial behaviors and interpretations. This is again issue 2 in the typology, this time from the perspective of the other group (see Lee et al., 1995; McCauley et al., 1980).

Third, I need to know whether my familiar cues and dimensions of individual differences will work in differentiating individuals in the new group. What are the markers of solidarity and status in the new group? Will behaviors that cohere in such familiar dimensions as neuroticism and extraversion cohere in the new group? As noted previously, we go far beyond the given in person perception, and we do so by applying a powerful inference structure that probabilistically links each person characteristic or cue with many others. The question is, how well will my familiar inference structure work in a different culture?

This question can be pursued either in terms of perceptions or in terms of facts. Does my inference structure depart from the one perceived in the new group? Does my inference structure depart from the facts of what goes with what in the new group? These questions are germane to issues 1, 3, and 5 in the aforementioned typology.

Fourth, I need to know the cues and dimensions of individual differences that are salient to members of the new group. Just as I am likely to use familiar cues for differentiating individuals in a new group, so too will members of the new group use their own familiar cues in evaluating me. Just as I am likely to use my own habits or schemas of person perception to go beyond the given in forming impressions of others, so too will members of the new group be using their own schemas of person perception to form an impression of me. This again is relevant to issue 1 in the typology, this time from the perspective of the new group.

The third and fourth needs of the sojourner, awareness of the structure of inferences in her own group and in the new group, are part of what was earlier identified as implicit personality theory. Whatever can be known about the validity of these social constructions is valuable; to be aware of the content of these constructions is essential.

Beneath these four issues is the metaphor of a double mirror. Our implicit personality theory and its academic counterpart (e.g., Big Five, or individualism-collectivism, or power distance) are our mirror for seeing ourselves in relation to others in our own and other cultures. We need to be alert to distortion when we use our familiar mirror to see our own group in relation to another or to see ourselves as individuals in relation to individuals in another culture. A rather different mirror may be familiar in another culture, and we will not understand our own image in the eyes of others if we are not aware of the mirror they are using. Successful interaction in another culture requires us to step through our looking glass to see ourselves in theirs (cf. Kenny, 1994). The contributors to the present volume have sought to organize research results for the benefit of those who would take this difficult step.

REFERENCES

Allport, G. W. (1937). *Personality: A psychological interpretation.* New York: Holt.

Almagor, M., Tellegen, A., & Waller, N. G. (1995). The Big Seven model: A cross-cultural replication and further exploration of the basic dimensions of natural language trait descriptions. *Journal of Personality and Social Psychology, 69,* 300–307.

Asch, S. E. (1946). Forming impressions of personality *Journal of Abnormal and Social Psychology, 41,* 258–290.

Ashmore, R., & Longo, L. (1995). Accuracy of stereotypes: What research on physical attractiveness can teach us. In Y-T. Lee, L. Jussim, & C. R. McCauley (Eds.), *Stereotype accuracy: Toward appreciating group differences* (pp. 63–86). Washington, DC: American Psychological Association.

Benet, V., & Waller, N. G. (1995). The Big Seven factor model of personality description: Evidence for its cross-cultural generality in a Spanish sample. *Journal of Personality and Social Psychology, 69,* 701–718.

Brown, D. E. (1991). *Human universals.* New York: McGraw-Hill.

Bruner, J. S., & Tagiuri, R. (1954). The perception of people. In G. Lindzey (Ed.), *The handbook of social psychology* (Vol. 2, pp. 634–654). Cambridge, MA: Addison-Wesley.

Buss, D. M. (1991). Evolutionary personality theory. *Annual Review of Psychology, 12,* 1–49.

Cacioppo, J. T., Gardner, W. L., & Berntson, G. G. (1997). Beyond bipolar conceptualizations and measures: The case of attitudes and evaluative space. *Personality and Social Psychological Review, 1,* 3–25.

Campbell, D. T. (1967). Stereotypes and the perception of group differences. *American Psychologist, 22,* 817–829.

Child, I. (1968). Personality in culture. In E. F. Borgatta & W. W. Lambert (Eds.), *Handbook of personality theory and research* (pp. 82–145). Chicago: Rand McNally.

Chinese Culture Connection. (1987). Chinese values and the search for culture-free dimensions of culture. *Journal of Cross-Cultural Psychology, 18,* 143–164.

Chiu, C-Y., Hong, Y-Y., & Dweck, C. (1997). Lay dispositionism and implicit theory of personality. *Journal of Personality and Social Psychology, 73*(1), 19–32.

Deaux, K., & Lewis, L. L. (1984). Structure of gender stereotypes: Interrelationships among components and gender label. *Journal of Personality and Social Psychology, 46,* 991–1004.

Diaz-Guerrero, R., & Diaz Loving, R. (1994). Personality across cultures. In L. L. Adler & U. P. Gielen (Eds.), *Cross-cultural topics in psychology* (pp. 125–138). Westport, CT: Praeger.

Dweck, C. S., Chiu, C. Y., & Hong, Y. Y. (1995). Implicit theories: Elaboration and extension of the model. *Psychological Inquiry, 6,* 322–333.

Eaves, L. J., Eysenck, H. J., & Martin, N. G. (1989). *Genes, culture and personality: An empirical approach.* New York: Academic Press.

Ekblad, S., & Olweus, D. (1986). Applicability of Olweus' Aggression Inventory in a sample of Chinese primary school children. *Aggressive Behavior, 12*, 315–325.

Eysenck, H. J. (1995). Creativity as product of intelligence and personality. In D. H. Saklofske & M. Zeidner (Eds.), *International handbook of personality and intelligence* (pp. 231–248). New York: Plenum.

Flanagan, J. C. (1954). The critical incident technique. *Psychological Bulletin, 51*, 327–358.

Funder, D. (1987). Errors and mistakes: Evaluating the accuracy of social judgment. *Psychological Bulletin, 101*, 75–90.

Funder, D. (1997). *The personality puzzle.* New York: Norton.

Funder, D., & West, S. G. (1993). Consensus, self-other agreement and accuracy in personality judgment: An introduction. *Journal of Personality, 61*(4), 457–476.

Goldberg, L. R. (1993). The structure of phenotypic personality traits. *American Psychologist, 48*, 26–34.

Goldman, W., & Lewis, P. (1977). Beautiful is good: Evidence that the physically attractive are more socially skillful. *Journal of Experimental Social Psychology, 13*, 125–130.

Granato, J., Inglehart, R., & Leblang, D. (1996). The effect of cultural values on economic development: Theory, hypotheses, and some empirical tests. *American Journal of Political Science, 40*, 607–631.

Hofstede, G. (1980). *Culture's consequences: International differences in work related values.* Beverly Hills, CA: Sage.

Hofstede, G. (1991). *Cultures and organizations: Software of the mind.* London: McGraw-Hill.

Ichheiser, G. (1949). Sociopsychological and cultural factors in race relations. *American Journal of Sociology, 54*, 395–401.

Ichheiser, G. (1970). *Appearances and realities: Misunderstanding in human relations.* San Francisco: Jossey-Bass.

John, O. P. (1990). The "big five" factor taxonomy: Dimensions of personality in the natural language and in questionnaire. In L. Pervin (Ed.), *Handbook of personality: Theory and research* (pp. 66–100). New York: Guilford.

Jussim, L., Eccles, J., & Madon, S. (1996). Social perception, social stereotypes, and teacher expectations: Accuracy and the quest for the powerful self-fulfilling prophecy. In M. Zanna (Ed.), *Advances in experimental social psychology* (Vol. 28, pp. 281–388). Orlando, FL: Academic Press.

Kagan, J., Arcus, D., & Snidman, N. (1993). The idea of temperament: Where do we go form here. In R. Plomin & G. E. McClearn (Eds.), *Nature, nurture and psychology* (pp. 197–212). Washington, DC: American Psychological Association.

Katz, D., & Braly, K. (1933). Racial stereotypes of one hundred college students. *Journal of Abnormal and Social Psychology, 28*, 280–290.

Kenny, D. (1994). *Interpersonal perception: A social relations analysis.* New York: Guilford.

Kenny, D., & Albright, L. (1987). Accuracy in interpersonal perception: A social relations analysis. *Psychological Bulletin, 102*, 390–402.

Lee, Y-T., Jussim, L., & McCauley, C. (Eds.). (1995). *Stereotype accuracy: Toward appreciating group differences.* Washington, DC: American Psychological Association.

Lee, Y-T., & Ottati, V. (1993). Determinants of ingroup and outgroup perception of heterogeneity: An investigation of Chinese-American stereotypes. *Journal of Cross-Cultural Psychology, 24*, 298–318.

Lee, Y-T., & Seligman, M. E. P. (1997). Are Americans more optimistic than the Chinese? *Personality and Social Psychology Bulletin, 23*(1), 32–40.

Linton, R. (1945). *The cultural background of personality.* New York: Appleton–Century–Crofts.

Linville, P., Fisher, G., & Salovey, P. (1989). Perceived distributions of the characteristics of ingroup and outgroup members: Empirical evidence and a computer simulation. *Journal of Personality and Social Psychology, 57*, 165–188.

Loehlin, J. C. (1992). *Genes and environment in personality development.* Newbury Park, CA: Sage.

Lynn, R. (1995). Cross-cultural differences in intelligence and personality. In D. H. Saklofske & M. Zeidner (Eds.), *International handbook of personality and intelligence* (pp. 107–124). New York: Plenum.

Magnusson, D., & Torestad, B. (1993). A holistic view of personality: A model revisited. *Annual Review of Psychology, 44*, 427–452.

Markus, H. R., & Kitayama, S. (1991). Culture and the self: Implications for cognition, emotion, and motivation. *Psychological Review, 98*(2), 224–253.

McAdam, D. P. (1992). The five factor model in personality: A critical appraisal. *Journal of Personality, 60,* 329–361.

McCauley, C. (1995). Are stereotypes exaggerated? A sampling of racial, gender, academic, occupational and political stereotypes. In Y-T. Lee, L. Jussim, & C. McCauley (Eds.), *Stereotype accuracy: Toward appreciating group differences* (pp. 215–243). Washington, DC: American Psychological Association.

McCauley, C., Jussim, L., & Lee, Y-T. (1995). Stereotype accuracy: Toward appreciating group differences. In Y-T. Lee, L. Jussim, & C. McCauley (Eds.), *Stereotype accuracy: Toward appreciating group differences* (pp. 293–312). Washington, DC: American Psychological Association.

McCauley, C., Stitt, C. L., & Segal, M. (1980). Stereotyping: From prejudice to prediction. *Psychological Bulletin, 87,* 195–208.

McClelland, D.C. (1961). *The achieving society.* Princeton, NJ: Van Nostrand.

McCrae, R. R., & Costa, P. T. (1990). *Personality in adulthood.* New York: Guilford.

Mischel, W. (1984). Convergence and challenges in the search for consistency. *American Psychologist, 39,* 351–364.

Ottati, V., & Lee, Y-T. (1995). Accuracy: A neglected component of stereotype research. In Y-T. Lee, L. Jussim, & C. McCauley (Eds.), *Stereotype accuracy: Toward appreciating group differences* (pp. 29–59). Washington, DC: American Psychological Association.

Ozer, D. J., & Reise, S. P. (1994). Personality assessment. *Annual Review of Psychology, 45,* 357–388.

Peabody, D. (1985). *National characteristics.* London: Cambridge University Press.

Pepitone, A., & Triandis, H. (1987). On the universality of social psychological theories. *Journal of Cross-Cultural Psychology, 18,* 471–498.

Putnam, R. D. (1993). *Making democracy work: Civic traditions in modern Italy.* Princeton, NJ: Princeton University Press.

Revelle, W. (1995). Personality processes. *Annual Review of Psychology, 46,* 295–328.

Saklofske, D. H., & Zeidner, M. (1995). *International handbook of personality and intelligence.* New York: Plenum.

Schwartz, S. H. (1994). Cultural dimensions of values: Toward an understanding of national differences. In U. Kim, H. Triandis, C. Kagitcibasi, S. C. Choi, & G. Yoon (Eds.), *Individualism and collectivism: Theory methods and applications* (pp. 85–119). Thousands Oaks, CA: Sage.

Stein, R. I., & Nemeroff, C. J. (1995). Moral overtones of food: Judgments of others based on what they eat. *Personality & Social Psychology Bulletin, 21*(5), 480–490.

Tagiuri, R., & Petrullo, L. (Eds.). (1958). *Person perception and interpersonal behavior.* Stanford, CA: Stanford University Press.

Triandis, H. C. (1972). *The analysis of subjective culture.* New York: Wiley.

Vexliard, A. (1970). *Caractère national.* Une structure en profoundeur. [National character: A structure in depth]. Istanbul: Universitesi Edebiyat Fakultesi.

Weber, M. (1930). *The Protestant ethic and the spirit of capitalism* (2nd ed., Parsons, Trans.). New York: Scribner's. (Original work published 1904).

Whiting, J. W., & Child, I. (1953). *Child training and personality: A cross-cultural study.* New Haven, CT: Yale University Press.

Wiggins, J. S. (Ed.). (in press). *The Five-Factor Model of Personality: Theoretical perspectives.* New York: Guilford.

Wiggins, J. S., & Pincus, A. L. (1992). Personality: Structure and assessment. *Annual Review of Psychology, 43,* 473–504.

Yang, K. S., & Bond, M. (1990). Exploring implicit personality theories with indigenous or imported constructs: The Chinese case. *Journal of Personality and Social Psychology, 58,* 1087–1095.

Author Index

Subject Index

9781138012462